RABBI ELYSE GOLDSTEIN is widely recognized as an innovative and thought-provoking teacher of Torah. One of the leading rabbis of a new generation, she is the director of Kolel, The Adult Center for Liberal Jewish Learning, a full-time progressive adult Jewish learning center. Goldstein lectures frequently throughout North America. She is also the editor of *The Women's Torah Commentary: New Insights from Women Rabbis on the 54 Weekly Torah Portions* and the author of *ReVisions: Seeing Torah through a Feminist Lens.*

The Women's
Haftarah Commentary

Jewish Lights books by Rabbi Elyse Goldstein

ReVisions:
Seeing Torah through a Feminist Lens

The Women's Haftarah Commentary:
New Insights from Women Rabbis on the 54 Weekly Haftarah Portions,
the 5 Megillot & Special Shabbatot

The Women's Torah Commentary:
New Insights from Women Rabbis on the 54 Weekly Torah Portions

The Women's
Haftarah Commentary

*New Insights from Women Rabbis
on the 54 Weekly Haftarah Portions,
the 5 Megillot & Special Shabbatot*

EDITED BY RABBI ELYSE GOLDSTEIN

JEWISH LIGHTS Publishing
Woodstock, Vermont

The Women's Haftarah Commentary:
New Insights from Women Rabbis on the 54 Weekly Haftarah Portions,
the 5 Megillot & Special Shabbatot

2004 First Printing
© 2004 by Elyse Goldstein

Library of Congress Cataloging-in-Publication Data
The women's haftarah commentary : new insights from women rabbis on the 54 weekly haftarah portions, the 5 megillot & special Shabbatot / edited by Elyse Goldstein.
      p.   cm.
    Includes index.
    ISBN 1-58023-133-0
    1. Bible. O.T. Pentateuch—Commentaries. 2. Haftarot—Commentaries. I. Title: New insights from women rabbis on the 54 weekly haftarah portions, the 5 megillot & special shabbatot. II. Goldstein, Elyse.
BS1225.53.W66 2004
221.7—dc22   2003024336

10 9 8 7 6 5 4 3 2 1

Manufactured in Canada

Published by Jewish Lights Publishing
A Division of LongHill Partners, Inc.
Sunset Farm Offices, Route 4, P.O. Box 237
Woodstock, VT 05091
Tel: (802) 457-4000   Fax: (802) 457-4004
www.jewishlights.com

Rabbi Hanina said:
"From my teachers I learned much,
from my colleagues still more,
but from my students most of all."
—Babylonian Talmud, Ta'anit 7a

With thanks to all my students for teaching me so much.

Contents

Bereshit / Genesis

Contents

Shmot / Exodus

Vayikra / Leviticus

Bamidbar / Numbers

Contents

Devarim / Deuteronomy

Special Shabbatot

Haftarot for Days of Awe

Contents

Holiday Haftarot

Five Megillot

Special Additional Selections

Index by Author

Acknowledgments

This book was inspired by my speaking tours for *The Women's Torah Commentary* (Jewish Lights). Each place I went, the question was always asked, "And what about the haftarot? You can't just do the Torah portions from a feminist perspective and leave the haftarot out!" Mothers of Bat Mitzvah girls would e-mail me from across the world wanting a quick "spin" on the haftarah portion their daughters were studying, since they were using *The Women's Torah Commentary* for their Torah portion. Some of the writers from *The Women's Torah Commentary* were ready for a new challenge, and rabbis who were not in that book were anxious to write for a new volume.

I am grateful to all the rabbis who put great time and effort into submitting their pieces. Being a rabbi is a busy and demanding career, and having the time to write is often, unfortunately, a luxury. Being asked to do a commentary piece, though, is a particular joy, since it means the writer must study and examine and probe the biblical section and its traditional commentaries carefully. And that is exactly what rabbis love—and yearn—to do.

A special thank-you to Stuart Matlins, publisher, and Emily Wichland, managing editor, of Jewish Lights, who envisioned this book while *The Women's Torah Commentary* was still in its first printing. They knew that the second volume was natural, and necessary, and

Acknowledgments

their encouragement convinced me to call for submissions. Alys Yablon was a marvelous help with her insightful editing.

Thank you also to my family for their unwavering patience and enthusiasm for my writing. My husband Baruch and my sons Noam (thanks especially for his spell-checking and editorial assistance), Carmi, and Micah are teachers of the Torah of life in their own right. They never fail to support me, and I am eternally grateful.

May the fiery and profound words of the prophets, prophetesses, and seers, kings and queens, heroes and heroines, challengers and contenders you will meet within this book inspire you, and may you always feel the passion for God, for Torah, for Israel, and for the people that the prophets felt.

Rabbi Elyse Goldstein

Introduction

Synagogue attendees, especially those who come for Bar or Bat Mitzvah ceremonies, will notice that, somewhere in the middle of the worship, there is a special moment when the Torah is lifted from its ark, taken out, and paraded around the sanctuary; then it is laid on a table in the front of the room to be read aloud. It is a moment of great solemnity for all those present. This Torah reading occurs each Saturday, Monday, and Thursday. But on Saturdays only, there is an additional reading that takes place after the Torah has been read, lifted, and redressed. At that point in the service, a person comes forward to read the haftarah, a special portion taken from either the Prophets or Writings sections of the Hebrew Scriptures, which come after the Torah (the Five Books of Moses) in the order of the Jewish canon.

While the institution of the public reading of the Torah goes back to the time of Ezra the Scribe, during the return from Babylonian exile around the fifth century B.C.E., the origin of the haftarah reading is unclear. The most common explanation is that, around the second century B.C.E., Antiochus Epiphanes prohibited the reading of the Torah during the days preceding the Maccabean revolt. Lacking the ability to hear the weekly portion read, the priests found certain portions in the Prophets that thematically tied them to what would have been that week's Torah reading. Thus, for example, in the week when the portion about Noah would have been heard, worshipers would instead hear a selection from Isaiah that mentions "the waters of Noah." Likewise, in the week when the story of the golden calf would have been read, the haftarah portion is from I Kings, the story of Elijah fighting against the priests of Ba'al. In both stories, Israel is threatened by the influence of foreign gods, and Elijah would remind the participants of the story of Moses.

Other scholars are of the opinion that the custom was instituted later as an anti-Sadduccean measure by the Pharisaic rabbis who claimed that the Sadduccean rejection of anything but the Five Books of Moses was heresy. Legislating a weekly reading from the books of the prophets would drive home the point that the prophets were as authoritative as the Torah. Either way, not only was the reading of the Haftarah considered to strengthen, and in a sense imitate, the Torah reading, but it also served as a potent tool for the teaching of values, ethics, and moral lessons contained in the prophetic portions chosen. It established the Prophets and Writings as important in their own right and as powerful adjuncts to the Five Books of Moses. The weekly Haftarah reading ensured that the people would learn the whole Jewish Scripture, not just the Torah.

The earliest reference to the synagogue tradition of reading the Haftarah is, interestingly, not in a Jewish source, but rather in the Christian Bible. In Acts 13:15 Paul is invited to deliver a sermon "after the reading of the law and the prophets." In the Talmud, the earliest reference to the specific selection process for the haftarot is in *Megillah*, which names the haftarot for the four special Sabbaths. However, nowhere in the Talmud is the specific order of haftarot for Sabbaths given. Those portions were not fixed until after the talmudic period, and there is reason to believe that the Haftarah readings might have varied from place to place. Even today, there is a difference in some weeks between what Sephardim and Ashkenazim read for their haftarah.

So unclear are we as to the origins of this now-common practice that we are not even sure what the word *haftarah* means. Some suggest that it corresponds to the Latin word *demissio*, since the service would have ended with the reading for the haftarah. Its three-letter Hebrew root is *p-t-r*, meaning "to take leave of" but it has come to mean "additional" or "added" as in the Passover Haggadah, *ain maftirin achar afikomen*, nothing should be added (or eaten) after the *afikomen*.

The haftarot have become a beloved part of the synagogue service, so much so that they factor heavily in the choosing of a Bar or Bat Mitzvah portion. The Bar or Bat Mitzvah child is called up to read the *Maftir* (also meaning "additional reading"), the last few verses of the Torah portion, and is then given the honor of chanting the haftarah. The haftarah is sung with its own special cantillation, and can be read directly from a vocalized book, making it somewhat easier to read than the calligraphed script of the Torah scroll, which contains neither cantillation marks nor vowels. Special blessings are said before and after the reading of the haftarah.

The Haftarah readings are rich in imagery: some poetic, some narrative, and some dark and brooding. The early prophets were prominent in society and often were advisors to the king, seers or oracles consulted in times of crisis or war, and influential in their relationships with mighty leaders. The prophets who lived before the destruction of the First Temple in 586 B.C.E. warned of the coming cataclysm in graphic terms. They firmly believed that the destruction and exile were going to be divine punishments for a people who had strayed, and they pleaded with the Israelites to mend their ways. These prophets did not elect to become prophets; it was not a job they sought out. Instead, they were called by God to convey a message, as unpopular or unpleasant as that message might be. Prophecy was not a trade that could be learned, but was "visited" upon the prophet directly by God. Thus the prophet was destined, set apart from the people, and duty-bound to be God's envoy. The prophets use strong and evocative language again and again to convey their themes. After the destruction of the Temple, the later prophets were called upon to deliver the message of consolation and even optimism to the people: They would be restored, and they would be redeemed. All was not lost. The prophets addressed the contemporary situation in which they lived with an unstinting insistence on morality, righteousness, and justice. They were the original "social activists"; in fact, the early Reform movement modeled its own call for a Judaism based on social activism on the prophets.

Also found in the haftarot are sections of biblical history, like the stories of David and Bathsheba, Saul, Rahav, and others. These narratives contain many of our heroes and antiheroes and reveal biblical society to us in a colorful way. This commentary also explores the Five Megillot. Though not haftarot in the classical sense, the Megillot are read on certain Jewish holidays, and each one has a special theme related to its own holiday. Ecclesiastes, with its existential questions on the meaning of life, is read on Sukkot, the time of year when we turn inward and prepare for the long winter ahead. Esther for Purim and Ruth for Shavuot introduce us to two heroines who become the symbols of female leadership. Song of Songs is read on Passover, and its sensual, pastoral imagery reminds us of love in the spring. And Lamentations, in which a female Jerusalem is mourned, is read on Tisha B'Av and marks a period of intense grief not only over the loss of sovereignty but over the loss of the Temple, the symbol of that sovereign nationhood.

Also included in this book are some of the haftarot that are commonly heard in synagogues on holidays like the major festivals, the High Holidays, or the Shabbat during Chanukah. Haftarot for the first day of each of the major festivals, as well as all the haftarot of the High Holidays, are offered, but there is no philosophical statement intended by not adding to the commentary from the second and last days' haftarot, or those of certain other holidays; it was simply a matter of space, volume, and wanting to expand the boundaries of the book but not to make it so large that it becomes unusable. The haftarot of the four special Shabbatot—Shekalim, Zachor, Parah, and HaChodesh—are also included, since these four take the place of a "regular" haftarah reading when those four special Shabbatot fall (Shekalim and Zachor before Purim, Parah and HaChodesh before Passover). And last is the section of special women found in the Prophets or the Writings, women the reader might not meet otherwise, since they do not get their own haftarah portion; they are unusual, feisty characters, and their stories give us a glimpse into the lives of our ancestors. We end with two pieces of biblical poetry that may be of special interest to women. First, the Woman of Valor section of Proverbs 31, which is traditionally sung praising the woman of the household on Friday nights, and is often recited at the funeral of a righteous woman. Many people believe this poem is only about a stereotypical "wife and mother," but a feminist analysis shows its depth. Then we close with a feminist look at Psalm 23, "The Lord Is My Shepherd." While this psalm has no overt feminine imagery, and is read at the funeral of both men and women, it offers a special solace when viewed through a contemporary lens.

The methodology of *The Women's Haftarah Commentary* is the same as that of *The Women's Torah Commentary*. Each essay is written by a different female rabbi, bringing her unique perspective to the text. These writers come from Reform, Conservative, and Reconstructionist seminaries. It is my great hope that one day Orthodox women will serve in some capacity as rabbis, but that has not happened yet, so their absence is felt in this book. The writers serve in congregations, schools, and organizations all over the world. You will find their biographies at the end of the book. The paths that brought each woman to the rabbinate are also part of their biographies, and give you a window into their extraordinary lives.

Translations from the Hebrew text are by the author of each particular essay. The writers seek to find something within the Haftarah text that speaks directly to them as women, so they can elucidate the meaning of the portion for today's girls and women. Where there are female characters, they put them into historical perspective and imagine what their lives may have been like. They search some of the more problematic texts—the sacrifice of Jephthah's daughter, for example, or the character of Jezebel, or the imagery of God as a jealous husband who "punishes" His wife—and find within them nuances and interpretations that help "balance" them and give them softer and more subtle meanings. In every generation it has been the duty of the commentator to bring the text to life for a society that may find its message threatening, daunting, or even superfluous. The feminist commentators in this book are no different. They seek to enlighten a biblical text, no matter how it may portray its women, or how it may imagine the God-Israel relationship.

This book is intended as a companion volume to *The Women's Torah Commentary*. They can be used side by side to explore a feminist way of looking at the complete weekly reading. They can both be used as tools to help a Bar or Bat Mitzvah grasp how his or her Torah and Haftarah portion are linked, and how each can be read for contemporary meaning. For the non-Jewish reader, many prophetic portions will be familiar, as they are read in the Christian liturgy as well. Now they will be infused with new Jewish and feminist significance.

Like the early codifiers of haftarah readings, it is my hope that using *The Women's Haftarah Commentary* will help to bring the Haftarah back to an honored position in the weekly life of the Jew, not just as an "adjunct" to the Torah reading but as a meaningful reading on its own. Many Haftarah commentaries are contained within the traditional commentaries on the Torah reading, but are little more than a few lines meant to tie together the Torah portion with its haftarah. When Rabbi W. Gunther Plaut published *The Haftarah Commentary* in 1996, it was one of the first progressive commentaries that delved deeply into the weekly Haftarah readings and did not rely almost completely on their connection to the Torah reading. Like Plaut's important commentary, this book is meant to advance the goal of providing readers with interpretations and explorations of the Prophets and Writings on their own terms. In reading them, both men and women may discover a whole new set of biblical stories, and thus a whole new possibility of increased joy in studying and learning.

Rabbinic Commentators and Midrashic Collections Noted in This Anthology

Solomon ben Moses HaLevi Alkabetz: b. 1505. A charismatic speaker who inspired his audiences with his kabbalistic knowledge. Best known for his composition of *Lecha Dodi*, the hymn of the Sabbath sung to welcome in Shabbat on Friday evenings.

Abraham Ibn Ezra: 1089–1164. Poet, grammarian, biblical commentator, astronomer, and physician from Spain, whose commentaries feature many etymological and grammatical explanations.

Gersonides: Rabbi Levi ben Gershon, 1288–1344. A philosopher, astronomer, mathematician, and biblical commentator also known as the *Ralbag*.

Rav Kook: Rabbi Abraham Isaac Kook, 1865–1935. First Ashkenazi Chief Rabbi of modern Israel, and modern commentator whose works include a high-level understanding of secular philosophy.

Maharsha: Rabbi Shmuel Eliezer Halevi Eidels, 1555–1631. Polish commentator on the Talmud and Rashi.

Maimonides: Rabbi Moses ben Maimon, 1135–1204. A Spanish physician and philosopher, known as a commentator and a halachist. He is famous for his legal code Mishneh Torah, his philosophical work *Guide for the Perplexed*, and many other works. His acronym is *Rambam*.

Malbim: Rabbi Meir Loeb ben Yechiel Michael, 1809–1879. An Eastern European scholar whose commentaries rely heavily on the belief that every single word is essential and conveys a necessary thought.

Metzudat David: Rabbi David Altschuler's eighteenth-century commentary (around 1782) on the Prophets, elucidating the meaning of the text.

Midrash Rabbah: A compilation of homilies on the stories of the Torah, from about the sixth century C.E.

Nachmanides: Rabbi Moses ben Nachman, 1194–1270. Born in Spain. He spent his last years writing his commentary in the Land of Israel. His acronym is *Ramban*.

Pesikta Rabbati: A medieval midrash on the festivals of the year, and on the biblical and prophetic lessons of the holidays, from the sixth or seventh century C.E.

Philo of Alexandria: 20 B.C.E.–50 C.E. A nobleman and philosopher who wrote in Greek and favored allegorical interpretations.

Pirkei de Rabbi Eliezer: A very early midrashic collection traditionally attributed to Rabbi Eliezar ben Hyrcanus who lived in the first century C.E.

W. Gunther Plaut: 1912–present. German-born Reform rabbi living in Toronto whose *Torah: A Modern Commentary*, published in 1985, is considered one of the greatest liberal Torah commentaries of our time, encompassing not only traditional commentary in translation but modern historical, sociological, psychological, and literary insights into the text. He is also author of *The Haftarah Commentary*.

Radak: Rabbi David Kimchi, 1160–1235. Commentator from France best known for his scientific philological analysis.

Rashbam: Acronym for Rabbi Shmuel ben Meir, Rashi's grandson, known for his piety and his strict insistence on retaining the most literal sense of the text.

Rashi: Acronym for Rabbi Shlomo Yitzchaki, 1040–1105, from France. Rashi is the most well known of the medieval commentators, famous for explaining the *peshat*, or plain meaning of the text, sprinkled liberally with stories, parables, and some fanciful suggestions of his own based on classical midrash. In traditional circles, Rashi is studied most often as providing the central vision of what the text really means.

Sifrei: Halachic midrash to the Books of Numbers and Deuteronomy, compiled at the end of the fourth century C.E.

Tanhuma: A fourth-century C.E. collection of midrashim ascribed to Rabbi Tanhuma of Palestine.

Tanna de Bei Eliyahu: A uniform work of midrash (not a compilation) concerned with the ethical and religious values of the Bible, dated anywhere between the third and tenth centuries C.E.

Targum: Bible translation. During the period of the Second Temple, many different translations appeared in Greek and Aramaic. Such translations also serve as interpretations.

Tosafot: Collections of comments on the Talmud arranged according to the order of the Talmudic tractates, relying heavily on Rashi's talmudic commentary. Rashi's pupils and descendants began to expand and elaborate on their teacher's talmudic commentary in the twelfth to fourteenth century C.E.

Bereshit /Genesis

RABBI AMY JOY SMALL

הפטרת בראשית
Haftarat Bereshit

Isaiah 42:5–43:10

*T*hus said God YHVH, Who created the heavens
and stretched them out, who spread out the earth
and what it brings forth, who gave breath to the people
upon it and life to those who walk thereon: I the Lord,
in my grace, have summoned you, and I have grasped
you by the hand. I created you, and appointed you a
covenant people, a light of nations. (ISAIAH 42:5–6)

THE PEOPLE OF ISRAEL, whose land was conquered, and who were thus
exiled to Babylonia, were a people suffering the double loss of their
autonomy and their home. It is hard for any of us who have not lived
through forced deportation and exile to imagine what this kind of loss
is like. Not only are the people forced to live as strangers in a strange
land, but also they must adapt to foreign rule and the subjugation of
their beliefs, customs, and lifestyle as well.

What was the emotional impact of this experience of loss, and the
accompanying necessity to adapt? One could imagine more than sadness—perhaps they lived in fear for the future. What would happen
next? How would they survive? In crushing uncertainty, the people
would have worried about all aspects of their future. The violent and
disempowering circumstances of their "resettlement" most likely left
them feeling lost and afraid.

3

The prophetic writings of that period illustrate the swirl of feelings that resulted from the exile experience. Sadness, fear, and despair seep from the poetic words of the prophets. Yet even more pronounced is the sense of confusion. You can almost hear the Judean exiles sitting in Babylonia, holding their heads in their hands, desperately asking, "How did we get into this mess anyway? What do we do now? Will God help us?"

In the discussions within their community about the circumstances that led to this fate, there must have been recriminations and blame for the destruction of the beloved Temple and the loss of the national home. Historians suggest[1] that the exiles to Babylonia were primarily the community's elite—its leaders and their community of peers. Perhaps they felt guilty for misdirecting their people; and in their feelings of loss and being lost, might not their collective self-worth have been battered?

Isaiah rose to address the people precisely at this terrible moment, offering interpretations of their experiences. In this portion, Isaiah exhorts: "Listen, you who are deaf; you blind ones, look up and see! Who is so blind as the chosen one, so blind as the servant of YHVH? Seeing many things, he gives no heed; with ears open he hears nothing" (42:18–20). After years of hearing the warnings that destruction would occur if the people were not faithful to Torah and prophetic cries of impending doom as punishment for being unfaithful to God, the people believe that they are victims of their own wrongdoing. In their despair, they turn to God, and to the Divine messenger, the prophet, to guide them out of the darkness. Speaking God's message, the prophet leads them toward clarity, hope, and a sense of purpose.

The image of a blinded nation being led toward the light is so resonant that there are three other references to it in this portion alone. We read, "Opening eyes deprived of light, rescuing prisoners from confinement, from the dungeon those who sit in darkness" (42:7). Just as God will redeem Israel from the darkness, Israel shall become a light to all nations. "Opening eyes deprived of light" is a metaphor for "freeing the imprisoned."[2] Isaiah tells his people that they will be rescued and that God will lead them down a road they could not discern alone: "I will lead the blind by a road they did not know, and I will make them walk by paths they never knew. I will turn darkness before them to light, rough places into level ground. These are the promises—I will keep them without fail" (42:16). "Setting free that people, blind though it has eyes and deaf though it has ears" (43:8). Clearly, Isaiah wants the people to know that God has heard their cry, that God understands their confusion and fear. They can feel assured that God will light the way and guide the people.

Even in this hope-filled portion, we hear echoes of God's displeasure with the people of Israel. "Who was it who gave Jacob over to despoilment and Israel to plunderers? Surely YHVH, against whom they sinned, in whose ways they would not walk and whose teaching they would not obey" (42:24). Using characteristically harsh language, the prophet speaks of how those who trust in idols will be driven back and utterly shamed. And yet, the haftarah overwhelmingly conveys the message of change and of hope for a bright future.

So why this turnaround?

We can read this portion as a conversation between a parent and a child. The child, Israel, has misbehaved (badly!) and been punished. In a midrash that imagines the behaviors warranting such a punishment, we are told that, "When people eat too much, drink too much, and become arrogant in spirit, all kinds of mishaps take place. Only when their eyes are opened to the spirit of Torah do they appreciate that they were like prisoners sitting in the darkness."[3] Even though the child was warned that certain unacceptable behavior would prompt a harsh punishment, and it occurred just as it was forecast, the child is still confused, lost, and fearful of what will happen next. Israel, still immature, needs help to find its way. Isaiah quotes God as saying, "Bring my sons from afar, and my daughters from the end of the earth— all who are linked to My name, whom I have created" (43:6–7). In this portrait, the people of Israel seem like adolescents, challenging the authority of the parent, seeking to find their "own way," and old enough to be capable of making a major mess of things! And yet, even in their rebelliousness, they still desperately need adult guidance. Most of all, they need unconditional parental love.

Thus, it is noteworthy that the prophet makes use of both masculine and feminine similes for God, indicating perhaps that God could be both Mother and Father. Use of female imagery for God is, in fact, a one of Isaiah's distinguishing characteristics.[4] "I have kept silent far too long, kept still and restrained Myself; Now I will scream like a woman in labor, I will pant and I will gasp" (42:14). The power of this verse is missed by the Sages. From a feminist perspective, one cannot help noticing this powerful birthing image in juxtaposition to the creation theme in the beginning of the portion, linking it to the Torah reading. The Creator is the Birth Mother of humanity, and, like all mothers, She continues to nurture her young. In seeing God as the Mother through our own lens, we find within that image a nurturing, loving parent who comes forth to comfort and guide her young. She is not unlike our own images of nurturing mothers.

Starting with the reminder that God was the creator of the world, who "gave breath to the people upon it" (42:5), the prophet begins this portion with the message of unconditional love. Isaiah seems to deliberately recall the images in *Parashat Bereshit* in these opening words, using the language of the Torah as a bridge: "God who created the heavens and stretched them out, Who spread out the earth and what it brings forth" (42:5). God is more than just the Creator; God who "gave [us] breath" is engaged and personal, in contrast to the lofty and impersonal image in *Bereshit*.[5] This portion thus begins with and then transcends the predominant biblical worldview, in which good or bad fortune in life supposedly results from supernatural reward and punishment. This child was brought into the world by choice, lovingly, and with a purpose.

This sense of unconditional love helps us to understand the complexity of the message of both disappointment and hope. We are most vulnerable in our relationship with our parents. Likewise, we are most uplifted when our parents show us love, and, as teenagers may grudgingly admit, we may be most influenced by lessons taught to us by our parents. In fact, during a phase of our lives when our fragile egos are developing through our experiences, it is not at all uncommon for teens to feel battered by any serious loss. The despair of the people of Israel is one such low personal moment.

Thus, this message of reassurance from the Mother is just what the people need. The prophet's reminder that the warnings that preceded the exile did in fact come true is communicated, so that they will see it as proof of God's wisdom and experience, in which they are encouraged to trust. God really does know what will happen if the people go astray, as in a parent who says, "I just know more than you do about this. Trust me." God is a solid rock in whom they can trust, having been there all along just waiting for the people to learn and to grow and to mature.

Yet these conversations between parents and children, especially teens, don't always go as well as expected. Even when parents intend to reassure and lovingly guide their child out of a difficult and frightening morass, they sometimes react with impatience and slip into anger. True to metaphoric role, this very emotionally engaged Mother is invested in the experience of the child. God says, "I have kept silent far too long, kept still and restrained myself" (42:14). It is a note of exasperation, as if to say, "I have waited for you to find your way, to see the light and behave according to your potential, but, oy, I have lost my patience!"

God's angry outbursts in this haftarah might make us uncomfortable and frightened. It would be nicer to hear the message of hope delivered lovingly, patiently, and gently by a consistently nurturing Mother. But we are human, and we hear God through human experience. Surely we would be impatient if we were the parent here!

The Mother's heart is breaking—as Her children suffer, so does She. As we listen to the conversation between parent and child, we hear the parent plead with the child to understand, saying, "I will not abandon you, I will save you and protect and preserve you because I love you. Even though you have more to learn, I will help you because I can see that you need me." As our rabbinic Sages imagine the dialogue, Isaiah's insight expands to mean, "'So you are my witnesses—declares YHVH—and I am God,' [Isa. 43:12]; and when you are not my witnesses then I, as it were, am not God."[6] Israel and God are part of each other's identities. God lives to be Israel's parent. The people can relax; the ordeal will soon be over. It is a message that we could imagine any child in a difficult spot would want to hear from his or her parent, and a message that still uplifts the community of Israel in moments of darkness throughout the ages.

RABBI JILL HAMMER

הפטרת נח

Haftarat Noach

Isaiah 54:1–55:5

*S*ing joyfully, barren one who did not give birth!
Burst out and sing, rejoice, you who never were in
labor, for more are the children of the abandoned woman
than of the wedded one, says God. Make wide the place
of your tent and the curtains of your tabernacles!
(ISAIAH 54:1–2A)

*N*oach and his sons went, and his wife and his sons'
wives with him, into the ark. (GENESIS. 7:6)

A MIDRASH SUGGESTS that when Noah, his wife, his sons, and their
wives entered the ark, "The men went alone and the women alone,
for they were forbidden from sexual relations because the world was
afflicted with suffering."[1] This midrash is part of a larger rabbinic
theme: women and men who forgo procreation because of their fear
that their children will know suffering. Adam and Eve, parents of
humanity, as well as Amram and Yocheved, parents of Moses, are said
to have separated for a time because of their fear that their children
would be born into a broken world.[2] We can read the haftarah of
Parashat Noach as an antidote to the fear of brokenness; the story of
Noah's unnamed, unexamined wife and daughters as they rediscover
hope, and as our own story of renewed faith.

9

The haftarah of *Parashat Noach* is Isaiah's vision of an exiled Israel redeemed and returned to her land. Isaiah understands the exile and decimation of the Israelites as Divine punishment for sin, but preaches the possibility that God will forgive. The prophet imagines Israel as a joyful, repentant wife, reunited with a God-husband no longer angry at her: "For a little moment I left you, and with great mercies I will gather you up" (Isa. 54:7). God reassures the desolate woman, symbolic of the Israelite nation, that though God sent her away and made her live in pain and humiliation, God has finished punishing her, and no one will ever harm her again. As a reward for her patience, her fertility will be so great that she will have to refurbish her tents in order to accommodate all of her offspring. The language is poetic, the imagery exquisite, but feminist scholars have pointed out a sinister side to Isaiah's potent words: There is a clear similarity between God's "discipline" of Israel and the cycle of violence in an abusive relationship, in which one partner victimizes and then comforts the other.

Naomi Graetz gives a particularly potent rendering of this disturbing textual metaphor in her essay "Jerusalem the Widow" in *Shofar: The Journal of Midwest and Western Jewish Studies* 17:2. If God is an angry husband who punishes his errant wife and then forgives her, why should human husbands not follow God's example? If this behavior is abhorrent to the Jewish community, how can we cope with a sacred text that ascribes it to God? Perhaps by transforming the text through creative interpretation, we can imagine Israel's wifehood in a new way.

Naamah and Her Daughters-in-Law

The women of *Parashat Noach*, Noah's wife and daughters, have only a small role in the narrative. Noah's wife is given a name in midrash—Naamah—but his sons' wives do not even have midrashic names. We do hear from rabbinic midrash that Naamah's deeds were pleasing to God,[3] and in her modern midrash *Noah's Wife: The Story of Naamah* (Jewish Lights),[4] Rabbi Sandy Eisenberg Sasso suggests that it was

Naamah who saved all the plants of the earth by collecting seeds. Yet from the Torah, we know only two things about these four women: that they went onto the ark with Noah and his sons, and that the daughters-in-law did not yet have children. In the text, God does not speak to the women, but merely commands Noah concerning their entry onto the ark. Yet, like Naomi and her daughter-in-law Ruth, these women are thrown together on a desperate journey, not knowing where they will find food or how their line will be continued. Their story is continued in modern stories we know well: immigrants crossing oceans, persecuted families in hiding, refugees from oppressive countries or abusive homes. Isaiah's words of pain and comfort, addressed to a feminine presence, seem to speak to old and new tales of women's survival and endurance.

What must these women have felt, closed into the wooden box that floated on the waves, separated from their spouses, torn forever from many of the people they had known and loved? It is easy to apply to these women Isaiah's words: "Storm-tossed, suffering one, not comforted" (Isa. 54:11). In their fear, they may have been grateful not to have had children who might have suffered in a terrifying reality where the raging sea was everywhere. We can imagine Naamah saying to them: "*Roni, akarah lo yaladah*; Sing, barren one who did not give birth!" (Isa. 54:1). She too is grateful for their childlessness, for how can she want grandchildren under these horrific circumstances? We can imagine others who have suffered feeling that same hopelessness.

In the midst of such turmoil, there is tremendous guilt and shame associated with survival. In times of tragedy, we may blame ourselves for our troubles. Sometimes we are justified in examining our actions. Yet sometimes we blame ourselves simply because it gives us a sense of control in a chaotic world. In a strange way, it makes us feel less vulnerable if suffering is our own doing. Women, in particular, are taught to hold themselves responsible, even if in reality someone else, or no one else, is at fault. This is how many abusive relationships are perpetuated, and it is also why many women and men spend their lives harassing themselves for not being perfect. It is this sense of unreasoning guilt that the haftarah addresses by insisting that God is no longer angry, and promising: "Fear not; you shall not be put to shame" (Isa. 54:4). Perhaps, by offering forgiveness for our past misdeeds, real or imagined, the haftarah asks us to move beyond our guilt and accept the covenant of Noah—the covenant of unconditional love. Perhaps, as Naamah and her daughters-in-law stood at the entrance of the ark and saw the rainbow in the sky, they were able to feel that they deserved to rebuild. For them, that was God's covenant of love.

We, too, are called to rebuild when we have been broken down. "All you who are thirsty, go out for water," God calls near the end of the haftarah (Isa. 55:1). How ironic to suggest that those who once feared the water should now be sustained by it! Yet God promises that fear can be overcome, and that water, which once caused death, can now be a source of life and hope. We can imagine Naamah and her companions, freed from the ark, tentatively, gingerly drawing a first bucket of fresh, life-sustaining water, relieved that it does not rise up and swallow them. So, too, after great sorrow and fear we must confront what overwhelms and grieves us, in order to rediscover hope.

There is a pre-Raphaelite painting by John Everett Millais titled *The Return of the Dove to the Ark*. Surprisingly, rather than picking Noach as his subject, the artist depicts two young women. One holds the dove with the olive branch while the other leans down to kiss it. Both look relieved and tenderly joyful. Millais's painting captures the moment of realization that God is present even in the darkest places. This is the moment of covenant—when new life becomes possible, when the abandoned one becomes fruitful. Rabbinic midrash tells us that though Noah and his sons boarded separately from Naamah and her daughters-in-law, they all left together. As the haftarah says: "You will call a nation you did not know, and a nation that did not know you will run to you" (Isa. 55:5). In Hebrew, the verb *yada*, "know," can mean "to make love" as well as "to understand or recognize." When we restore hope, we can form relationships with one another—the first step necessary to building a future.

ℑhe Message of *Haftarat Noach*

"Rabbi Oshaya said: Why is Torah compared to the three liquids—water, wine, and milk—as it is written: All who are thirsty, come to the water. . . . Come and buy wine and milk [Isa. 55:1]? Just as these liquids are only found in the humblest of vessels, so words of Torah are only found in one whose mind is humble."[5] By quoting *Haftarat Noach*, Rabbi Oshaya reminds us that Torah is not for the arrogant. We must read this haftarah not as a text that supports the self-justification of abusers, but as a text that comforts the suffering of survivors and refugees. If we imagine *Haftarat Noach* as the story of all who come through the storm, we learn that God's covenant is with those who struggle through their own guilt and fear to find new life in difficult times: "Like the water of Noah this is to me; as I swore that the waters of Noah should no more go over the earth, so I have sworn that I will not be angry with you or rebuke you. . . . My covenant of peace shall not be removed" (Isa. 54:9). We can transform the haftarah's powerful image of God as spouse—"Your husband is your Maker"—from rageful patriarch to partner in the renewal of life. In this haftarah, we imagine the women and men throughout the ages who sought God in the midst of the sea. *Haftarat Noach* is a reminder that in spite of our brokenness, where hope reigns, anything is possible—even rebuilding a life after the harshest of storms.

RABBI SUE LEVI ELWELL

הפטרת לך לך
Haftarat Lech Lecha

Isaiah 40:27–41:16

Why do you say, O Jacob,
Why do you assert, O Israel,
My way is hidden from the Eternal,
My claim is ignored by my God?
Do you not know?
Have you not heard? (ISAIAH 40:27–28)

AS MICHAL SHEKEL teaches in *The Women's Torah Commentary*, *Parashat Lech Lecha* is a portion of journeys, both physical and spiritual.[1] The first journey is that of Abraham and Sarah, if one accepts Sarah Sager's suggestion that the curiously doubled imperative that gives this portion its name includes Sarah in the challenge to go forth and leave all that is familiar.[2] Our ancestors travel to Egypt, presaging subsequent descents into the land of the pharaohs. They take the measure of the land, hoping to lay claim to property that will become a home to them and their descendants. The road to the creation of the next generation, however, is not as easily traveled. Infertility becomes the impetus for Abraham and Sarah to enlist Sarah's servant Hagar to serve as the birth mother of Abraham's first child, but Sarah interprets Hagar's successful conception as an affront. When Hagar flees from her mistress, God appears to her and reassures her that she will bear a son who will live among his brothers. God's presence, or absence, is significant in each of these journeys.

14

The complementary prophetic portion, composed during the period of the Israelites' exile in Babylonia, is a composite of sources that address God's role in Israel's journeys. The haftarah expands the metaphor of journey beyond the patriarchal narrative to speak to the entire Jewish people, wherever they may find themselves. This haftarah begins with a cry of invisibility, a cry that could have been uttered by any one of the biblical characters whose journeys are described in the Torah portion *Lech Lecha*. "Why do you say, O Jacob, / Why do you assert, O Israel, / My way is hidden from the Eternal, / My claim is ignored by my God?" The prophet Isaiah sets up the question in anticipation of the answer that he will provide: The omnipresent One, who does not tire nor age, gives strength to those who trust in God's deliverance. These opening verses clarify the extent of God's dominion as both spatial and temporal: "Creator of the earth from end to end, [Who] never grows faint, never grows weary." The Holy One is portrayed as omnipresent and omnipotent, qualities that reassure every weary traveler, any seeker who has lost her way. These words are addressed to all the Israelites, but the use of the particular names Jacob and Israel underscore that the collective is named for a single patriarch whose life, and name, like those of Abraham and Sarah, was changed by his encounter with the Divine. The prophetic charge to the people is effective precisely because each individual is addressed as capable of an encounter with God that can determine the future direction of her life.

Isaiah promises the energy and prowess enjoyed by the young to those who put their faith in the Holy One, invoking the majestic symbol of an eagle to illustrate the image of power. In Exodus 19:4, it is God who is portrayed as lifting the people on eagle's wings. Here the Holy One endows all who trust in God with the ability to "soar on wings like eagles." When we remember that all travel in the ancient world was on foot, we too are elevated by this image of soaring above the earth, with the speed and grace of a majestic eagle. Scholars point out that while this haftarah includes several voices or oracles, the message of the portion is singular: The Holy One is first and last, more enduring than natural formations or human creations.

A second metaphor employed by the prophet is particularly challenging to the modern feminist reader. Masters of various crafts are described as coming together to help one another, encouraging one another to excel. These cooperative workers are juxtaposed with "You, Israel, my servant/ Jacob, my chosen one . . ." This is an Israel whose primary connection is not with other mortals, but with God. Twentieth-century theologies of mutuality celebrate the holiness that can develop between two individuals who commit themselves to a shared goal or vision or task. Isaiah's image seems to undermine such a spirit of mutuality, offering the contrasting and unsettling image of shame and contention that can result when two individuals clash or compete with one another. The lowest blow seems to come when Israel is called *tolaat Ya'akov*, which is often translated as "the worm Jacob." Israel is reduced to the lowliest of creatures, and our humility is magnified by God's greatness. God promises that God will transform this ineffectual creature into a force so considerable that mountains are turned to dust, and hills become chaff. The images of abject meekness and raw power provide an uncomfortable contrast with the cooperative laborers, and seem to take us to a world of gross inequities, a world in which invisibility may be preferable to partnership with a bully.

How are we to resolve this discomfort? How are we to understand this reiteration of the One and the worm as a relationship that will outlast and outlive the seemingly more vibrant engagement of peer cooperation? The final couplet of the haftarah provides a typical *nechemta*, an attempt to comfort the reader and the traveler alike. If we read this portion as a collection of texts assembled intentionally to assist the weary traveler, we may see that the prophet's vivid images reflect the sights and insights of the wandering Jew. The prophet helps the traveler make sense of the complex and troubling worlds we all encounter. When we return to the beginning of the portion, we realize that the opening verses of the haftarah have set the tone for the entire portion: "Do you not know? / Have you not heard? / The Holy One is God Eternal, Creator of the earth from end to end" (40:28). This God is the One who has been with us since the beginning of time, and, we learn as we continue our journeys, God's work does not end with creation. As we learn, as we make our way through our lives, the world is full of examples of successful partnerships between individuals. Human beings can find both pleasure and profit in working, playing, and building lives and homes together. But the prophet's words take us beyond our own experience, expanding our perspective from the narrow boundaries of our own perception. The prophet's questions take us into God's time and the vastness of eternal space, beyond the reach of human endeavor. Isaiah challenges us to imagine a connection that is deeper and more gratifying than the companionship or shared achievement of mortals. The prophet opens our eyes to the possibility of spiritual partnering, partnering between God and each individual human soul.

The image of the cooperative laborers acts as a foreshadowing, a preview of true cooperation. A true partnership, a covenantal *brit* between God and every Jew, is even more powerful, more mutually beneficial, than any partnership between mortals. Unlike the human partnership, which yields fine carpentry or metalware, God's partnership with human beings is a source of spiritual support and the creation and nurturing of hope: "I, the Eternal, your God / Who holds your right hand / I say to you, Have no fear / I will help you." This *brit* transcends time and space. This *brit* is mysterious, for it can transform mortal experience into something greater and, finally, more enduring. Many of us who are survivors of loss and trauma have known the blessing of human support. And many of us have sensed, too, the deep comfort of God's healing hand, God's sheltering arm. This haftarah teaches us that we need not journey alone.

When this haftarah is read along with the *parashah* it complements, we glimpse the genius of the Rabbis, our teachers. Human beings, even the most noble among us, cannot see beyond the limits of our own experience. Reaching for truth, we clumsily bring pain and even shame to one another. As Abraham and Sarah begin their journey, we, their heirs, ready ourselves for the next stage in our lives. This portion challenges us to consider how God can become our traveling companion, and how traveling in God's presence may transform the way we encounter ourselves and our world. In a world of connections that are too easily broken, these words point toward a relationship with God that can nourish and renew the spirit. Isaiah offers a model of a connection and a perspective that can nourish and sustain us for days and years to come: "For you shall rejoice in the Holy One / and glory in the Holy One of Israel" (41:16).

RABBI PAULA JAYNE WINNIG

הפטרת וירא

Haftarat Vayera

II Kings 4:1–37

*B*ehold, I perceive that this is a holy man of God . . .
(II KINGS 4:9)

IN THE HAFTARAH for *Parashat Vayera*, we read of the ascendancy of the prophet Elisha, disciple of Elijah, following Elijah's rise to the heavens in the fiery chariot. Elisha is known for the miraculous cures he brings to people, and particularly for the ten miracles he performed during the period of his prophecy. In our story from II Kings, chapter 4, we read of two of Elisha's ten miracles. In this set of stories we see Elisha helping two women regain hope and dignity. These stories tie the haftarah and Torah portions neatly together, as they both show women achieving goals that are otherwise unattainable. A third story often associated with this *parashah* is the story of Hannah from chapter 1 of the Book of I Samuel, read on Rosh Hashanah.

At the beginning of this tale, Elisha encounters a widow of one of the disciples of the prophets, who is too poor to support her family. A creditor is ready to enslave her and her two children in order to pay off their debt. Sensing the woman's desperation, Elisha makes certain that as he performs the miracle necessary to assist her, he does so in a manner that preserves her dignity. When he meets the widow and she confides her problem to him, Elisha responds by asking her what she has in her home. She tells him that she has only one jug of oil. Elisha tells the woman to borrow as many vessels as she can from her neighbors and

19

then close the door and together with her children use their jug of oil to fill the other vessels. Though the original jug of oil was small, it sufficed to fill all the vessels she had collected. Elisha then instructs the woman to go out and sell the oil so that she will have enough funds to support her family.

This quaint story helps to illustrate one of the nicest qualities of the Elisha stories: that heroes can be miraculous and still mortal. Rather than giving her riches, Elisha helps the widow to help herself. In the eleventh century, Maimonides emphasized that this was the most important type of *tzedakah*. This story seems to convey a sweet, simple lesson; it also reminds us that faith and belief are often not so much miraculous as a factor of our own choices. While certainly the fact that the oil kept flowing until all the vessels were filled is miraculous, it could not have happened had the widow not been open to the possibility that life could and should be better. This distraught widow had many choices as to how to respond to her downtrodden state. She could have given up on life and become embittered. She could have accepted her fate and become enslaved. Instead, she looked for a positive way out of her situation, and was ready to recognize the help Elisha, as God's prophet, could offer her.

The second miracle recounted in this haftarah portion directly connects it to *Parashat Vayera*. Elisha travels to the village of Shunem where a wealthy woman lives. This woman always invites Elisha to share a meal whenever he passes through Shunem. Believing him to be a man of God, she offers him hospitality by fixing up a place for him to stay in her home whenever he comes to their village. This act of hospitality mirrors the hospitality Abraham showed his visitors in our *parashah*. Elisha is so grateful to the Shunemite woman for her generosity that he inquires of his servant, Geichazi, what he can do to repay her for her kindness. Geichazi asks if perhaps the Shunemite woman needs Elisha's support with the king or the army commander. Humbly, the woman replies that she lives among her own people and requires no such intervention. She clearly did not feel it necessary to be compensated in any way for her hospitality to Elisha and Geichazi.

Elisha is not satisfied and wants to reward her. Geichazi knows that the woman "has no son, and her husband is old," and tells Elisha of her predicament. Elisha then speaks to the woman, saying, "At this season next year, you will be embracing a son." The Shunemite woman, like Sarah in our Torah portion, is incredulous at this news and replies, "Please, my lord, man of God, do not delude your maidservant." As is usual in the Bible, despite her doubts, the Shunemite woman does conceive and gives birth to a son. But in a dramatic turn of events we read that after the child grows up, he goes to see his father in the field one day, cries, "Oh, my head, my head!" and then collapses. The servants carry the unconscious boy to his mother and he lies in her lap for a few hours and then dies. His mother was not willing to believe that her son could be taken from her in this manner.

Immediately, the Shunemite woman rushes to find Elisha to see what he can do to help. As she approaches Geichazi in search of Elisha, she hides her distress from him, perhaps fearing that Elisha might not want to assist her. But when Elisha finally sees her and notices her dismay, she cries out to him, "Did I ask my lord for a son? Didn't I say 'Don't mislead me?'" In her distress, she feels that she would rather not have had the son than to see him die prematurely. Elisha urges her to return to her son quickly, giving her his staff to place on the face of the boy, in hopes of reviving him. The Shunemite woman refuses to leave without Elisha. As it turns out, Elisha's staff is not enough to revive the boy, as Geichazi discovers while Elisha and the boy's mother are on their return journey. However, when Elisha arrives, he breathes into the boy's mouth, warms his body, and after sneezing seven times, the boy is revived. The Shunemite woman's choice to believe that Elisha could help her son, and her effort to bring him back to her home, make it possible for Elisha's miracle to work. Had she not believed in his abilities to heal, and believed that her son deserved to be healed, her son would have died.

The women in these stories may seem like straw figures, chosen because they fit necessary categories: widow, barren woman, and distraught mother. But as is always the case with biblical stories, no one character—particularly a female character—is given so much attention unless we are meant to learn something special from her. The women of the stories help demonstrate the importance of faith, commitment, and belief. They also remind us of the basic humanity and decency needed to build a true community. The widow needed means of support. The wealthy barren woman, willing to share her food and home with a stranger, finds completion with a child, until his life is threatened and she can't bear the thought of this loss. When their lives are changed through miraculous means, they are each grateful, and acknowledge God's role in the restoration of their fortunes. Yet had they not sought out assistance, and been willing to involve themselves with God's prophet, they would never have been able to change their lives.

Like these women in the Elisha tales of the Second Book of Kings, we too will only see the miracles life has to offer us if we are open to the possibility that miracles can happen for us, even in our darkest moments. While it would be presumptuous of us to assume that there is a prophet waiting around the corner to improve our lot in life, there are certainly many people we encounter who can help us throughout the joys and challenges of our lives. These miraculous stories remind us that we have a choice to believe, to act on our beliefs, or to remain skeptical of the world around us. By believing that God's prophets have the power to help and to heal, the women of these stories regain faith, dignity, and hope. By believing that our tradition, our people, and our community can help us find faith, dignity, hope, and support, we too can find the strength to overcome our difficulties and create blessed lives.

RABBI BETH JANUS

הפטרת חיי שרה
Haftarat Chaye Sarah
I Kings 1:1–31

*K*ing David answered, "Get Bathsheba." (I KINGS 1:28)

KING DAVID IS ONE OF THE pivotal characters in Jewish history. Not only is he considered the greatest king of Israel, he has also become the archetype for the Messiah. The Rabbis say that the Messiah will be a direct descendant of David. *Haftarat Chaye Sarah* tells of David's last act: the passing on of the throne to his son, Solomon. However, David does not accomplish this succession alone. Nathan, the prophet, and Bathsheba, David's wife, play central roles in this historical transition.

Bathsheba first appears in II Samuel 11. David sees Bathsheba while she is bathing on her roof. The text illuminates her great beauty. David sends for her. They lie together, and she becomes pregnant. Because Bathsheba is already married, David devises a plan to have her husband, Uriah, killed in battle. The death of Uriah enables David to marry Bathsheba. Significantly, this episode is told over two chapters, which is substantial for a biblical story. There is a considerable amount of action and dialogue between David, Uriah, Nathan, and the commander-in-chief, Joab, but none with Bathsheba. In the middle of this story, Bathsheba says only one thing, "I am pregnant" (II Sam. 11:5). Even David's unnamed servants have more lines than this. Little is known about Bathsheba from this episode, and it would seem from this introduction to her character that she is only an agent in this story;[1]

she seems to exist simply to propel the story of the principal figure, David.[2]

The next time mention is made of Bathsheba is in this portion, *Haftarat Chaye Sarah*. David is now old and ailing, and his eldest living son, Adonijah, declares himself king. David is unaware of this. Nathan devises a plan to alert David, so that David can pass the kingship on to his younger son, Solomon. Nathan approaches Bathsheba, explains the situation of Adonijah's alleged kingship, and asks her to speak to David. He furnishes her with the exact words to say. She is to remind David of his promise that her son, Solomon, would succeed him as king, and then ask David about Adonijah as Nathan enters and confirms what she has said. The scenario plays out, and subsequently, David declares Solomon to be king.

On first glance, it appears that this haftarah is a story in which the men are the central characters, and the women are only there to support them. Bathsheba receives her lines, she "performs," and her part is over. However, a careful reading reveals a different narrative.

At the beginning of this haftarah, there are details about Adonijah's rebellion. Nathan is the first to respond, and his initial response is to go to Bathsheba. This is the first indication that Bathsheba is seen as a crucial factor in Solomon's ascent to the throne. Nathan wants her to go to David and prevail on him to declare Solomon king, spoiling Adonijah's aspirations.

Nathan knows that David is unaware of Adonijah's self-appointment. It appears that in his old age, David is oblivious to the political turmoil regarding his successor. Nathan does not want to tell David that he fears that David does not know what is happening in his own kingdom. This would be too disrespectful to the king. So instead, Nathan calls on Bathsheba to give David the information, without pointing out that David does not know what is happening. Behind his back, he tells her to say to David, "My lord, the king, did you not swear to your servant by saying, 'Solomon your son will rule after me, and he will sit on my throne.' So why is Adonijah now ruling?" (I Kings 1:13).

If Bathsheba were simply an agent, she would have used the exact words that Nathan had given her. She would have humbly been Nathan's mouthpiece. Instead, she changes the language slightly, and this subtle change reveals her power and character. Bathsheba begins where Nathan directs her: She reminds David of the promise he made to her regarding the kingship of her son, Solomon. But instead of couching her language in describing Adonijah's rebellion, or leaving it out altogether, she speaks plainly. She says, "And now, behold Adonijah has become king, but my lord, the king, does not even know" (1:18). She confronts David in his weakness and senility. She believes Solomon should be the next king and does what she can to achieve that goal in a clear, direct manner.

She then provides David with more information about Adonijah's actions. She goes beyond what Nathan has asked of her and speaks to David, not from a script, but from her own mind. She tells David: "The eyes of [all of] Israel are upon you to tell them who will rule after you" (1:20). She is unafraid to place the facts before the king. She wants David to comprehend the gravity of the situation. She continues to speak until Nathan comes to interrupt, as is the plan.

When Nathan begins talking to King David, Bathsheba is presumably sent out of the room. Nathan corroborates Bathsheba's narration, and only when he finishes speaking does David speak for the first time since Bathsheba arrived. His first words are, "Call in Bathsheba." Not only does Nathan look to Bathsheba immediately during this crisis, but the king does as well.

What do we learn from this? On the simplest level, Bathsheba is a powerful woman. Although she does not speak often in the Bible, if we look critically at the words she does say, we see that she is an important character in the story of King David. She truly influences the course of Jewish history.

On a deeper level, we also see an egalitarian model for leadership. We tend to assume that political systems from thousands of years ago follow a strict form of hierarchy. We might assume that King David, as the person with control, would have ruled within this structure of power. But *Haftarat Chaye Sarah* reveals that David did not rule alone. It would be easy to dismiss this story as the exception to the years of King David's rule, because he is ailing and old. Perhaps he only needed help at this point, near the end of his days. But this story can also suggest a long-term relationship between Bathsheba and David, as political leaders *sharing* power. Nathan, Bathsheba, and David all refer to an earlier promise David made to Bathsheba regarding Solomon's future kingship. This points to just one discussion between David and Bathsheba about crucial political decisions, while there may have been many. Nathan and David would not each immediately turn to Bathsheba at the peak of David's vulnerability, if David had not done so in the past. The Rabbis agree that the sharing of responsibility is the ideal, as in a midrash that comments on Ecclesiastes 4:9–12 ("Two are better than one . . . A threefold cord is not readily broken.") "Rabbi Judah, Rabbi Nehemiah, and the Rabbis comment. Rabbi Judah says: [Two] refers to David and Bathsheba, and *a threefold cord* to Nathan the prophet . . ."[3]

David, Bathsheba, and Nathan are models for us because they share power. It is obvious that each individual has points of weakness no matter how high her or his position. If we each recognize our weaknesses, and the weaknesses in those around us, then we can surround ourselves with people who strengthen our leadership. We can complement each other. A complete leadership is rarely filled by one person. Few of us will ever be good leaders unless we can first admit vulnerability and allow others to lead with us. Nathan saw David's weakness, but admitted that Bathsheba had to join with him in order to influence David's actions. David, after being confronted and informed, admitted his weakness and turned to Bathsheba. Together they formed an influential threefold cord.

RABBI CAROL E. STEIN

הפטרת תולדות

Haftarat Toldot

Malachi 1:1–2:7

*A*nd the Torah of truth was in his mouth . . .
(MALACHI 2:6)

THE PROPHET MALACHI speaks in the days of the Second Temple. As do many of his fellow prophets, Malachi criticizes the conduct of *B'nei Israel*, particularly in their "religious practice," such as the inferior quality of the animals offered for sacrifice. In this haftarah the rebuke comes in the form of an imagined conversation. God speaks on behalf of Heaven and on behalf of *B'nei Israel*, as God imagines they would speak for themselves. It is as *B'nei Israel* that the reference to Jacob and Esau appears. This reference to Rebekah and Isaac's twins is the connection to the Torah reading for this week. In the *Parashat Toldot* reading from Genesis, Jacob appears before his ailing father. Claiming to be his brother Esau, Jacob seeks and receives the blessing that was due the firstborn.

In the second chapter of Malachi, the rebuke of the people (actually, the men, because they are responsible for fulfilling the sacrificial and ritual obligations of Torah) has concluded, and the tribe of Levi is being cautioned to fulfill their duty: to glorify God's name (2:2). God reminds them that God relies on their awe (*yirat HaShem*) in making the covenant with them. God warns of curses and other unpleasantness as punishment for the failure of the *Levi'im* to satisfy this one requirement. At 2:6, it is the *Levi'im* who are being described. "The

Torah of truth was in his mouth and iniquity was not found on his lips . . ."

The resonance of this verse in Malachi can be heard in Proverbs 31:26 and 30 of *Mishlei*, the part of the Book of Proverbs popularly referred to as *Eshet Chayil*, Woman of Valor. This is what is said about the woman of valor: "Her mouth opens with wisdom and the Torah of loving-kindness is on her tongue" (verse 26) and "a woman in awe of God, she is to be praised" (verse 31). The woman here appears to have precisely the qualities God expects from the *Levi'im*, those who serve as priests and those who assist the priests: a Torah of truth on their lips.

In what ways are women of valor like those who serve God? First, the woman spoken of in *Mishlei* is a woman who reveres God, just as the *Levi'im* were selected for a special relationship because of their awe and reverence for God. It is worth noting here that the tribe of Levi was separated from the remainder of *B'nei Israel* in several ways. They were separated in the performance of their jobs, when the *Levi'im* served as assistants to the *Kohanim*, the priests. Only the Levites and the *Kohanim* could touch the ritual objects. Others—the remainder of *B'nei Israel*—were prohibited from touching them. Additionally, the tribe of Levi was not counted in the census, whose purpose was to number those eligible to serve in the army. The *Levi'im* and *Kohanim* did not go to war.

Traditionally, women too have different jobs than men and were not counted on to be soldiers. Although many women today have jobs outside the home, and are eligible to serve in the armed forces of many countries, including Israel, the analogy still holds: Those in attendance at the place of worship and those attending to the family home are indispensable and could not be spared for battle.

The other significant similarity between the tribe of Levi and the woman of valor is that the words of Torah fill their mouths. The priests and their assistants were fully occupied with the needs of the sanctuary and altar. Their knowledge of Torah—the religious guide—was assumed as a necessary part of their work. It is expected that, because they had to know the contents of God's teaching, their mouths would be filled with those words, and no words of injustice. So too the woman of valor, who, according to the words of *Mishlei,* is not only filled with wisdom but with kindness as well. And having this knowledge, she speaks it. When might she speak it? Whom does she see? As the chief administrator of the home, this woman of valor would speak with vendors, and those who might be working around her family's home. She might also speak to the neighbors and other women with whom she might join to do work best shared by many hands.

A woman of valor has the responsibility for educating her children, and how better to do so than with words of Torah and loving-kindness? The priests and *Levi'im* were responsible for running the Temple in Jerusalem and the *mishkan* in the wilderness, and, just like the woman of valor, they too had to guide those coming to offer sacrifices or to worship. Similarly, the Rabbis throughout the ages since the destruction of the Second Temple have been charged with keeping alive the worship traditions and providing religious education. The woman of valor has carried that responsibility since the time of Sarah, as both wife to Abraham and then mother to Isaac.

Malachi speaks to men only in chapter 1. He speaks only to those who are required to bring sacrifices, specifically, unblemished animals, the best of the herd (Lev. 1:3, 10). Yet, the qualities of those to whom God is speaking are articulated. Those same qualities are found in *Eshet Chayil.* Just as the Levi is called a messenger or angel of the Lord of Hosts (Mal. 2:7), so too is the woman of valor—and all the women of valor today. Might we not see the valorous women in our lives, who preserve our heritage, as the *Levi'im* of Judaism today?

RABBI KATHY COHEN

הפטרת ויצא

Haftarat Vayeitze

Hosea 12:13–14:10

I will love them freely . . . (HOSEA 14:5)

LIKE MOST PROPHETIC PORTIONS, the haftarah for *Vayeitze* outlines the sinfulness of Israel, expresses the forthcoming punishment for those sins, and closes with a note of comfort for the future relationship between God and the people of Israel. Of particular note in this reading are both the use of imagery and the general background of the prophet Hosea.

The reading begins with a clear link to the Torah portion of the week, a reminder that Jacob has fled to the land of his mother's family to find a wife. There appears to be no further connection between the Torah portion and the haftarah portion than this bit of history, but thematically the connection is stronger than we may first notice. The very concept of marriage, albeit as a metaphor, is central to Hosea's understanding of Israel's relationship to God. Hosea is less interested in the happenings of the past than he is in warning of the future degradation.

Living during the eighth century, Hosea rails against the Northern Kingdom of Israel, which he refers to as *Ephraim*. The eighth century was a period of general wealth and prosperity for the people of both the Southern and Northern Kingdoms. Hosea preached that this wealth had caused a decline in the steadfastness of the people. Idolatry was again taking hold in the kingdom, and prosperity was leading to moral laxity. People were less attuned to the will and the ways of God. With Assyria becoming a nation of rising power, Hosea prophesied that the Northern Kingdom would see its destruction at the hands of Assyria.

Hosea is the first prophet to use the beautiful imagery of Israel as God's bride, a very powerful concept, since the husband/wife relationship is viewed as a sacred bond. The midrash[1] suggests that Hosea understood the power of this attraction through his own foible. When the Holy One said to Hosea, "Your children sinned," Hosea should have replied, "They are Your children, children of those You greatly loved, children of Abraham, Isaac, and Jacob. Let the measure of Your mercy roll over them." Not only did Hosea not speak in this way, but he actually dared say to God, "Master of the universe, all the world is Yours [to do with as You like]. Put another people in their place." The Holy One said, "What shall I do with this so-called Sage? I will tell him, 'Take yourself a whoring wife, who will bear you children in whoredom.' Later I will tell him, 'Send her away from you.' If he is able to do so, I, too will send Israel away [from Me]." So Hosea went and took Gomer the daughter of Diblaim (a woman of ill repute) to be his wife. After two sons and a daughter were born to him, the Holy One said to Hosea, "Should you not follow the example of your teacher Moses who separated from his wife as soon as I began speaking to him? You too should live apart from yours." Hosea replied, "Master of the universe, I have children by her. I cannot send her away or divorce her." The Holy One replied, "You—whose wife is a whore and whose children are the children of whoredom, so that you do not know whether your children were fathered by you or by others—still reply in this way. Yet you dare to say of Israel who are My children, children of those tested by Me, children of Abraham, Isaac, and Jacob, Israel who are one of the four masterpieces—Torah, heaven, and earth, the Temple and Israel—I wrought in My world, yet you dare to say of them, 'Put another people in their place!'" Thus made aware that he had sinned, Hosea started beseeching mercy for himself. But the Holy One rebuked him: "Before beseeching mercy for yourself, beseech mercy for Israel."

Thus many of the writings by Hosea stress the importance of the relationship between a husband and a wife. Hosea is horrified by the possibility that Israel has broken that sacred marital trust with God. In this imagery the "wife" has strayed, but with appropriate instruction will see the error of her ways and return to the loving husband. God's punishment of the people is comparable to that of a loving parent, consequences meant to set the child back on the proper path without causing harm. These are not actions born of anger or retribution, but rather of pure commitment to Israel. God's love is understood to be unconditional, even when angered by the actions of the people.

In this haftarah portion Israel breaks the sacred trust in two manners. First, the reversion to idolatry is a proverbial slap in God's face. It is akin to an adulterous affair. Israel's first and only love is meant to be to God. The presence of these idolatrous practices threatens that sacred bond. Israel's second transgression is the desire to be ruled by a human king, which is viewed as a weakness in the relationship between God and the people. Though the presence of the king does not break the marital bond, it creates distance between the people and God—a distance that God does not desire (Hosea 13:11).

God's anger is kindled by this distancing of Israel from the marital bond. The imagery used to describe the outcome of this anger reflects another important relationship—that of a woman to her children. The bond between a woman and her child(ren) is almost indescribable. The power of feeling life growing within, the pain of birth, and both the joy and trepidation of nurturing offspring lead to a connection of tremendous power. Throughout history women have been willing to lay down their lives to save their children. In the Book of Maccabees (II Macc. 7) we read about a most unusual mother who encouraged each of her sons to face the death of a martyr rather than submit to idolatrous practices. She watched as each was killed and then she submitted to the same fate. This woman was made to choose between the sacred marital bond between God and Israel and the maternal bond to her children.

The fate awaiting those who have incensed God is even more ferocious than that of the woman in the Book of Maccabees. Hosea declares in 14:1 that the young children will be destroyed and the pregnant women will be cut open. The imagery is overwhelming. It is meant to bring tears to the eyes. It is a mother's worst nightmare, a parent's dreaded fear. The maternal relationship—born of hope and joy—will soon be the cause of the greatest mourning known on earth. These words are intensely personal. They are much stronger than warnings of pestilence or starvation. These words strike at the heart of one of the most powerful relationships known to humanity.

The strong language in this section effectively emphasizes the point that the destruction of the marital bond with God will lead to the destruction of all other human relationships based on love. If the people are not capable of loving God, then they are not truly capable of loving each other.

Hosea prophesies that the people will return to God and that they will reestablish that sacred bond. Forgiveness will be granted, and once again the people will live in the glory of God's protection. It is in 14:5 that the greatest comfort is offered. Hosea reports that God says, "I will love them freely." In this short sentence there is an assurance that both the marital bond and the maternal bond will be reinforced.

Surely it is in relationship to God and people that life remains meaningful. Hosea learned this in the midrash cited above. The fact that this haftarah portion is read on the same day as the Torah portion that reveals Jacob's search for a wife has an underlying purpose. As Jacob searches for the person with whom to create that sacred marital bond, God demands that Israel be faithful to the Divine marital bond.

It is likewise interesting to note that part of this portion is also read on *Shabbat Shuva*, the Sabbath between Rosh Hashanah and Yom Kippur. It is on this Shabbat that we are most conscious of repairing our relationship with God. We strive to see ourselves as God's partner in the unfolding of creation. We instinctively know that our actions during the previous year have created distance between God and us. On *Shabbat Shuva* we read this portion and strive to repair the sacred bond with our Creator.

Hosea's imagery of marital fidelity provides the modern reader with a context in which to understand the depth of relationship that is possible between a people and their God. It is important to understand that Divine marital fidelity incorporates concepts that differ from human marital fidelity. Whereas we can place our complete trust in God's wisdom, this is generally not the case among people. We are imperfect by nature, and we are capable of making imperfect choices in our love lives. When love is no longer part of a marriage or when abuse is present, we recognize that those bonds are already broken. With pain and sadness, the marital relationship may dissolve. Yet, we strive to bring into our lives, both with God and with a loving spouse, a relationship built on the highest standards of our tradition. When bonds of love are treated with integrity, the world stands in balance.

RABBI NINA BETH CARDIN

הפטרת וישלח
Haftarah Vayishlach

Hosea 11:7–12:12

*J*e wrestled with an angel and prevailed; he cried and entreated him . . . (HOSEA 12:5)

A LONG TIME AGO, crying was sacred. In desperate moments, in times of great sorrow, when overcome with emotion, our ancestors cried. Abraham cried when Sarah died; Esau cried when Jacob stole his birthright from him; Jacob cried when he first kissed Rachel; Joseph cried when he saw his brother Benjamin again. In this haftarah, in Hosea's retelling of the story of Jacob wrestling with the angel (Gen. 32), one of the two rivals cried.

Most of the biblical characters who cry are men. But crying in the Bible is far from unmanly. Throughout the Bible, crying was not only an acceptable accompaniment of powerful emotions; often, it was a necessary accompaniment. Tears authenticated the emotion. "Looking about, Joseph saw Benjamin, his brother, the son of his mother . . . and he was overcome with emotions. On the verge of tears, he hurried out, went into a room and wept there" (Gen. 43:29–30).

This was the case with emotions, and all the more so with prayer, itself often an impulsive verbal response to emotions. But why would prayer need to be authenticated? Because prayers can be conjured up any time they are needed. Although often spontaneous and genuine, they can also become routine, formalized, and calculated. Imagine if we found ourselves being called by a prophet to repent. We could dig into

35

our satchel of pious words, riffle around until we found particularly pen-
itent-sounding phrases, and deposit them in the prayer slot. But tears,
before they were devalued as the coin of women, were seen as authentic. So much so that while prayer might not be accepted without tears,
tears could be accepted without prayer: "R. Eleazar said: On the day
that the Temple was destroyed, the gates of prayer were closed . . . But
though the gates of prayer are closed, the gates of tears remain open . . ."
(*Berachot* 32b). Tears penetrate the very heavens. They come from a
deep place and thus enter a deep place. Their source enables them to
achieve their destination. And that destination is before the very
throne of Heaven.

What happens then? What happens to our tears? They are collected, counted, preserved. In one of the most poignant verses of the
entire Bible, the psalmist writes: "God, You put my tears in Your pouch,
in the place of all [ac]countings" (Ps. 56:9).

Our tears do not go unnoticed. God scoops them up, as it were, and
places them in a watertight pouch so they should not be lost, so they
should not be wasted. No matter what other response our crying may
produce, the psalmist allows us to imagine that, at the very least, God
cares about our tears. God tends to our distress with such care that each
of our tears is precious, gathered up like precious droplets of rain or dew
in a parched desert. And with each tear harvested, our pain is ever so
tenderly soothed.

Sometimes, our tears are meant to be more than soothing. They are
meant to be theurgic; that is, they are meant to move God to do what
we want.

> The prophet Isaiah, son of Amos, came to King Hezekiah,
> saying: Thus said the Lord, set your affairs in order for you
> are going to die, you will not live. Thereupon Hezekiah
> turned his face to the wall and prayed to God: "Please,
> God, remember how I have walked before You sincerely
> and wholeheartedly, and have done what is pleasing to
> You." And Hezekiah wept and wept. Before Isaiah had
> gone out of the middle court, the word of God came to

him: "Go back and say to Hezekiah, Thus said the Lord, I have heard your prayer, I have seen your tears. I will heal you" (II Kings 20:1–5).

That is secretly what all of us hope for, but we know that such miraculous responses are likely beyond our reach. Still we cry, even when we know there is nothing more that can be done. At such times, we cry not to make things come out differently, but simply because there is nothing else for us to do. Tears are our only release, our only response. And though they may not heal, they may ease the grip of the ache.

Remarkably, our tradition tells us that such crying is not only a human response, but a Divine one as well. *Lamentations Rabbah* tells us that when God saw the destruction of the Temple, God cried.

> At that time the Holy One, blessed be God, wept and said, "Woe is Me! What have I done? . . ." Metatron [a chief angel] came, fell upon his face, and spoke before the Holy One, blessed be God: "Sovereign of the Universe, let me weep, but do Thou not weep." God replied to him, "If you do not let me weep here, I will repair to a place where you cannot go and weep there." (Prologue 24)

Sometimes we just need to cry. Sometimes we seek to cry alone. Other times, we choose to cry in the presence of others, to have them witness our sorrow and comfort us in our pain. It is often hard for others to see us weep, but as this midrash teaches, it is a gift to be present at another's weeping. And we dare not ignore tears that are shed in our presence.

To feel a tender hand upon our face, to be gently stroked and have our tears dried, is to feel the power of a loving, strong presence. And more than just any presence. For this intimate gesture conjures up memories of the very first person who dried our tears, and kissed them away. Even as our mother and father once comforted us, so God will one day comfort us. Tears in the Bible and Midrash were true, redemptive, regenerative, releasing.

And yet, over time, and over many cultures, tears became associated with women, and, once associated with women, they came to be seen as a sign of weakness, a tool of manipulation, and thus they lost much of their power. A curt Hasidic story drives home the point: "A widow was sued for rent before the Sachatzover Rebbe. She began to weep copiously. The Rabbi refused to hear the case on the ground that he had learned from the Kotzker that tears are a form of bribery."[1]

Indeed, tears can be manipulative, as can prayers. But we don't devalue prayer. We learn instead to pray truthfully, and to discern genuine from manipulative prayers. So we must again do with tears.

RABBI HARA E. PERSON

הפטרת וישב

Haftarat Vayashev

Amos 2:6–3:8

*C*an two walk together without knowing? (AMOS 3:3)

THE PROPHET AMOS raised his voice and cried out against the wrong-doings of Israel. In the section of the Book of Amos used as the haftarah for *Parashat Vayashev*, Amos speaks out against a multitude of ethical and ritual crimes, including legal corruption, improper treatment of the poor, and forcing wine on the Nazirites, those pledged to not drink any wine at all in the service of God. Amos calls the people to account, reminding them of their special relationship with God, and demanding that they take responsibility for their actions while warning them of God's punishments should they not take heed.

Amos connects the relationship between the people and God to the relationships between one person and another. He asks, "Can misfortune come to a town if Adonai has not caused it?" (Amos 3:6). God will be the *cause* of all the bad that befalls the Israelites, but not the *reason*. The reason lies in the improper behavior of the Israelites. At the very beginning of the Torah, in Genesis, we are taught that all people are created *b'tzelem Elohim*, in the image of God (Gen. 1:27). Forgetting that there is a spark of the Divine in each person leads people to treat each other like objects measured by their usefulness, rather than as human beings. The righteous are sold for a quick financial gain (Amos 2:6). Women become objects of sexual gratification for men (Amos 2:7).

39

And in ignoring the fact that each person is created in the image of God, the ideas of holiness and ethical actions become forgotten and discarded as well. God's holy places are defiled (Amos 2:8) and God's laws are abrogated (Amos 2:12). Amos saw this behavior, and it concerned him greatly. He understood that a lack of ethical behavior was a reflection of the state of their relationship with God, and that the relationship was in trouble. Unable to connect with God properly, the people were unable to connect with each other and vice versa.

The *parashah* of Vayashev teaches that "They sold Joseph for twenty pieces of silver to the Ishmaelites, who brought Joseph to Egypt" (Gen. 37:28). In the haftarah we read, "Because they have sold for silver those whose are righteous" (Amos 2:6). In rabbinic tradition, Joseph is commonly referred to as a *tzaddik*, or righteous person[1] and this idea gives support to reading Amos 2:6 as a reference to Joseph. The midrashic collection *Pirkei De Rabbi Eliezer,* in chapter 38, takes this connection one step further, tying the reference to sandals in the continuation of line 2:6 of the haftarah to the selling of Joseph into slavery. The midrash states, "[The brothers] sold him to the Ishmaelites for twenty pieces of silver, and each one of them took two pieces of silver . . . to purchase shoes for their feet . . ."

The connection, however, seems to go deeper than simply the mention of slavery noted by the rabbinic commentary and midrash. On another level, what the Torah and haftarah are concerned with is the mishandling of personal relationships, in often disturbing and even unethical ways. *Parashat Vayashev* contains within it three significant stories about Joseph. The first, in Genesis 37, is the story of the young Joseph being sold into slavery by his brothers. The second, in Genesis 39–40, tells the story of Joseph's early years in Egypt, in which he is taken in by Potiphar and winds up in jail. These two tales of Joseph bracket the story told in Genesis 38, the puzzling story of Joseph's brother Judah and his daughter-in-law Tamar.

That a group of brothers would so despise and resent one of their own that they would sell him into slavery, lie to their father, and cause their father great pain by reporting his son's death is an obvious example of a problematic relationship. In the story that features Judah in Genesis 38, he too is embroiled in a web of unethical relationships. When his first son dies and leaves his wife Tamar a childless widow, it is Judah's duty, according to the laws of levirate marriage outlined in Deuteronomy 25:5–10, to marry her to his second son so that she can have a child to care for her in her old age. That son would also act as an heir for her first husband. When that second son subsequently dies as well, without having produced a child, Judah refuses to marry his third son to Tamar. Tamar, unwilling to give up the dream of a child that should be hers by right, concocts a plan and seduces Judah himself, finally securing for herself not just one child but twins. A third important story in Vayashev recounts how Potiphar's wife tries to ensnare Joseph into a sexual relationship with her. When Joseph refuses, trying to act correctly, she accuses Joseph of attempting to seduce or rape her, for which he is thrown out of Potiphar's house and into jail.

Amos speaks out against "Father and son going to the same girl" (Amos 2:7). Read against the text of the *parashah*, this statement recalls Judah's encounter with Tamar and raises the question of how Judah could not have known who Tamar was, even in her disguise. Did he notice but not care, thinking only about the momentary sexual satisfaction? Or did he not even notice, having never properly known her for who she was, having seen her only as an adjunct to his sons, despite her having lived in his household? Is she invisible to him as a person, but now visible as a sex object? Judah is seeing Tamar as a thing, a prostitute, rather than as a person created in God's image. Amos also brings to mind Joseph's unfulfilled episode with Potiphar's wife that appears later in this *parashah,* for while not father and son, there was a close relationship between Joseph and Potiphar, similar to that of a mentor and protégé. As related in Genesis 39:3–6, Potiphar had tremendous trust in Joseph and left his entire household to his care. Not only would a relationship between Joseph and Potiphar's wife have been morally compromised because she was already married, but Joseph would also have been betraying the incredible trust placed in him by Potiphar.

Amos speaks of breakdowns in relationships on many levels. Using the example of a father and son going to the same young woman, he connects that breakdown to the profaning of God's holy name (2:6). It is significant that the Hebrew word used here to denote the kind of woman visited by the father and son is *na'arah*, best translated as "girl," or "young woman." It is not just her gender that is implicit in this word, but also her youth. What is emphasized here is not just that the father and son are sexually involved with the same person, but that she is young as well. Rather than finding satisfaction and pleasure in relationships based on true partnership and friendship, the father and son are engaged in extramarital sexual relationships based on easy gratification. In addition, they use a *young* woman to achieve this gratification, an allusion to an unequal power relationship, one in which she is being taking advantage of by these men.

This kind of a relationship profanes the name of God because what is missing is the mutual love and care that should be part of an ethical relationship. By taking advantage of this young woman and using her for their own gratification, this father and son are profaning God's own divinity, not recognizing the spark of the Divine that flickers within her.

The story from the *parashah* of brothers selling another brother into slavery serves as an analogy in the haftarah to people in a society not taking care of each other. Having been created by God, all people are, on some level, siblings. All people are responsible for each other. When the poor are not cared for, when a piece of silver or a pair of sandals becomes more important than human life, this is an example of abusive, unethical relationships in which our humanity is lessened. And when our humanity is lessened, the Creator of humanity is also diminished.

Amos cries out against these kinds of relationships, teaching that these relationships cause a society to lose its ethical compass and fall apart. "Can two walk together without knowing?" he asks, using a form of the verb *yadah*. In Hebrew this verb means "to know" on a deep level, as opposed to simply "being familiar with." This is true knowing, knowledge based on intimacy. Can two people carry on a real relationship without that deeper level of knowing and caring about each other, without seeing the spark of the Divine in each other? Amos's question also speaks to the relationship between the people and God. Can the people walk with God, professing to follow God's laws, while breaking those very laws? The answer, of course, is no. It is not enough to superficially walk with God; to truly walk together with God people must live in a way that acknowledges God's presence in their lives on a deeper level.

When men engage in relationships with women that are not those of caring partners but of use, of satisfying physical needs but not caring for the other, God is angered and society itself crumbles. The same is true when communication breaks down and people cannot talk and cannot listen, and when family members don't take care of each other. Amos warns the people to listen well, for, if not, the lion will roar and they will truly have something to fear.

Through Amos, God reminds the people of their long and rich history with the Divine. God is angry, but God has not turned away. It is up to the people to restore their relationship with God by reestablishing relationships with each other based on trust, caring, and ethical behavior. It is only when we stop selling each other for silver, when we stop using each other, that we can know the love of God intimately and fully.

RABBI ZOE KLEIN

הפטרת מקץ

Haftarat Miketz

I Kings 3:15–4:1

*S*o the king said: Fetch me a sword. They brought a sword into the king's presence. Then the king said: Cut the living child in two, and give half to the one, half to the other. But the real mother was churning with compassion [*rachamim*] for her son, so she pleaded with the king: Please, my lord, give her the living child; whatever you do, don't kill him! But the other said: No, it will be neither yours nor mine; cut it in two. The king spoke up: On no account kill the child—give him to the first woman—she is the real mother. When Israel heard of the decision of the king, they held him in awe, seeing that he had within him Divine wisdom to do justice [*hochmat Elohim b'kirbo la'asot mishpat*].

(I KINGS 3:24–28)

SOLOMON'S VERY FIRST COURT DECISION is the heart of *Haftarat Miketz*. It is perhaps the most famous example of Solomon's wisdom. At the end of our haftarah, it is concluded that "He had within him Divine wisdom to do justice." The Hebrew for "Divine wisdom to do justice" is *hochmat Elohim la'asot mishpat*. The Sages believed that the two different names of God, *Elohim* and *YHVH*, each referred to different aspects of God. *Elohim* was God as Judge. *YHVH* was the God of love and mercy. The kind of wisdom that Solomon possessed came from the aspect of God that judges. Let us imagine that there is also another kind of wisdom in the world—*hochmat YHVH la'asot rachamim*, "Divine wisdom to do mercy." Our challenge in this text is first to understand Solomon's wisdom, and then to recognize a wisdom to do mercy that stems from a God of love.

King Solomon is renowned for his wisdom. The Sages credit him as the author of the Song of Songs, Proverbs, and Ecclesiastes. Legends abound about his keen insight into problems and riddles. Midrash tells of the Queen of Sheba traversing the desert terrain with caravans of gifts to test his majesty's brilliance for herself. She asks him, "What has ten openings, and when one is opened, nine are closed, but when nine are opened, one is closed?" Solomon knows immediately that the answer is a person, for a person has ten openings: two eyes, two ears, two nostrils, a mouth, a naval, and two for excreting. Nine are closed in the womb, but the naval is open to receive nourishment through the umbilical cord. Upon birth, the naval is closed and the rest are opened and ready to function. The Queen of Sheba is amazed by Solomon's wisdom and insight, and lauds him with spices, tapestries, and exotic birds in gold cages. It is curious that the Queen of Sheba is not recorded in history as a pillar of wisdom herself. Solomon only solved the puzzle, but she came up with the clever riddle in the first place.

In verses 15 and 16 of the haftarah, there is a striking juxtaposition between the abundance of riches that must have filled the halls for the king's sumptuous banquet, and the two destitute women who come heartbroken, afraid, and angry to the palace for help. We can imagine the contrast in their dress to that of the banquet's official guests. Rabbi Levi ben Gershon (known as the Ralbag) suggests that God brought the prostitutes as Solomon's first case to rein in the ego of the king, to teach him that not only would he pronounce judgment on high officials, but he would judge the salt of the earth as well. Here, we can admire Solomon for lending his discerning ear to the uninvited women.

It is interesting to note that the woman does not refer to her housemate by name, rather only as "this woman." They live in the same house together and they were each present for the birth of the other's child, and yet they don't know each other's names. Their aloneness is emphasized in the woman's presentation. It would have been enough for her to say, "We were alone," but she adds "no one else was with us," and "just the two of us were in the house." From a legal standpoint, it is important for the king to understand that there were no witnesses. This is a case of one woman's word against another woman's word. But why so much emphasis on their aloneness? The woman is talking about an existential aloneness that defies legalisms. She and her house-mates are prostitutes. The men come and go and care little, if at all, about them. All they have in the world is each other. No one else understands how alone they truly are, except for each other. They are companions in this sad life, in their sad house. No one came to help with the baby. There is no father, only "she was there with me . . . we were alone." Of course they know each other's names! They have an intimate, sharing friendship. When we listen with Solomon's *hochmat Elohim la'asot mishpat*, we hear the important point that there are no witnesses. When we listen, however, with *hochmat YHVH la'asot rachamim*, we imagine the first woman's pleading, "This isn't only about the child, King Solomon! This is about my terrible fear that I have lost my friend, that I've lost my companion and I am truly alone!"

When we listen with *hochmat Elohim la'asot mishpat*, we are aware of a criminal act. It is an accusation of one of the most disturbing crimes one can commit—kidnapping. However, when we try to listen with *hochmat YHVH la'asot rachamim*, we have an inkling of the unfathomable sorrow that guides her actions. She wakes up in the night, her infant son is snuggled against her bosom. She nudges him, but he is still. His little lips are not rooting around to suckle warm milk; in fact, in the moonlight, they seem blue. The truth becomes all too clear. The boy is dead. She believes that she suffocated him in the night by rolling over in her sleep. And so the woman is struck all at once by an enormity of grief and guilt. Perhaps she runs to her friend's room crying and clutching her heart. Perhaps she just tiptoes to her friend's bedside ashen and pale as a ghost. Perhaps she wants to find comfort there. Perhaps she picks up her friend's son for solace and then just can't bear the thought of letting go of his warm, snuggly body. She takes the boy gently, for her friend is not stirred out of her sweet slumber, and brings him into her bed and nurses the living child. Just to nurse one more time, just to be needed by someone, to kiss his innocent little brow. Perhaps she is crazy. Perhaps she is criminal. When we approach her with the wisdom of mercy, we can never underestimate the profundity of absolute despair.

Why does Solomon repeat the testimony in verses 22 and 23? Commentary suggests that it is important for a judge to repeat testimony to be sure he has heard correctly. Malbim, however, looks more closely and says that Solomon is acknowledging the different ways the women prioritize. He points out that one woman prioritizes "the living one," while the other woman prioritizes "the dead one." In this way, it is possible that Solomon was already ready to make his decision, that he already knew that the woman who prioritized the living one was the true mother.

We know that the women are prostitutes, and so we assume that they have a lot of contact with men, and that the contact is more often less than loving. The king before whom they plead their case offers them a violent solution. Granted, the king never intended to cut the child in two. His is a brutal justice. The male presence throughout this story is unloving, except for these two little baby boys who offer their mothers, at long last, a pure and complete and gentle love. They lie snuggled into their mothers' bosoms, the first bed companion that promises not to hurt, not to leave. And then one leaves, and utterly abandons his mother. And so the one little baby boy only a few days old seems the last remaining shred of hope for both of these women, to save them from their savage solitude.

Rashi suggests that Solomon heard a *bat-kol*, a "heavenly voice," that told him, "This one is the mother." Does Rashi think that the test was not a perfect one? Is it possible that the woman who wanted the child cut in two could have been the child's mother? We assume that the biological mother would never want to hurt her child. It is a widely accepted stereotype that women are naturally nourishing, organically embracing, and motherly. But it is dangerous to assume that all women are motherly. Furthermore, between the two women, the extreme stereotypes of women are represented; one is seen as compassionate, merciful, loving, nourishing, and motherly; and the other as murderous, vengeful, irrational, angry, and dangerous. We see this in the age-old distinctions between Eve and Lilith, angel and demon, virgin and whore. Maybe Solomon's test was designed not to elucidate who was the biological mother but, as he said, the "real mother," the mother who "churns with compassion." The Hebrew for "compassion" is *rachamim*, coming from the Hebrew root for "womb," *rechem*. The biological mother carried her son in her *rechem*, her womb, but the "real mother" is the one who will carry him throughout his life in her *rachamim*, her compassion.

You are the sovereign ruler. Two prostitutes come before you and plead this very case. They are weeping. They are trembling and afraid. They are terribly sad. The baby boy, rosy and beautiful, is wiggling about in his basket. He smells like milk and sugar. You have a sword at your side. You have arms to embrace. You have an open heart and an open mind. Both of these women woke up to a dead baby, and only one realized that the baby was not hers. A *bat-kol* has told you which woman is the real mother, and so you know. How do you now proceed? What sort of divine wisdom would you give to those who stand trembling before you? Is there a way to decide in favor of both justice and compassion?

RABBI MARSHA J. PIK-NATHAN

הפטרת ויגש

Haftarat Vayigash

Ezekiel 37:15–28

*A*nd you, mortal one, take a stick and write on it,
"For Judah and the Israelites associated with it"
and take another stick and write on it "For Joseph—
Ephraim—and all the house of Israel associated with it."
Bring them close together, so they are as one in your
hand. (EZEKIEL 37:16–17)

THE WORDS OF *Haftarat Vayigash* are from the Book of Ezekiel the prophet, exiled from Jerusalem to Babylon shortly before the destruction of the Temple in 586 B.C.E. As a member of the priestly class, his greatest concerns revolved around national unification, and the restoration of the Temple and its cultic practices.

Haftarat Vayigash presents us with one of Ezekiel's unique prophetic acts. In this brief text, Ezekiel reveals God's command to him—to take two sticks, one representing the Southern Kingdom of Judah, and the other representing the Northern Kingdom of Joseph, and to join them, bringing them together as one.[1]

God anticipated that people would ask the prophet about the meaning of this unusual action, and Ezekiel is to explain it as a symbol: that just as the two sticks are joined together in Ezekiel's hand, so too will God gather the dispersed Israelite people—that is, those of the ten lost tribes—and bring them back together with Judah to re-create a single nation in the land. Further, God tells Ezekiel to explain to the people that this single nation will be a pure nation, which would "never again defile themselves by their idols, and abhorrent images, and other transgressions," and that God "will cleanse them." Then they will be, says God, "My people, and I will be their God." God also instructs Ezekiel to tell the people that they will be united under the rule of a king from the Davidic dynasty. God commits to the ultimate fulfillment of this vision, echoing the ancient Divine promise: "they will remain on the land which I gave to my servant Jacob and in which your fathers dwelt; they and their children and their children's children shall dwell there forever . . ."(37:25). Finally, God promises: "I will make a covenant of peace with them. . . . I will place my sanctuary in their midst forever. My presence shall rest over them . . ." (37:26). While a beautiful and passionate prophecy, Ezekiel's vision has not been fulfilled. The ten tribes have not been reunited, and those of our people who were lost in 722 B.C.E. have not been found. Is it a prophecy that will need to wait for another era? Is the world not yet ready for the fulfillment of this prophecy? Rather than dismissing Ezekiel's words as prophecy unrealized or fantasy unfulfilled, we might look more deeply to glean the true relevance in the subtlety of the prophet's message.

Looking closely at the text in verse 17, we see that at first Ezekiel is told to take the sticks and bring them close to one another so they become *l'achdim*—as one—in your hand. The Hebrew phrase is an unusual one; it includes the *l* prefix, connoting "toward" and puts the word for "one" (*echad*) into the plural (*achadim*). This odd word makes us wonder: Is the idea here to put two sticks together to make one new unbroken whole, or, perhaps, allowing the sticks to come together *toward* being *as* one? Read this way, we can see the individual sticks remaining inherently independent and retaining their own identities. In the plural form ("onenesses"), there is room for more than one. It implies or, better, invites room for multiplicity, even in this call for unity. The strange usage of this word invites us to explore the notion of unity altogether. With "onenesses," we challenge the usual assumption that unity means sameness, and can explore the idea of unity in more pluralistic ways, extending the grammatical cue to our lives.

The idea of unity in Ezekiel's vision is to bring back "home" those who have in some way wandered far from familiar paths or become estranged. Is it a viable vision to expect thousands of people—men, women, children, old, young—after centuries (or perhaps millennia) of living in other lands and assuming multiple identities to be able to return "home"? Can they then gather pieces of ancient collective memory and weave them into an identity into which they can seamlessly slide? And—more strikingly—is it even a desirable vision? Ezekiel's vision uses a backward gaze, returning to the time of the Temple and its reverence for cultic activity: priests, sacrifices, purity rituals, and the rule by a single royal dynasty. It is a static image, returning to the way things had been as if that is the only way they could possibly work. What would it look like if Ezekiel's image of a "family reunion" looked forward instead? To do so would be to sew from their experience not a seamless garment, but one that is stronger *because* of its seams.

To reimagine this idea of unity in Ezekiel's context challenges us to think of notions of unity in our own time. While the establishment of the State of Israel in 1948 was a paradigm-shifting event in history, it certainly was and continues to be very different from Ezekiel's vision of the unified state; we are all well aware that the Jewish people, even living in the Promised Land itself, are deeply divided. While many of us long for a time when the differences do not polarize us, we might not agree that our dream is represented by the image of two sticks coming together as one. What would Israel, as a contemporary nation—not an abstract vision—be without the vibrant and creative tension between Ashkenazim and Sephardim, religious and secular, conservative and liberal viewpoints on a wide spectrum of issues and passions?

The patriarchal vision of returning to the status quo would be challenged by a feminist vision of unity. In such a vision, the call for unity would not depend on a single means of getting there, and would not hearken back to past standards of what works and what doesn't work. In such a vision, unity would not mean uniformity. As Jews we view the notion of K'lal Yisrael (the totality/unity of the Jewish people) with reverential, perhaps wistful ambivalence. As much as we want to all get along and think we are operating from shared assumptions, we know all too well that we do not. To say that we have the same starting point and shared destination is to run the risk of setting up *K'lal Yisrael* as a static, unyielding straw idol that we must inevitably knock down. Rather, reality reflects back to us that while we come from a multitude of origins in our religious beliefs, political loyalties, and lifestyles, we strive to come together as Jews, continuing to evolve in our definition of what that entails. A beautiful midrash poignantly illustrates how multiplicity can be inherent in and strengthen unity. It speaks of the moment in the Book of Exodus when the Jewish people gathered at the foot of Mount Sinai to receive the word of God:

> Observe how the voice issued forth. It came to each Jew according to his capacity—the elderly, the young men, the children, the infants, the women—each according to his capacity . . . even pregnant women heard according to their capacities.[2]

Not only at Sinai, but each day, there is no monolithic understanding that works for all of us as Jews. Some of us hear God's voice calling us primarily through traditional religious observance, some through social action, some through commitment to Israel, others through the cultural and artistic expression of our Jewishness, and still others through creating tradition anew. What a blessing that, as at Sinai, God's voice continues to call to us in such a multiplicity of ways!

As women, too, we are blessed with the understanding of how many voices contribute to our understanding of the world, and how our lives would be lacking without this diversity. We have come a long way from the early understanding of women's liberation as defining "us" against "them" to an embracing not of "Feminism," but of the many feminisms that reflect the varied dreams of women. Like Ezekiel's sticks, we can, as feminists, come together in unity, but not uniformity—understanding that a vision that allows everyone to actualize her potential is true freedom, but that not everyone can, will, or should do that in the same way. Poet Adrienne Rich tells us, "Isn't there a difficulty of saying 'we'? . . . there is no collective movement that speaks for each of us all the way through."[3] We must be careful to note, then, our "location," as contemporary feminist scholars call it. Even as Jewish women, we speak from a wide array of such "locations"; ironically, the *truly* radical notion is that there is not just one Jewish feminism, but, as with feminism itself, many Jewish feminisms. From Orthodox women striving to find a feminist voice within halachah, to Jewish feminist scholars in the academy, to Jewish lesbians attempting to bridge worlds that have traditionally been at irreconcilable odds, we continue to shape a Jewish feminist vision that allows us to respect those whose visions differ from our own.

In our haftarah, the final word is God's, not Ezekiel's. As the text ends, God promises to make a *brit shalom*, a covenant of peace with Israel. As God's covenant with Noach was sealed by a rainbow, with its dazzling array of colors—the modern symbol of celebrating diversity—so too can we trust that under the sheltering wings of God's oneness, we have the freedom to explore all the joy and wonder of our own "onenesses."

הפטרת ויחי
Haftarat Vayechi
I Kings 2:1–12

Now David's days grew to a close, and he instructed [*vayetzav*] his son, Solomon, saying: "I am going the way of the earth. You shall be strong and be a man [*vehazaktah vehayitah l'ish*]. Keep the charge of YHVH, your God, walking in God's ways and observing God's laws, commandments, rules, and warnings, so that you may succeed in all that you do and wherever you turn."
(I KINGS 2:1–3)

THE HAFTARAH FOR THE PORTION *Vayechi* gives us a glimpse into a very private moment in the life of two of the Bible's most prominent public figures: King David and his successor, his son Solomon. This short haftarah portion of only twelve verses describes a critical series of events: David's deathbed message to his son, followed by his death, and Solomon's accession to the throne.

While a great deal of Jewish literature looks at the biblical kings as models for the ethics of war and conflict, contemporary readers can look to the story of David and Solomon as a model father-and-son relationship. In fact, the linking of this narrative with the Torah portion in which Jacob addresses each of his sons on his deathbed encourages the reader to focus on the parent-child relationship.

David is fully aware that he is about to die, and begins his speech by telling Solomon so, ensuring that his son will listen to him carefully, since these are the final words he will hear from his father. According to the Divine prophecy, Solomon has been singled out as David's royal successor from among his many brothers. While in the Torah portion Jacob speaks to all twelve of his sons on his deathbed, David reserves all his words for Solomon alone. After a lifetime together, what does David want to convey to his beloved son? His words can be interpreted in two primary ways: as political orders or personal advice.

One could argue that David's message is not an intimate one, but rather a series of orders designed to ensure that Solomon will uphold his father's religious and political loyalties. This interpretation hinges on the use of the term *vayetzav* in the opening verse, which comes from the verb "to command." In verses 5 to 8, using military language found elsewhere in the Tanakh, David instructs Solomon with regard to two primary matters: exacting vengeance against Yoav ben Tzeruiah and Shimei ben Gera, two men who wronged David years earlier; and rewarding the kindness of Barzillai, one of his supporters, by dealing graciously with his sons.[1] According to commentators, David dies obsessed with his legacy and preoccupied with events of long ago. He speaks to Solomon on his deathbed not because of a special father-son relationship between them, but because Solomon is his designated political successor. He does not take advantage of the opportunity to honor his relationship with his son through a sharing of intimate words, and he leaves the reader dissatisfied with the lost potential of the moment and troubled by the violence that David has commanded his son to carry out. This seems to be a stereotypical moment involving an emotionally absent father speaking to his son of "practical details" rather than love.

Yet David's message can be understood differently. The verb *vayetzav* can also mean "to instruct" and is used several times in the Tanakh in reference to instructions at the time of death.[2] Perhaps David's final message to Solomon was his way of teaching his son one last time. Though his words lack emotional power, a careful reading of the text reveals that David is attempting to convey his deepest values and beliefs to his son, and expresses his sincere wish for Solomon's success in all his future endeavors. David seems to want Solomon to know that he has confidence in him and his abilities, a knowledge that will guide and comfort him as he loses his father and begins his reign as king.

David's opening words to Solomon are general but also personal, "be strong and be a man *(vehazaktah vehayitah l'ish).*" The instruction to "be a man" jumps out at us, and challenges us to put aside modern connotations in order to contemplate what this phrase meant in its context. The same words are used in the plural in I Samuel 4:9, as a prebattle "pep talk" for the Philistine army, who are afraid to fight against Israel. In that context, the command to "be a man" emphasizes bravery. Yet there are other possible interpretations of *vehayitah l'ish* in our haftarah. Juxtaposed to the other half of the phrase *be strong,* the command to "be a man" implies that while maintaining strength one should also remember to be human and humane, valuing life over might; for David understood from his own experience that leaders can easily begin to feel larger than life and lose their moral grounding and humility. Gersonides interpreted this phrase as "do not act like a child,"[3] in which case David's charge is similar to the charge of "Today you are a man," given to a Jewish boy at Bar Mitzvah. This charge is not about masculinity, but rather an indication of responsible adulthood. *Be a man* here means *zie a mensch*—strive to be the best person you can be.

David goes on to express his desire that Solomon obey the Torah. David exemplified a kind of piety that one would not normally expect from a political and military leader, and devotion to God and Torah was central to his being. As a parent, he seems to be saying to his son: "I'll no longer be around to be your role model. I want you to understand what it is I value most, and I pray that you will value the same things. I have found blessing, meaning, and direction in my life because of my devotion to Judaism, and I hope that you will as well." David is expressing his wish that Solomon will succeed in all his endeavors, not only in the military realm.

Finally, David instructs Solomon to punish Yoav and Shimei, whose crimes were perpetrated many years ago. It is a surprising message, for it seems that the great and pious king is bearing an old grudge of which he simply cannot let go, even as his death approaches. Some traditional commentators, wary of criticizing David, have argued that his motive was not selfish, but rather a protective gesture based on his wise intuition that Solomon would be in danger if these orders were not carried out.[4] Another interpretation is that, although David's primary concern was to express his wish that Solomon be a good person guided by the Torah, David feared how he would be remembered, and he mistakenly thought that exacting vengeance against his former enemies would bring honor to his memory. Perhaps David wanted to emphasize to Solomon the lasting power of wrongful actions, and warn the young man to think of the future consequences of his choices. David also instructs Solomon to reward the sons of Barzillai, teaching him that acts of kindness are vitally important in the world and have lasting impact. Amid his specific instructions, David does indicate his confidence in Solomon's wisdom and judgment, "for you are a wise man *(ish hacham atah)* and you will know what to do with him" (I Kings 2:9).

David's deathbed message for Solomon still lacks a great deal of intimacy by our contemporary standards. There are no phrases like "I love you. I'm proud of you!" in David's address. His reservations reflect the norms of the time, old scars of having loved and lost other sons. Nevertheless, as feminists we understand that praising someone's actions is not the same as validating her as a person, and that our feelings for those we love cannot simply be understood; they must be verbalized and actualized. However, we also know that words can never sufficiently express the power of our holy relationships. Solomon was blessed to receive guidance from his father and have a precious few final moments with him. Surely this encounter was a source of comfort to him as David died, and a source of strength as he embarked on his new role as king.

This haftarah portion encourages us to think about the messages that we give to our own loved ones. For many generations, Jews have expressed their deepest hopes and dreams in ethical wills read by their children after their death. Whenever we stand with our children in times of transition—such as when they go away to camp or leave for college, and certainly at the end of our lives—we have an opportunity to teach them about our values and the importance of Judaism and Torah in our lives. We should always strive to express our confidence in their abilities, and to tell them that we love them. We must honor the holiness of those moments in our lives by fulfilling their potential with kind words for those we love.

Shmot / Exodus

הפטרת שמות

Haftarat Shmot

Isaiah 27:6–28:13; 29:22–23

*T*he days are coming when Jacob will take root,
   and Israel will bud and blossom,
and fill the face of the earth with fruit. (ISAIAH 27:6)

THE NEW FRONTIER for sophisticated, socially conscious individuals is the clash between the authentic development of our intellectual, spiritual, and emotional lives and the compulsion to remain within traditional boundaries set by our families and communities. Often, as mothers, daughters, and partners, we encounter the same sense of alienation that so many frustrated artists, musicians, and dreamers experience, as we find our aspirations sidelined when we struggle to fit into the roles everyone else expects us to play.

How many of us feel constrained by our constant attentiveness and accommodation to the needs of those around us? How many fear that our dreams and aspirations have been permanently tabled for the sake of others? How many sense a lack of deliberation and direction in our lives as a result? For some, this disconnect is distinctly manifest in our religious lives: We just don't have time to take the class we want to; our partners feel threatened by our desire to develop a more meaningful spiritual life; our children think we're crazy when we suggest a deeper observance of Shabbat or kashrut. As a result, we may end up living lives that are only shallow sketches of what we dream they could be. Ultimately, many of us find ourselves engaging the world in ways

61

entirely foreign to our sense of self, which can be unfulfilling at best, downright painful at worst.

In *Haftarat Shmot*, Isaiah speaks to this sense of estrangement. He articulates the great promise that the nation will be transformed from being *Jacob*—afraid or incapable of fulfilling its potential, systematically undermining itself—to being *Israel*—self-actualizing, living in full dignity. Isaiah describes Jacob as a flower, the root of which is invisible to passersby, and therefore trampled by history. Yet this very root will become the source of redemption, blossoming into the catalyst for all change in the world. It is, as the psalmist projected, the very rock that was rejected that will become the cornerstone (Ps. 118:22). What could be a more promising vision for a nation that is demoralized, humiliated, afraid? What could be a more critical message for individuals who are lost, lonely, brokenhearted?

How does a person, or a nation, allow herself to leave behind a life of unfulfilled potential, of self-alienation, of "Jacobness," and become Israel? Isaiah declares that the path to redemption begins with hope. God has promised us that there will be an end to our agony: "Therefore the Lord said to the House of Jacob, who redeemed Abraham: No longer will Jacob be shamed, no longer his face grow pale" (Isa. 29:22). Our challenge is to hear this promise, and allow ourselves to believe that there is another way to live, that no pain is interminable, that there will be a redemptive light that emerges at the end of even our darkest nights.

Isaiah's promise of Israel's escape from degradation is brilliantly juxtaposed to the corresponding Torah portion, *Parashat Shmot*. In the exact moment in which we read about Israel's descent into slavery in Egypt—"Let us deal harshly with them, so that they may not increase!" (Exod. 1:10)—the haftarah offers us the prophetic vision of a people redeemed, living in a world in which torment and affliction are but a memory: "The days are coming when Jacob will take root, and Israel will bud and blossom and fill the face of the earth like fruit" (Isa. 27:6). The prophet dares us to dream that the world will one day look different than it does today, compelling us to envision an existence unburdened by grief and anguish. And he instructs us that the only way to preserve faith in this dream is to refuse to succumb to despair, despite our profound sense of loss. Precisely as the story of our national trauma begins to unfold in Shmot, Isaiah forces us to imagine the unimaginable: that our debilitating exile will end in a massive ingathering, a celebration of the promise of freedom fulfilled.

To read Isaiah on this level is to engage in one of the deepest theological claims of the Jewish people. But what comfort does this prophetic vision offer those of us who suffer daily from a different kind of exile and loss? Isaiah's message of redemption must be read on multiple levels. We encounter exile first as a nation, enveloped in the memory of the staggering traumas of slavery and forced eviction from our homeland. But, many of us also experience our own personal exile, as we recognize the depth of our own self-alienation. Who am I? What am I doing with my life? What happened to my dreams? Will I ever be able to be the person I need to be in the world?

Self-alienation, though painful, is not analogous to the communal catastrophe described by Isaiah. But in his brazen insistence that we don't have to accept our lives as they are, Isaiah awakens us to the ever-present possibility of change, growth, and rebirth. "And in that day, a great ram's horn will be sounded, and those who are lost, who are in the land of Assyria, and those who have been expelled, who are in the land of Egypt, shall come and worship the Lord on the holy mount, in Jerusalem" (Isa. 27:13). How do we make manifest the possibility of real change? Is hope enough to save us from our own personal exile? How can we recover meaning in our lives? How are we to heal our own broken hearts?

In *Netivot Shalom*, Hasidic master Rabbi Shalom Noah Barzovski suggests that Shabbat is the key, offering the possibility of redemption from *both* types of exile. He writes:

> Shabbat has the power to bring redemption *to each and every individual in her personal life*. During the six days of the week, one feels as though she is in exile (this means

that she feels herself far from the Holy One, the Source, the Center). But on Shabbat, one is able to return and bring herself closer to the Holy One. And this is the redemptive vision, reliving the Exodus from Egypt (escape from the narrow place) . . .[1]

He begins with the remarkable affirmation that it is completely normal for a person to feel distant from herself, to lack direction, to feel a loss of self-understanding. But one must never give up hope. Shabbat comes to afford us the opportunity to confront the searing questions we have about our lives, to reconnect with ourselves, our families, our dreams—to reconnect with God. Physical and spiritual transformation await us, if we only allow ourselves to awaken to their possibility. By reintroducing us to our core values, reigniting our passions and desires, and giving us the opportunity to reclaim our sense of self, Shabbat offers us the power to effect change in our lives, to touch the essence of what we once dreamed might be possible, to journey from stagnation to spiritual mobility.

But Isaiah's dogged insistence on national transformation suggests that, ultimately, our individual redemption is not enough. *Netivot Shalom* continues:

Every Shabbat has the power to bring redemption *to the world*. . . . It is incumbent upon every Jew to remember and truly know [the experience of the liberation from slavery] . . . but this is not just for the sake of memory. Rather it is for the sake of actually doing the work of Shabbat. A Jew must rise up from a place of degradation, and find within herself ultimate freedom. . . . The essence of Shabbat is the memory of *Yetziat Mitzrayim* (the liberation of those enslaved) because it is [incumbent] upon every Jew to remember that it is her life's work to leave Egypt, and with the strength of the holy Shabbat, to bring redemption *to the world*.[2]

In other words, liberation from our personal exile, combined with the memory of our people's liberation from slavery, will ultimately transform the world. The crushing experience of our personal and collective invisibility must necessarily leave us with a commitment to help nurture the seemingly invisible roots that surround us.

As people who have struggled to overcome our own social enslavement, it becomes our life's mission to identify and work toward the liberation of those who remain vulnerable to the stranglehold of society. The real promise of transformation, then, is that our redemption leaves us with an obligation to redeem, our freedom leaves us with an obligation to free. This is how we are able to fulfill the great promise that we might one day be an *or l'goyim*—"a light unto the nations" (Isa. 49:6), a people who has emerged from the depths of night to comfort the world with the unabashed insistence that there *will* be a dawn. Ultimately, our escape from exile, our personal and national transformation out of the narrow constraints of *Jacobness*, is resolutely linked to our mandate as *Israel* in the world.

RABBI ANDREA CAROL STEINBERGER

הפטרת וארא
Haftarat Va-era

Ezekiel 28:25–29:21

*T*hus says the Lord God:
I am against you, Pharaoh king of Egypt,
Mighty monster, sprawling in your channels,
Who said, My Nile is My own; I made it for myself.
(EZEKIEL 29:3)

EZEKIEL LIVED IN THE DAYS before the destruction of the First Temple
and Israel's exile to Babylon, at a time when Israel may have hoped to
form an alliance with Egypt in order to avoid its own destruction.[1] This
haftarah portion is drawn from a larger text (Ezek. 25–32), in which
Ezekiel preaches against the nation of Egypt, rebuking them for their
disloyalty toward Israel in its time of trouble.

The haftarah reveals the prophet Ezekiel's vision of the destruction
of Egypt as a result of its lack of faith in YHVH. The beginning and end
of the haftarah are framed, in contrast, by a prophecy of hope for the
children of Israel, who will live in safety and security as a result of
their faith in God.

Two phrases in particular provoke interpretation. In 29:3 Ezekiel
refers to Pharaoh as a "mighty monster" because Pharaoh so selfishly
proclaims that he, himself, has created the Nile River. To make matters
worse, Pharaoh boasts of the Nile River, saying, "My Nile is my own. I
made it for myself." A more accurate (and certainly fascinating) translation of verse 3 might be, "I have made myself." What might Pharaoh

have meant by the claim, "I have made myself"? Is Pharaoh likening himself to a god, equating himself with the Nile? What are the consequences one faces when one looks at a creation and proclaims, "I have made myself"? Perhaps there is a lesson inherent in the text about the danger present in "making ourselves." What danger does this statement pose for us as women?

Indeed, it is possible to say that women have made themselves over, in the image of society. Social scientists continue to debate between nature and nurture, and women continue to wonder, "What is our image supposed to be?" Is it the male model, the image of a business suit, the CEO of a company, strong and professional and capable of rising to the top of the work world? Or is it the feminine model of the mother, the loving and kind woman who is capable of raising children and making a home? It is not clear if women are made to be "feminine" or if society has taught us to be this way. This is precisely why women have, in the last century, sought to make themselves over into something they had not been before.

This makeover poses the question: Have we women come into our own, or simply shifted the focus of the social expectations we try to live up to? If we follow the feminine path, traditionally thought of as a home life based on taking care of children, we may be accused of not living up to our full potential as human beings, and of simply succumbing to society's expectations of the classically feminine woman. If, however, we play according to male rules, wearing the business suit, living at the office, denying ourselves the experiences of childbearing and creating a home life, aren't we also simply fitting ourselves into society's expectations for men?

This situation is a clearly a conundrum for us. Just as Pharaoh says, "I have made myself," women, too, have redefined ourselves and redefined our roles in society. And equally troubling for us is that the haftarah rejects Pharaoh's claim, calling him a mighty monster for his haughtiness. It is as if the haftarah is warning Pharaoh: "Do not see yourself as the last definer of life, of what it is possible and impossible to do. There is inherent danger in what you are doing, Pharaoh." The haftarah challenges us too: Have we made an idol of the male models of success, claiming that only the male model of the work ethic appropriately defines us? Or, conversely, have we made an idol of femininity, arguing that making a home is the preferred role for women?

The challenge of (re)making ourselves as women leads us to a discussion of the "mighty monster." There are indeed mighty monsters for us as women. While Pharaoh's mighty monster is his boastfulness, ours is the tendency to try to "do it all"—striving for both career and home. Some therapists report that their female patients express frustration and exasperation, lamenting that while they had been educated to believe that they could achieve it all, both professionally and personally, they simply were unprepared for the tremendous amount of work it would take to create a personal life. They had been prepared for the years of school that a degree required and for the time in the workplace it would take to achieve professional success. Yet no one had prepared them for the tremendous pressure they would feel to become wives and mothers, to devote the same energy and drive to creating a household as they had to establishing a career. They see the irony in it all. They are bright, college-educated women with impressive careers, and yet they are disillusioned with their own personal lives.

A recent article in *Lilith*, an independent Jewish women's magazine, reported: "The latest statistics report that a wife performs 70 to 80 percent of the unpaid household tasks even if she works full time at a paying job."[2] If this statistic is true, it is no wonder that women feel the weight of a mighty monster—the monster of unresolved identity. The woman seeks and achieves equality in the workplace, but then feels utterly overcome by the tasks of raising children and making a home.

In our haftarah portion, Ezekiel rebukes Pharaoh for claiming, "I have made myself." We create our lives; yet we also have the capacity to create other lives—other human beings. What happens when we become overwhelmed with the double tasks of our profession and a family? How are we able to share the tasks of raising healthy, stable children with others? How can our partners, family, friends, and caregivers share in this Divine task of maintaining a healthy family? Only when we acknowledge the incredible miracle inherent in the ability to create our lives as God's gift will we also be able to identify each person's inherent strengths. It is then that we are able to assign the appropriate tasks to each person, according to his or her unique talents and capabilities, for the greater good of the family and the world. When we are able to share our load, and when men share it with us, the task of maintaining two worlds—that of our career and of our family— becomes easier. Only when we are able to work together as a community will we combat this mighty monster of the pressure to create and sustain two worlds by ourselves.

Our haftarah ends with God's pronouncement of strength for the children of Israel, which translates as: "I will cause a horn to sprout for the House of Israel, and I will grant you an opening of the mouth." Why does the haftarah use this imagery of an open mouth? The answer lies in the strength of finding one's voice. When women (and men) are able to achieve this balance between work and caring for our families, we too will be blessed with strength and security. Our mouths will be open and we will find our voices, and they will be clear. We will learn to ask more, to demand more, to expect more. We will live in safety and security, with faith that ultimately it is in God's image that we are created, not our own.

RABBI DENISE L. EGER

הפטרת בא
Haftarat Bo

Jeremiah 46:13–28

*F*ear not, . . . for I am with thee. (JEREMIAH 46:28)

IN THESE FEW PASSAGES from the Book of Jeremiah we learn of the prophecy against Egypt. This is one of the last prophecies made by Jeremiah, targeting the alliance made by Israel with Egypt in an effort to fend off the Babylonian army of King Nebuchadnezzar invading from the north. Jeremiah foretells of the eventual Babylonian triumph over the Jewish state and the ultimate fall of Egypt.

This haftarah reading is linked to its Torah portion Bo, in the Book of Exodus, which outlines the final plagues inflicted by God on Egypt during the era of the Israelites' enslavement. The two sections share a strong anti-Egyptian tone. In his condemnation of Israel's aligning with Egypt, Jeremiah hints that Israel should never have entered an alliance with our ancient archenemy. The prophet paints a picture of doom, disaster, and humiliation born of Egypt's arrogance. So, too, in the Torah portion, the arrogance of Pharaoh and the Egyptians lead to their destruction in the Reed Sea. Thus the haftarah and Torah portions both show how God's plan to defeat the Egyptians is inevitable.

This section of Jeremiah utilizes feminine imagery, such as *bat-Mitzrayim*—daughter of Egypt—to describe Egyptians throughout the haftarah. Alternatively, Egypt is described as either the weak woman or the calf ready for sacrifice, while YHVH is referred to as the king. It is YHVH, imagined in masculine terms as Master of All, who is directing the Babylonians, the invaders from the North. Jeremiah's images of the events that will befall Egypt are violent. He emasculates the warriors of the Egyptian army by calling them calves rather than bulls. He points out their immaturity and impugns their courage: "The daughter of Egypt shall be shamed and given into the hands of the people of the North" (Jer. 46:24). These emasculated men can no longer "protect" their women. Jeremiah uses male domination of women as the metaphor of fulfillment of God's plan against Egypt. The conquering Babylonians, however, are described as woodcutters, strong and manly, ready to destroy the forest and the serpent within.

But one can also understand the *bat-Mitzrayim* as the goddesses of Egypt. The imagery that Jeremiah uses in these verses can be traced to ancient Egyptian goddesses.[1] All of these metaphors—the young female calf, the trees of the forest, and the serpent—are literary images that bring to mind different goddesses of Egypt. The young female calf is the consort of the Egyptian bull god, Apis.[2] The trees of the forest to be cut down by the woodcutters are associated with the Egyptian goddesses Hathor, Isis, and Nut, who were often portrayed as trees. And the serpent is the ancient Egyptian goddess Wadjet, the cobra-headed goddess. Thus the prophecy of Jeremiah can also be read as a condemnation of the pagan worship of the Egyptians, and, by association, Israel's alignment with pagan worshipers will be her undoing.

Interestingly, in earlier sections of the Book of Jeremiah, the prophet uses female imagery to describe Israel. Alternatively, Israel is a bride (2:1–3)—a positive image—or a harlot (3:1–10)—a negative one. In this haftarah, we see only negative female imagery when Jeremiah describes Egypt.

We know a great deal about the personal life of Jeremiah, more than most of the other prophets in the Bible: He became a prophet at a young age and devoted his entire life to his faithful mission. He never married, he was imprisoned for a number of years, his prophetic visions were rarely heeded, and he was almost put to death. It seems that Jeremiah stood in opposition to everyone in his day—priests, other prophets, and kings. He must have been a man of great faith to sustain his spirits despite his often dark and desolate prophecies of the impending destruction of Jerusalem. But one also gets a sense of Jeremiah's utter isolation in his reflections. One wonders what might have been if Jeremiah had had a family or a significant partner in his life. Would the harshness of his visions have been tempered by a stronger sense of loving presence? Jeremiah's words in this haftarah portion especially convey an anger and even utter contempt for the leadership of the Jewish people and their plan to align with Egypt. Jeremiah's anger seems overwhelming, as if he were consumed by that rage. It seems he has no love for the Jewish people in his anger at their idolatry. But so, too, Jeremiah's own isolation by imprisonment and by distancing himself from the nation of Israel, fuels that anger.

The *parashah* ends with two verses of hope for Israel. Although clearly God will mete out punishment for Israel's idolatrous behavior, and for aligning with Egypt, in the end Israel will be preserved and find a place of tranquility.

It is difficult to imagine how one can draw from this prophecy a message of hope, given these brutal images of Egypt and Israel. It is difficult to imagine that a loving God would inflict such harm on any of God's children. Yet one cannot read these verses in isolation. Elsewhere in the Book of Jeremiah, the prophet does preach a strong message of relationship between the people and YHVH. Jeremiah writes of his soul weeping and God's pain for Israel's captivity (13:15–17). One might imagine a parent who punishes a child for misbehavior while saying, "This is going to hurt me more than it does you." Jeremiah rails against the idolatry that has crept into Israelite religion, yet he offers a vision of an eternal covenant that will remain in place even when Jerusalem falls.

If Jeremiah had used a tactic other than harsh words and oracles against Israel and the other nations, would his message have been received differently? Could the nation of Israel actually have repented of its idolatry without such dire language? Could that repentance have staved off the destruction of the Temple and the exile into Babylonia? Most of all, would the people of Israel have understood the value of the Temple, and their own independence as a nation, without the captivity in Babylonia? And, of course, the ending words of the haftarah bring us, finally, comfort: "Fear not, my servant Jacob, for I am with thee." This consoling line is repeated twice (verse 27 and 28), as if to say, "I was angry, very angry, but I will never revoke my parental protection."

This haftarah's prophetic message actually comes to pass generations later. In Jewish tradition, the captivity in Babylonia ends when Darius the Mede defeats the last Babylonian king, Belshazzar. His successor, Cyrus, authorizes the return of the Jewish exiles to Israel and the rebuilding of the Temple. Following Cyrus, King Ahashuerus, who eventually marries Esther, ascends the throne. In Jewish tradition, Darius, the next ruler of Persia, is said to be Esther's son. It is Darius who authorizes the Temple's completion. In this haftarah Jeremiah has emphasized the evil of aligning with Egypt and has urged the connection to Babylonia. Perhaps Jeremiah the prophet knew that, ultimately, when the Babylonians would meet defeat, it would be their conquerors who would help the Jews renew and restore their national life. Perhaps this is one reason that Jeremiah condemns Israel for aligning with Egypt but not with the Babylonians. Jeremiah's emphasis on the eternal covenant taught that, though punished, the Jewish people would not be deserted. Thus, Jeremiah had prophetically seen the future enough to understand that God's ultimate plan was for the Temple to be rebuilt. Tradition teaches us this very message.

RABBI DEBORAH J. SCHLOSS

הפטרת בשלח
Haftarat Beshalach

Judges 4:4–5:31

*I*arose, a mother in Israel . . . (JUDGES 5:7)

UNFORTUNATELY, STEREOTYPING pervades and influences many aspects of our world, both ancient and modern. In Jewish life, "often the ideas that men held about women were more stereotyped and limited than the actual roles of the women warranted."[1] *Haftarat Beshalach* and its rabbinic commentary provide us with many ripe illustrations of this popular, yet potentially destructive phenomenon.

Haftarat Beshalach, like the Torah portion to which it is partnered, celebrates victory over tyranny. Both culminate in a song of praise and thanksgiving. Judges 4:4–5:31 is unique in that it is the only haftarah portion that focuses more on the initiative of women than of men. In the first line of our portion we read: "Deborah, wife of Lappidoth, was a prophetess, she was a judge in Israel." The Rabbis have a much easier time accepting Deborah's role as a prophet than as a judge. The Talmud describes six other prophetesses, in addition to Deborah.[2] But Deborah's position as a judge is disconcerting to the Rabbis. They simply cannot tolerate a woman in this powerful, hierarchical, leadership position. The limiting and confining of women's behavior in traditional Jewish life is not, as our Sages of old lead us to believe, because of stringencies in Jewish law, but rather, the result of contemporary social attitudes.[3]

As a Jewish historian relates: "Custom became master, and custom is a tyrant. Custom survives the circumstances which give it birth, and because the retention of it is based on sentiment, it is not amenable to the assault of reason." [4] It is from this tyranny of mind-set that the Rabbis infer that Deborah really was not a judge, directly contradicting the *peshat* of our text, as well as establishing the basis for the rabbinic disqualification of women to serve as judges.[5] This inability of women to serve in a judicial capacity was one of the major obstacles to the ordination of women rabbis in the Conservative movement.

At the opening of *Haftarat Beshalach*, the loose confederation of Israelite tribes are beleaguered, having endured the oppression and violence of Canaanite King Jabin for twenty years. He had attacked and conquered the land in which they were living, the land promised to our ancestors by God. Sisera is the army commander for a coalition of tribes united under King Jabin. In this unstable living situation, people are afraid to live in open places and walk in the streets. So Deborah sends for Barak and tells him to gather together ten thousand men on Mount Tabor. Then she draws Sisera and his troops and chariots toward them, enabling Barak and his men to defeat the Canaanites and deliver Sisera to his death.

Barak appears unsure of himself and the entire scenario. After all, the Canaanites had nine hundred iron chariots, which in and of itself was a great advantage, not to mention the large organized infantry that so outweighed the beleaguered and disjointed Israelite tribes. Barak tells Deborah that he will go only if she accompanies him. Deborah replies, "I will go with you, but you won't get any credit for the victory, because God will hand Sisera over to a woman" (Judg. 4:9). Deborah is all too aware of the social milieu in which she operates.

A strong rain traps Sisera's iron chariots in the mud, enabling Barak's men to kill the Canaanite troops; Sisera alone flees. During this time, the Canaanites have an alliance with the Kenites. Heber and his wife, Yael, break away from their fellow Kenites who live in the South, and each has a tent nearby. Sisera approaches Yael's tent, seeking protection. She gives him soothing milk, and after he falls asleep she takes a hammer and drives a tent peg through his head. Sisera is killed by a woman, just as Deborah predicts. Only then does Barak's army continue to Hazor, killing King Jabin in his capital.

The Israelites do prevail, just as in Deborah's prophecy, but instead of acknowledging her prowess, or the peace and stability that the Israelites enjoyed for forty years as a result of Deborah's leadership, the talmudic Rabbis paint her negatively. Rabbi Nachman calls Deborah a hornet, based on the Aramaic translation of her name, *ziborata*.[6] Names of people and places in the Bible and Talmud were perceived as quite significant because they were believed to give insight into one's personality or the character of a place.[7] Rabbi Nachman states, "Of the hornet it is written, 'And she sent and called Barak, instead of going to him.'"[8] He is presuming a haughtiness in Deborah that is simply not supported by the text. Deborah had a great deal of pressure and onerous responsibilities in her dual role as prophet and judge. Clearly it was not expedient, let alone safe, for her to travel to Barak.

Toward the beginning of the Song of Deborah, one of the oldest and most eloquent poems in the Bible, we read, "Deliverance ceased, ceased in Israel, until I arose, Deborah, arose, O mother in Israel!" (Judg. 5:7). During this time the Israelites must have been desperately aching for a strong leader. Several verses later we read, "Awake yourself Deborah, awake yourself, awake yourself and sing a song" (Judg. 5:12). In the Talmud the Rabbis state that if a Sage is boastful, his wisdom can leave him, and if prophets are boastful, their gift of prophecy can leave them.[9] The Rabbis explain that because Deborah boasts that she is a mother of Israel, she is punished by God's spirit departing from her.[10] Their interpretation of "Awake yourself Deborah" is that her ability to compose her song temporarily left her, due to her presumed pride in referring to herself as mother of Israel.

I believe that Deborah, clearly understanding the gender dynamic within the Israelite culture, refers to herself in the most sensitive, inoffensive, unobtrusive way possible when composing her song. It's ironic that *mother* is a traditionally accepted role for a woman, yet the Rabbis punish her for this appellation. But the sixteenth-century Safed mystic Solomon Halevi Alkabetz read no negativity into Judges 5:12. He used this verse in his beautiful song *Lecha Dodi*, which Jews sing every Friday evening during *Kabbalat Shabbat* services: *"Uri uri, shir dabberi,"* "Awake, awake, sing a song [to God]."

It would have been both interesting and instructive if the Rabbis had indicated how they thought Deborah should have referred to her-self in her song.[11] Indeed, Deborah begins her song with blessing and gratitude to God: "I bless the Lord! I will sing, will sing to the Lord . . ." (Judg. 5:2–3). In fact, praise and thanks to God permeate her song. She enumerates each of the miracles God performed for the Israelites. What a beautiful lesson we can glean from Deborah's humility: While it would have been justifiable for Deborah to honor her role in bring-ing peace to the Israelites, the only Being she praises and glorifies is God. After we accomplish something noteworthy, besides feeling pride in ourselves, we would do well to follow Deborah's lead and remem-ber to acknowledge how God enabled us to reach our new height.

Haftarat Beshalach illustrates that behind shattered stereotypes lie surprise and success. Although it was unconventional to have a female judge and military leader, Deborah superbly leads the Israelites to victory and to a forty-year peace. Although Sisera thought he was safe among a Kenite ally, Yael kills him. Although the Israelite army is greatly outnumbered and technically inferior, it wins. And ironically, Rabbi Akiva, one of Judaism's most venerated Rabbis, was a descen-dant of Sisera. As Rabbi Joseph Telushkin explains, "A descendant of this great enemy of the Jews becoming a great rabbi and scholar rep-resents the Jews' ultimate victory over their ancient Canaanite opponent."[12]

Just before Deborah is introduced, we read: "The Israelites *again* did what was offensive to God . . . so God delivered them into the hands of King Jabin of Canaan . . ." (Judg. 4:1–2). This is a common refrain in the Book of Judges: It is a way of introducing each new oppression the Israelites face in the land. However, after the forty-year peace the Israelites experienced as a result of Deborah's leadership, we read: "The Israelites did what was offensive to God, and God delivered them into Midian's hands for seven years" (Judg. 6:1). Missing in this second text is the word *again*. The fact that after Deborah's tenure the text does not state: "The Israelites *again* did what was offensive to God" illustrates that they were given a fresh start as a direct result of Deborah.[13]

As Rav Simon says, "anyone who experienced a miracle and praised God may be certain that all his sins will be forgiven and that he will become a new person."[14] Deborah's acknowledging and praising God for the Israelites' victory enables the Israelites to move forward into their future, unencumbered by their past behavior. Like Deborah, our lives can be imbued with appreciation and thankfulness for both the subtle and more palpable ways that God operates in our lives and in our world. Deborah shatters the stereotype of her time, and, in doing so, helps us shatter ours.

RABBI SHIRA STERN

הפטרת יתרו

Haftarat Yitro

Isaiah 6:1–7:6; 9:5–6

*I*n the year that King Uzziah died, I looked at God seated on a high and raised-up throne; and the fabric of God's robe filled the Temple. Around God, angels stood at attention, each of whom had six wings; with two, they covered the face; with two, they covered the legs; and with two, they would fly. And one would call out to another: "Holy, Holy, Holy, is the God of Hosts; God's glory fills all the earth!" The doorposts would quake at the sound of that voice, and the house was filled with smoke. Then I said, "Woe is me, for I am lost! Because I am a man of unclean lips and I live in the midst of people with unclean lips, and nevertheless, I have seen God with my own eyes." Then one of the angels flew to me with a red-hot coal, which he had taken from the altar with tongs; He placed it on my lips and said: "Now that this coal has touched your lips, your guilt is removed and your sin gone." Then I heard the voice of the Eternal, saying, "Whom shall I send? Who will go for us?" And I answered, "Here I am—[*Hineni*]—send me." (ISAIAH 6:1–8)

THE TORAH PORTION of *Yitro*, both the *parashah* and its matching haftarah, describes awe-inspiring flashes, transformational moments so searing that we, generations later, can still feel the heat and see the light. Moses and the community of Israel see the lightning and smoke and hear the thunder and blare of the horn as God first reveals the Torah at Sinai. Isaiah experiences this vision even more intimately, feeling the Divine encounter so strongly that when God asks for a ready prophet, Isaiah answers without hesitation, "I am here."

The direct connection between the Torah and haftarah portions is in the simple *peshat:* God's opening up to us through text, both spoken and transcribed. But the more subtle connection involves subliminal suggestions through the underlying message.

Some modern advertising agency might take credit for the invention of delivering subliminal images, but, in fact, the practice is ancient. Literary allusions to another story in another time and place reinforce the message: This vision of Isaiah's is powerful, authentic, and prophetic. How is this done? The text is filled with references to Moses, the one who stands apart as the greatest prophet of all, the one who broke the mold because, as we read in Deuteronomy 34:10: "Never again did there arise in Israel a prophet like Moses . . ." He is obliquely referred to three separate times in this section. First, Isaiah's experience of seeing God reminds us of Moses as he confronts God's presence at the top of Mount Sinai. Second, Isaiah physically evokes Moses' first encounter with God at the burning bush by reminding us that he is "a man of unclean lips—who lives among people with unclean lips" (verse 5), a reference to Exodus 4:10 in which Moses is described as "slow of speech and slow of tongue." And third, both he and Isaiah come into contact with a burning coal—albeit in a midrash (*Exodus Rabbah* 1.31), which surely reminded the Rabbis of Isaiah's experience. In Isaiah 6:7ff, the prophet's sins are seared away when the angel touches his lips with the red-hot coal. Moses, according to the midrash, is saved from death at the hands of Pharaoh when an angel directs his hand toward coals and away from gold in a significant test.

But Moses isn't the only prophetic model for Isaiah: Abraham too is recalled by the use of the simple word *Hineni*—"Here I am." We hear the voice of Isaiah, but our minds make the leap to our first patriarch, who uttered *"Hineni"* as a response to God's call. These allusions to the past lend legitimacy to Isaiah's position as a leader worthy of God's attention.

Moses and Abraham, however, present a particular challenge if we read the text with a feminist eye, because both men temporarily abandon their wives in some fashion in response to God's call. They may have been outstanding Jewish leaders, but they were both poor models as husbands. Moses leaves his wife (and uncircumcised infant son) when God asks him to return to Egypt, ignoring her until his father-in-law Jethro reunites the family in this very Torah portion. And Abraham, then Abram, arranges for Sarah to cross the border of Canaan and Egypt as his sister lest he be killed by the king who might desire his wife and kill him to get her (Gen. 12).

In addition, the image of God presented at the beginning of our haftarah is highly anthropomorphic: a being with a face and legs, wearing a robe and sitting on a throne, holding court like a king. This is the vision that opens Isaiah's eyes, the central experience of his life, and it is difficult to imagine an image more thoroughly male. This is exactly the traditional image of the "bearded old man on the throne" that so many moderns now reject. Can women encounter God as Isaiah did?

We can, if we read this haftarah text differently, watching for clues that might broaden the definition of *revelation*. Many of us understand the words *revelation* and *covenant* in personal terms, all of which are relational: We experience God in relationship to ourselves. *Revelation* might mean seeing God through a prism we have never used before. Seen through the prism of Isaiah's personal experience, his representation of God is a reflection of his own life and relationships. Isaiah, during his forty-year career, had close ties with the palace and the king, and it would be natural for his dream to mirror that reality. But his dream doesn't have to be ours.

Can women step up to the plate and say, *"Hineni"*? Grammatically, the word *hineni* is a first-person singular construction: It means "Here

I am," and it is not gender specific. *Hineni* is the verbal raising of the hand, the "Pick me, pick me" of biblical language. But with the blessing of being chosen comes responsibility. Abraham does active recruiting for God's people; Moses takes us out of Egypt and draws the blueprint of Torah, and Isaiah parlays his vision into a lifelong attempt to bring about profound political and social change. We have more limited examples of women who experience Divine revelation in a personal way: Rebekah prays for guidance while pregnant, and, based on an answer only implied in the text, engineers Jacob's ascendance as patriarch. Miriam keeps the Israelites together, providing for them both spiritually and physically, with her wandering well.[1] But the text is silent about how she becomes a prophetess; there is for her no *Hineni*. Perhaps one reason for this silence is the intimate nature of women's experience of revelation: Our female ancestors simply translated these private moments into acts, and it is through their actions, not their conversations with God, that we share their visions of God.

So what can Isaiah teach us? When he cries out, "Holy, holy, holy is the God of Hosts, the whole earth is filled with God's glory" (verse 3), he experiences the very public, demonstrative divinity; when he says, *"Hineni,"* he reminds us of how each of us individually can create a personal, private connection to God. And because he offers us both means of viewing God, all of us—men and women—now have a new spiritual lens through which to sense divine intent. He offers the grand view along with the narrow, the extraordinary along with the ordinary, as spiritual moments.

Some women, having experienced revelation by praying, studying, grappling with, and probing our tradition with other women in a completely different way than ever before, have begun to articulate that awe-filled sensation. Rabbi Laura Geller describes it in her essay "Encountering the Divine Presence" in *Four Centuries of Jewish Women's Spirituality*, edited by Ellen M. Umansky, as "Diving deep and surfacing, remembering and inventing, wrestling and loving, being wounded and being blessed. . . ."

We may envy Isaiah's clear communication, his ability to respond appropriately to his vision, despite his protests of "unclean lips." Often, because women have been left out of the biblical narrative and therefore out of the liturgy as well, we speak the words that are holy, and yet they do not reflect exactly what and how we feel. Esther Broner, who helped pioneer the Women's Seder, describes the way many women have felt, unable to find themselves in the text and respond to it:

> I begin the journey into my history.
> I journey with other women.
> To those on the other shore, not able to risk the plunge.
> To the raising high of women who were laid low.[2]

Isaiah tells us: Start with your own experience. Find the spark in you that, connected with others, makes a bigger light, one that will reach those who have not yet been able to discern it. Isaiah reminds us that we all—individually—can receive Torah as revelation; that when we hear the message, we can use it to connect to the community of women. We have the power to, as Broner says, "raise high the women who were laid low." We have the power to be prophets.

RABBI LORI COHEN

הפטרת משפטים
Haftarat Mishpatim

Jeremiah 34:8–22; 33:25–26

*E*ach person was to set free his Hebrew male or Hebrew female slaves; no Jew should be a slave for another. Now when all of the officials and people who had entered the covenant heard this, each of them released their male and female slaves, agreeing that none of them would again enslave them. But after a while they changed their minds and took back the ones that they had freed and forced them back into slavery.
(JEREMIAH 34:9–11)

*T*hese are the rules that you should set before them: If you acquire a Hebrew slave, only six years he will work and in the seventh year he shall go free, without a payment [of redemption]. (EXODUS 21:1–2)

THIS HAFTARAH IS PART OF the prophet Jeremiah's admonitions to the Israelite people, a prophecy about what will happen if they fail to follow God's commands. It is tied to a very specific historical context, and therefore we can date it accurately at 588 B.C.E. This was a prosperous time, but Judah was caught between the two superpowers of the era—Babylonia and Egypt. Zedekiah, the last king of Judah, reigned from 597 B.C.E. until the destruction of Jerusalem in 586 B.C.E. During his reign, he vacillated in his loyalties between Egypt and Babylonia. Jeremiah counseled Zedekiah to accept the rule of King Nebuchadnezzar of Babylon, believing that the "foe from the North" was part of God's judgment against the unrepentant people.

In 589 B.C.E. the Babylonians invaded Jerusalem, and the Israelite ruling class agreed to release all of their Hebrew slaves, according to the toraitic rule written in Exodus, "If you acquire a Hebrew slave, only six years will he work and in the seventh year he shall go free." They felt that this act was a means of appeasing God and persuading God to be merciful. The Book of Jeremiah indicates that previously the people had not been faithful to these laws of release. When the Babylonians retreated from the city a year later, and they again felt safe and secure, the slave owners reversed their decision and forcibly took back their slaves. Jeremiah is incensed with this act, this breaking of the covenant, and foretells the complete destruction of Jerusalem.

Slavery in Biblical Times

After having been recently released from bondage in Egypt, the Israelites were commanded by God to be especially sensitive to the needs of the slave. We see this moral connection in the language of the first of the Ten Commandments: "I am the One who took you out of Mitzrayim [Egypt], out of bondage." The connection is also made in the haftarah: "Thus says the Eternal, the God of Israel: I made a covenant with your ancestors at the time that I took them out from Mitzrayim, from the house of bondage, saying: In the seventh year you will set free your fellow Hebrew slaves, the ones who have sold themselves to you" (Jer. 34:13–14). Ancient society understood the economic benefits of the institution of slavery, and the Israelites shared part of that worldview. However, within Israelite society the relationship between master and slave was ambiguous; the slave was both a human being with feelings and rights, as well as property, having monetary value.

Under biblical law, there were different categories of slaves. An *eved ivri*, or male Hebrew slave, could be a slave by order of the court for criminal behavior, or by volunteering himself for bondage in order to pay off a debt or to escape poverty. A *shifcha*, or female slave, was often a minor who was sold into slavery by her father for household duties and marriage. There were foreign slaves bought from other nations or from resident aliens: "Male and female slaves you may have from the nations who surround you, from them you may buy male and female slaves" (Lev. 25:44). Also, there were children of slaves who were born in their master's house, "the children that are born in your household" (Lev. 25:45): They were considered the property of the master.

There is a distinction throughout the Torah texts between Hebrew slaves—or, probably more correctly, indentured workers—and foreign slaves. Often Hebrew slaves were treated as members of the master's household: They would celebrate the holy days, be circumcised, and at times inherit property if there were no immediate heirs.

According to biblical law, Hebrew slaves were to be released after six years of labor. According to Deuteronomy 15:12–14, "If a fellow Hebrew slave, male or female, is sold to you, he will work for you for six years and on the seventh year you will set him free. But when you set him free you will not send him away empty-handed. Provide for him from the flock, the threshing floor, and the vat, from that which God blessed you with." Thus he would go free with an abundance of food in order to start anew. Philo remarks that "the Hebrew legislation concerning the Hebrew bondsman breathes kindness and humanity throughout."[1]

It appears from the haftarah that both officials and the upper class were not making a distinction between their Hebrew slaves and their foreign slaves. The Hebrew slaves were not receiving the "kindness and humanity" that was due them. The Hebrew slaves did not choose to stay in bondage but were forced to return, *Vay'yich'b'shum l'avadim v'lish'fachot.*

The Message

Imagine for a moment the plight of those men and women who had been taken into slavery, or who had sold themselves into bondage to cover their debts. Among them were also young girls who had been sold by their fathers, in hope that they would be given the basic necessities of life or find a husband. They were in the most vulnerable social position, totally at the whim of their overseers. God's laws for release had not been heeded. They knew the stories of their ancestors who had been freed by God from bondage in Egypt, that frightening place where the Israelite people were born, and yet they were back in slavery—not to foreigners but to their own brothers and sisters, fellow Israelites. They must have believed that the sound of their crying reached God's ears when King Zedekiah made a covenant with the people in Jerusalem to proclaim freedom for them—*likro la'hem d'ror*. There was dancing in the street when all of the slaves were released. However, after several months, the people changed their minds, no longer afraid of invading forces, and forcibly took all of them back into slavery. God did not go back on the covenant made with the Israelites when they were taken out of bondage, but the Israelites themselves broke their covenant with their fellow Hebrews. Freedom had been proclaimed, but was denied.

The Hebrew word for freedom, *d'ror*, means an abundant flowing of liquid, which can refer to milk or tears.[2] An outpouring of milk represents our responsibility to feed and care for the hungry; feminine imagery of nursing and nourishment. An outpouring of tears is the empathy that is felt when we understand the plight of the weak and downtrodden in our society.

In Midrash *Eicha* 1:23 we read about the difference between false tears and real tears. It says in Lamentations 1:2, "The desolate city of Jerusalem weeps bitterly." Rabbi Shimon bar Yochai said to Israel, "You cry frivolous tears; but in the end you will cry real tears." When did the people cry frivolous tears? We read in the following verses: "And Moses heard the people crying" (because they did not have meat during the wandering in the wilderness) (Num. 11:10), and "The whole community broke into loud cries and the people wept that night" (hearing the report that the inhabitants of the land were like giants) (Num. 14:1). And when did they cry real tears? Once in Ramah and once in Babylonia. In Ramah, as it says, "A voice is heard in Ramah, Rachel weeping for her children" (Jer. 31:15). In Babylon, as it says, "By the rivers of Babylon, there we sat and wept when we remembered Zion" (Ps. 137:1). According to Rabbi Avyu, God said, "As a reward for these tears, I will redeem you."

At the time that the officials and the people agreed to release their slaves, there was a proclamation of liberty, but not one that resulted from abundant flowing of concern or empathy. Rather, this liberty was based on ulterior motives. The people only wanted to protect themselves from God's anger.

We are a people who have vacillated between real tears and frivolous tears, and acted out of both proper and selfish motivations. Sometimes we have been concerned only with our own survival, and sometimes we are moved by the plight of others. God heard our cries, and saw our real tears, and freed us from bondage in Egypt; God promises that in the future, response will come with real heartfelt emotions. There is a difference between crying for ourselves alone and crying for others. When we concern ourselves with the fate of others, we tie our destiny to theirs. When we align ourselves with the needs of the weak and the downtrodden, we are crying tears of liberty.

As women, we have historically been free to cry and to express our emotions, and therefore to empathize fully with the feelings of others. Jeremiah, in his historical context and as a spokesperson for God, does the same. It is incumbent upon us as women to make sure that we encourage others to express their passions and their sentiments. We often try to succeed in a masculine world by suppressing our emotions, yet we must not conceal our real tears or try to muffle the tears of others. Jeremiah knew that true freedom would come only when we responded fully and truly to the tears of others; only then could we expect God to be touched by ours.

RABBI ELISA KOPPEL

הפטרת תרומה

Haftarat Terumah

I Kings 5:26–6:13

When the House was built, only finished stones cut at the quarry were used; no hammer or axe or any iron tool was heard in the House when it was being built. (I KINGS 6:7)

REMEMBER, FOR A MOMENT, a time when you've seen a construction site become an actual structure. Think about the transformation of an empty lot into a building. Get a picture in your mind of the wonder of piles of wood and cement becoming a place where people live, work, study, play, or pray. Now, imagine the building of the Temple. Imagine not what the structure itself looked like—many an artist has done that—but what it was like while Solomon was directing the builders. Imagine the workers taking the beams and putting up walls. Imagine people piling up the finished stones, cut even though no iron tools could be used at the Temple site.

But how could these stones have been cut? In the Talmud, the Rabbis imagined Solomon asking his advisors how he could possibly cut the stones without iron tools. The advisors answer that he could build it if he had the *shamir*.[1] According to tradition, the *shamir* was a creature the size of a grain of barley, which could cut through any substance. It was created, along with a whole collection of mysterious objects, at the twilight of the first Shabbat during the week of creation.[2] This wormlike creature's original purpose was to engrave the stones that were on the priestly vestments, because the stones are described as being both "in their entirety" and "engraved."[3] After Solomon used it to build the Temple, it ceased to exist. The *shamir* was used in order to make the seemingly impossible become possible. Indeed, all the items that God created directly before resting on Shabbat, according to midrash, are items that seem to be contrary to nature. One of those created items was the rainbow, which marked the end of the seemingly endless flood, the symbol that God would never again make something contrary to nature's regular system occur. The mouth of the ass that spoke to Balaam is another such item, turning a normal animal into a talking one. Likewise, the *shamir* was created so that the Temple and the priestly vestments could be made, enabling human beings access to God that they otherwise would not be able to possess.

But these items, formed at the last moment when God could create, are not the only objects of opposition. All of creation, in fact, is so: light and darkness on the first day; waters divided from waters on the second; earth and sea, seed-bearing plants and trees on the third; and so on. As each step of creation takes place, an opposing pair comes to exist. Finally, at the last moment, God creates those items that do not fit neatly into any of these pairs, creating—perhaps—a final pairing between the natural and the unnatural, necessary for the course of history, and thus the world, to exist. Conflict comes to be the nature of creation, and thus the nature of the world. It is, though, a conflict within which peace can exist, and in which an ultimate peace can be achieved.

The *shamir* came into being in order to bring order out of conflict, resolution out of contradiction. The creature itself is full of internal conflict. That something so small can be so strong is surprising, although this is often the case in real life, as well as in legend. According to the Rabbis, the creature was wrapped in tufts of wool and placed in a lead tube full of barley bran.[4] Because the *shamir* could cut through any hard substance, only the softest substances could house it. The story of how Solomon acquired this creature raises conflicts of its own.

When Solomon needed to find the *shamir*, his advisors told him to take a male and female demon and press them hard against each other, until they told him where it could be found. When Solomon did so, the demons told him that they did not know, but that he should go to Ashmedai, king of the demons, who might know. Ashmedai lived on a mountain, where he had dug himself a pit, filled it with water, covered it with stone, and sealed it with his signet. Each day, he examined the seal, opened the pit, drank from it, resealed it, and went on his way. Solomon immediately sent for Benaiah to capture Ashmedai, giving him a chain and a signet ring, with God's name written on both. He also provided him with a wool fleece and jugs of wine, sending him off to Ashmedai.

Benaiah went and dug a ditch from below to Ashmedai's pit, draining the water into the ditch. Then, he stopped up the ditch with the wool fleece. Above the pit he dug another ditch, through which he poured the wine into Ashmedai's pit. He covered both ditches with earth, climbed a tree, and waited there. When Ashmedai came, he examined the seal, opened the pit, and found the wine. He did not want to drink the wine, but he eventually became very thirsty. So, he drank, became drunk, and fell asleep. Then, Benaiah came down, threw the chain over him, and bound him, taking him back to Jerusalem. After keeping him as a prisoner for a few days, Solomon finally asked him for the *shamir*. Ashmedai answered that he did not have the *shamir*, because it was given to the prince of the sea, who gave sole charge of it to the wild cock, who used it to split mountains, after which he scattered the seeds of trees in the crack, in order to attract settlers. They sought out the nest of the wild cock, and finding fledglings in it, they covered it with white glass. The wild cock came, tried to get into the nest, and couldn't, so he went to fetch the *shamir*. Just when the wild cock was about to set it down upon the glass, they threw a pebble at the cock, causing him to drop the *shamir*, which they immediately took from him.[5]

This Talmudic story teaches us that in order to get the one thing he needs to build the structure of ultimate goodness, Solomon must go to Ashmedai, the most evil of creatures. The *shamir* is brought by

Solomon so that no iron tool would be heard in the House of God; the material of weapons could not be brought into a place of peace. The lesson of the *shamir* is that it is only through conflict that true peace can exist. We often try to avoid conflict, when in fact inconsistency is necessary and even useful to our growth and development. It is only when we embrace the conflict and contradiction in our lives that we are able to find the peace that we seek. Solomon had to go through a turbulent quest in order to find the *shamir*. So, too, it is often only after we endure our own tests that we can find the key to building our own Temple.

RABBI ALISON B. KOBEY

הפטרת תצוה
Haftarat Tetzaveh

Ezekiel 43:10–27

*A*nd when they are guilty [ashamed] of [all their sins] that they have done, show them the plan of the Temple. (EZEKIEL 43:11)

IN *HAFTARAT TETZAVEH*, we read about God's command to Ezekiel to reveal the blueprints for a future Temple to the people of Israel. Ezekiel hopes to make the new Temple a permanent structure, standing as a pathway to God. Through Divine assistance, Ezekiel is precise in his detailed description of the "House." Moreover, in contrast to the First Temple, which was destroyed because of the people's transgressions, this new Temple is meant to be a permanent structure. In Ezekiel 43:11, we read that after the First Temple was destroyed, "when they are guilty [ashamed] of [all their sins] that they have done," the Israelites will be able to see the plan of the Temple with all its ensuing regulations. With the acknowledgment of the people's remorse, there will be forward movement into a new era with a permanent Temple. Furthermore, by having the codes in writing, the people will be able to more easily follow the structural plans and laws in their entirety. After this essential introduction, we read about the details of the structure, and the sacrificial rituals that must occur within its walls.

Ezekiel's belief that the people must first feel guilt in order to rebuild the Temple is a key concept in the haftarah. We read in the Talmud,

93

"If one commits a sin and is ashamed of it [literally conscience-stricken], all one's sins are forgiven."[1] One who does something wrong, feels guilty over the wrongdoing, and then truly seeks repentance should indeed be forgiven. The causal relationship makes sense. Guilt is often an important emotion that leads us to accept responsibility for an action, and allows us to move forward more easily. However, what about the times when guilt is not warranted? What about when our actions do not seem to result in direct consequences? Is everything cause and effect? In other words, did our sins really cause the First Temple to be destroyed?

We often struggle with this theological model because it challenges us. Do our behaviors inevitably lead to other events? Most people would agree that some do, but some do not; and, as a result, many of us reject the idea of "punishment theology," which suggests that God directly punishes our actions. Sometimes, there is no causal relationship (at least that we can understand) between actions and events. Good things happen to bad people, and bad things happen to good people.

In verse 11, Ezekiel is deliberate in his choice of the word *nichlimu*, meaning guilt or shame, depending on translation. Is our translation of the word based on gender? Do men and women perceive shame and guilt in the same way? Do we react differently? One rabbi noted the frequency of women using the phrase, "I thought I was doing something wrong. I felt I deserved it" in his counseling sessions.[2] The idea of shame can be pervasive among women. When we read the text, however, our assumption is that Ezekiel is talking to a group of men. More often, men translate the word *nichlimu* as *guilt*, an emotion that supports Ezekiel's idea. When one feels guilty, it is usually because he or she did something wrong. Ezekiel's vision is based on the direct link between the Israelites' actions and the destruction of the Temple. He is using the sins of the Israelites to intellectualize the destruction of the First Temple. Ezekiel's point is purposeful: We must acknowledge the past in order to move forward. However, what if our initial assumption was wrong? What if women were present? Would we translate the word *nichlimu* as *shame*, rather than *guilt*? The idea of shame is a heartfelt emotion, but sometimes we feel shame even when we do nothing wrong.

Women often experience a feeling of misplaced shame. Although the people sinned, that is not the real reason for the loss of the Temple, which can also be explained as a result of the war between the Israelites and their neighbors. The Talmud teaches that "a woman solicits with her heart, the husband does so with his mouth."[3] In other words, women tend to emotionalize experiences, which may make healing a longer process, while men tend to intellectualize them. Ezekiel thinks about the issue more like a traditional man: He intellectualizes the experience, asks the people to apologize, and then moves forward to build another Temple.

In verses 12 through 27 of this haftarah portion, Ezekiel describes a clear vision for the new Temple, with specific dimensions for the altar, and the various sacrifices meant to occur there. The altar's purpose is to "offer to God burnt-offerings and to cast blood on . . . [the altar]" (Ezek. 43:18). The priestly descendants were commanded to "dwell near to Me [God] to serve Me" (43:19) with various sacrifices. We know from the text that the priests are descended from Zadok, and that they are male. But, in the Hebrew, *ben-adam*, literally "son of Adam," refers to all of humanity. Ezekiel's vision, which originated from God, is therefore ambiguous.

So, what if both men and women were present to hear Ezekiel? What if both women and men were priests? The experience of the destruction of the First Temple and the resulting emotions may have been different. Women and men acknowledge past events in different manners and share emotions in various ways. Ultimately, Ezekiel's goal is to generate hope, and to eliminate sins, by envisioning the perfect and more permanent Temple.

This vision may have yielded an alternative space if both men and women had been priests and priestesses. The sanctuary and the altar might have looked different, and the function of the space might have been different. Whereas the men were focused on the structural details of the sanctuary, we can imagine the women emphasizing other pathways to draw nearer to God. Imagine, for a moment, our own modern visions of the sanctuary. Would it have matched Ezekiel's ideas? If we had a vision from God about the Temple, how exactly would it look?

We Jews have all moved from the days of the ancient Temples, away from animal sacrifices, and, in many cases, away from punishment theology. In today's world, when one enters a liberal synagogue, one may see the same rituals being performed by either male or female rabbis. We participate on the bimah, read Torah and haftarah, counsel, participate in life-cycle events, and more. Admittedly, we are still not completely equal as clergy. When we are truly equal, our gender will not be the start of our titles, as in *woman rabbi*. On the other hand, as women, we are often viewed by our congregants as more approachable, and provide new entry points for people to come to synagogues and engage in ritual, prayer, and Jewish life. We can be vehicles for people to "dwell near to . . . [God] to serve Me" (43:19) and we have certainly brought a new vision to prayer and to sanctuaries. Although we would not want to surrender the positives, we do deserve to be treated as fully equal. It is our humanness that differentiates our genders. From a Divine perspective, we are equal.

As Ezekiel teaches, we need to remember our wrongdoings, feel guilty, and repent when appropriate, but we are not meant to bury ourselves in unnecessary layers of shame. We are all meant to take personal responsibility for our ethical and religious lives, and are all intended to find means to draw near to God. When we, men and women, equally access these pathways toward God, then, "says the Eternal God, I will desire you."[4]

RABBI VALERIE LIEBER

הפטרת כי תשא
Haftarat Ki Tissa

I Kings 18:1–39

Now gather all of Israel and send them to me at Mount Carmel as well as the 450 prophets of Ba'al and the 400 prophets of Asherah who eat at the table of Jezebel. (I KINGS 18:19)

IF THE TORAH CONDEMNS the worship of the golden calf in *Parashat Ki Tissa*, then the haftarah sounds the alarm about how quickly idolatry can seduce the multitudes with empty promises. This portion from the Book of I Kings presents Queen Jezebel and the prophet Elijah as foils against one another: Elijah is the staunchest supporter of YHVH, and Jezebel is the devoted patron of the heathen god Ba'al and the goddess Asherah. Elijah proves in this haftarah portion the impotence of the god of Queen Jezebel and King Ahab and the omnipotence of YHVH. This is not only a challenge of God against god, but also a challenge of the humble prophet against the powerful, morally bankrupt monarchy.

The description of Jezebel, the strong woman who leads the cause against the one true God YHVH, challenges Jewish feminists. Here is one of the few women in the Bible who is named, wields power, and dominates several scenes. As feminists, we want to find characteristics in her to emulate. Nevertheless, it is difficult to respect this queen who has the Jewish prophets slaughtered, and who gives financial support to the prophets of idols.

Neither Jezebel nor Elijah can be fully understood without the other. They are opposites. Jezebel is a foreigner from Phoenicia, while Elijah is a native. She is the daughter of the king of Phoenicia, but he is without lineage. She is so wealthy she can support hundreds of prophets, and he is so destitute he must often beg for food.[1]

The Bible introduces Jezebel two chapters prior to the section in our haftarah portion: "Ahab, the son of Omri, did evil in the eyes of YHVH, more so than any [king] who came before him. He walked in the sins of Jereboam, son of Nebat [his predecessor], he married Jezebel, daughter of King Ethbaal of the Phoenicians, and he pursued and worshipped Ba'al and bowed down to him" (I Kings 16:30–31). The Torah warns repeatedly of the dangers of marrying pagan women, lest they convert their husbands to heathen religious life. The assumption is that such women hold strong domestic sway over their husbands, even over their religious and spiritual lives.

Jezebel's very name is a reference to the god Ba'al. In the Ugaritic language, *Jezebel* means, "Where is the Prince?" This is part of the ritualized question that was called out in times of drought in the Phoenician religion. The full cry was, "Where is Ba'al the Conqueror? *Where is the Prince*, the Lord of the earth? For Ba'al the Conqueror lives; the Prince, the Lord of the earth, has revived."[2] Jezebel's name proclaims her faith in Ba'al, and her belief that he can reverse drought. Jezebel's life mission is to spread the faith of Ba'al. Conversely, Elijah's very name, *Eli-ya-hu*, is a declaration of his Jewish faith: "YHVH is my God." Elijah's life work is to spread the belief and teachings of YHVH. Jezebel and Elijah are like walking billboards for their respective God. While their backgrounds are diametrically opposed, their fervor for their religion and the lengths they go to show their devotion are almost identical.

Jezebel does not appear in the action of the haftarah; nonetheless, she pervades it. She is the prime financial supporter of the hundreds of prophets of Ba'al who try, without success, to get him to accept their sacrifice at Mount Carmel. In this story, Elijah alone vanquishes the prophets of Ba'al. Judaism triumphs over idolatry. YHVH proves to be the only real God and thus Jezebel is defeated. The haftarah ends here, but just a few verses later we read that Elijah slaughters the prophets of Ba'al, just as Jezebel had killed Elijah's fellow prophets of YHVH. The Rabbis chose to end the haftarah before Elijah's murders to bolster the portrayal of Elijah as all good and Jezebel as thoroughly corrupt. While the Rabbis tried to keep the separation between good and evil very clear, the Tanakh reports the story with less judgment.

Jezebel does not retreat. In a later episode in I Kings 21, she urges King Ahab to seize a vineyard from one of his subjects, Naboth. She concocts a scheme charging the innocent man with blasphemy, and the townspeople stone him to death. King Ahab then takes his land. Here Jezebel proves to be determined, clever, and ruthless. We forgive Rebekah, Tamar, Michal, and Sarah for these very same characteristics. Out of concern for the future of the Jewish people, they tricked their husbands, sons, fathers-in-law, and kings. Jezebel's guile, however, serves only her husband's career and her own drive for power.

Rabbinic literature emphasizes Jezebel's seductive nature to explain how King Ahab could be driven to such base behavior. Many midrashim that condemn Jezebel begin with a verse from the story of Naboth's vineyard, "There had never been anyone like Ahab, who devoted himself to doing evil in the eyes of God at the urging of his wife Jezebel" (I Kings 21:25). Here Jezebel is the instigator. In one midrash she is said to have attached erotic pictures to Ahab's chariot to stimulate his libido.[3] In another she is said to have been co-ruler with Ahab.[4] Even more threatening to the Rabbis of Jewish tradition than a woman who flaunted her sexuality was a woman who achieved control over men through such allure. In some circles even today *Jezebel* is used as a slur to suggest that someone has loose sexual morals.[5] To emphasize the sexual nature of Jezebel's power of seduction is to detract from the real goal of her ambition: the triumph of Ba'al in Israel. She sought to lure the Jews into religious infidelity, not sexual infidelity. Yet Jezebel is often remembered as a harlot because of two later scenes.

After the death of King Ahab, Yoram, Jezebel and Ahab's son, rose to the kingship of Israel. Elijah had passed the mantle of prophetic leadership to his disciple Elisha. Elisha helps to stage a coup, anointing Jehu, an officer of Yoram's army, king. Jehu confronts Yoram in the very field Yoram's parents had wrested from Naboth. Suspecting nothing, King Yoram asks, "Is all peaceful, Jehu?" Jehu replies, "How can there be peace with your mother Jezebel's harlotry and widespread sorcery?" (II Kings 9:22). Jehu proceeds to kill Yoram and assume the throne. Jehu's are easy insults to sling. We might expect that her son's challenger would slander Jezebel's name with such accusations even if she had been innocent of them.

Many readers of the Bible look to Jezebel's final scene as further proof of her sexual promiscuity. Jehu rides his chariot to her and, hearing of his approach, she applies makeup, coifs her hair, and sits in her window. Because prostitutes would wear cosmetics and sit in windows to ply their trade, many accuse Jezebel of being a bona fide harlot.

However, a better explanation is that she was sitting in her window not to seduce Jehu, but to defy him. Upper-class women regularly wore cosmetics. Jezebel applies them now to give herself a striking appearance so that when Jehu rides into Jezreel, he will recognize her as Queen Jezebel—the daughter and widow of kings. When Jehu arrives, Jezebel taunts him, calling him *Zimri*. Zimri, like Jehu, was a usurper of the throne, but he lasted as king for only seven days, until Ahab's father Omri killed him and became king. Defiant to the end, Jezebel's own servants shove her out her window, and she is trampled by Jehu's horses. Jezebel's recalcitrance suggests that she knows that Jehu (and the prophets of YHVH) will triumph over her, but hopes that this victory will be short-lived. Peter Ackroyd writes: "This story portrays her [Jezebel], rather unexpectedly, [as] a woman, a queen mother—a figure of status. . . . Whatever else tradition has said about Jezebel, and all of it [is] negative, it records a courageous woman, with dignity to face certain death with no loss of face."[6]

Had Jezebel been on the side of Judaism and a supporter of YHVH, she would be praised for all the attributes for which she is maligned. She is condemned by tradition for everything she does well, because she acts on behalf of monotheism's enemy. While Elijah leaves the world in a chariot of fire with a reputation for courage, compassion, and goodness, Jezebel's courage, loyalty, and power are usually forgotten. Yet without Jezebel, Elijah would not have risen to glory, nor captured the imagination of the Jewish people. Without Jezebel's opposition, the final words of this haftarah portion would be less powerful: "The Eternal alone is God; The Eternal alone is God" (I Kings 18:39). These are the words with which we end our Yom Kippur prayers each year, a reminder of our own fidelity to the One God.

הפטרת ויקהל

Haftarat Vayakhel

I Kings 7:40–50

*H*e made the table of acacia wood, two cubits long, one cubit wide, and a cubit and a half high; he overlaid it with pure gold and made a gold molding around it. (EXODUS 37:10–11)

OUR SHORT HAFTARAH—a mere eleven verses—deals exclusively with the fashioning of the Temple and its accessories. Bronze columns, gold tables, and door sockets dominate the text, while their makers, Hiram and Solomon, are mentioned only briefly.

The haftarah focuses on a centerpiece of the First Temple—a gold table that holds the loaves of Temple bread. But in the period after the Second Temple, the Rabbis of the Talmud begin to discuss this table and its significance, and the one table grows into ten: "Our Rabbis taught: Solomon made ten tables . . . and Solomon made ten candlesticks" (*Menachot* 99a). And not only do the Rabbis multiply the number of Temple tables—all made of gold—but they decide that one of them belonged to none other than Moses himself. The Temple accessories, in the minds of the Rabbis, grow bigger and shinier and possess profound historical significance dating back to the time of Jews wandering in the desert. Diagrams abound on the pages of Talmud, with each Rabbi suggesting the perfect spot for his perfect table.

For the Rabbis, the Temple and its accessories represent the ultimate *makom kodesh*, holy place. For us, while we're drawn into their imaginings and can fantasize about Temple grandeur, the Temple remains only a fantasy, an image, an ancient, sparkly world made of gold and bronze and crimson velvets. Yet the Temple imagery causes us to question whether our own homes and our own spaces can be a *makom kodesh*.

The Rabbis' imaginative spirit regarding the placement and locations of things like gold tables and crimson curtains suggests that we too must put care into our own homes. If we all live in our own mini-temples, our kitchens and tables serving as places to seek God and make blessings over bread, then we too should concern ourselves with our own temple accessories. If Hiram, King Solomon, and the talmudic Rabbis were in the business of decorating their holy places in the name of God, then so should we.

But we are often overwhelmed at the idea of creating our own *makom kodesh*, our own mini-temple. When we don't build the perfect home, we feel as if we've fallen short of what we should be doing. Spatial order and symmetry give way to clutter and the busy lifestyle. A life where our homes surround us, comfort us, and inspire us in the way the temple did for the priests is indeed a rarity. While we have the desire to act as Hiram and Solomon do in our haftarah—creating beautiful decor for our homes, fashioning our own candlesticks—we lack the time and energy. So we often do what the Rabbis do in *Menachot*—we imagine a world more beautiful and more ordered than the one that actually exists.

The Rabbis, in a sense, are like us. They push the Temple to bigger and better things. They "super-size" the Temple accessories. One gold table becomes ten tables—nine tables plus a rare antique—the table that Moses himself built for the *mishkan* in the days of wandering in the desert. They fantasize when they cannot have perfection. But not Solomon. In our haftarah, he "left all the vessels [unweighed] because of their very great quantity; the weight of the bronze was not reckoned" (I Kings 7:47). Solomon is able to leave well enough alone. He is capable of recognizing the value in what somebody else has created, in what already exists. His Temple—the First Temple—is simple.

His Temple contains only one instrument for each purpose. While elaborate for its time, his Temple still reminds us that one table is sufficient. If ten tables aren't necessary to worship God, then we certainly don't need ten to serve our families.

Our haftarah ends with a brief description of the Temple doors: "and the hinge sockets for the doors of the innermost part of the House, the Holy of Holies, and for the doors of the Great Hall of the House, of gold" (I Kings 7:50). Even the hinges of a holy place matter. They are an invitation to enter. This ending is an invitation from King Solomon himself, an invitation to enter into the imaginative, organized, detailed, creative world of the *Beit Hamikdash*. But the only way in for us today is the simple doorway of our own home. Even the hinges matter there, too. If we enter our own homes with the same reverence as our ancestors entered the Temple, we could turn even the everyday accessories into instruments of spirituality.

RABBI Y. L. BAT JOSEPH

הפטרת פקודי

Haftarat Pikudei

I Kings 7:51–8:21

*T*hese are the records of the *mishkan* [sanctuary] . . .
(EXODUS 38:21)

*W*hen all the work that King Solomon had done in the
House of Adonai was completed . . . (I KINGS 7:51)

THE COMPLETION OF the *mishkan* ("sanctuary") in the wilderness—the
subject of this *parashah*—paralleled the completion of King Solomon's
Temple in Jerusalem, the subject of the haftarah. The narrative of the
haftarah is replete with references to the past. Basing our lives on the
tradition of our patriarchs' tents, on the Torah revealed at Sinai, and
on the customs that took root through the ages is a central tenet of rabbinic Judaism.

Solomon begins by bringing the wealth his father, King David, had
accumulated for the Temple's construction and upkeep into the Temple treasury. As Solomon notes in his inaugural address, it was David
who first conceived the idea of building a permanent home for God in
Jerusalem. Although God did not permit David to construct the Temple himself, he nevertheless paved the way for its creation under the
guidance of his son, Solomon.

The procession to the new Temple includes the ark containing
the Tablets of the Law (the Ten Commandments) as well as the Tent of

Meeting and all its sacred vessels, thereby maintaining the continuity between the sanctuary in the wilderness and the sanctuary of the Promised Land.

Most notable among these listings of treasures, accoutrements, and investiture is the absence of women. Neither the haftarah nor the Torah portion makes mention of them. Miriam has no role in the *mishkan* of the wilderness, and there is no description of a role for women in Solomon's Temple.

Historically, the realm of the *mishkan*—and later, the synagogue—was the realm of men. Men served as priests and later as cantors and rabbis. In modern Rabbinic courts, women are not given the role of judge, nor are they counted as credible witnesses in most instances. In the traditional synagogue, women are not counted as part of the minyan, the quorum of ten required for public prayer services. And even in this era of egalitarian congregations, we often find ourselves perceived and described as "taking on the roles or duties of men."

Is there anything in these texts that can provide a point of connection and meaning for women? The word *mishkan* is frequently translated as "tabernacle," a platform for sacrifices. But its root is a word that means a "dwelling" place. Indeed, both the *mishkan* in the wilderness and the Temple in Jerusalem were dwelling places of the Divine presence—the presence known in Hebrew as the *Shekhinah*, a feminine word from the same root as *mishkan*. The Hebrew word for *altar* (a platform for sacrifices) is *mizbei'ach*, a word that provides an important connection between the historical/traditional domain of women and the *mishkan*.

When we break bread on Shabbat, it is a Jewish custom to sprinkle the challah with salt before eating it. Many participate in this custom without knowing why. While the salt is a reminder of the Temple and the sacrifices offered there, it is more specifically a reminder to us that every table is a *mizbei'ach*; every home is a *mishkan*. With the dinner table as the altar, the Jewish home becomes a microcosm of the ancient Temple, with women effectively serving as the Levitical priests. The Levites tended the fires of the ancient altars in Jerusalem, offering sacrifices of pleasing odor to God. Women traditionally tend the home fires, preparing meals of pleasing odor and great nourishment to their families. The Levites ensured that all the ritual laws were meticulously followed and the routine of the Temple maintained. Women ensured and continue to ensure the smooth running of their households and the fulfillment of daily home rituals both religious and secular. The *Kohein Gadol*, the high priest, also served as arbiter and judge in matters concerning Temple law. Women, as the *Kohein Gadol* of their homes, often mediate and arbitrate disputes concerning the laws of the house or family. The high priest was expected to be of the highest moral character, a role model for the society. Mothers face equally stringent expectations.

The home, as much as the synagogue service, became a focal point for Jewish ritual and Jewish spirituality. It is, traditionally, the place where our Jewish education begins. We light candles, and join in Pesach seders and Friday morning challah baking long before we fully appreciate the religious significance of these rituals. Among Jews who identify with our people only on a cultural level, the connection to one's home is all the more vital. For many, this is the only focal point for any kind of Jewish ritual. It is a sad irony that the significance of this dimension of Jewish spiritual life has come to be undervalued in the postmodern era. Our grandmothers and great-grandmothers understood the importance of their role in Jewish continuity and the Jewish education of both sons and daughters. They did more than bake cookies and serve tea. They exposed generations of Jewish children to folklore, holiday rituals, prayer, and song. They were, indeed, the *Kohein Gadol* of the home in their day.

The Temple is gone, as are the ritual sacrifices. They have been replaced, ostensibly, by the synagogue and daily prayer service with rabbis and cantors conducting the ritual affairs of the community in place of the Levitical priests. The tributes brought for the Temple treasury in ancient times are analogous to contemporary acts of *tzedakah*, "charity." The grandeur of the past has been muted, but the values endure. We have endured as a people because our imagination has allowed us to envision and reenvision the Temple as a metaphor, which has meaning and direct application to our daily lives.

Recent generations of Jewish women have been blessed with expanded roles in contemporary Jewish life. We are equal partners in the sanctuary and enjoy a wide range of roles as Jewish professionals. We may be rabbis, cantors, educators, and Jewish board members in addition to being partners, mothers, and the *Kohein Gadol* of our homes.

If every table is indeed a *mizbei'ach*, then every home is potentially a *mishkan*—a dwelling place where the *Shekhinah*, the Divine presence, is welcomed not simply as an honored guest, but as an integral part of the household. The haftarah records that King Solomon completed his work with the dedication of the *mishkan* in Jerusalem. In truth, the task of dedication can never be completed. Each generation has the obligation to pick up where Solomon left off and dedicate our homes anew as sanctuaries of Jewish learning, Jewish ritual, and Jewish continuity.

Vayikra / Leviticus

RABBI TINA GRIMBERG

הפטרת ויקרא

Haftarat Vayikra

Isaiah 43:21–44:23

Now [if you think I don't recall your goodness]
remind Me! Let us arrive at judgment! Tell [your
story], so you can become righteous! (ISAIAH 43:26)

THE HEAVENLY COURT was unusually crowded that morning. Right after
the angels finished singing their morning praises to God, they settled
noisily in their pews and waited for the hearing to begin. On this morning God was judging the children of Israel, for they had turned away
from God and sinned by worshipping idols and other gods. The large
chamber was full of important witnesses and guests, men of great distinction. Abraham in his beat-up leather sandals, Isaac with the scarf
around his neck, Jacob reclining against the back of his chair, Moses
with his white, uncombed hair and shining face, and many more were
present. They were there to testify on behalf of the children of Israel
and help to spare them. The room was filled with murmur and whisper,
but turned silent when God entered. In the whole of Paradise not a
bird chirped, not a creature made a sound. Those who were present at
Mount Sinai when the tablets were given recognized this awesome
silence.

Seated on the large leather throne, God made a motion to begin.
Abraham was the first to come forward. Plucking his beard and rending
his garments, he pleaded with God on the behalf of the children of
Israel: "Holy One, you have exiled my children and destroyed their

place of worship. Will there be an end to their sufferings? Will You not have mercy for my sake?" But the Holy One replied sternly: "They have transgressed against my Torah. . . . I cannot forgive them," and remained unmoved. Then Isaac came forward and began to plead: "Maker of the Universe, I too served You full-heartedly. Will You not have mercy for my sake?" But the Holy One remained unmoved. Isaac was followed by Jacob, Jacob by Moses, and Moses by Jeremiah, each offering his tale of sacrifice and devotion. However, their pleas went unheeded. The Divine mercy seemed to have left Paradise, and God remained unmoved.

Seeing that their pleas were futile, all the forefathers began to weep. Realizing Israel's grim predicament, the angels added soft and tearful cries. All seemed lost, and the children of Israel's fate was just about to be sealed, when suddenly the room gasped. Through the crowd of sweaty male bodies, Rachel, the mother of Israel, broke through, "Maker of the Universe!" she cried out: "It is revealed and known to You that Your servant Jacob cherished a great love for me, and yet my father conspired to substitute my sister for me. I was hurt and bitter, but yet I overcame my pain and left jealousy and anger behind. Now if I who am flesh and blood, dust and ashes, was not angry and bitter, then why should You, the Ruler of the Universe, whose love has no end, and whose kindness is great, not be able to overcome Your anger and find mercy for Your children?" To everyone's surprise, Divine mercy returned to Paradise to fill the court with its presence, and God was moved. "For your sake, O Rachel, I will restore Israel to their place. They are forgiven."

The midrash from *Lamentations Rabbah* (poem 24) poses a valid question in light of the haftarah: "Why was mother Rachel's plea more potent than that of the patriarchs?" Did not all the witnesses—Abraham, Isaac, Jacob, and the others—show their love for God though sacrifice and self-denial? What set mother Rachel's plea apart from all the others was her address to God's attributes of mercy and forgiveness. These virtues are prevalent in every good parent, but are particular to a mother.

The text of *Haftarat Vayikra* is full of references to the maternal qualities of God. In Isaiah 44:2 we read: "Hence says YHVH, your Maker, who formed you from the womb [and who] will help you: Have no fear, Jacob, My servant . . ." Words like *form* and *womb* evoke strong images for the reader—images of pregnancy and maternity. Torah does not waste words and does not use them superfluously; therefore, the use of the word *yatzar,* meaning "to form, to create" three times in chapters 43 and 44 is significant. These words reach out to us and remind us of God who is a nurturer and a giver of life.

This haftarah, however, is not the only place in Second Isaiah where the reader finds the vocabulary of motherhood. Isaiah 40–66 is full of maternal references: "Alas for him who says to his father, 'What are you begetting?' And to [his] mother, 'To what are you giving birth?'" (45:10) and "'Now' says YHVH, 'I will scream like a woman in labor. I will inhale, and I will exhale simultaneously'" (42:14).

Why is Second Isaiah so particular in the use of feminine language? Mayer I. Gruber proposes the following theory: Isaiah's predecessors, Jeremiah and Ezekiel, often called Israel a harlot or an unfaithful wife who was involved in idolatrous cults and lusted after other gods. These foreign cults were desirable to Israelite women because the female qualities of the foreign deities were positively represented, but the Temple service excluded women's participation and involvement. In an attempt to address Jeremiah and Ezekiel's insensitivity, Gruber suggests, Second Isaiah deliberately stresses women's imagery in his writings.[1] Mother-sensitive language continues all the way to the end of the book: "I shall comfort you like a man whose mother comforts him, and you shall be comforted through Jerusalem" (Isa. 66:13).

Rachel's feminine plea, her sensitivity to the motherly qualities of God, resonates with Isaiah's message. Mother Rachel comforts her children by ensuring their restoration in God's favor, and God comforts the children of Israel by offering them the possibility of *teshuvah,* "repentance," by letting them tell their story.

In Isaiah 43, God asks the children of Israel to engage in a debate: "Now [if you think I don't remember your goodness] remind Me! Let us arrive at judgment! Tell [your story], so you can become righteous!" It is possible that in the process of this telling, the nation will realize their mistake of pursuing emptiness by serving idols: "Tell your version, that you may become righteous," urges God. The process of storytelling becomes a process of self-redemption. The story leads to a key realization and a change of behavior.

Telling one's story with a purpose of self-discovery, healing, and change has been practiced by humanity from the beginning of time. As Frank McConnell writes: "You are the hero of your own life-story. The kind of story you want to tell yourself about yourself has a lot to do with the kind of person you are, and can become."[2] The process of storytelling encourages the children of Israel to become who they were always meant to be—better Jews and better human beings. Telling a story can be a profoundly religious experience.

Hasidim have adopted storytelling as a spiritual discipline. One of the basic tenets of this practice is teaching through examples or role models. The stories about the noble qualities of great moral men and women, called *tzadikkim*, and the way they loved and revered God, served as a lesson and an example to follow. The power of their example was to be found in their honest struggle with life, its complexities, and its temptations: "It is a good sign for a person if when he hears stories praising the virtuous deeds of the tzadikkim and their sincere and holy service of God, blessed be the One, his heart becomes aroused and inflamed with hope that he too might serve God sincerely. This is a sign that God is with him."[3]

As sinful Israel begins to tell their story to God, like all storytellers, they begin from the beginning, remembering and retelling the story of their ancestors and their glorious past. So as the Israelites told the tales of patriarchs and matriarchs whose lives were filled with challenges and tribulations, they also remembered their own steadfastness. They remembered that their heroes and heroines remained devoted to God and to each other. Despite life's complexities, Jacob reconciled with Esau, Joseph with his brothers, and Rachel learned to live side by side with her fertile sister Leah. In those struggles they encountered God face-to-face and encouraged the following generations to do the same. The stories about their ancestors would have inspired the sinful Israelites, awakening their hearts and setting them on fire, arousing them to turn back to God.[4]

In this way, Isaiah hearkens back to mother Rachel, encouraging the people to be faithful to both God and themselves. His pleas for *teshuvah* and his promise of reconciliation reminded them of her open arms, and thus of God's own embrace.

הפטרת צו

Haftarat Tzav

Jeremiah 7:21–8:3; 9:22–23

*S*o shall I cause the sound of joy and the sound of
gladness, the voices of bridegroom and bride, to pass
away from Judah's cities and Jerusalem's courtyards, for
the land shall be barren. (JEREMIAH 7:34)

THE SONS AND DAUGHTERS of Judah shall die, slaughtered at the hands
of their parents and burned in fire. In her cities, the songs of bridegroom and bride will fall silent, and with them the promise of new generations and new life. When the bones of Judah's elders are brought
from their graves, scattered under a scorching and unforgiving sun,
none shall gather them together and return them with honor to the
earth.

Such is the vision of the prophet Jeremiah, who—according to
Jewish tradition—spoke these words near the Holy Temple in
Jerusalem twenty-two years before it was defiled and destroyed by the
armies of Babylon. His words reflect the traditional understanding that
Jerusalem fell not because of Babylon's might, but because of our ancestors' refusal to heed the word of God; specifically, the Torah's ethical
commandments. A nation that does not take care of its own needy—
the widow, the orphan, the poor—cannot rise up in strength united
to stave off an enemy invader. And, in the end, as Jeremiah warns, a
nation that abandons its needy will destroy the memory of its elders
and the promise of its youth.

Jeremiah's prophecy is vivid and frightening, dreadful in its detail; we almost understand why the rulers of his day preferred to seek his death rather than heed his terrible warnings. It was unthinkable to them that the proud nation of Judah might fall so horribly, that its prosperous and powerful might be cast into exile. Interestingly, however, it is not only to the ruling class that Jeremiah speaks here; he charges both the leaders and the citizenry of Judah equally with the downfall of their nation if they do not turn back to God's ethical commandments.

Male biblical prophets do not generally preach to the women of their day. It is in fact bold to imagine that the wives, mothers, and daughters of Judah were even gathered to hear Jeremiah's Temple oration, let alone to assert that Jeremiah spoke to them directly. Yet if we read selected passages from this haftarah in the context of Jeremiah's prophetic career, we find license to understand some of his words as bearing particularly upon the women of Judah.

In these chapters, Jeremiah fills his oracle with images and language that are commonly considered of concern to women. He speaks in detail of the sacrifice of children (7:31); the cessation of joyous wedding celebrations (7:34); and the figurative abandonment of the elderly (8:1–2), in his depiction of the bones of the dead, disinterred and dishonored. The sanctity of the family unit is destroyed, and the links between the generations are severed. Thus does Jeremiah draw a parallel between a broken family and a fallen nation; indeed, Jeremiah uses the phrase *hamishpacha hara'ah*, "the wicked family" to describe the nation of Judah. Such an oracle was perhaps intended to convey the gravity of Judah's danger to the nation's women, who might best be able to relate to Jeremiah's warnings through images and phrases that evoked their primary responsibilities of making a home and tending to their children. Jeremiah makes his point quite clearly: Just as a family cannot survive if it fails to protect and nurture its children, ensure its continuity through the forging of committed relationships, and honor its elders, so too will such abdications of duty doom an entire nation.

Yet Jeremiah does not appeal to the women of Judah only through his language and images. Because Hebrew is a gendered language, one can discern if the "you" being addressed is masculine or feminine by noting the verb forms and noun suffixes employed. And in this haftarah, one remarkable verse (7:29) clearly applies specifically to a female audience. Jeremiah proclaims, "*Gazi nizreich v'hashlichi,* Cut off your hair and cast it away," with all three Hebrew words appearing in the feminine form. While this usage may appear in part for poetic reasons, it is worth noting a similar phrasing in Micah 1:16, which is undoubtedly intended to apply to a feminine object. There Micah speaks specifically of the kingdom's sinful cities, which he personifies throughout the chapter as women. Interestingly, his charge to "cut off" hair occurs in connection with the loss of one's (figurative) children; that is, the coming exile of the cities' inhabitants. The other prominent place in the Bible where someone cuts off hair as a sign of mourning is Job 1:20, where Job does so upon learning that his children have died. Thus, although this practice is considered a common rite of mourning, its most-cited mentions in the Bible occur in relation to child loss and/or in the feminine form.

Yet unlike Micah, Jeremiah is not speaking to a female-personified city; rather, he specifically addresses real women, calling them to action. Jeremiah continues to compare the imminent fall of Judah with the shattering of a family unit, choosing the words *gazi nizreich* to evoke an image of lost children, knowing that image would effectively galvanize his female listeners.

The argument that *gazi nizreich* is addressed to women is all the more strengthened as we read the word that follows: "*Hashlichi,* cast [it] away." This passage marks the only time this particular form of the verb *sh-l-ch,* to cast away, appears in the Bible; and the form, as Radak notes, is unmistakably feminine. The rest of the verse—likewise employing the feminine command form—urges Jeremiah's listeners to cut off their hair, cast it away, and "raise lamentation upon the high hills." This order also reflects the fact that women traditionally served as the formal mourners and bewailers of their communities.

This simple grammatical evidence is fortified when one considers it in light of Jeremiah's prophetic career. According to Jewish legend, the very first person to whom Jeremiah revealed prophecy was his mother, before whom he launched into a diatribe against the citizens of Judah as he emerged from the womb.[1] Jeremiah was also a relative of Huldah, an esteemed prophetess who delivered oracles to the women of the city.[2] Jeremiah understood the value of addressing his words to women.

That Jeremiah concerned himself with female listeners is striking in itself. Yet it is even more important to ask why. In a time and place where virtually all social, economic, and political power was held by men, why would a major prophet direct his oracle to women? What tremendous change in Judah might Jeremiah hope to effect by addressing the city's women as well as men?

Let us imagine that the women left the house and the marketplace, their husbands and children, and ascended together to the hills of Judah, ripping their hair from their scalps and raising their voices in wailing and lament. Let us imagine that the men of the city stared in bewilderment as their wives and daughters took up Jeremiah's cry, refusing to fulfill their traditional duties of home and children as long as their husbands refused to follow God's ethical law. Let us imagine that days and nights passed, the sultry noon heat and the cool midnight air carrying the rebuke of Judah's women, as households went unattended and children unfed. Let us imagine that the women's message at last was heard, that their men at last understood the relationship between family and nation, that both were reunited and rededicated in the name of God.[3]

To be sure, the women of Judah were not the locus of its social, economic, or political authority. Yet they were the ones who fed, clothed, and supported the men who held—or who would grow up to hold—such authority. This simple fact granted these women a power they may not have known they possessed, a power that, if used fully and passionately, might indeed have been sufficient to turn the attention of their husbands and sons to the truth of Jeremiah's words. Perhaps

Jeremiah—who addressed his first oracle to a woman and who counted among his kin a prophetess who preached to women—understood the power these women might have exercised. Perhaps Jeremiah hoped that these women would employ their unique, feminine power to bring Judah back to the ethical and the just path. Perhaps things might have been different if they had.

הפטרת שמיני

Haftarat Shimini

II Samuel 6:1–7:17

*M*ichal, Saul's daughter, had no child until her dying day. (II SAMUEL 6:23)

KING DAVID'S TRIUMPHANT return of the Ark of the Covenant to Jerusalem, the core of *Haftarat Shimini*, is marked by two unsettling incidents. The first, the death of Uzzah, parallels the untimely deaths of Aaron's sons Nadav and Avihu in *Parashat Shimini*. The second marks the end of David's marriage to Michal, his first wife.

On the face of it, Michal's life is a tragedy, summed up by the last verse of her story, "Michal, Saul's daughter, had no child until her dying day" (II Samuel 6:23). In the context of the haftarah, it is hard to view this verse as anything other than a punishment. In II Samuel 6:16, we read that Michal saw David dancing and she "despised him in her heart." Verses 21 and 22 capture their final argument as she sarcastically comments that David does not have the royal stature of her father King Saul, and he retorts that, nevertheless, God chose him to replace her father as king. This is immediately followed by the verse revealing Michal's childless state.

But this statement can be interpreted differently as well, for the verse itself is not pejorative. It does not say that Michal is being punished. It merely makes a statement of fact—Michal never had children. How we choose to view her childlessness is up to us. If we choose to see Michal through the lens of pity, we view her as the pawn of both her husband and her father. Her barrenness is the final chapter in an unful-filled life. But there is another way to read Michal's story. The Samuel narratives and the rabbinic portrayal of Michal in the Talmud show us a complex woman, difficult to categorize, one who cannot be defined in simple terms no matter how much the text seeks to circumscribe her.

One of the significant characteristics of Michal is that the text reg-ularly seeks to place her in a definable role based on who she is in rela-tionship to the men in her life. Michal's name occurs eighteen times in the Bible: Ten times she is described as "the daughter of Saul," twice as "David's wife," and once as both. There are only five instances in which one of these phrases is not appended to her name, yet in each of those cases it is clear which relationship role she plays. Despite all this, the text fails to decisively connect her to either man. The most telling example is found in I Samuel 25:44 where we read that Saul has given "his daughter Michal, David's wife" to another man.[1] Michal is both "Saul's daughter" and "David's wife." She cannot be neatly placed into either category. As "Saul's daughter" she falls in love with David, who pays a bride-price of two hundred Philistine foreskins for her. Then, as "David's wife," she defies her father when he wishes to kill the man she loves. She helps David escape and then deceives her father, telling his messengers that David is sick in bed. In both of these narratives, Michal is consciously casting her lot in with the man her father views as a threat and an enemy.

In contrast to the early portrayal, where Michal allies herself with David, in this haftarah she is very much her father's daughter. As David dances publicly and ecstatically when the Ark is brought into Jerusalem, Michal views him with contempt. Her mental image of the king of Israel is based on her father, a man who never would have engaged in such behavior. She cannot appreciate David's joy as the Ark's exile comes to an end. She only sees that he is leaping about like a fool before the humblest of his subjects. The dignity that she expects from a king is lacking in David's behavior, and she hates him for it.

How do we reconcile the two different images of Michal? Is she the loving wife of David or the proper daughter of Saul? Clearly she is both and neither. An unsympathetic interpretation might look at the psychodynamics of the family relationships, and suggest that Michal's problem lies in not settling into a single role. As both daughter and wife she is unable to be fully daughter or fully wife. This reading of the text, of course, ignores the reality of our modern lives. All of us play many roles as we go through life. One moment we may be acting as a parent to our children, and the next as a child to our parents. Our family of origin may place one demand upon us, while the family we create may have completely contrary expectations. As Saul's daughter and David's wife, Michal finds herself in a place that is very familiar to anyone who has tried to navigate the shoals of relationships. Just as you seem to be moving in one direction, an eddy whirls you around and points you toward the other shore. Do you follow the current or try to row against it? The traditional demand that Michal be either fully wife or fully daughter mirrors our own society's insistence on women choosing to fully identify with their newly created family once married.

Michal does not follow the current. Described again and again as the daughter of Saul and the wife who loves David, she is neither the dutiful daughter of one king nor the supportive spouse of another. In a world where women are valued for the children they bear, she bears no children. She doesn't fall into any of these expected female roles, yet the Rabbis of the Talmud have a positive view of her.

Michal is one of the women in our tradition who is described as a wearer of tefillin.[2] What suggested to the rabbinic eye that Michal, of all the possible biblical women, should do something so distinctive?[3] Michal doesn't fit the standard "womanly" roles, and therefore she is the only kind of woman the Rabbis can imagine performing a male mitzvah. Unable to categorize her, the Rabbis do not know what to do with her. Michal is a strong woman. How better to situate her strengths than by identifying her with a public male mitzvah?[4]

In *Sanhedrin* 19b the Rabbis discuss a problem they find in II Samuel 21:8 where Michal is described as the mother of five sons and they say: "Surely it was rather Merav who bore them! But Merav bore and Michal brought them up; therefore they were called by her name.

This teaches that whoever brings up an orphan in his home, Scripture ascribes it to him as though he had begotten him." In our haftarah, Michal is defined by her childlessness. Yet in the Talmud, she becomes the paradigm of the adoptive parent. Although not a biological parent, Michal finds a way to share herself and her life with the next generation.

When we look at the wider context of Michal's life, it does not seem a tragedy at all. We see a woman who is not confined by people's expectations but rather self-defined. She loves the man she marries even as the text makes it clear that her father would have preferred anyone other than David. She saves David's life through lies and trickery at the expense of her relationship with her father. Although given to a second man in marriage, she returns to David, apparently untouched. She has a vision of how a king should act and she stands by her belief, even though it means the end of her marriage. Rather than living the barren life implied by the words she "had no child until her dying day," she has a life filled with family and productivity.

Should we pity Michal? It is easy to look back on our lives and say what we should have done. It is more difficult to say the right thing, or make the right move at the moment. Michal does a remarkable job dealing with the circumstances life hands her. She does not become bitter about roles that do not fit her. Instead, she moves forward, and creates herself anew as an adoptive mother and a teacher to future generations. She is not constrained by a tradition that does not allow women to use tefillin. She makes the choice to wear them, and the texts support her choice.

Michal is a model for those of us whose lives do not follow expected patterns. Those of us who cannot fit into a tidy category, or a two-word summary, can find in Michal an example of a woman who transforms her lack of a single, definable role into an abundant, productive, fertile life. She teaches us that we do not have to be defined by what we are not; that we can create and re-create ourselves as we go through life.

RABBI MARY LANDE ZAMORE

הפטרת תזריע
Haftarat Tazri'a
II Kings 4:42–5:19

Naaman, commander of the king of Aram's army, was highly valued by his king and was held in great esteem, because through him YHVH had given victory to Aram; he was a mighty soldier who had *tzara'at* [leprosy].[1] Once, when the Arameans went out on a raid, they brought away a young maiden from the Land of Israel, and she became a servant to Naaman's wife. She said to her mistress, "If only my master could go to the prophet in Samaria! Then he would cure him of his leprosy." Naaman went and told the king, "Such and such said the servant girl from Israel." And the king of Aram said "Go and I will send a letter [with you] to the king of Israel." So he went, taking with him ten talents of silver, six thousand shekels of gold, and ten changes of clothing.
(II KINGS 5:1–5)

FOR NAAMAN, THE COMMANDER of the king's army, the spiritual journey that leads to his acceptance of YHVH starts with illness and the advice of an unnamed Israelite servant girl. The Talmud upholds Naaman as one of the greatest *gerei tzedek*—those who convert to believing in YHVH alone—standing above even Jethro, Moses' father-in-law, the Midianite priest.[2] It is the Israelite servant girl who propels Naaman toward his revelation. Her pivotal role in this haf-tarah raises the question as to why she goes unnamed in the Bible and almost unaddressed in the commentaries. She is "the woman behind the man." While her full personality and story remain hid-den, the text itself gives us a few clues, allowing the reader a glimpse into this Israelite girl's untold story.

The unnamed servant girl and the role she holds remind the read-er of Joseph—another Israelite forced into slavery in a foreign land. Like Joseph, this girl offers insight into the situation of those around her, therefore providing the strangers among whom she lives with help and guidance. A brief comparison of Joseph and the Israelite girl will help us learn more about her.

In Genesis 39:1, Joseph is taken as a slave to Egypt and sold to Potiphar, a high-ranking official in Pharaoh's court. The unnamed Israelite girl, too, was captured as plunder in conquest and now serves Naaman's wife. Joseph quickly earns the respect of Potiphar and his household. Even in jail, his skill of dream interpretation allows him to become Pharaoh's right-hand man. While the text does not tell us how it comes to be, it is clear that everyone in Naaman's household respects the Israelite girl.

One can easily imagine that the household of Naaman, the high-ranking officer in the Aramean army, is in an uproar, for the master of the house has been stricken with *tzara'at*. The mistress of the house is greatly distressed over the matter; the servants are buzzing with the gos-sip over what should be done. Finally, the Israelite servant girl comes to her mistress suggesting that Naaman visit the prophet in Samaria. Later, we learn that the prophet to whom she refers is none other than Elisha, the disciple of Elijah.

Amazingly, the text clearly outlines that everyone from Naaman's wife to Naaman himself to the king is readily listening to and taking the advice of an enslaved Israelite girl. While the servant is highly respected, the text does not tell us why. In the Joseph narrative, the text is explicit as to why he thrived in Potiphar's house. We are told:

> YHVH was with Joseph and he was a successful man. . . .
> When his master saw that YHVH was with him and that
> YHVH made everything he did successful in his hand,
> Joseph found favor in his eyes . . . (Gen. 39:2–4).

Joseph is successful because of his relationship with God. Perhaps that is the key to the Israelite girl as well.

The girl's suggestion that Naaman go to Israel to seek out YHVH's prophet for a cure reveals the depth of her faith. The emphasis in this haftarah is on belief in YHVH. That faith is often expressed as confidence in YHVH's human prophets and their ability to perform the task at hand. Despite being cut off from her people and forced into servitude, the Israelite girl retains her confidence in Elisha's power to heal. While the text does not make it explicit, the reader can easily infer that her faith in YHVH has not been shaken by her life experience.

On the other hand, Naaman's confidence in Elisha is not as unshakable. Naaman obtains permission from the king of Aram to visit the prophet. He takes with him silver and gold, as well as valuable garments, anticipating that this cure will come at a price. Naaman also brings with him a letter of introduction from the Aramean king. Upon his arrival in Israel, Naaman has an odd interaction with the king of Israel. Elisha learns of the situation and forwards the king a message, asking for Naaman to be sent to him. Elisha does not say, "Send the man to me so that I can cure him of his *tzara'at*," but rather he declares, "He will know that there is a prophet in Israel" (5:8). Here we see the theme of faith again. Knowledge of the prophet leads to knowledge of YHVH. To have trust in God's prophet and to witness and acknowledge the prophet's power is to believe in God. Therefore, the point of this entire section is Naaman's conversion experience through his interaction with Elisha.

When Naaman arrives at Elisha's home, the prophet gives him the prescription to bathe seven times in the Jordan River. Rather than following Elisha's advice, Naaman becomes enraged and leaves. While storming out, he declares, "Behold, I thought he would surely come out and stand and call out the name of YHVH his God and wave his hand over the place and cure the leprosy" (5:11). Naaman has not received the cure he expected, and so he further complains, "Aren't the rivers of Damascus better than all the waters of Israel?" (5:12). He had enough faith in the Israelite girl's advice to come to Elisha, but he is unwilling to follow his unexpected instructions. At this juncture, his servants step forward and convince him to follow Elisha's instructions. Naaman immerses himself in the Jordan River seven times—like the later rabbinic practice of conversion through mikveh—and he emerges from the water a cured man. Notice that all of the servants seem to hold a deeper understanding than the master. This is an indirect commentary on the fleeting power of human lords in relation to the eternal power of YHVH.

Now, as a healed man, Naaman believes. He declares to Elisha, "Behold now I know that there is no God in all the Earth, but in Israel . . ." (5:15). There is a brief interaction in which Naaman wishes to give Elisha the presents of silver, gold, and clothing that he brought, but Elisha will not accept these payments. This, of course, reinforces the message that Elisha is a true prophet of YHVH. Knowledge of God is the ultimate goal, not the praise or payment of God's prophet.

The haftarah ends with an interesting request from Naaman, the new convert to YHVH. He asks for YHVH's forgiveness in advance, for Naaman knows that his continued duties for the king of Aram will include accompanying him to the temple of Rimmon to worship. There, the king leans on Naaman's arm, forcing Naaman to bow in worship with him. Naaman says, "YHVH, please forgive your servant for this one matter" (5:18). At this, Elisha tells him to go in peace.

Midrash *Tahuma* on *Parashat Tazri'a* suggests that Naaman's disease comes as punishment for his capturing and enslaving the Israelite girl. Naaman's punishment and salvation, then, are both as a result of her. The servant girl becomes the unrecognized role model for Naaman. After his conversion experience, Naaman sadly foresees a lonely life separated from the Land of Israel and, in his view, YHVH. In truth, he becomes like the captured servant girl, fated to be separated from her people yet compelled to maintain her religion on her own. Ironically, Naaman is to live the very life he imposed on his servant. When Naaman immerses himself seven times in the water and emerges, we learn that "his flesh was clean as the flesh of a young boy" (5:14). This description of a young boy—*na'ar katan*—is merely the male version of the servant girl's description—*na'arah k'tanah*.[3] Naaman and the Israelite servant girl now share the same God and the same challenges of maintaining their faith.

The Israelite servant girl, like Joseph in Pharaoh's court, becomes the model of true faith. Belief in YHVH can be maintained and nurtured despite the odds. That is why her suggestion that Naaman seek out the prophet in Samaria is so important. Her belief that Elisha can heal her master reflects her unwavering belief in YHVH. The Israelite servant girl is "a lily among the thorns" (Song of Songs 2:2). Faith like hers is what has sustained and inspired the Jewish people through the hard times of involuntary dispersion.

הפטרת מצרע
Haftarat Metzorah

II Kings 7:3–20

*T*here were four men, all with *tzara'at*, at the entrance to the gate. They said to one another, Why should we sit here until we die? (II KINGS 7:3)

HAFTARAT METZORAH takes place during a time of war between the Northern Kingdom of Israel and the Southern Kingdom of Judah. Samaria, the capital of Israel, is under siege by the army of Aram. The king of Israel and his people are in a state of panic. A strategic alliance between Syria and Judah has left Israel starving and helpless. The famine becomes so harsh and bitter for Israel that mothers are forced to eat their children.

*T*he Four Men and Their Adventure

Our haftarah begins with four men with *tzara'at* (often loosely translated as "leprosy") waiting at the gate of the city. Rather than waiting by the entrance of the starving city, the men decide that it would be best to risk their own lives and desert to the Aramean (Syrian) enemy camp where resources are abundant. The four men enter the Aramean camp, and there is not a soul to be found. Adonai has caused the Arameans to hear the sounds of a large army approaching with horses and chariots. They assume that the king of Israel has paid the kings of the Hittites and of Egypt to attack. Out of fear, they immediately abandon camp.

The four men enter two of the tents and find food and drink to consume. They also find clothing, silver, and gold that they decide to hide for themselves. Then they undergo change of heart. They say to one another, "We're not doing right!" Their shared conscience instructs them to inform Israel of their found treasures. They immediately head back to the gate of the city to spread the news of good fortune.

When the king receives a report of the four men's adventure, he is suspicious that the Arameans have set up a trick to ambush his people. The king decides to send forth two scouts on horseback to investigate. When they arrive, the scouts discover that the four men are indeed telling the truth, and there is an abundance of food at the camp. Israel receives relief from its suffering.

*W*hat Is This *Tzara'at* and Who Are These Four Men?

The Rabbis of our ancient and medieval texts viewed *tzara'at* as a spiritual affliction, which manifests itself physically. Nehama Leibowitz states: "Medical research fails to associate the biblical *tzara'at* with any known disease. Its diagnosis as leprosy is rejected by modern medicine."[1] Rabbinic text associates *tzara'at* with a multitude of wrongdoing, including "a look of pride, a dishonest tongue, killing an innocent person, devising wicked thoughts, and bearing false witness." One of the most popular rabbinic interpretations of the cause of *tzara'at* is *lashon ha'ra,* which literally means an "evil tongue or speech," or "idle gossip." While it is difficult to think of anyone who does not at times resort to idle gossip and hurtful chatter, still the Rabbis see *tzara'at* as a punishment for not holding our tongues.

The biblical text of II Kings does not provide information about these four *metzoraim* (men with *tzara'at*), their pasts, or why they became stricken. Some Rabbis suggest that these men may be Geichazi, the servant of Elijah, and his three sons.[2] In biblical times, one had to possess righteous qualities in order to become even the servant of a prophet. The Talmud teaches us that even though Geichazi was a great scholar of Torah, he possessed three negative personality traits that led to the loss of his place in the world to come (heaven): an evil eye, sexual licentiousness, and disbelief in Elisha's prophetic ability to resurrect the dead.[3] Whether or not the four stricken men were Geichazi and his sons, these heroes who brought relief to Israel were downtrodden outcasts of "mainstream" society.

But why were they outcasts? The midrashic interpretation of *tzara'at* as punishment for speaking out gives rise here to a new interpretation. When we don't use our words thoughtfully, whether or not we are telling the truth, we often promote uncomfortable social situations for ourselves, which may actually affect our health. And the talmudic Rabbis' definition of idle gossip may have been entirely different from our own contemporary sensibilities. Sometimes it is important to speak the truth, even if we become ostracized for challenging a social system. Many of us have experienced a kind of social *tzara'at* for taking the risk of challenging authority.

Perhaps we can see the four men as truth-speakers. Within the midst of starvation and misery, they decide to take control of their own destinies by speaking the truth about what they needed to do to survive. Instead of welcoming their deaths passively, they take proactive measures and set forth on a journey to find comfort and nourishment, despite grave risks.

In our story, the Arameans hear an entire army approaching. They hear the rumble of chariots and horses and run for their lives. How is it that the eight feet of four outcasts can cause such a stir? The four men refuse to give in to the weaknesses that either they possess or society has inflicted on them. In deciding to desert to the enemy camp, which may be seen as an immoral decision, they also desert the label of inadequacy that has been attributed to them in their "home" territory. They step away from what is familiar and stifling and venture forth toward new treasures and true sustenance. Even the Arameans can hear the roar of their determination and courage.

The four heroes of our story do not succumb to the label that has been placed upon them, and courageously decide to walk toward their cure. The decision to nourish their own souls and bodies ultimately brings relief to the entire Kingdom of Israel. These men remind us, as women, to triumph over societal labels and limitations and to defy the ways in which we are defined. As we join forces together on this path, as our mouths speak the truth about authority, and as our footsteps create a roar of change, we will cure the *tzara'at* of inaction, silence, and disempowerment. Imagine the relief the world would obtain if all women, and therefore all individuals, were to become courageous enough to venture forth toward the new treasures and the true sustenance found in compassionate truth telling. While difficult at the onset, speech for the sake of freedom, and courageous acts for the sake of change, have the potential to bring about ultimate personal and communal healing to our world. The four men of *Haftarat Metzorah* encourage us to take our chances.

RABBI NINA H. MANDEL

הפטרת אחרי מות
Haftarat Acharei Mot

Ezekiel 22:1–19

You have brought on your day; you have reached your year. (EZEKIEL 22:4)

THIS PHRASE, "You have brought on your day; you have reached your year," is commonly understood as an admonition by God against the people of Israel. The message, via the prophet Ezekiel, is that the people have engaged in idolatrous and sinful acts and have brought upon themselves rejection and punishment by the God to whom they previously looked for protection. In essence, this phrase suggests that they are getting what they deserve. This sentiment fits closely with the opening of the Torah portion, *Parashat Acharei Mot*, with which this passage of Ezekiel is associated. The portion opens with a brief retelling of the story of Aaron's sons, Nadav and Avihu, who, in their religious zeal, "drew near to the presence of God" and consequently died (Lev. 16:1). By worshipping in a way that was considered outside the norm, they earned their just punishment.

What does it mean to women to hear "we have brought on our day"? This idea of deserved punishment for rebellious acts is morally problematic in the same way that defenders of rapists have claimed that rape victims "asked for it" by dressing provocatively. Assertive and self-advocating women are labeled with old stereotypes of being castrating, shrewish, scheming, or just plain unladylike. Even from an essentialist standpoint, when women step outside the norm they are often castigated for denying their own biological imperatives and putting society at risk. These offenses include the irrational behavior of a menstruating woman, the damage done by a mother who does not stay home with her children, the woman who puts off childbearing for her career, and the woman who neglects (or neglects to find) a husband. In reading this passage from Ezekiel, it is important to consider exactly what it means to willfully commit an act that threatens the norm and bring about a punishment.

Though this haftarah portion enumerates the sins of males, their sinful acts are intertwined with the females among them. Men have had sexual relations with menstruating women, their daughters-in-law, and their sisters; they have neglected widows and humiliated mothers, turning the city of Jerusalem into a city of bloodshed. The inhabitants of the city have become *tameh*, "impure," in need of purification, because of sexual acts involving women and because of the creation of fetishes (*gilulim* in the Hebrew) that are now being worshipped idolatrously. In a later verse, Israel is described as a land in need of purification by the rain (Ezek. 22:24), bringing to mind the rituals with water and the mikveh, which restore the balance of purity after sex acts, menstruation, childbirth, and death.

These two themes, idolatry and sex, are not unique to Ezekiel, nor is it unusual to find them relating to women. Idolatrous women frequently lead men astray in the Torah (see Num. 25). Similarly, women are frequently portrayed as makers of fetishes and idols (see Jer. 19) that are purported to threaten the sanctity and power of God's dominion. The notion of women's sexuality as a locus of temptation and contamination is one that had a strong hold not just on the biblical, but also on the rabbinic imagination. A good portion of Jewish law prescribes the separation of women as sexual objects from the vulnerable eye of the otherwise righteous man. The righteous man, as described in Ezekiel 18:1–13, does not commit any of the offenses we find in our portion, while the Sages who "turn their thoughts to fetishes" incur the wrath of God (Ezek. 14:3).

The phrase *bringing on your days* is unique to Ezekiel; we find it nowhere else in this form. Its interpretation as an admonition is found in just a few later commentaries. Radak relates it to the destruction of the Temple and the state of exile that the Jews brought on themselves. *Bring on days* refers to the initial exile; *reaching your year* signifies the gravity of the matter. The exile will be doubled, as this phrase reminds us, during the initial time of suffering. In a later commentary, *Metzoret David Yehzekiel*, the connection between the national responsibility, sin, and the destruction of the Temple is repeated. However, the focus is on the nature of that responsibility: "You, yourself, bring about days of punishment and days of reward."

This reading adds a redemptive note to the idea of "bringing on what you deserve," in that we also bring on our own reward, our own liberation. That note can also be found in the root *k-r-v*, "to come or bring near," and is often used to describe the offering of sacrifices. When the text of Ezekiel says, "*vatakrivi yameich*, you, yourself, bring your days near," the issue of responsibility is introduced. But *k-r-v* also means "to come," and it suggests that the causative act of bringing something near can have positive connotations. We see *k-r-v* in *Parashat Acharei Mot*, describing the action that leads to the deaths of Nadav and Avihu—*karvatam*. They drew near for sacrifice, but crossed into the space of "too near" and were punished for it. It is crossing the line of accepted/expected behavior that can move "nearing" from a positive to a negative action.

What is interesting to note is that despite the pressure in the Jewish tradition for boundaries and conformity, most of the women who are given names, whose stories are told and exalted in the Torah, are the women who dared to step outside the norm, to "draw near" in ways that challenged established authority.

Often, this crossing of the line happens precisely around women and sexuality. In Genesis 38, for example, Tamar poses as a prostitute and uses her sexuality to exact justice from her father-in-law, Judah. In turn, Judah publicly recognizes her rightful stance (38:26). In another story, the prostitute Rahav hides Joshua's spies and allows them to escape from their pursuers. As a reward, she and her family are protected from the ensuing attack by the Israelite soldiers (Josh. 2). In the book of Judges, Yael lures the enemy Sisera into bed with food and drink, then kills him when he falls asleep (4:17–20). Despite later concern for the dangerous power of women's sexuality, the power of these women is that they are portrayed as both sexual and heroic.

We also find examples in which women rebel against authority in ways that seem surprising in the biblical context, but that end up being lauded as particularly brave or insightful. The first rebels in the Exodus story are the midwives Shifra and Puah who go against Pharaoh's orders to kill male Hebrew babies (Exod. 1:16–21). Their actions earn them protection from God. In Numbers 27, the daughters of a man named Zelophehad challenge Moses' division of land among the men. Because their father had no sons, they argue that they should receive the portion of land that would have gone to the male heirs. Again, the challenge to authority is commended when it is in service to a greater good.

Alongside the prohibitions, warnings, and frustrating silences, Torah provides us with women who "draw near," who take risks, make sacrifices, and subvert expected behavior. For the most part they are taking control and asserting their right to control their own fate not by being like men, but by unapologetically being women. If early Jewish feminist studies emphasized equal access to the tradition for women, we can now look at the ways the women rebels in our texts and lore have broken new ground while not undermining themselves as female beings. We can be rebels while at the same time "drawing near."

When we women bring near our days and reach our years, we have the potential to bring about the punishment or the reward. When we draw ourselves near through acts of rebellion and passion, when we are unapologetically unbound by expectations not our own, then we can bring on our days of constructive change, our years of power— not as victims blamed for our own suffering but as cherished partners rewarded for our commitment.[1]

RABBI RONA SHAPIRO

הפטרת קדשים
Haftarat Kedoshim

Amos 9:7–15

*T*he plowman shall meet the reaper . . . (AMOS 9:13)

THE OPENING WORDS of this haftarah are among the most startling words of the prophets: "To Me, O Israelites, you are just like the Ethiopians—declares the Lord. True, I brought Israel up from the land of Egypt but also the Philistines from Caphtor and the Arameans from Kir." It is hard to imagine a more sweeping rejection of Jewish chosenness. The Exodus from Egypt, our very claim to fame, our moment of greatest intimacy and surest certainty of God's presence, is here called into question. "You are not the only ones whom I have redeemed," thunders God, "Going free from a place of exile is not unique to you. Yes, I have redeemed you from Egypt, but redemption, even miraculous redemption, is not a unique event. I care about everyone."

And yet these opening lines seem to be contradicted by the latter part of the haftarah reading. God promises to mend the fallen sukkah of David, to "restore My people Israel. . . . They shall rebuild ruined cities and inhabit them; they shall plant vineyards and drink their wine; they shall till gardens and eat their fruits. And I will plant them upon their soil, nevermore to be uprooted from the soil I have given them . . ." (Amos 9:14–15). Amos once more asserts Israel's chosenness. It is almost as if Israel were an eldest child. Once cherished and adored by her parents above all other living creatures, she is suddenly

138

thrust from glory, forced to share her throne with one or more inter-lopers in the familial love triangle. Suddenly, the child is not special anymore—no different from her siblings.

But hopefully the child grows up. As a child progresses through the middle years, she reaches a more mature understanding of her place in the family. She is special to her parents just as Israel is special to God; she still has a chosen place, a chosen land, and, in fact, the intimacy of the relationship remains constant. The only thing that has changed is the wider context—the child is special and unique to her parents, but now realizes that her siblings are too. Similarly, Israel comes to know that others share her "special relationship" with God.

In that context, the image of *sukkat David hanofelet* (Amos 9:11), the "fallen booth of David," is interesting. A sukkah is the most inti-mate of structures. We build it with our own hands and then dwell in it, living close to God, as it were, for the eight days of the holiday. To say that God will restore the fallen sukkah of David is to say not only that we will dwell in intimacy with God, but also that, this time, in this messianic sukkah, it will be "firm as in days of old." In other words, our intimacy with God will not be premised on the false notion that we are God's only beloved; it will be based in the mature knowledge of our place in the world family, and so it will be enduring. In fact, Sukkot is the only biblical holiday on which Israel offered sacrifices on behalf of all the *other* nations. This holiday on which we dwell in our sukkot, in intimacy with God, is not about our exclusive intimacy with God but about our intimacy with God alongside the other nations.

This haftarah offers, in fact, a powerful antidote to its Torah read-ing. *Parashat Kedoshim* concludes: "You shall be holy to Me, for I the Lord am holy, and I have set you apart from other peoples to be mine" (Lev. 20:26). The Torah portion of *Kedoshim* reflects our infancy, when God took us out of Egypt, fed us in the desert, and we believed that we were God's one and only. The haftarah of *Kedoshim* compels us to grow up, and to revise that self-image.

Why does Amos need to tell us that we are not uniquely chosen? It is not only Jews who have mistakenly come to believe in a God-given superiority. Perhaps it is inherent in the human condition that we need to believe that we are the best, that others are in some way destined to serve us. Whites, until very recently, and with disastrous consequences, asserted their "superiority" over other races. Inherent in many kinds of nationalism is the belief not only in the right of each nation to exist but in the superiority of that nation. And there are Jewish men who have believed that God determined that they, and not women, should study the holy words, lead the prayers, and decide on all matters of importance. Perhaps it was understandable that Jewish men, feeling downtrodden in the secular world, needed to assert superiority over someone. In a world of scarcity, eldest and youngest fight to the death. We have only to turn back to Genesis and recall the examples of Cain and Abel, and Jacob and Esau. But in a world of abundance, which Amos envisions and which we must help to create, this is neither necessary nor desirable.

We as women have fallen into the same trap, believing men to be inferior in the things we consider "feminine," like empathy, caring, and connection. When women claim "natural" superiority in matters of intuition, cooking, child rearing, and caregiving, have we not merely turned the tables?

What might Amos offer to combat this dangerous tendency? The conclusion of the haftarah envisions not a time of miracles, but a time of fertility—the plowman shall meet the reaper because the harvest season has lasted so long that planting has again begun. "They shall plant vineyards and drink their wine; they shall till gardens and eat their fruit" (Amos 9:14). The imagery of the sukkah is one of harvest. To create abundance, Amos suggests, we must each take our place in the world as *unique* but not *better*, *special* but not *alone*. The very imagery Amos chooses implies that the reaper needs the plowman just as the trader of grapes needs the one who plants the grapes. We cannot all be plowmen or traders—each is valued for her unique contribution. Like the oldest child we, as men and women, must wrestle with the demon of wanting to be the only one, the one best loved, so that we can join with one another to build the fallen sukkah and dwell within it together.

RABBI RACHEL ESSERMAN

הפטרת אמר

Haftarat Emor

Ezekiel 44:15–31

*T*hey [the priests] shall not take a widow or a
divorced woman for a wife; they shall take only a
virgin of the seed of the House of Israel and the widow
of a priest. And they shall instruct My people in [the dif-
ference] between the sacred and the profane and they
shall make known [the difference] between the pure and
the impure. . . . They will not become impure for a dead
man; but for a father or mother, or son or daughter, or
sister who does not have a husband, they may become
impure. (EZEKIEL 44:22–25)

THE BOOK OF EZEKIEL opens with a vision of heaven, of fabulous winged
creatures and radiant fire; it closes with a prophetic vision of Israel's
glorious return from exile in Babylonia. The haftarah read with
Parashat Emor comes from the later section of the book, and outlines
the priests' obligations and duties once the Temple in Jerusalem is
rebuilt. It ties closely into the Torah portion that also deals with the
laws of the priestly class.

Since ancient Israel used sacrifice as their main form of worship,
and only priests were allowed to perform these sacrifices, the priests had
to be well versed in the laws of ritual purity. Only that which was pure
and sacred could be used in these holy rituals. Priests were held to a

higher standard of purity than the rest of the population, because they performed these holy rites.

When speaking of the priests, the Torah refers only to the men. Women could not be priests, nor officiate at sacrifices, nor judge sacred matters. Their only connection to the priestly class was either by blood (if their father was a priest) or by marriage (if their husband was a priest). They were strictly defined by the status of the men in their life. For example, in Leviticus 22:3 we learn that if a daughter of a priest marries a nonpriest, she loses her right to eat from the food tithes (the taxes) that belonged solely to the priestly class. If a woman whose father was not a priest married into a priestly family, her status changed, and she was allowed to eat from the tithes. After marriage, a woman's priestly or nonpriestly status was solely determined by her husband's status.

The section of Ezekiel found in this haftarah specifically deals with two priestly matters that affect women: marriage and burial. While all Israelites were subject to the laws of forbidden marriages found in Leviticus 18:6–16, priests were subject to additional restrictions.[1] Only a woman who was a virgin or the widow of another priest was acceptable for marriage to a priest. If a priest married someone outside those definitions, he defiled himself, and was therefore unfit to perform his duties at the Temple. Thus, women who had been with men who were not priests, or who had behaved in an inappropriate manner (by not remaining virgins) carried with them a blemish that also stained the priest. Conversely, the priest's purity would be ensured by marrying a "pure" woman.

How did the purity laws work? Ritual objects that were dedicated to God and the Temple achieved a state of purity; thus, to use them for any other purpose made them impure. In a similar way, the priests belonged to God. They had to keep their hair trimmed and weren't allowed to shave their heads. They couldn't drink wine before going into the inner court, nor could they wear anything in the inner court that would make them sweat. They had to avoid anything that would prevent them from performing their tasks in a state of purity—that included contact with dead bodies, and being married to the wrong women.[2]

A priest was allowed to become impure only for the burial of a close relative. The haftarah specifically lists his father and mother, son and daughter, brother and unmarried sister. He is not allowed to defile himself for a married sister, for her change in status from virgin to married woman effectively negates the familial connection. Since the verse makes no mention of his wife, commentators have asked whether or not he can attend her burial.

Classical commentators note that the laws in Ezekiel differ from those in Leviticus. Rashi notes that while Leviticus allows priests to marry any widow, Ezekiel allows them to marry only the widows of priests. He wishes to reconcile the differences in these two texts, and deals only with the legal aspects of the verses. However, in his commentary to Leviticus 21:2 (which deals with the same topic), Rashi opens a debate about the obvious missing relative in both the lists: the priest's wife. The list of relatives in the Torah portion of *Emor* includes the phrase *kin close to him*, which is not found in the haftarah list. Rashi claims that *kin close to him* includes his wife, so he can attend her funeral. But Rashbam disagrees, and says that the priest may *not* attend his wife's funeral, since she is not specifically listed. The different opinions of these two commentators reflect the difficulty in determining a wife's status. On the one hand, she is part of the priestly class by virtue of her marriage; on the other hand, she is not a blood relative. Rachel Biale notes:

> The priests were forbidden to marry divorcees (Lev. 21), though they were not forbidden to divorce their wives. This strange asymmetry can only be understood if we understand the prohibition on marrying a divorcee as part of the strict laws of purity by which priests are bound. The same term applied to a divorcee as to various agents (corpses, reptiles, etc.) which cause ritual impurity. For the priests . . . a woman who had sexual relations with another man (i.e., a divorcee or a *zonah*, one who

had sexual relations outside of marriage) was "defiled" and forbidden. Perhaps there was actually some theory of priestly "purity of blood" which extended the meaning of ritual impurity to encompass sexual relations and familial lineage.[3]

The verses in Ezekiel classify women much like the animals that were brought to the Temple to be sacrificed: the permitted or the prohibited. Dividing women into categories of "allowed" and "disallowed" made it easier for the priest to know who was permitted to him. The system was willing to err on the side of disallowing large groups of women rather than taking a chance on mixing priestly blood with blood that might taint the priestly heritage, since that "communal" heritage mattered more than any one individual's desire.

This haftarah raises many questions for feminists. How does not being a virgin make a woman inappropriate for marriage? What exactly *is* a wife's relationship to a husband? How do we define—or redefine—notions of purity and "bloodline" for today? And, most important, how can we be a "kingdom of priests" yet not exclude, not rely on hierarchy, and not judge some as "tainted"?

An idea of purity that excludes large groups of people may be troubling for those who believe in an egalitarian society that offers equal opportunity for all. However, the problem lies not in the idea of physical purity as an approach to God, but rather in how the idea was translated into law. Using our bodies as a vehicle for closeness to God could bring a new type of spirituality into our lives, opening paths we've never before considered. However, when physical purity is translated into laws that separate those "pure of body" from those "impure of body," when they render some privileged and some disadvantaged, then the whole notion of purity itself becomes tainted. Perhaps we can imagine using physical purity to expand our connections to God; treating all human beings as if they were holy vessels. Imagine treating one's body as holy—as a priestly vessel—by not abusing alcohol or drugs, and by eating, drinking, and exercising properly. Imagine treating all humans as holy to God and no longer subjecting them to verbal, physical, or sexual abuse. Everyone—women and men, young and old, those with mental or physical disabilities—would then be vessels holy and sacred to God.

RABBI NANCY WECHSLER-AZEN

הפטרת בהר
Haftarat Behar

Jeremiah 32:6–27

*J*eremiah said: The word of Adonai came to me saying, Hanamel, the son of your uncle Shallum, will come to you and say: "Buy my field in Anathoth, for the right of redemption is yours to buy it." And just as Adonai had said, Hanamel came to me in the prison compound and said to me, "Please buy my field that is in Anathoth, in the territory of Benjamin; for the right of inheritance is yours and the redemption is yours. Buy it for *yourself.*" Then I knew it was the word of Adonai. (JEREMIAH 32:6–8)

TELLING THE TRUTH, especially to those in power, has never been an easy task. For the forty years leading up to the destruction of Jerusalem in 586 B.C.E. by the Babylonians, Jeremiah warned kings and commoners of impending disaster. Son of the priest Hilkiah, Jeremiah preached against idolatry, empty sacrifice, and even localized worship in the Jerusalem Temple. His preaching nearly cost him his life; the people of his own village, the national leaders and priests, other prophets, and even family members seem to have been involved in the plot to get rid of him. Later he would be thrown into a pit of muck, only to be rescued just before being fatally submerged.

While confronting corruption and trying to avert disaster present enormous challenges, Jeremiah never sank into abject despair. Even more difficult perhaps than telling the truth to those in power is the ability to see hope in the face of desolation. Locked in a stinking, scorching prison compound in the midst of a summertime siege of Jerusalem, knowing the city is about to be destroyed and the rest of the land conquered, Jeremiah buys land anyway. Despite his gloomy predictions of the destructive results of Israel's faithlessness, Jeremiah ultimately clings to the optimism of the Eternal. "Thus says Adonai of Hosts, the God of Israel: Houses and fields and vineyards shall yet again be bought in this land" (Jer. 32:15).

Based on the right of redemption to reclaim family land, as stated in the Torah portion, Jeremiah's cousin Behar (Lev. 25:25–28) comes to ask him to make the claim. To purchase land that is about to become Babylonian territory seems the height of absurdity, especially for an imprisoned man, yet Jeremiah's purchase of the field in Anathoth promises a future for Judaism.

While unlikely that he will ever live on that land during his life-time, he never gives up his belief that God's mercy will one day prevail. The Jews will someday return to the essential belief in one God and adherence to one Torah. God will take them back and return them to the land. Jeremiah's purchase ensures a stake in that future possibility, and stability for generations to come. Spiritually, Jeremiah's purchase of land represents the belief that, despite all darkness, the light of truth will one day abide.

To report accurately on the prophetic career of Jeremiah, we must also reclaim another speaker of truth from the same era. Her career may have even exceeded Jeremiah's and yet we know little about her life. The prophetess's name was Huldah, and she was Jeremiah's aunt.[1] She is the only prophetess mentioned during the period of the monarchy. It says in *Pesikta Rabbati:* "Jeremiah was one of three prophets who proph-esied in that generation—Jeremiah, Zephaniah, and the prophetess Huldah. Jeremiah prophesied in the city squares, Zephaniah in the Temple and synagogues, and Huldah among the women."[2] Not only a prophetess but a scholar as well, Huldah conducted an academy in Jerusalem, we learn from the Targum on this passage. The Gate of

Huldah in the Temple was formerly the gate leading to Huldah's schoolhouse.[3] Not only on earth, but also in the world to come, Huldah is named as one of the nine women who supervise classes for women in Paradise.[4]

We learn about Huldah specifically from II Kings 22:14, written during the tumultuous reign of King Josiah in the middle of the sixth century B.C.E. Prior to King Josiah was the evil King Amon, who followed in the sinful footsteps of his father King Manasseh. The priest Hilkiah discovered the Book of the Law in the Temple and brought it to the attention of King Josiah. Shocked by its teachings and realizing how lapsed the Jews had become, King Josiah initiated numerous reforms in the hopes of restoring and saving Jerusalem from God's wrath.

King Josiah commands Hilkiah the priest and several contemporaries to inquire of God and how God was going to punish them because they were not following the Divine law. Interestingly, it is not to his son the prophet that Hilkiah turns for advice, but rather to his sister-in-law, the prophetess Huldah. "So Hilkiah the priest, and Ahikam, and Achbor, and Shaphan, and Asaiah, went unto Huldah the prophetess, the wife of Shallum, the son of Tikvah, the son of Harhas, keeper of the wardrobe—now she dwelt in Jerusalem in the second quarter—and they spoke with her" (II Kings 22:14).

Despite the Tanakh's endorsement of Huldah as prophetess and the Targum's recognition of her work as *Rosh Yeshiva* (head of an academy), Huldah's life was devalued by the later Rabbis. Midrashic interpretations attribute Huldah's gift of prophecy not to her personal merit, but rather to her husband's character. "Huldah's husband Shallum, the son of Tikvah, was a man of noble descent and compassion. Daily he would go beyond the city limits carrying a pitcher of water from which he gave every traveler a drink, and it was a reward for his good deeds that his wife became a prophetess."[5]

In contrast to her husband's lofty status, Huldah's very name is used against her, since one of the meanings of its root, *ch-l-d* is to dig or to cover with earth. From this the Rabbis linked Huldah's name to the word *choled*, which means "weasel." *Megillah* 14b states: "Eminence is not for women; two eminent women are mentioned in the Bible, Deborah and Huldah, and both proved to be of a proud disposition. Deborah was haughty toward Barak, and the prophetess Huldah spoke of Josiah as the 'man' without giving him the title of king. This 'unpleasant' feature of their character is indicated by their 'ugly' names; the former was called Deborah (bee). And the latter was called Huldah (weasel)."

This unattractive association for Huldah is derived from an encounter between Hilkiah and company who had come to ask the prophetess about the future. She said to them, "Thus says Adonai, the God of Israel: 'Go tell the man that sent you to me . . .'" (II Kings 22:15), referring to Josiah as a man, not as the king. Rather than seeing Huldah's astute statement as a commitment to person over title, the Rabbis interpret this as a sign of disrespect. She becomes a "weasel" for undermining the royal position, rather than honored for reminding everyone that kings are human too.

With Huldah thus painted in a diminished light, the Rabbis ask how anyone could choose Huldah's prophecies over the oracles of Jeremiah. In *Megillah* 14b we read: "But if Jeremiah were there, how could she prophesy? It was said in the school of Rab in the name of Rab: Huldah was a near relative of Jeremiah, and he did not object to her doing so. But how could Josiah himself pass over Jeremiah and send for her? The members of the school of Rabbi Shila replied, 'Because women are tenderhearted.'" The Maharsha[6] comments that *tenderhearted* means that she would pray for them.

Did Hilkiah believe he could negotiate a more gentle rebuke because Huldah was female? The midrashic description of Huldah as tenderhearted is actually an insult to her integrity as a prophetess. As women, we must be conscious that, at least initially, we are often taken for a patsy because of our gender. And when we prove that we will not be manipulated by anyone's insistence that we are so very "tenderhearted," we may be rejected and told we are acting not like a woman but like a man.

On the other hand, there is the Maharsha's acknowledgment that Hilkiah chose Huldah for her oracle because she was willing to pray for their well-being. Through the Maharsha's commentary on the meaning behind *tenderhearted,* we surmise that he viewed Huldah's spirituality as a positive trait. She was a prophetess who voiced the word of God, but she was also a human being whose spirit would respond in prayer to the pain of those seeking her advice.

It is possible that the heavy hand of patriarchy disempowered Huldah's role because she prophesied a similar message to the one preached by her nephew Jeremiah. Jeremiah was only eighteen years old when he began to preach. I like to imagine it was the wise matriarch Huldah who taught her young nephew to develop his ability to keenly feel God's presence and hear God speak. Perhaps over the years she inspired him to stand firm in his convictions and believe in a Zion restored, even from his dismal prison cell. As Huldah was Hanamel's mother, she may have been the one to prompt him to go to Jeremiah and request the reclamation of the land.

A different rendering of Huldah's name can bring some much-needed dignity to her life and prophecies. The root *ch-l-d* also means "duration" and "world."[7] Huldah taught in Jerusalem about the world and the proper ways to be involved in earthly life. Combining these images with the previously mentioned definition of digging or hollowing out,[8] Huldah can be seen as the prophetess who burrows through obstacles and, by doing so, offers spiritual guidance to the world.

Telling the truth, especially to those in power, has never been an easy task for women who are already in a powerless position in society. Many times, early midrashic writers and commentators invested in the quiet eradication of powerful women's contributions. While we will never know if a Book of Huldah ever existed, by remembering her today, we reclaim a piece of our spiritual landscape as powerful women. The oracle of Jeremiah has led us to a revival of Huldah. Her truth now resounds.

RABBI HANNA GRACIA YERUSHALMI

הפטרת בחקתי

Haftarat Bechukotai

Jeremiah 16:19–17:14

*T*hus says the Eternal One:
Cursed are those who trust in mortals,
making mortal flesh their strength,
turning their heads from the Eternal . . .
Blessed are those who trust in the Eternal
and whose trust is in the Eternal!

(JEREMIAH 17:5–8)

JEREMIAH LIVED JUST BEFORE the Babylonian destruction of Jerusalem and the exile of the Israelites. His sermons and lessons, therefore, mostly preach doom and destruction. A reluctant spokesperson for God, Jeremiah's words are emotional, passionate, and revelatory. While the Israelites continually worshipped idols, acted immorally, and strayed from God's path, Jeremiah exhorted them to change their ways. He reminded them of God's demand that they keep their part of the covenant, which started with Abraham and was reaffirmed through Moses, the Exodus, and the desert experience. A consequence of their evil ways, exile was inevitable if the Israelites did not repent and return to God. Jeremiah's prophecy was realized when Jerusalem fell in 586 B.C.E. and the Jews were dispersed from their homeland.

Most scholars agree that the haftarah portion for *Bechukotai* is a series of unconnected pieces of prose and poetry.[1] There are, however, several verses that are noteworthy. Jeremiah begins the portion by proclaiming that the peoples of the earth will come to acknowledge God. Isaiah and Micah preach similar words.[2] A familiar concept, it was also preached by Zechariah: "On that day, God shall be One, and God's name will be One" (14:9), a verse that is included at the end of the *Alenu* found at the conclusion of the daily prayer service. The portion ends with a verse requesting healing, words that were subsequently incorporated into the eighth blessing of the traditional weekday *Amidah*.[3]

Perhaps the most compelling verses in this portion are those that address the concept of blessings and curses, which correspond to the Torah portion with which this text is paired. In the Torah text (Lev. 26:3, 14–15), rewards and punishments are described in great detail and understood as direct consequences of behavior. So too, in this haftarah portion, Jeremiah reminds the Israelites:

> Thus says the Eternal One: Cursed are those who trust in mortals, making mortal flesh their strength, turning their heads from the Eternal. They shall be like a stunted tree in the desert, never seeing when good comes, dwelling in dry places in the wilderness, in a salt land where no one dwells. Blessed are those who trust in the Eternal and whose trust is in the Eternal! They shall be like a tree planted near water, sinking its roots by a stream, never noticing when the heat comes, its leaves green, careless of times of drought, never failing to bear fruit.[4]

In this dramatic description, God presents two scenarios for the Israelites: Follow My teachings and you will be blessed; turn away by worshipping idols or men of mere flesh and blood and you will be cursed.

Though these two categories are very distinct in the biblical text, in real life, the notions of blessings and curses are much more blurred. A folktale illustrates this point: A man in a small village in China acquired a beautiful horse. "How wonderful," exclaimed the villagers.

"What a blessing has come to you!" He said, "What seems like a blessing may be a curse." The villagers, puzzled by his reaction, went on their way. Some time later, the man awoke to find that his beautiful horse had run away. The villagers rushed to his side to comfort him on the loss of his prized possession. Again, he puzzled them by saying, "What seems like a curse may be a blessing."

Sure enough, some time later, his horse returned, surrounded by a whole herd of beautiful stallions, worth a huge fortune. The villagers, struck by the man's extraordinary luck, congratulated him. The man replied, "What seems like a blessing may be a curse." Some time later, the man's son, riding on one of the stallions, was thrown from his mount and broke his leg. The villagers rallied to offer support to the man on his son's injury. The man was calm, saying, "What seems like a curse may be a blessing." Not long afterward, all the young men of the village were conscripted into a terrible war far away, in which they were killed. But this man's son had not been sent to the war because of his broken leg. What seems like a curse may be a blessing! This story illustrates that the line between blessings and curses is not always clear in our lives.

In our modern context, it is not always possible to make such definitive distinctions between blessings and curses. These concepts seem borrowed from another time and place. Yet, we often refer to good things—health, family, love, and friendship—as blessings. The converse is not always true. When an illness, loneliness, or poverty enters our lives, we regard this as "bad luck," more than as "curses" we must endure. Do we therefore dismiss the message of this haftarah portion as simply another ancient text with little relevance? Perhaps this portion just reminds us that blessings and curses, and our *perceptions* of them, surround us daily. At times, they may even describe *every* individual experience. If we step away from the Jeremiah text and simply examine these two sides of the same coin, is there something for us to discover?

For many women, the word *blessing* conjures up the traditional image of a woman uttering the candlelighting blessing to usher in

Shabbat and the festivals. The word *curse* brings to mind the slang term for menstruation, namely "the curse." This is a simple way to understand the words *blessing* and *curse*. But how else can these two words relate specifically to women's lives?

We can examine the two words as they relate to motherhood. It is a common assumption that there is a time of no greater bliss than that of motherhood. Our culture depicts pregnancy, childbirth, and motherhood in glowing images, glossing over challenges and emphasizing the positive aspects of this experience. Indeed, in countless ways, most of society perceives motherhood as a "blessing."

There are many gifts that are associated with this time in a woman's life,[5] such as nurturing another living soul within one's own body; the miracle and wonder of birth; nursing and thereby sustaining another person through one's own body; gentle and sweet caring of a newborn; teaching hand motions, songs, first steps, and positive behavior; tender moments of hand-holding; first hugs and blown kisses; comforting a heart-wrenching cry; and inspiring exploration, courage, and independence. These can indeed be the blessings of motherhood. Society and culture teach us that these are the natural events of womanhood available to all of us. To put it in biblical terms, if you are a woman, become pregnant, and give birth to a child, as a result of your behavior, you will be granted these blessings.

But what is the other side of this coin, the dark side of these "blessings," the "curse" of motherhood? The answer is one that has little to do with motherhood itself and much to do with how motherhood is portrayed in our culture. Because there is such a wide gap between the image of a mother bequeathed to us by previous generations and the reality that faces women today, women are often muted from expressing their true emotions and feelings about motherhood. This muteness is the curse of motherhood.

The iconographic image of a mother is a woman who is nurturing, patient, kind, resourceful, ever-available, and always prepared and who finds absolute meaning and purpose in her role. What happens, however, when a woman's experience does not match this image? To whom does she turn? In whom can she confide? Society teaches that women ought not complain about their role, give voice to feelings of hardship, or emote about pangs of regret and loss. Often, some women feel as though they are not allowed to express their feelings of uncertainty because that would characterize them as "bad" moms. Though a woman's instinct is to talk about her emotions and reactions to this life experience, sadly, few do. People's perceptions, and, more important, the reactions of mothers themselves to these perceptions, shut down the process of communication. This is the curse of motherhood—the unspoken side of becoming a parent.

Author Naomi Wolf observes "how the experience of becoming a mother, as miraculous and fulfilling as it is, is also undersupported, sentimentalized and even manipulated at women's expense."[6] In her book titled *Misconceptions: Truths, Lies and the Unexpected on the Journey to Motherhood*, Wolf explores the hidden truths about impending motherhood. She notes that women are better served with a reality check about the difficulties of pregnancy, childbirth, and mothering than with the sugarcoated messages we often get from our contemporary culture.

Why is it so difficult for women to open up and be honest about this time in their lives? A few generations ago, women were taught to maintain a stiff upper lip about their roles in their families. Often women would become mothers in their early twenties, well before their identities were fully established or their careers begun. Today, our culture is different. Women have more choices and often delay childbearing until personal growth is further along and careers are well under way. As a result, women who have distanced themselves from the domestic role suddenly find themselves facing the daunting tasks of child rearing and housekeeping. So, when children are introduced, and women assume household responsibilities, life may require a huge adjustment.

This still does not address our question as to why speaking frankly about the challenges mothers face is such a taboo. Here is an example of when we, women, can become our own worst enemies. We do ourselves a disservice when we conceal our earnest, conflicted feelings about motherhood. We are sometimes judgmental of each other and reluctant to confide about hardships. We fear betraying our inner selves. We feel inadequate, ill-prepared, and fearful of sharing our feelings. We worry about being accused of acting in a selfish, self-centered, ill-informed, and naïve manner. We struggle with feelings of guilt when we crave time alone. We're confused because we don't intuitively know what to do with a crying baby. There are even some women who are so competitive about who is the "better" mother that they often dissuade others from being open and confronting challenges, as well as triumphs, in an honest way.

Among the myths of motherhood is the notion that a woman will instantaneously bond with her newborn. In a book titled *Love Works Like This: Moving from One Kind of Love to Another*, author Lauren Slater describes her feelings about her three-week-old daughter:

> I am a mother, but I don't look like a mother. I don't feel like a mother. Over and over during the day, or at night when I watch her sleep, I whisper, "I am a mother, mother, mother," as I did when I was pregnant, and I've grown accustomed to the word, but it stays a distance from me. I thought I would be smashed flat, or heaved high, mythically altered for this, the most mythic of roles but, shock of all shock, here I am, still me. And the baby? I have come to like her a little bit. That's it. A little bit.[7]

Is Slater's reaction typical? Probably. But we do not usually hear this perspective from mothers in our culture. Societal expectations drive us to hide our real feelings and live private lives of doubt and uncertainty. Here is the curse of motherhood—the muting of our true feelings!

How do we transform this curse to a blessing? For the ancient Israelites, a change in behavior brought about a change in fortune. All they had to do was repent, refrain from certain objectionable practices, and their curse gave way to a blessing. Perhaps the answer is the same for women who experience pregnancy, birth, and motherhood.

How do we change our own behavior and culture so that giving voice to negative feelings is acceptable, so that seeking help is encouraged, so that the job of mothering and caregiving does not overwhelm us? One answer is to join forces. Mothers can help and support each other by taking turns caring for each other's kids, through play dates, preparing double-portion meals to be shared, and keeping each other company during the trying times. By providing an outlet for each other, women can feel less alone, less isolated, and less frustrated by the daily grind of mothering.

This is just one example of how this "curse" can give way to a blessing. However, only through a more accurate representation of the reality of mothering will real change take place. Authors Wolf and Slater help us to understand that women have many different perspectives on motherhood. Our TV sitcoms use humor to shed light on the "real" family, creating a more honest characterization. Sadly, even our recent exposure to the victims of postpartum depression has taught us that women must have a safe environment in which to express feelings of inadequacy, helplessness, and fear.

The other answer is to start listening carefully and speaking openly about the other side of motherhood. As a society, we need to offer new moms—and dads—more resources for support, financial as well as emotional. As women, we need to help each other, be less judgmental, and more sympathetic. When we can truly and honestly identify with one another, without the sugarcoating, without buying into the myths, without muting our emotions, then hope too will be born and nurtured for a vastly different experience than that of previous generations. When mothers can create this kind of community for themselves, maybe then the curse of inadequate feelings and unexpressed doubts will give way to a welcomed blessing of openness, integrity, and truth. When this kind of community is created, mothers will feel more secure, like the trees planted by the waters in Jeremiah's biblical vision.

Though our discussion has taken us far away from Jeremiah's vision, let us again look to his words and read them to mean: Cursed

157

are those who do not rely on others, blessed are those who allow the Divine presence in their lives. Perhaps we can reinterpret Jeremiah's words to mean: Cursed are those women who trust in the image of a blissful motherhood, and who are judgmental and competitive toward other women, putting up self-righteous walls and not allowing others to confide in them. Blessed are those women who seek out support, who allow themselves to accept it and give it to other women and men, and who refuse to experience the hardships of parenting alone.

It is said that when two people discuss Torah, the *Shekhinah* dwells between them. How much more so it is possible to say that when two people discuss the care and love and difficulties of caring for a precious gift of life will the Divine presence dwell between them. For in sharing their stories—of pain and of joy—the presence of God will be nurtured between them. So perhaps, we can reread Jeremiah's words to mean not "Do not trust in mortals," but rather, "Do not trust in the passing judgment of mortals." Trust, instead, in the holiness that comes from two mortals recognizing the beauty, the frustration, and the utter, indescribable joy that comes from motherhood. As Jeremiah reminds us, only then will our roots sink deep and our trees give forth their ripe fruit. Only then will our curses give way to blessings.

Bamidbar / Numbers

RABBI RACHEL LEILA MILLER

הפטרת במדבר

Haftarat Bamidbar

Hosea 2:1–22

*R*ebuke your mother! Rebuke!
For she is not my wife,
And I am not her husband . . .
And on that day God will say:
Call me "my man";
Do not call me any more "my husband."

(HOSEA 2:4, 18)

THE PROPHECY OF HOSEA is a parable in which the relationship of Hosea and his wife Gomer is analogous to the relationship of God and the people of Israel. This allegorical relationship is threatened from the start by disloyalty. In the first chapter of Hosea, God commands the prophet to take a prostitute as a wife, with the understanding that she will continue her promiscuity. Hosea concedes, and the following chapters present his chastisements of the Israelites using the metaphorical language of the straying wife.

Our haftarah tells the Israelites as individuals to rebuke their "mother"—here, the Israelite collective—for her dalliances. The statement is not merely a pronouncement of divorce. A play on words transposes the notions of false gods and false husbands: Both can be referred to as *ba'alim*. Divine wrath, however, is short-lived. God, through the prophet, encourages the adulterous people to return to

God's ways. With mercy, God promises to welcome back the repentant partner. The haftarah closes with a message echoed in the liturgy: God is always ready for our *teshuvah* (repentance). Rather than greeting our return with hostility, God provides as betrothal gifts righteousness, justice, kindness, mercy, and faithfulness (Hosea 2:21–22)—the very qualities demanded of an ideal partnership.

God in Our Image: Understanding God through Human Experience

Rabbis of the past have struggled with God's motivation for the initial command of Hosea to seek out a harlot for a wife. Medieval commentators such as David Kimhi and Abraham Ibn Ezra suggest that God would not afflict Hosea in such an unjust manner, particularly knowing the resulting cuckoldry, so they conclude that Hosea's prophecy begins with a dream or vision. Through this vision, Hosea is able to sympathize with God's disappointment and is prepared to deliver the prophetic message. According to this view, the entire first chapter of the book, establishing the parable, did not occur. Hosea never really took Gomer as a wife nor suffered her continual disloyalties.

The Sages of the Talmud disagree. While they clearly also perceive the problem of God's apparently strange command, the Sages resolve this by providing a motivation for God. In the talmudic interpretation of Hosea, we learn that God's command was preceded by a lack of compassion on the part of Hosea. In *Pesachim* 87a, we read:

> The Holy One of Blessing said to Hosea, "Your children have transgressed." [Hosea] should have said to [God], "They are Your children! They are the children of Your favored ones—the children of Abraham, Isaac, and Jacob. Cause Your mercy to flow onto them!" [Were it] not sufficient that he did not say thus, rather [Hosea] said to God, "Ruler of the Universe, the entire universe is Yours—Might you exchange them for another people?"

The Sages identify a reason for Hosea's suffering: He is unable to convey God's message without first learning to embrace the characteristic of mercy. In the continuation of the talmudic passage, once God puts him through this trial, Hosea is himself unwilling to abandon his wife and children, despite their questionable parentage. Through this process, he discovers within himself the ability to understand the Divine qualities of patience *(erekh apayyim)* and mercy *(rachamim)*.

While both points of view—that of the medieval commentators and that of the Talmud—offer satisfactory responses to the problem of God's strange command, they raise an additional difficulty. Each answer suggests that God can be understood through human relationship, whether in prophetic vision or actual interaction. We can know God through human existence. In the analogy posited by Hosea's parable, God is, as it were, a jilted husband.

God's perspective is depicted as male because Hosea is male. This literary quality of the Tanakh challenges us. The biblical prophets' masculine voices influence their messages. If we each see God through the lens of our own experience, then our gender inevitably impacts how we understand God's relationship to the world.

A Marriage of Intimates

God's image in Hosea may also be male because God's role as a husband is expected to teach humans how to be husbands. The second chapter of Hosea is not a psychological portrait of an actual couple. We never witness the accusations, arguments, revenge, and pain that are the legacies of adultery, nor do we delve into its causes. Hosea does not provide a prescription for absolute forgiveness in the face of disloyalty. In fact, biblical law forbids a man to return to his faithless wife (e.g., Num. 5:11–29, Deut. 24:1–4). Therefore, this story illustrates that God's extremity in welcoming repentance is not expected of human beings.

On the other hand, Hosea's prophecy offers a provocative redefinition of marital roles. God promises a day when God will no longer be called by Israel *Ba'ali* (my husband/my master), but rather, *Ishi* (my man) (Hosea 2:18). *Ba'al* is the usual word for the male partner in a marriage. However, as noted by Radak, *ish* appears elsewhere in the Tanakh, also with the meaning of husband. (Hannah's husband, Elkanah, is called her *ish* in I Samuel 1:8 and 23.) Clearly, a distinction is made between these two types of husbandry. What makes *ish* ideal? What does God reject about being a *ba'al*?

The word *ba'al* conveys a sense of mastery, dominion, and ownership. As mentioned before, false gods are called *ba'alim*. One reason for the rejection of the term comes from the next verse: "I will remove the names of the gods from her mouth . . ." (Hosea 2:19). To refer to her husband as *ba'al* is too close to pagan imagery.

The commentators push this distinction further. Rashi says (on verse 2:18), "'You shall worship me from love, and not from fear.' *Ish* is the language of [sexual] intimacy and the affection of youth." Malbim (Meir Leibush ben Yehiel Michel) elaborates on this contrast. He attributes the lapse of Israel into idolatry to the lack of intimacy between God and the feminine *Knesset Yisrael*. Without the perception of God's closeness, one seeks intermediaries. As with the golden calf, Israel's idolatrous acts are fumbled attempts to reach a Ruler perceived as distant and disinterested. The prophetic vision offers the messianic hope that, in a better time, Israel will be united with God as a man and woman unite.

This vision assumes a model of marital relationship to which we should aspire. What is the nature of this union? We know from the text that the relationship of Gomer and Hosea is a failure. Without delving deeply into the psychology of infidelity, one imagines that Gomer's betrayals were motivated by her inability to reveal herself to her husband and her belief that he was unapproachable and aloof. Her husband, however, is not blameless; he has played the role of master, enforcing the emotional distance between them. Malbim and Rashi both imply as a solution the ideal established by Song of Songs: an intimate relationship that unites partners in sexual ardor, youthful enthusiasm, verbalized appreciation, and complete attention. By pursuing a passionate relationship of this type, we imitate God and hasten the time of redemption.

*B*eing Intimate with God

Returning to the Divine-human relationship, it is obvious that Hosea questions the characterization of God as a distant master or king. The prescription of intimacy deepens one's personal relationship with God. For some, it may be fulfilling to submit to the command of an omniscient, transcendent Being. For others, it may be difficult to feel any sort of connection to a God of this type. Hosea challenges us to open our hearts to a more passionate experience of God.

Every weekday, those who wear tefillin quote Hosea's words: "I betroth you to me eternally" (Hosea 2:21). Yet, it is rare for Jews to imagine themselves as lovers of God. Allowing oneself to develop a joyous attachment to God transforms life into something more vital than rote service to the higher good commanded by the King of Kings. Prayer becomes an ecstatic experience, a love song. Torah study is a sharing of secrets and the script for a struggle with mutual disappointments and longings. Mitzvot gain immediacy as they become gestures to meet the desires of a Lover one longs to please. Transgression is forgiven in a loving embrace.

The idea of the Jewish people, and individual Jews, being God's loving partner also places added weight on human action. Along with intimacy come responsibility and growth. Our relationship with God is fertile: We actively participate in God's ongoing creation of the universe. Let us hope to see a fulfillment of Hosea's prophecy, a day the world will be transformed by commitment among humans, and between humans and God, that is joyful, passionate, and accepting.

RABBI JUDITH Z. ABRAMS

הפטרת נשא
Haftarat Naso

Judges 13:2–25

*T*here was one man from Tsor'ah, of the family of Dan, and his name was Manoach. And his wife was barren; she'd not given birth. And God's messenger appeared to the woman and said to her: Here, please consider this: You are barren and have not given birth but you will conceive and bear a son. And now, take care please, that you drink no wine or hard liquor nor eat anything ritually impure. For behold you have conceived and will bear a son. And let no razor come up near his head, for the lad will be a Nazirite of God from the moment of his conception in your belly. And he will be the first to save Israel from the hand of the Philistines.
(JUDGES 13:2–5)

MANY OF US KNOW the famous promise of a pregnancy to our matriarch Sarah, when an anonymous angel comes to her with the news (Gen. 18:10). In *Haftarat Naso*, we see a parallel situation. Here, God's anonymous messenger not only promises an unnamed woman that she will bear a son but tells her, as well, that she must be responsible for his prenatal experiences so that, from conception on, this boy is the perfect, lifelong Nazirite.

The idea of Nazirite vows connects the haftarah portion to *Parashat*

Naso, which outlines how Nazirite vows are made (Num. 6:1–21). Nazirites are not to drink any alcohol, cut their hair, or come into contact with the dead for the period of the vow of Naziritehood. The Torah portion does not mention anything about lifelong Nazirite-hood, such as that in which Samson, the promised babe of our haf-tarah, will engage. It is because of Samson's special destiny to be a lifelong Nazirite that his mother is warned by the angel to follow the rules of the Nazirite herself so that the fetus is pure even as it develops in her womb.

Today we recognize how important prenatal influences are for the developing fetus. Ironically, modern women are advised to follow some of the Nazirite rules during pregnancy, for example, not drinking alcohol, which could hurt the fetus's development.

Haftarat Naso has much to teach us, not only about Samson's mother, but also about our tradition's belief that the fetus is both a part of the mother and yet an independent entity. What *is* the status of a fetus? There is no unanimity in our sources on this question. On the one hand, the fetus is considered to be a limb of the pregnant woman. In Exodus 21:22, we learn that if two men are fighting and they strike a pregnant woman who then miscarries but experiences no other trauma, the perpetrator must pay civil damages to the husband but is not accused of murder. This would seem to imply that the fetus is not considered to be a separate human being. Indeed, the fetus is not considered to have the status of a living human being until its head emerges from the mother's body (M. *Oholot* 7:6).

While the Sages had a profound respect and passion for life, they also understood that, in some situations, the fetus in the womb needs to be sacrificed. The Sages also felt that the fetus was only potential life while the mother had an actual life that took precedence. So, for example, if a woman experienced a difficult birth, the fetus's life could be sacrificed for the mother's:

> [to help] the woman who suffers a hard birth [process], the
> fetus may be cut into pieces in her womb and they bring it

> out limb by limb because her life takes precedence over his. [But if] the majority [of his body] came out [of the mother's body], we do not touch it, for one life does not supersede another life. (M. *Oholot* 7:6)

Neither forceps nor safe cesarean sections were available when this teaching was formulated, and the Sages did not know of the many other options now available for dealing with a fetus that cannot be delivered by a routine vaginal birth.

However, the Sages also taught that the fetus is not simply another body organ but a nascent soul. In BT *Sanhedrin* 91b, Rabbi Yehuda Nesia debated with a Roman theologian about whether the soul enters the fetus at the time of conception or at the time when the fetus's body takes shape. Both authorities come to agree that the soul enters the fetus at the time of conception but that the Evil Inclination does not enter the child until the moment of birth. Otherwise, the fetus would keep kicking in the womb, causing a premature birth.

God's participation in conception raises an animal act into a holy one: "[Human] creatures offer up a decaying drop in private and the Holy Blessed One returns to them praiseworthy, perfect souls in public" (*Leviticus Rabbah, Tazri'a* 14:2). It is God who transforms human body fluids into a soul. God is a partner in the process of creating a child. All the things that we consider unique to human beings are given to us by God:

> Our Rabbis taught: There are three partners in a person, the Holy Blessed One, its father, and its mother. Its father sows the white [substance, i.e., semen] out of which [come the child's] bones and sinews and nails and the brain in its head and the white in its eye; his mother sows the red [substance, i.e., blood] out of which [come the child's] skin and flesh and hair and blood and the black of the eye. And the Holy Blessed One gives it spirit and breath and beauty of face and seeing eyes and hearing ears and walking legs and understanding and insight. When the time comes for the child to depart for the world, the Holy

Blessed One takes away the Divine portion and leaves the portions of its father and mother with the child. (BT *Niddah* 31a / BT *Kiddushin* 30b)

Without God's animating spirit, we are nothing but dust and ashes. And God's spirit comes to the fetus while it is still in the womb. One thing that experience teaches us is that our children are born with their own distinct characters already installed on their "hard drives." Some babies are quiet; some cry all night. Some children are born with physical disabilities while others are born whole. Each fetus's character may be attributed to God, who comes to visit the fetus while it is still in the womb.

> [During the period of gestation] a light burns above the fetus's head, and it looks and sees from one end of the world to the other. . . . And you [can find] no better days for human beings than these days [in the womb]. . . . And they teach [the fetus] the entire Torah. . . . And when [the fetus] comes into the air [outside the birth canal], an angel comes and slaps [the baby] on its mouth so that it forgets the entire Torah. (BT *Niddah* 30b)

Not only does the fetus live in the physical comfort of the womb, but it lives a life of pure spirituality with the Torah. The cry a baby first gives after being born is unlike any other sound on earth. It is the sound of new life which, within ten seconds, turns into a cry of outrage. It is as if the baby were saying, "What is this? I had a nice, warm, dark environment in which to live and now there are all these bright lights, loud noises, and all sorts of unpleasant procedures."

At certain dramatic moments in the life of Israel, even the fetuses take part in the community's life:

> Whence do we know that even the fetuses in their mothers sang the song [at the Reed Sea]? [From the text] that says, "In convocations bless the Lord God from the source of Israel" (Ps. 68:27). But could [the fetuses] see [the miracle]? Said Rabbi Tankhum: The womb became for them

like a window pane [filled with] light and they did see it.
(BT *Sotah* 30b–31a)

The nameless angel and woman in this haftarah portion are a part of this great tradition of acknowledging that the spark of God is present in the creation of every human being.

One of the most profound spiritual experiences one can ever have is that of gestation and birth. When one feels the baby "quicken" for the first time, it is a moment filled with awe. A pregnant woman can viscerally experience how one can be oneself and another person at the same time. A pregnant woman lives on many levels. She is a vessel that holds something precious and holy. But she is also, in her own right, a complete person. This is a very high spiritual level: to be many things at once; to be aware of existence's multifaceted nature. It gives us a glimpse of how, perhaps, God experiences the world. Maybe we are all contained in God and the universe is God's womb. We are in God and of God at the same time. Thus, like Samson's mother, we can take pride in that which we nurture while taking comfort in the gentle and holy space we occupy in God's womb.

RABBI MARGOT STEIN

הפטרת בהעלתך
Haftarat Behalotecha

Zechariah 2:14–4:7

R̲oni vesimchi bat-Zion / Sing and rejoice O daughter
of Zion! (ZECHARIAH 2:14)

ZECHARIAH 2:14 OPENS our haftarah with a plaintive cry to the women
of Israel, calling them forth to praise God in a uniquely feminine way:
through singing and dancing.[1] In the verses that follow, the prophet
attempts to reassure the returning exiles that God will be with them
as they begin the sacred task of rebuilding the Temple. Why invoke
women's song and dance as part of that reassurance? Is this opening
line merely poetic window dressing to the vision that follows, or is it
somehow central to the prophet's message?

Women's role as sacred singers and dancers is well documented in
the Bible. Their song is often connected to successful military action,
serving a celebratory role in the ritual reenactment that followed such
a victory. They were known for their singing, dancing, and a skillfulness with words that ranged from soaring poetry to stinging rebuke.

Perhaps the greatest prophetess, poet, and musician in the Bible is
Miriam, sister of Moses and Aaron. It is Miriam who remembers to
bring her *tof* (timbrel) as the Israelites scurry out of Egypt, amid the
anguished cries of the bereaved parents of firstborn sons. It is Miriam
who finds the words to express the Israelites' sentiments at the shores
of the Reed Sea:[2]

> And Miriam, the prophetess, the sister of Aaron, took a timbrel in her hand, and all the women went out after her with timbrels and with dances. And Miriam sang to them:
>
> Sing to the Lord, for he is highly exalted:
> The horse and his rider has he thrown into the sea.
>
> (Exod. 15:20–21)

As a cultic figure, it is Miriam who leads the song and dance of victory over Pharaoh. The other women follow her, also singing and dancing. The men, most likely, joined in the singing, but refrained from the dancing, as the Hebrew *ve-ta'an lahem* (and she sang to them) uses the masculine plural for the direct object, whereas the word *va-tetzena* is a strictly feminine plural form of "going out [after her]." This may indicate the uniqueness of women's role as ritual dancers. Men were known to sing, for example, in the Psalms that attest to male Levitical singing but not to dance. More specifically, the call-and-response format of biblical poetry may indicate antiphonal singing on the Temple steps (where group A sings one line and group B responds with the next line). The notion that men were to sing but not to dance is also seen in II Samuel 6:16, where King David himself suddenly attempts to dance in victory, causing his wife Michal to express disgust. Yet I Samuel 18:6 tells us the women sang and danced, to greet both Saul and David after their victory. Thus a picture begins to emerge of an essential function reserved for women during times of ritual celebration.

That picture is brought into focus through the story of Deborah in the Book of Judges. Deborah, a prophetess and a judge, is also a military advisor and a cultic figure, displaying juridical, military, and political power when she accompanies Barak into battle, and prophesies his victory over Sisera. Although contemporary readers may assume it was unusual for a woman to fulfill these roles, especially in regard to military activity, the text itself does not indicate any surprise. In general, it was quite common for military leaders to be accompanied by prophetic advisors, and in that she was fulfilling a typical function of her position.[3]

The prose account of the events of Judges 4 is followed by the Song of Deborah in Judges 5. This epic poem is testimony to her skillfulness with words, part of the prophetess's requisite abilities.[4] Perhaps, as in the case of Miriam at the Shores of the Sea, Deborah did not compose the entire song, but rather the original kernel of poetry that later grew into the full-length song. However, its attribution to her is significant. It acknowledges her power as prophet and poet, two functions that unite to perform what is the prophet's greatest task: turning a military victory into a theological one, bringing together the disparate tribes of Israel with passionate words, and reminding them of Sinai. The song calls her a "mother in Israel," but the song itself performs motherhood by giving life through commemoration of Deborah's activities; she brings order out of chaos by means of her words.[5] Corroborating women's role in cultic celebration, it has also been suggested by scholars that this poem was composed for performance at a religious ceremony at a later date.[6]

An example of women's participation in the ritual celebration of military victory that later turns tragic is found in the story of Jephthah's daughter in Judges 11. Jephthah prays to God for military victory and promises in return that he will sacrifice "the first thing" that greets him upon his return home. Disastrously, the first thing turns out to be his daughter, who, following the ritual protocol established by female religious figures before her (and female relatives of male military heroes), rushes out to greet him "with timbrels and with dances." To keep his promise, he must sacrifice his daughter, who begs for two months' respite with her women friends to "bewail [her] virginity." This request is significant because it confirms her innocence and youth, a status similar to the "daughters of Zion" invoked by Zechariah.

With these examples in mind, Zechariah's clarion call, "*Roni vesimchi bat-Zion* / Sing and rejoice, O daughter of Zion," becomes a strategic request for women's ritual participation in his prophecy, an essential element in reaching that prophecy's successful conclusion. It is a way of articulating a hoped-for political and military victory within the context of a theological triumph. In Zechariah's case, the hoped-for outcome is the peaceful return of Israel from exile, and the restoration of the Temple in Jerusalem. His prophecy suggests that women would be needed to culminate this return in a suitable celebration that would, in essence, ease the nation's transition from a wartime mentality to the peaceful rebuilding of the Temple he so desires.

On the heels of this prophecy comes a second vision to Zechariah. In this vision, he describes a golden candelabrum with olive trees on either side, symbols of peace and agricultural rootedness in the Land of Israel. The second vision reinforces the first: Military victory must be followed by profound peace. It is this deeper harmony that will allow for a flowering of the spiritual life of Israel. God's words to Zechariah underscore the importance of this message:

"*Lo bechayil, v'lo bekoach, ki im b'ruchee* / Not by might, nor by power, but by My Spirit" (Zech. 4:6).

Women's timbrels and dances, their singing and celebration, are necessary to make the transition from military might to peaceful coexistence. These cultic activities signal the closing of one phase and the opening of a new one, where Spirit becomes more central. Then, and only then, can the people experience God's final promise in this haftarah: "*Chen! Chen lah!* / Grace! Grace unto her!" (Zech. 4:7).

RABBI PAMELA WAX

הפטרת שלח לך
Haftarat Shelach Lecha

Joshua 2:1–24

*J*oshua son of Nun secretly sent two men as spies from
Shittim, saying, "Go, have a look at the land—and at
Jericho!" So they set out, and they came to the house of
a harlot named Rahab and lodged there. . . . The king of
Jericho sent for Rahab, saying: "Bring out the men who
came to you and entered your house, for they have come
to explore the whole country." The woman had taken
the two men and hidden them, but she said, "Yes, the
men came to me . . . [T]he men went out and I don't
know where they went". . . . To the men she said, "I
know that YHVH has given you the land . . . Indeed, we
have heard how YHVH dried up the waters of the Sea of
Reeds before you when you left Egypt . . . Indeed,
YHVH your God is the only God in the heavens above
and on the earth below." . . . She secured the crimson
cord to the window. (JOSHUA 2:1, 3, 4, 5, 9, 11, 21)

*S*o the young spies came and brought out Rahab,
her father, her mother, her brothers—everything
that belonged to her and her entire family, they brought
out!—and left them outside the camp of Israel.
(JOSHUA 6:23)

HAVING BEEN UNABLE to convince ten of his fellow scouts and the rest of the Israelites of the desirability of entering the land in his original scouting mission in the Book of Numbers, chapters 13–14, Joshua undertakes another reconnaissance mission approximately thirty-nine years later, recorded in what has become the haftarah portion for the original story. If the first mission was characterized by a lack of faith on the part of ten of the twelve scouts, Joshua and Caleb excluded, and, by extension the entire Israelite community to whom the scouts reported their findings, this second mission bodes no better for the two spies sent to Jericho by Joshua. Yet their reconnaissance mission to a brothel, which might have turned comic,[1] is, instead, a brilliant move; it is the spies' good fortune to happen upon Rahab, a Canaanite prostitute who bolsters their resolve and teaches them about faith in YHVH. It is she who shows them the inevitable worthiness of their mission.

Rahab's success is demonstrated by the fact that the Israelite spies keep their promise to save her and her family, despite earlier Mosaic law in Deuteronomy 7:2 and 20:16–18 not to make agreements with any of the peoples of the land. Just as in the Ruth story, in which love and *chesed* conquer a seemingly inviolable law against intermarriage with a Moabite, the story of Rahab seems to suggest that there is such a thing as "situational ethics," in that Rahab's kindness to the spies deserves a reward (in this case, an agreement with an inhabitant of the land) despite an injunction against such a reward. Nonetheless, the spies are afraid of repercussions, blaming Rahab rather than their own desperation for the pact, claiming, "We are guiltless in this oath of yours which you have made us swear" (Josh. 2:17). The encouraging words that Rahab had earlier spoken to them in Joshua 2:9 are repeated nearly verbatim in their later report to Joshua: "YHVH has delivered the whole land into our power; in fact, all the inhabitants of the land are quaking before us" (Josh. 2:24), further proof of her success.

The rabbinic tradition totally recasts Rahab in one of three ways. The first suggests that *zonah*, harlot, can also mean "innkeeper."[2] This interpretation protects the Israelites' reputations, lest they be sullied for consorting with her. The second reformulation, however, thoroughly sexualizes Rahab. She becomes a sort of fantasy for the Rabbis, the eternal temptress, as we learn in *Megillah* 15a:

> The Rabbis taught, There have been four women of sur-passing beauty in the world: Sarah, Rahab, Abigail, and Esther. . . . Rahab inspired lust by her name. . . . R. Isaac said, "Whoever says, 'Rahab, Rahab,' at once has an issue." Said R. Nahman to him, "I say, 'Rahab, Rahab' and nothing happens to me!" He replied, "I was speaking of one who knows her and is intimate with her."

In this recasting, the Rabbis also turn Rahab's prostitution into a saving grace for the Israelites who, after all, would benefit from the knowledge to which she was privy in the bedroom.[3] Most fanciful of all, the Rabbis' third alternative re-creates Rahab as a righteous con-vert who marries Joshua and becomes the ancestress to priests and prophets, including Huldah and Jeremiah.[4]

If we think about Rahab's economic status, we can imagine that she was poor with few choices other than prostitution, or the oppo-site, that she was a woman of independent means, unbeholden to others. If the former, we might view her dalliance with the Israelite spies as a necessary and convenient means of pulling herself and her family out of poverty. If the latter, we might view her choice as an unselfish act of righteousness and vision, rather than as an act of eco-nomic necessity.

We need not second-guess Rahab's motives, for there are clues to the mystery in the text itself. First is her name, for the meaning of a name is always significant in the Bible. *Rahab* means "broad" or "wide." Her profession gave her the opportunity to meet a lot of people, and Rahab's ability to see broadly, to be open to possibility, and to entertain the unknown in her thinking may be what enabled her to see the merit of the spies' mission. Thus she, like Ruth the Moabite, throws her lot in with theirs, accepts their God, and ultimately saves her own family. Interestingly, Rahab lives directly inside the city walls. Rather than making her a true insider, however, one suspects that by profession and by residence, Rahab is, in fact, an outsider even in her own community, thereby making her alliance with Israel a bit less surprising.

Rather, the surprise lies in the Israelites' making an alliance with her! Shittim, from where Joshua sends his two spies, was the place where the Israelites became involved with forbidden Moabite women (Num. 25:1). This reference to Shittim is therefore a warning: The Hebrew word *zonah*, meaning "prostitute," is often used in the Bible to describe idolatry, or "whoring after other gods," a pagan practice most often associated with its women.[5] Being a Canaanite woman should have made Rahab all the more suspect to these Israelites. Not only was there the potential of her seducing them into idolatry, there was the added memory from the story of Tamar in Genesis 38 of Canaanite women as tricksters! She might indeed have seduced them sexually, as Tamar seduced Judah. Like Tamar, Rahab attains security for herself and her family within the community of Israel; each marks her success with a crimson cord. Tamar, of course, "played the harlot" in order to achieve her goal. One midrash suggests that the two spies were, in fact, Tamar's twin sons, Peretz and Zerach, and that the crimson cord that Rahab hangs in the window was given to her by Zerach: "It was the scarlet thread that the midwife had bound upon his hand to mark him as the child that appeared first and withdrew."[6] Though the language is sexually charged, Rahab ultimately didn't need to use sex to achieve her goals, as Tamar did.

Another clue to Rahab's motives is the larger context in which her story appears. Two other citations of women in the Book of Joshua undermine the notion of Israel's absolute patriarchy: Caleb's daughter Achsah (Josh. 15:16–19), who demanded and received land of her own from her father, and the daughters of Zelopchad (Josh. 17:3–6), who apparently need to remind the authorities to give them a portion of land as previously promised in Numbers 27. In this larger context of women and land in the Book of Joshua, the story of Rahab may be seen as the story of one woman's failed attempt to receive land in Israel.[7] Does this fact then lead us to believe that Rahab was self-serving in her attempt to help the spies?

Yet another parallel story in the Book of Joshua may help us here. In Joshua 10, another group of outsiders, the Gibeonites, are the ones who praise God, while the Israelites in the story never do, just as in the Rahab story. Together, the stories of Rahab and the Gibeonites seem like an attempt to show that the boundaries between Israelite and non-Israelite are perhaps more permeable than one might think, that sometimes an outsider is more of an insider than an insider is! In other words, throughout the Book of Joshua are scattered scraps of tension pointing to changes in Israel's self-perception, or in Israel's reality to the outside world. The story of Rahab, then, is a story that helps to build on the "Ruth" strand of Judaism, opening the boundaries and letting outsiders in. The thrust of the story, then, invites us to trust Rahab's purest motives.

Lastly, the Rahab story contains allusions to the Exodus story. As an amalgam of both Yocheved and the midwives Shifra and Puah, all three of whose efforts were needed in order to save Moses for his role as deliverer of the Israelites, Rahab makes another exodus possible for the Israelites themselves and for her own family, as well. Additionally, she saves her family with the use of the crimson cord, which is reminiscent of the blood on the doorposts of the houses when the angel of death passes over. Perhaps most significant of all is Rahab's willingness to lie to the king about the whereabouts of the Israelites and do what she can to save them, just as the midwives did in Exodus 1:15–21.

That Rahab cites the Exodus from Egypt and the crossing of the Reed Sea as things she knows of YHVH's might adds to the sense that she is herself significant as an actor in yet another exodus story. Just as the midwives received "houses" from God for their efforts, so does Rahab get rewarded.

Rahab teaches us about faith, kindness, loyalty, and about not judging a person by her profession. She also makes us aware of the permeability of the boundaries between Israelite and non-Israelite, a permeability with which we live daily in contemporary Jewish society.

הפטרת קרח
Haftarat Korach

I Samuel 11:14–12:22

*A*nd Samuel said to all Israel, "Behold, I hold hear-
kened to your voice, to all you have said to me, so
I have set a king to rule over you." (I SAMUEL 12:1)

SO WHAT OF SAMUEL, the last of the judges, and one of the first of the prophets? He has guided the Israelites, in so many ways, toward the kind of peoplehood and mode of governance that seemed a natural progression from the past and viable for the future. In the process, he created a new and united nation out of chaos. The Israelites, living previously as a loose confederation of tribes vaguely united by charismatic leaders, were now, under Samuel, shaped into a semblance of a nation. They were more cohesive than before, and it is clear from Samuel's oration in the haftarah that he labored diligently and selflessly for the good of the people.

However, his time as leader is up. The people, who under his guidance lived through enormous changes in their self-perceptions, begin to ask the kinds of questions that come to all groups in times of transition. Who are we? What constitutes our current identity? And how do we wish to see that develop or change in this new phase of our existence? What kind of a system do we wish to use, and what will be our models of leadership? These are some of their burning concerns as they prepare for the retirement of Samuel and for the beginning of the age of monarchy.

Samuel clearly disapproves of the avowed next phase for the people, the monarchy. However, as a faithful servant of the people, and against his better judgment, he responds to their expressed desire and anoints Saul as the first Israelite king. He registers his dissent on the basis of two concerns. First, he takes the desire of the people for a king as a personal attack on his integrity, as the people reject his model of guidance and ask for a different kind of leadership. He begs that they remember that he only worked for their good, and was honest and just in all his dealings. He is soothed and somewhat mollified by the reassurance of the assembled people, who acknowledge his honorable character.

But this is not enough. Second, Samuel proceeds to berate the people for clamoring for a king, and his objections concern the integrity of God—God who alone should be their ruler, and against whom they so often rebel. He goes so far as to call this *ra'ah*, an evil course to have taken, and calls upon God to display great might and power over the cosmos to frighten the people into submission. Samuel then calms them down and tells them that they will have their temporal ruler, but urges them to remain obedient and faithful to their Supreme Ruler above all other sovereigns.

In these and other passages in the Bible, such as the corresponding Torah portion *Korach*, both biblical authors and later rabbinical tradition inveigh against such rebelliousness and confrontations to the established order. In our Haftarah, this disapprobation is conveyed by means of thunder and rain (I Sam. 12:18); in the corresponding Torah portion, Korach and his crew are swallowed up by the earth (Num. 16:31–33).

The "Inherited Wisdom"

Judaism is, in many ways, a proscriptive religion. Certainly our tradition protects our "freedom of conscience" and does not intrude upon our private beliefs. But in the public sphere, Jewish life is heavily circumscribed. We are taught, and we also inherit, our rituals and practices, our prayers, our models of rabbinical leadership, and our organizational styles, because people who have reflected on these concepts believe they know what is the appropriate way for others to behave, and also believe that their insights are ordained by God. And perhaps in the past, this sufficed. Perhaps in times of flux and insecurity, when leaders attempt to construct the identity of the group, pressures toward conformity become prominent and seem most appropriate.

From biblical times through today, there have been decent leaders with powerful visions who have worked to mold groups in their image, ascribing the authority for their positions to God. Women—especially those who identity themselves as feminists—who wish to reconstruct Judaism and redefine what constitutes a Jewish identity, have often had to rebel against the established order. In order to establish an inclusive identity and comfortable forms of leadership, practice, and language, as human beings and as Jews they sometimes find themselves at odds with the dominant Jewish culture.

The modern Jewish world has been struggling with a monumental change in form and content, and it is still in flux. An example from the world of the female rabbi will illustrate this. The "traditional" contemporary model of the (male) rabbi has been a pyramid, with the rabbi as the managing director of the corporate synagogue. The rabbi has the final word (unless the synagogue places the board or executive at the top of the pyramid and assigns ultimate authority to them) and is certainly the *marah d'atra*, the final arbiter on halachic matters. Such a model of leadership creates a hierarchical organization in which power and precedent are controlled by the rabbi. The rabbi is the "boss." Many women rabbis have reflected deeply on the nature of power. These women view themselves as facilitators and partners in renewing Judaism, and are willing to divest themselves of the traditional type of authority granted to rabbis. Rabbis who seek to work in a more cooperative way find that this is not always welcomed by their communities. Many people are confused by this tack, and they either insist that the rabbi exert power in various situations, or they engage in aimless power struggles, seeking to fill the void.

Feminism as a contemporary philosophical/theological recasting of traditional Judaism, and the sociological shift due to the presence of ever-growing numbers of women rabbis, cantors, scholars, lay leaders, and the like, have offered powerful challenges to the inherited wisdom, to the way things have always been.[1] Women have reflected on how to lead in an enabling manner, how to reimage God as more immanent, and how to read our historical texts in ways that both construct new images and deconstruct discriminatory and unpalatable ones. No other contemporary Jewish movement has had quite the same overarching effect as the women's movement in Judaism.

And how have these challenges been met? Sometimes our leaders have reacted as Samuel did, perceiving them not as possible alternatives to be explored, but rather as threats to Judaism's essential ideology. One can understand Samuel's initial emotional reaction. Many of those who cling to the past are decent people who have, like Samuel, served the Jewish people and their own communities with immense commitment and personal investment. The association of one's identity with one's life work and ultimate values is intense, and thus, the threat of disruptions to the "way things are" is taken personally. As in the case of Samuel, there can be anxiety that their motives have been misinterpreted, and defensiveness about the pursuit of a path now called into question. We feminists need to be aware of how these changes affect people and find ways, as the people did for Samuel, to reassure them about our indebtedness to them, and our recognition of the value of their work.

If that were the only way in which anxiety and disapproval were expressed, then there would be far fewer battles and far fewer bruises. But, too often, the leadership does what Samuel did and calls upon God to suppress dissent and frighten those who question, those who, like the people at the threshold of the monarchy, clamor for change. This is a very potent way of silencing people.

Many women and men who engage in feminist analysis desperately wish to remain within the tradition and understand their theologies and innovations as organic developments. But struggles for change can become battles that rend communities, and who would want to feel that they have violated sacred tradition, split a community, and even engaged in *khilul haShem* (profanation of YHVH)? Threatening to open the earth up under these challengers, and sending thunder and lightning are effective methods of ensuring that the tradition continues and the community is not ruffled. But the new world beckons, and, as in Samuel's day, different forms of leadership and organization will arise.

Were some of Samuel's dire predictions about abusive kings correct? Certainly they were. In choosing the monarchy as their form of government, the people subjected themselves to an oppressive earthly hierarchy that would often rob them of their autonomy and disempower them. Jewish feminism is a critique of hierarchies and the language of subjugation, and seeks to empower people and strengthen them in their autonomy. In this respect, Samuel himself might have recognized the prophetic nature of Jewish feminism.

But the Israelites and their kings were subject to the same Divine ethical precepts, thus transforming the ancient model of the Divine monarch. Tradition teaches that the messianic age of peace and harmony will be ushered in by a monarch, a scion of King David. So the Bible and later Jewish tradition made its peace with monarchy.

Perhaps contemporary Jewish tradition and Jewish leaders will someday make peace with feminism and its insights, and recognize the ways in which most Jewish feminists have retained strong links to the tradition and have attempted to reshape Judaism in an organic, symbiotic, but profound manner. Such recognition could, in itself, help bring the messianic age a step closer.

הפטרת חקת

Haftarat Chukkat

Judges 11:1–33

W hatever comes out from the door of my home to meet me when I return in peace from the Ammonites, then to God will I offer it as a sacrifice.

(JUDGES 11:31)

THE HAFTARAH FOR *Chukkat* comes from Judges 11:1–33. These verses relate the story of Jephthah, a mighty warrior who will become the next judge of Israel. However, in the Bible, Judges 11 continues for a few more verses. If we read these verses, we will discover a story about a young woman that parallels the Genesis account of the binding of Isaac. But our story ends with the tragic human sacrifice of that young woman and leaves us questioning our responsibility to break the silence of her story.

Jephthah lived during the time when Israel had not yet established a monarchy and the Israelite tribes were constantly battling with their enemies, the Philistines, the Canaanites, and the Ammonites. Jephthah is a mighty warrior, but his brothers force him to leave their home because they do not want him to share in their father's inheritance. Jephthah leaves and many years later, his brothers find themselves losing their battle to the Ammonites. Remembering Jephthah's military ability, the brothers negotiate with him until a deal is made; if Jephthah successfully leads them in battle, they will make him their leader, the next judge of Israel. The narrator of Judges informs us that the spirit of God passed to Jephthah. We know that God will enable him to win the war.

Jephthah then vows to God: "If you give me the Ammonites in my hand, then whatever comes out from the door of my home to meet me when I return in peace from the Ammonites, then to God will I offer it as a sacrifice" (Judg. 11:30–31). In the ancient Near East, vows that included the use of God's name were not made lightly, since people did not have a way of retracting these vows. Jephthah makes a vow that he knows he cannot retract. What will greet him when he comes back from battle? Will it be one of his sheep or goats? Jephthah wins the war, and the haftarah ends.

It is the section not read in synagogues that introduces his daughter. In verse 34, Jephthah returns from battle and his daughter, known only as *Bat-Jephthah*, the daughter of Jephthah, comes to greet him. She greets her father with timbrels in her hands. She is dancing and rejoicing at the sight of her father returning in victory from battle. Her actions are honorable, loving, and normative. It was the custom of ancient Israelite women to greet their men returning from battle by going out in the street and welcoming them with song.[1] It seems reasonable that, given this custom, Jephthah might have guessed his daughter would come greet him. Why, then, would he make such a potentially dangerous vow?

The verse continues, "And she was *his only*, besides her, he had no other son or daughter" (emphasis added). The narrator pointedly releases information about Bat-Jephthah, and this information heightens our sensitivity to her fate and the injustice of her father's vow. The first part of the sentence—that she is his only child—seems to reflect the fact that besides her he had no son or daughter. Why do we need both parts of the sentence if the first would suffice? Why is her being the only child emphasized? *Metzudat David* explains that Jephthah's wife had children from a first husband, but Jephthah had no other child but this one. So the emphasis is necessary, or the reader might think that the wife's children from the first marriage were also

Jephthah's children. They are not. He had only one child. Only Bat-Jephthah.

Looking back to Genesis 22:2 we find God instructing Abraham: "Take your son, *your only* one" (emphasis added). The same Hebrew word for *only* is used in both stories. Bat-Jephthah and Isaac are both referred to as the *yehid* (masculine) and *yehida* (feminine) of the father. They are both the children of fathers who were willing to sacrifice them to prove their loyalty to God.

Yet, aside from their status as only children, the lives and fates of Isaac and Bat-Jephthah are nearly opposite. We know a great deal about Isaac. We know very little about Bat-Jephthah. Isaac is the male child with a proper name. Isaac is thirty-seven years old; his age can be deduced from the biblical accounts in Genesis 25. Isaac's life will be the fulfillment of God's promise to Abraham that his descendants will be as innumerable as the stars in heaven (Gen. 15:5). In Judges, the child is a female, with no name. There is no way to figure out her age. Her death is the fulfillment of a man's vow to God, with not one descendant. In Genesis, Isaac's life is saved. In Judges, Bat-Jephthah's life is not.

One could only imagine the terror the ancient audience experienced when it heard this story of Bat-Jephthah. It was the same terror Jephthah experiences as the text continues with Judges 11:35: "For when he saw her, he rent his clothes and said, 'Woe, my daughter, you have brought me to my knees, you have troubled me, for I have opened my mouth to God and I cannot go back.'" The rending of the clothes and falling to the floor are ancient signs of mourning, and Judaism today still retains vestiges of these traditions.[2]

Jephthah starts mourning for his living child, whom he has doomed to die at his own hands. Bat-Jephthah does not protest, but she does negotiate with her father. She asks to go away for two months to be with her friends and weep for her youth. Her request is granted.

We do not know where Bat-Jephthah went, or what she did, or even with whom she went. We do not know if her leaving was a ploy to encourage her father to change his mind. Maybe he would miss her so much that he would not carry out his vow at the end of the two months. There is an audible silence in this text. Did no one protest this human sacrifice? Did no one come to her defense? Was a whole community silent? Did that silence condone this violence?

Two months pass. Bat-Jephthah returns to her father. The text does not tell us, as it does in Genesis, that the father built an altar, piled up the wood, placed his daughter on the wood, and stood over her with a blade raised in his hands. Perhaps the writer of Judges is subtly protesting this human sacrifice by never explicitly stating that Jephthah killed his daughter, or that his daughter died. We are left to fill in those blanks when we read: "He did to her by his vow that he vowed" (Judg. 11:39). The Rabbis, discomforted by the possibility of a human sacrifice, suggest that Jephthah should have offered a monetary consecration in place of his daughter.[3] The next verse concludes the chapter by informing us that "It was custom in Israel for the daughters of Israel to go and mourn for the daughter of Jephthah for four days each year."

We do not know where they went—perhaps to the same place Bat-Jephthah went, a place long since forgotten. It is a place and a ritual that does not exist in our books, as Bat-Jephthah's story does not exist in our haftarah. Her story would never come to light in the synagogue unless we, like the ancient Israelite women who annually mourned her fate, make sure that her story survives. We must redeem her story every year, so her life and death have meaning.

How many more anonymous women, women whose lives and deaths are taken for granted, remain hidden from us? We shall never know. The challenge of including Bat-Jephthah's story as part of the haftarah is that we, as a community, must face the awful fact that child sacrifice might have actively existed in ancient Israel long after the story of Abraham and Isaac taught us not to sacrifice our children. We might have to wonder about a father willing to kill his own daughter to prove he can fulfill a vow to God. We might speculate about the Israelite men who accepted Jephthah as judge of Israel after murdering his own daughter. We might question the women who mourned Bat-Jephthah annually but were silent or silenced during her lifetime.

When Bat-Jephthah is not mentioned on *Shabbat Chukkat*, we participate in the conspiracy of silence that glorifies Jephthah's military victory, while negating his responsibility to his daughter. Then it is our responsibility to give voice to her story and acknowledge that violence is condoned through secrecy.

RABBI JANE KANAREK

הפטרת בלק
Haftarat Balak

Micah 5:6–6:8

*F*or I brought you up out of the land of Egypt,
I redeemed you from the house of slaves,
And I sent before you Moses, Aaron, and Miriam.
(MICAH 6:4)

WE BEGIN OUR STORY of Miriam in a dream, a life-giving dream of richness and redemption. Pharaoh's cup bearer, imprisoned, has a dream
that he cannot interpret. He dreams of a vine with three branches
that blossoms, its clusters immediately ripening into grapes. Under
the interpretive imagination of the ancient Rabbis, this dream
becomes a vision of Israel's future redemption from slavery. The vine
is Israel. The three branches are Moses, Aaron, and Miriam. The act of
blossoming is the arrival of Israel's redemption.[1] Who is this woman
who appears in a dream as a savior to all Israel hundreds of years before
her birth?

In the haftarah of Balak, the prophet Micah provides us with a tantalizing hint of Miriam's greatness as a leader, a greatness that God cites
as proof of God's unceasing care for the Jews. God condemns those
among the Jews who use sorcery and worship idols, and Micah exhorts
not only the people but the entire earth to listen to God's case against
Israel. Arguing defensively, God dares the people to name any way that
God has caused them hardship. In place of travails, God has only acted
righteously: God brought them out of Egypt, sent before them Moses,

Aaron, and Miriam, defeated King Balak, and enabled them to cross the Jordan. Such acts merit loyalty, not the worship of foreign gods. Miriam's leadership, then, as the dream predicted, is one of the reasons that God merits Israel's everlasting devotion.

Miriam is mentioned by name seven times in the Bible.[2] Tradition also accepts her as the nameless sister who watches her brother Moses from a distance, when their mother hides him in the Nile. Despite this sevenfold mention, the prophet Micah is the only biblical figure who presents her as a leader alongside her siblings, Moses and Aaron. Even more strongly, he uses a verb—*shalach*, "to send"—typically used in connection with a prophet or a Divine messenger.[3] In a similar historical passage in I Samuel 12:6–8, the prophet Samuel lists only Moses and Aaron as the leaders whom God sends to bring the Israelites out of Egypt. Yet the tracings of her biblical story do reveal Miriam's centrality to the Exodus and desert narratives. Even more, a filling-in of that outline with rabbinic traditions about her life will enable us to imagine why Micah, in contrast to others, includes her as a paradigmatic leader.

According to one midrash, Shifrah and Puah, the two midwives who refuse to follow Pharaoh's decree to kill the male newborns, are none other than Yocheved and her daughter Miriam. The word *puah* means "to blow" or "to cry out." Practicing a tradition passed down from mother to daughter, Miriam knew from a young age the art of bringing life into the world. She would make the sound *puah* to the child as it came forth from the womb, with her breath, comforting and delighting that new life as it emerged. Perhaps she continued to practice the art of midwifery in the desert and taught it to other women.[4]

According to another reading found in the same passage, Miriam's other name, *Puah*, literally encoded her prophetic abilities: She would cry out her Divine knowledge that her mother was destined to bear the child who would one day save Israel. It is in the surety of this knowledge that we see Miriam demonstrating one of the traits vital to a leader: outspokenness in the face of injustice. The Rabbis write that when Pharaoh decreed that all male newborns be thrown into the Nile, Amram decided to divorce his wife Yocheved. Never having any more children, they would be spared the horror of carrying out Pharaoh's decree. The men follow Amram's example and also divorce their wives. But Miriam chastises her father, telling him that his decree is even more severe than that of Pharaoh's. "Pharaoh," she says, "decreed only against the males, but you have made a decree against males and females alike." On hearing her words, Amram remarries Yocheved. The other men then also remarry their wives.[5] This reunion of Amram and Yocheved results in Moses' birth. With the courage to speak harshly to her father, her elder, Miriam can see what he cannot. Not only does she know that a male savior will be born to her family, but she also understands that even if the Egyptians succeed in killing some of the boys, girls will be born and girls will live. They will one day give birth, and they will one day pass on the traditions of her people to their children. As a midwife, Miriam knows that one death-bearing decree must not be responded to with another and that life, even in the face of terror, must continue. So when Moses is hidden in the Nile, Miriam stands guard over him from afar to see if he will live.

But Miriam also recognizes that resistance against terror comes through planning for joy. Miriam first appears by name in the biblical narrative when she leads the women in song and dance in celebration of the Israelites' crossing of the Reed Sea. "Miriam the prophet, the sister of Aaron, took a timbrel in her hand and all the women came after her, with timbrels and dances. Miriam sung to them, 'Sing to God for God has triumphed, horse and rider God has hurled into the sea'" (Exod. 15:20–21). Where, though, did the women get these timbrels in the desert? As Exodus 12:34 informs us, the Israelites had to leave Egypt in such haste that there was not even time for their bread to rise. We can imagine that Miriam had the forethought to instruct the women that when the moment came to leave Egypt, no matter what they took with them, they had to carry instruments of song. The way will be a hard one, she must have warned them, and to survive we will need to sing, for it is not by bread alone that people are sustained. Following their leader, the women brought timbrels and danced at the sea in celebration, praising God.

The tradition records that in reward for Miriam's Song at the Sea, the people merited a miraculous well that followed them in the desert as long as Miriam lived.[6] As a result of the well, the desert flowered, bringing forth figs, grapes, and pomegranates.[7] These fruits are the same ones that God promises will grow in the Land of Israel. Miriam comprehends that the people need spiritual sustenance on their long journey. Because she sustains them with joy, God in turn sustains them with food, food that acts as a reminder of the redemptive goal of their travels.

Like all leaders, Miriam's actions are watched and judged in minute detail. Numbers 12 records the troubling story of Miriam and Aaron's outspokenness against Moses because of his marriage to a Cushite woman. The biblical text is enigmatic about their accusation, but what is clear is that Miriam is punished more severely than Aaron by the infliction of leprosy upon her. Responding to the use of a singular verb—*va-tedaber*, "and she said"—when the plural "and they said" would have been more appropriate, Rashi explains her punishment by citing the tradition that it was Miriam who first spoke evil words about Moses because he had separated from his wife Zipporah.[8] Perhaps Moses' action reminds her of their father's earlier divorce of their mother, and, seeing the same conduct, the same loss of future life from her brother, she quickly speaks out against him.

However, her critical conduct is now an example for all those journeying in the desert, and it is as a leader that she is judged. As the Sifrei observes: Miriam's words about Moses were spoken not in his presence, but rather privately, for his benefit, in praise of the Holy One, and for the sake of building the world. If even with all this to her credit God chastises her, all the more so will God punish a person who publicly derogates another.[9] Miriam is an effective reminder to the people precisely because they consider her their leader. In fact, she is so much their leader that the people refuse to continue on their journey until God heals her of the leprosy and she can rejoin the camp. She is, in the image of the cup-bearer's dream, one of the branches upon whom the people depend.

Why, then, Miriam's unique mention here by the prophet Micah as a leader of the people? The haftarah concludes with the famous exhortation in Micah 6:8 that what God demands of us is to do justice, love goodness, and walk humbly with God. Miriam, as a leader, has done all three. She has done justice by demanding that her parents challenge Pharaoh's decree, and by rebuking her brother privately to Aaron. She has loved goodness by bringing comfort to all the children she brought into the world, those in Egypt and those in the desert, and by telling the women to bring musical instruments with them on the arduous desert journey, and by leading them in song. She has walked humbly by hiding in the bulrushes to watch her brother and by accepting her punishment, yet continuing as the people's leader. As the ancient dream predicted, Miriam has led and sustained her people on the long journey of liberation out of Egypt, through the desert, and up to the borders of the Promised Land.

RABBI SUSAN P. FENDRICK

הפטרת פינחס

Haftarat Pinchas

I Kings 18:46–19:21

*A*nd after the fire, a still, small voice. (I KINGS 19:12)

IT IS TRADITIONAL when studying Torah to examine all the possible connections, both obvious and not, between a given Torah portion and its assigned haftarah reading. In the case of *Haftarat Pinchas*, one thematic connection between it and *Parashat Pinchas* stands out clearly, but we shall see another connection of special interest to women.

Parashat Pinchas is chiefly associated with the character after whom it is named, Pinchas, although his fame (or infamy) is established at the end of the preceding portion, *Parashat Balak*. There Pinchas fatally stabs a man and his Moabite or Midianite lover, in connection with the idol worship toward which these nations had enticed the Israelites. Pinchas's actions ostensibly stave off a far more severe plague than the one the Israelites would soon suffer.

In *Haftarat Pinchas*, too, we find zeal on God's behalf displayed by Elijah the prophet. Here, too, the Israelite nation has gone astray—and here, too, a foreign woman is at the core of their idolatry. Queen Jezebel, the wife of King Ahab, has persuaded him and his people to worship Ba'al, either a false or a competing god to YHVH.

While Pinchas acts on his own initiative—the rabbinic tradition

195

walks a fine line between praising his intervention and warning that it is not to be imitated or repeated[1]—Elijah is on a Divine mission, sent to turn the Israelites from their idol worship to the worship of the One God. He is demoralized at the difficulty of his task, and God strengthens his resolve, encouraging him to eat and drink to fortify himself for the ongoing, difficult prophetic challenge of turning people from sin to sanctity. Elijah's retreat to Mount Horeb, associated with the same mountain called Sinai elsewhere in the Hebrew Bible, is one of forty days and forty nights, echoing Moses' journey up the mountain. This association further reinforces Elijah's greatness by connecting him to the greatest of all Jewish prophets.

Like *Parashat Pinchas*—and because of its connection to it—*Haftarat Pinchas* might easily be known as the story of a great man taking up a difficult task in defense of the Holy One. But its teachings are greater and deeper, its lessons less dramatic but no less profound.

There on Mount Horeb, God appears to Elijah, asking him, "*Mah l'cha po, Eliyahu*—Why are you here?" I Kings 19:10 reports Elijah's answer—an answer he will give a second time, in exactly the same words again in 19:14: "I have been very zealous for YHVH, the God of hosts, for the children of Israel have forsaken Your covenant, thrown down Your altars, and slain Your prophets with the sword. And I alone am left, and they seek my life, to take it away."

Why does God ask Elijah again at the end of verse 13, "*Mah l'cha po, Eliyahu?*" And what are we to make of the fact that Elijah's reply is identical in every way? What happens in the intervening verses suggests the reason that the question must be asked a second time. The next verses demonstrate the weakness of even the great prophet Elijah in offering an identical answer, and—most important for our purposes—hint at a path of listening and responding that Elijah implicitly rejects, but that Jewish feminists must embrace and teach as a Jewish response.

The first time Elijah describes why he is in retreat, demoralized by the difficulty of his work and daunted by the task before him, how does God respond?

> And behold, YHVH passed by, and a great and strong
> wind split mountains, and shattered rocks before YHVH;
> but YHVH was not in the wind. And after the wind, an
> earthquake, but YHVH was not in the earthquake. And
> after the earthquake, a fire, but YHVH was not in the fire;
> and after the fire a *kol d'mama daka* [commonly translat-
> ed as "a still, small voice"]. And so it was, when Elijah
> heard it, that he wrapped his face in his mantle, and went
> out, and stood in the entrance of the cave [in which he
> had been lodging]. (I Kings 19:11–13)

While in verse 9 it had been "the word of YHVH" that came to
him—*v'hinei d'var YHVH elav*—now with a small change it is simply "a
voice"—*v'hinei elav kol.*

The words *kol d'mama daka* have invited many translations over the
years, including the best-known "a still, small voice," but also "a sound
of gentle stillness" and "a still voice of silence." Whatever it was, and
whatever it might have sounded like to others had they heard it, the
kol d'mama daka appears to have absolutely no effect on Elijah. The
wind, the earthquake, and then the stillness neither transform nor move
Elijah. What we have instead is a striking *lack* of transformation.

We might imagine that Elijah, like Pinchas who favored grand gestures over subtle action, felt the great wind and the splitting of the
mountains and the shattering rocks. He experienced the earthquake
and lived through the fire, and perceived in these dramatic actions
the God he knew himself to be serving, missing entirely the fact that
God was indeed not in the wind, nor in the earthquake, nor the fire.
And after the fire came a *kol d'mama daka*—a voice of quiet and stillness, modified by no such disclaimer. Elijah could not see, could not
hear what we as readers cannot help hearing: God crying out to him
through a voice of stillness. It is as if God wants Elijah to understand
that, as the author of Ecclesiastes might have put it, "There is a time for
great gestures, and there is a time for gentle voices." This was God's
message to Elijah: Not only by mighty acts can God be known. God is
often known in the quietude *after* the greatness.

The second *"Mah l'cha po?"* might better be understood as: "Elijah, *now* what do you have here? What have you seen, felt, learned here in this manifestation of the Divine? What has this meant to you?" The text, as it were, "knows" that there is something significant in the *kol*, the voice, because this second time it is not the "word of YHVH" but "a voice" that calls to him. But Elijah himself cannot hear the difference, does not understand that God is giving him an opening to see things in a different way.

Elijah's identical response indicates that he has not been changed by his experience. And God, recognizing the limitations of even one of God's greatest prophets, realizes that it is time for Elijah to have a successor. After Elijah offers this second response using the same words, God tells him, among other things, to anoint Elisha in Elijah's place. Perhaps relieved, perhaps realizing himself that it was time, Elijah does so swiftly and without hesitation.

The *kol d'mama daka*: What is this gentle voice that Elijah didn't hear, didn't understand as the voice of the Divine? The search for an answer brings us back to *Parashat Pinchas*, and to a story of women raising their own voices. While the *parashah* begins with the conclusion of the story of Pinchas, it has at its center two brief but significant stories: one of women seeking justice, and the other of Moses anointing his own successor.

The daughters of Zelophehad—Mahlah, Noa, Hoglah, Milcah, and Tirzah—bring a case before Moses. Their father has died, leaving behind no sons, and they want to inherit their father's property rather than having it all go to their male relatives, which was the legal norm at the time. Moses immediately brings their case to God's attention, and God responds by saying that indeed these daughters should receive a share of their father's inheritance, along with his other relatives. Moreover, the law in general is to be changed: If a man has no sons, his daughters shall inherit.

From our position many years later, it seems like a small gain. It affects only one family, and the results are hardly revolutionary, since women are to inherit only in the event that they have no brothers.

Yet when we see the similarity between God's next instruction to Moses and God's last instruction to Elijah in *Haftarat Pinchas*, we know something else about the *kol d'mama daka* that Elijah missed. The *kol d'mama daka* is the voice of the Divine heard not only in the grand sweep of nation building and in the dramatic gestures of those zealous on God's behalf; the *kol d'mama daka* is heard wherever we take seriously questions of justice and ethics, where the claims of even a few are heard as so important that God might care about them, and where change is possible even if it does not achieve everything in a moment.

Moses knew all this, and responded in a way that Elijah did not. Therefore God's instruction to him to appoint Joshua as his successor is not, as in the case of Elijah, a recognition of his limitations, but rather an illustration that a person's life work can reach its pinnacle not just in the great moments, but in small moments of listening and responsiveness. For his part, Elijah, like Pinchas, was only comfortable in one mode—the dramatic and the grand. Moses' greatness lay in his ability to lead in different ways in response to different needs. Hearing the *kol d'mama daka*—knowing God and acting as God's emissary in the smaller moments—was perhaps more than Elijah could do.

While contemporary Jewish feminists may at times long for and work for swifter change and revolutionary transformation, we also know too well the hard and holy work of listening slowly to the quieter voices in our midst, pressing for justice and change in small yet sacred ways, and recognizing in them the voice of the Divine. This challenges us to act in the Divine image as it appeared to Elijah: to hear—and sometimes to speak with—a *kol d'mama daka*, a gentle, still, passionate voice.

RABBI RACHEL R. BOVITZ

הפטרת מטות
Haftarat Mattot

Jeremiah 1:1–2:3

*B*efore I created you in the womb, I knew you. And before you emerged from the womb, I sanctified you, I appointed you a prophet for the nations.
(JEREMIAH 1:4–5)

HAFTARAT MATTOT, with its moving scene of Jeremiah's Divine commission,[1] returns us to an era when the leaders of the Jewish people were prophets ordained by God. Since the destruction of the Second Temple, however, Jewish leaders have been appointed through rabbinic academies. Unlike many Christian denominations, which maintain that God is involved in a clergyperson's "calling to the ministry," in the Jewish faith, rabbinical candidates self-select to apply to seminaries with the goal of serving as leaders of their people.

While we have been blessed with great leaders who have sought to be "teachers and sages in Israel,"[2] the self-selection system does not ensure that the greatest number of potential leaders will serve our Jewish communities in the future. There are many reasons exceptional individuals may not nominate themselves for the rabbinate, including lack of confidence in their abilities, fear of the unknown, and a general hesitancy to self-promote. Because many of these potential leaders do not self-select, we miss the benefit of a full pool of potential leaders. We may miss out on a significant segment of people who could make important contributions to our local and global communities.

ᴀ One-on-One Solution from Jeremiah

We hear a solution to this problem reverberating in God's words to Jeremiah—a call for meaningful mentorship of the next generation of Jewish and secular leaders alike. In fact, it may be *only* through mentorship that we can ensure that the greatest number of talented leaders will emerge.

This is especially true for women, who are still so new to many vocations. A number of contemporary articles and books have pointed to the value of professional mentorship by women for women. Researcher and author Carolyn Duff speaks of the unique female mentoring relationship:

> Fostering is a term that frequently comes up when women probe the meaning and potential of woman-to-woman learning connections. . . . She fosters when she cares about another's vision and encourages her to realize her vision. . . . Woman-to-woman mentoring encompasses the benefits and values of both mentoring, in the traditional sense, and fostering.[3]

So let us consider the notion of women mentoring women for positions of leadership. What does this entail? We can glean some guiding principles for mentoring from God's commissioning of Jeremiah. Although there are only a brief seven verses that speak to this experience, they reveal an exemplary model.

> And the word of YHVH came upon me saying: Before I created you in the womb, I knew you. And before you emerged from the womb, I sanctified you, I appointed you a prophet for the nations.

> And I said, "Alas, my master YHVH, I really don't know how to speak, because I am just a young man."

> And YHVH said to me: Don't say I am just a young man, for all that I send you to do you will go about doing, and

201

all that I command you, you will speak. Don't be afraid in front of them, because I am with you in order to save you, says YHVH.

And YHVH sent his hand out toward me and touched my mouth.

And YHVH said to me: Here, I have put my words in your mouth. See that I have assigned you this day over the nations and kingdoms to pull up and break down, to destroy and to tear down, to build and to plant. (Jer. 1:4–10)

This text reminds us that we may have in our midst a number of women who see themselves as Jeremiah did. And we are reminded that for those women who may not radiate self-assurance or excel at self-promotion, a mentoring relationship can be particularly crucial. As God does with Jeremiah, we must challenge these women with a mission we know they are both capable of and destined to achieve. It follows that the community benefits when we seek out and mentor this new source of potential leaders.

Returning to the Womb and Identifying Specialness

How can one encourage a talented woman to consider a profession that may appear too daunting to attempt? Again, God's mentorship of Jeremiah provides some important tips. For example, to illustrate that Jeremiah has been predestined for prophetic leadership, God does not remind Jeremiah of merits from his childhood or teenage years, but instead recalls for him his earliest identity, as an embryo in his mother's womb. God points to Jeremiah's unique essence as the main reason he should become the moral leader of the Jewish people. And in anticipation of Jeremiah's reluctance to accept his new, powerful role, God's statement is fourfold: "I created you, knew you, sanctified you, and appointed you." It forms a compelling argument: If you believe in me, you must believe in yourself. The effect is to make God's claim of Jeremiah's potential for leadership indisputable.

Similarly, the first step for woman-to-woman mentoring is for the mentor to articulate to her protégé the latter's intrinsic value and worth. Our Jewish tradition maintains that every person is made in the image of God and therefore is holy and special. Moreover, as God said to Jeremiah, each of us is created by God, known by God, sanctified by God, and thus well positioned to assume an important role in this world. Finally, just as God persuaded Jeremiah to look deep within himself, a good mentor will help a potential candidate understand that her unique essence may be destined for a kind of greatness she may not have envisioned on her own.

Another important hint about effective mentoring can be found in the Jeremiah story's use of the womb as a female metaphor. The womb imagery implies that Jeremiah's first experience with God is nurturing and life-giving. Inside the womb a fetus develops and grows, shielded from the outside world and its impending challenges. So, too, a woman mentor should provide a safe environment for her protégé to grow and learn before facing larger and more critical audiences. With this nurturing support, a woman enters the "jungle out there" with confidence and experience.

It is also noteworthy that God tells Jeremiah "I knew you" while in the womb. As biblical scholar Angela Bauer points out, "The root *y-d-ay*, 'to know,' connotes intimacy, and is used frequently in covenant language. So, beyond intellectual knowledge, God's 'knowing' of Jeremiah embodies a closeness that will characterize their interactions throughout the book."[4] Similarly, developing a true closeness with the woman we are mentoring is also a crucial step; we form our own kind of covenant.

Touching the Mouth and Giving Voice

In the story, God touches Jeremiah's mouth to give him the words he will need. Interestingly, there is another reference to this depiction of the prophet-God relationship in Jewish tradition. The Talmud speaks of a similar experience occurring at the birth of every child:

> [While in utero] they [the angels] teach it [the unborn child] the entire body of God's teachings. . . . When it comes out into the air of the world, an angel arrives and strikes it on its mouth and this causes the baby to forget the entire body of God's teachings.[5]

Accordingly, we each have hidden somewhere within us *kol hatorah kula*—the entirety of Torah. The general human experience is to forget that we have God's teachings within us. But there is hope in this lesson as well. Note that the wording is explicit. The entirety of Torah is not *destroyed* at the moment of birth, but merely *forgotten*, lost in the depths of our souls when as infants we awaken to the world around us. As we acquire wisdom throughout our lives, we seem to regain bits and pieces of that deeper knowledge that was lost to us. This may be why we often have some faint sense of having "heard that before." At these moments our greatest learning resonates with the forgotten teachings of the womb.

This notion—that there is "the entirety of Torah" within us, that this great gift merely lies dormant and hidden, like a frequency that we can't quite hear unassisted—has some key implications for mentoring. Think of the person who needs our help in realizing her true inner value. As we mature, we all tend to realize how little we know. For some, this awareness can be motivating, while others find it paralyzing. Mentoring can help someone overcome this paralysis. It can facilitate the discovery or the rediscovery of her own inner voice. A good mentor helps her protégé find her authentic self, her inner wisdom, and the confidence to display both.

Unlike God in Jeremiah's commissioning, a mentor does not put the words into her subject's mouth. Her goal is not to duplicate herself. Instead, a mentor reinforces the talmudic understanding that riches lie within each of us. Having been guided to this awareness, a potential leader who has previously not recognized her talents will be far more likely to give voice to her ideas, her inner Torah.

Imitating God and Ushering in New Prophecy

As Jews, we dream of one day ushering in a messianic age of peace and harmony on earth. Yet we also simultaneously work on creating a better world in the here and now, through acts of loving-kindness and following God's mitzvot. We rely on the leaders of our community to inspire and direct us in this mission of *tikkun olam*, healing the world. Since God no longer speaks directly through chosen prophets, we must dedicate ourselves to enabling ethical, courageous, and thoughtful leaders to speak to us. We must seek out women whose inner wisdom may be hidden from us. And if they are reluctant, we have an obligation to encourage and mentor them to fulfill their potential to join the ranks of our leadership in the future.

Even more so than Jeremiah, Moses was a reluctant leader–turned–great prophet. God spoke to both of these men and made them aware of their inherent abilities to direct and serve the Jewish people. Through loving mentorship, we can inspire more women and men to realize and bring forth their talent, wisdom, and compassion. This will bring greater leadership to the Jewish community, as well as to our world at large. God may no longer speak through prophets. But through mentorship that assures us a greater diversity of new leaders, we may yet experience prophecy in our own day.

RABBI JENNIFER ELKIN GORMAN

הפטרת מסעי

Haftarat Ma'asei

Jeremiah 2:4–28; 3:4

*F*or two evils My people have done; they left Me, the
Source of Living Water, to carve for themselves cisterns, broken cisterns, which cannot hold water.

**Although you wash with lye and use soap, the stain
of your guilt is before Me, says the Lord God.**
(JEREMIAH 2:13, 22)

HAFTARAT MA'ASEI is one of only a few haftarot that do not relate to the
weekly *parashah*, but instead to their occurrence in the calendar. The
middle of the three haftarot of admonition, *Haftarat Ma'asei* is read
during one of the Shabbatot between the seventeenth of Tammuz and
the Ninth of Av, a period called *Bein HaMitzarim*. *Bein HaMitzarim*
literally means "between the straits," but is also a reference to labor and
childbirth. When a woman is in full, active labor, she is said to be *bein
hamitzarim*. The theme of the haftarah is one of rejection of God's
covenant in favor of the sin of idolatry. One might therefore ask, "How
is it that the time leading up to the destruction of Jerusalem and the
Holy Temple is named after the labor for childbirth, which brings life?"

In any true labor there is a turning point toward the end result.
In childbirth this is appropriately called *transition*, when labor moves
from a preliminary point into active childbirth. This is a critical time.
Birth cannot occur without it; however, if it proceeds adversely, there

206

will be dire consequences for the mother and the new life still inside her. From this point we move toward a new life or, if complications arise, death for the mother and/or the child. In the middle of *Haftarat Ma'asei*, Jeremiah, speaking for God, laments, "They left Me, the Source of Living Water, to carve for themselves cisterns, broken cisterns, which cannot hold water." Here is our transition, our turning point. In the middle of *Bein HaMitzarim*, in the middle of the middle haftarah, we read of Israel's denial and forsaking of God. What stands out in this verse is the name used for God, *M'kor Mayim Hayyim*, the Source of Living Water. *Mayim Hayyim* is also the highest level of mikveh.[1]

The laws of mikveh are found in Leviticus 15. These laws deal with spiritual reentry into the community for anyone with a bodily emission, such as menstruation or ejaculation. The means by which one is spiritually cleansed is by bathing in water, specifically in the water of a mikveh. Over time, the requirement of mikveh remained only for women after menstruating. As such, it is the only mitzvah that can truly be called a women's mitzvah.

In reading this haftarah, we can see God, the Source of Living Water, calling out through the prophet in order to reestablish the covenant. In reclaiming mikveh in a positive way, women can continuously restore our connection to *M'kor Mayim Hayyim*. Through the prophet, God reaffirms our covenant; so too do women reaffirm a unique covenant through mikveh. As Tikva Frymer Kensky writes:

> In considering child-bearing, two Jewish themes seem to cry out for such reinterpretation [to be brought into the sanctified realm of Judaism]. One is the biblical notion of covenants sealed in blood, both the blood of the covenant of circumcision, and the sprinkling of the people with the "blood of covenant" as they accepted the covenant of Sinai. Menstrual blood should also be seen as a sign of the covenant, the covenant between God and woman, by which women become and continue to be the bearers and shapers of new life. God affirms this covenant

in the blood of menarche, and women affirm it as they undertake a pregnancy.[2]

Women can also affirm this covenant outside of pregnancy when we attend mikveh, for with our attendance we reaffirm our partnership with God through a return to M'kor Mayim Hayyim. "Being in a mikveh is a state of suspended animation between past and future. We are asked to trust that the water, as symbol of the source of life, offers an opportunity for spiritual regeneration."[3]

It is especially appropriate that the reference to M'kor Mayim Hayyim is found in the middle of the middle haftarah during Bein HaMitzarim. When we act as in Jeremiah, rejecting M'kor Mayim Hayyim, we reject the cycle of holiness, purification, and covenant. The transition takes its turn for the worse. We are left with death and destruction, as follows in the days leading up to Tisha B'Av and the destruction of the Temple. However, following this time is a seven-week period of nechemta, of comfort, of teshuvah (repentance), and of rebirth, leading up to the Yamim Noraim (High Holy Days), and especially Yom Kippur. At this time we are given a chance as a people to renew our covenant with God, and on Yom Kippur God renews the covenant with us. Appropriately, the month of Elul is a time many choose to attend the mikveh, to cleanse themselves in preparation for the new year, a time of spiritual rebirth.

For women, mikveh can be more than an annual opportunity. Attendance at the mikveh can be a monthly appointment with God, a connection to the yearly cycle, and to the generational cycle. "It is a tangible connection to past, present, and future generations in a uniquely woman's way, as well as a link to other women across space and time today."[4] Additionally, attendance at the mikveh requires women to learn to tend to their bodies, as well as to their souls. Among mikveh-observant women, attendance at the mikveh is often the time for their monthly breast self-exam. Indeed, many mikvaot have posters on how to perform a self-exam. One may also find flyers from abuse hotlines.

Mikveh is ripe as a source for new rituals surrounding women, their sexuality, and their fertility. It can be used as a tool for recovery, reconnection with God, and the reclaiming of one's sexuality after rape or abuse. Rather than leaving God, the Source of Living Water, mikveh can provide an acceptance of God back into one's life. Where soap and harsh cleansers cannot clean away sin or guilt, the water of the mikveh can provide a womb from which to be reborn. It can provide a healing experience after surgery or in conjunction with fertility treatments. It can act as a reclaiming of one's body after birth. It can also be an expression of gratitude.

As this middle haftarah leads the calendar through *Bein HaMitzarim*, we can see in the imagery of labor, stillbirth, and death a way to reclaim God through the act of mikveh. We can look toward the period of *nechemta* and Elul, renewing our covenant with M'*kor Mayim Hayyim*, the Source of Living Water, through all the frightening, and enriching, transitions of our lives.

Devarim/Deuteronomy

הפטרת דברים

Haftarat Devarim

Isaiah 1:1–27

*A*las, she has become a harlot, the faithful city, that was filled with justice. (ISAIAH 1:21)

*E*very Jew carries her/his own Jerusalem within her/his heart. (LEVI ESHKOL)

ON THE THREE SHABBATOT that precede the commemoration of the destruction of the First and the Second Temple of Jerusalem, the prophets Jeremiah and Isaiah warn the people of Israel about the consequences of sin. Rabbinic literature refers to the period from the seventeenth of Tammuz to the ninth of Av as *bein haMitzarim*, "between the straits." Those are three weeks of admonition. The city of Jerusalem feels the desolation of this terrible event and she is abandoned by her people. She becomes imagined as a prostitute, crying out of her anguish and sorrow. Who is Jerusalem? What happened to her? Why is it that the prophet Isaiah in *Haftarat Devarim* declares: "Alas, she has become a harlot, the faithful city, that was filled with justice"? (Isa. 1:21).

In II Samuel 5:7–9, we learn that "David took the stronghold of Zion the City of David, and David dwelt in the stronghold." Since then, Jerusalem has historically been the centerpiece of Jewish spiritual topography. Jerusalem is more than a place and a location, it is immaculate, pristine, unique, a bride, a queen, respectable, and decent. How terrible, then, to imagine this clean, wholesome city as a common prostitute! Jerusalem is almost always referred to in the feminine by the prophets. What makes this city seductive enough to be compared to a woman?

The Sages of the Talmud offered an explanation: "Abram called the site *Yireh* (Gen. 22:14), which means 'God will see and protect the City.' Shem, son of Noach, called the same site *Shalem*, which means complete, whole, and perfect. From these two names, the name *Yerushalayim*, 'Jerusalem,' was formed."[1] Is Jerusalem a female because of the combination of wholeness and being within the protective sight of God? Or perhaps Jerusalem is a She-City because of her beauty: "One who has not seen Jerusalem in her glory has never seen a beautiful city."[2] Or perhaps, Jerusalem is a She because of the combination of laughter and tears, calmness and passion, conquests and invasions, pleasure and pain. Often we imagine the feminine as being unique, able to envelop all these contradictions.

Jerusalem is also a symbol of the love between husband and wife, between God and God's people, and the connection of engagement and consecration in the covenant of love. The Shulchan Arukh notes: "When a man marries a woman, he takes a bit of ash and smears it on his forehead, and in some communities he breaks a glass under the bridal canopy. All these measures are taken to remember Jerusalem, as is written, 'If I forget thee, O Jerusalem, may my right hand forget its cunning'" (Ps. 137:5).[3]

Jerusalem became the protected place, the untouchable capital of God's presence; in essence, the favored daughter. Jerusalem became the *Shekhinah*, the dwelling of the Jewish people, a shelter. This is expressed in Psalms 122:3: "Jerusalem that is built like a city together." Our Sages in the Talmud explain: "Jerusalem—a city that joins all the Jews together in friendship. Jerusalem unites all elements of the Jewish people and symbolizes our unity. The ingathering of the exiles and the gathering of Jews from all countries, even as a city is reconstructed, is the most tangible expression of unity."[4]

We are dealing here with a mystery: How can an incorporeal God have real involvement with a city? Somehow, as the psalmist declared,

"In Judah God is known" (Ps. 76:2). Zion had become a bridgehead for Divine communication. If the wider world were to be drawn into the knowledge of God, it would come about through Jerusalem in some way: "The law will go out from Zion, the word of the Lord from Jerusalem" (Isa. 2:3).

So the people wondered if the city was inviolable because of the Divine presence there. This perception of the blessed city was promptly denounced by the prophets Micah (3:12) and Jeremiah (7:1–15), who instead warned of Divine judgment upon the city. Prophets denounced Jerusalem for her idolatry and disregard of God (Ezek. 8:3) and for her corrupt leaders and oppression of the poor (Jer. 13:13; Mic. 6:9–16). Isaiah compared Jerusalem to Sodom in Isaiah 1:9, and Ezekiel likened the city to an Egyptian prostitute called Oholibah in Ezekiel 23:4. The fall of the city to the Babylonians in 586 B.C.E. then fully vindicated this criticism. God, so Israel came to understand, had acted in judgment against this precious city. Because God's beloved gift had been abused, it had been taken away. Jerusalem was clearly not immune. God's presence, God's holiness, was not a talisman. Rather, it was a call to righteousness. The presence of God in Jerusalem was conditional, and upon understanding this, the people lament having taken God's favor for granted.

Jerusalem is now seen as a harlot not because she chose to be one, but as a consequence of her abandonment. Jerusalem the favored daughter is now an uncovered whore, a wife gone bad. Yet the haftarah cries out to her: "Your husband will not abandon you, your children will return and your nakedness will be covered with a clothing of peace." Through our daily prayers we try to persuade her husband: "Have mercy and return to Jerusalem, Your city. May your presence dwell there as You have promised. Build it now; in our days and for all time. Reestablish there the majesty of David, Your servant. Praised are You, Adonai, who builds Jerusalem" (from the *Amidah*).

And when husband and wife—God and Jerusalem—are reunited, beauty once again radiates, unity is once again possible, and, as it says in Lamentations 5:21, "Our days will be renewed as of old."

RABBI SHERYL NOSAN-BLANK

הפטרת ואתחנן
Haftarat Va'etchanan

Isaiah 40:1–26

*G*et yourself up to a high mountain, *m'vaseret*
[female messenger of good tidings] to Zion, raise
your voice with strength, *m'vaseret* to Jerusalem;
fear not . . . (ISAIAH 40:9)

SHE HAS BEEN STANDING, alone, on a high mountaintop, for a very long
time. Before her, she can see Jerusalem, but it is cloaked in a dark,
dense fog. In the distance, through the mist, she can just make out
more remote villages and towns of Judah. Generations have heard her
comforting message, a healing balm for their wounded souls; but the
same generations have refused to see her, intentionally or uninten-
tionally denying her womanly strength, spiritual insight, and wisdom.
Commentators, translators, and grammarians have attempted to veil
and vanquish her, but, throughout, she has remained a steadfast and
faithful woman. Who is this solitary woman, unfailingly providing her
strong, gentle message of comfort and hope?

We meet the messenger in *Haftarat Va'etchanan*, which is read on
Shabbat Nachamu. *Shabbat Nachamu* ("the Shabbat of Comfort") is
the Shabbat immediately following Tisha B'Av. Unlike most other haftarah portions, selected primarily for their thematic relationship to
the weekly Torah portion, *Haftarat Va'etchanan* was selected because of
its proximity to Tisha B'Av. Tisha B'Av is a time of mourning, and
Shabbat Nachamu is a time of comforting. It is named for the first words

216

of the haftarah portion, which are uttered by God: "*Nachamu, nachamu ami*"—"Comfort, comfort my people!"[1] (Isa. 40:1). God's instructions for comforting continue in the next verse, wherein God personifies Jerusalem as an anguished woman:[2] "Speak wholeheartedly[3] to Jerusalem, and declare to her that her term is served, her iniquity is expiated . . ." (Isa. 40:2).

In response, voices call out, on God's behalf, in verses 3 to 8. These Divine voices, which Rashi defines as emanating from *ruach ha-kodesh*, the "Holy Spirit," or *Ha-Kodesh Baruch Hu*, the "Holy, Blessed God," are ultimately *not* the voices that comfort Zion. Rather than relying solely on Divine but disembodied voices of solace, God turns to a messenger of flesh and blood. In verse 9 God calls to the *m'vaseret* (female messenger of good tidings), saying "Get yourself up to a high mountain, *m'vaseret* to Zion, raise your voice with strength, *m'vaseret* to Jerusalem; fear not . . ." (Isa. 40:9).

It is not surprising that God calls on a female messenger to console woeful-woman Jerusalem. In Hebrew grammar, cities are always female and, in the Bible, Jerusalem is frequently referred to as a woman, as in Isaiah 52:1–2 and Lamentations 1:8. Mark E. Biddle asserts that:

> The personification of Lady Jerusalem, sometimes virtuous mother, sometimes widow, sometimes harlot, provides the biblical author with an additional character. While in "objective" terms, she may be a figure representing the people . . . in terms of the dynamics of biblical poetry, her independence and integrity must be recognized and she must be allowed to play out her role in the drama.[4]

Stereotypically, women communicate easily and compassionately with other women. Thus, the female messenger—*m'vaseret*—is the voice the female Jerusalem can hear clearly. It is surprising, then, that the female form for the word for *messenger* occurs nowhere in the entire Bible except here, in Isaiah 40:9. This verse is also the only place where we hear her words. Even more surprising is the consistent, unabashed attempts to hide her as a woman for centuries, while heeding her as a messenger.

The denial or denigration of the *m'vaseret* as a female can be traced to Targum Yonaton. There, *m'vaseret tzion* is translated into Aramaic not as "[female] messenger to Zion," but as "[male] prophets who herald Zion."[5] Rather than recognizing the *m'vaseret* as a woman, Radak and Kimchi explain that the *m'vaseret* is Zion itself, conveying God's message. Ibn Ezra states that *m'vaseret peshat* is certainly not to be understood as female or even as a word written in the feminine grammatical form. Rather, it should be seen as merely a feminine conjugation because it refers to *adah*, meaning "congregation" (a feminine noun in Hebrew). Thus, Ibn Ezra renders the phrase "congregation of Zion" rather than "messenger of Zion" in obvious violation of the text's plain meaning.[6]

Rashi alone contemplates seeing the *m'vaseret* as a woman, but in denigration of the female. In his commentary on verse 9, he reminds us that in Isaiah 52:7 we read, "How beautiful upon the hills are the feet of the *m'vaser* [male messenger]." According to Rashi, the masculine and feminine forms are employed in the two verses to set up a contrast. He explains that if the children of Israel are worthy, God's messenger will come "swift as a male," but if they are not worthy, the messenger will be "weak as a female and will delay 'his' steps until the end."

Even contemporary, liberal scholars appear to be dumbfounded by the notion of the *m'vaseret* being female. Modern commentators ponder the verse and conclude, "The phrase is difficult."[7] But we can see the phrase as quite simple: After the heavenly voices ring out in verses 3 through 8, God calls on a woman to bring comfort to the woeful woman, Jerusalem. The difficulty commentators face is the radical shift to the image of a strong, solitary woman, able to discern and carry the word of God to bring comfort to those in need.

The *m'vaseret's* gift to us is comfort, with a caveat. She has long urged us to be consoled, but as a woman of insight and observation, she sees through the barriers contemporary women build, which may keep us from finding solace. We are educated, empowered, and independent; she reminds us not to let these desirable qualities hinder our healing. Her message seems to be that, unlike God, we haven't "weighed mountains in a scale and hills in a balance" (Isa. 40:12); still, we shouldn't let lack of understanding impede our healing. We may be influential in our spheres, but to God, even the "nations are like a bitter drop from a bucket" (Isa. 40:15); so our pride shouldn't impede our healing either. The messenger realizes that we value our strength and independence, but tells us that if our hearts and souls are open to being comforted, we may be able to hear God call us, and support us, even as "God calls all [the stars] by name . . . and not one is lost" (Isa. 40:26). She tells us that if we are receptive, the Holy One will embrace, nurture, and guide us, "like a shepherd tending the flock, gathering arms-full of lambs and carrying them close to the bosom, gently leading the mother sheep" (Isa. 40:11). The *m'vaseret's* message to modern women is to let our able minds and active hands rest, as we open our hearts to the Comforting Healing Presence of the Holy One.

But just as there are two utterances of *nachamu*—"comfort!"— there are two messages the *m'vaseret* offers us. Her second message is simply offered through her being: Her presence as a woman we can, and must, emulate. As she follows God's command to "get . . . [her]self up to a high mountain" (Isa. 40:9), she models for us the ability to rise above the distractions and demands that can distance us from our Spiritual Source. As she overcomes fear and "raises her voice with power" (Isa. 40:9) to spread truths with conviction and passion, so too must we. Most important, as she is a comforter, so too must we be.

The *m'vaseret* is a partner with God, following the mitzvah of the Compassionate One, to bring comfort. God's message shapes her words, God's direction guides her feet, and perhaps God's help is delivered through her hands. As God comforts Rachel, weeping for her children (Jer. 31:15–19), and as Ruth comforts Naomi, bitter from her losses (Ruth 1:16–17), so does the *m'vaseret* comfort woeful-woman Jerusalem; so too can we comfort those who weep, live in bitterness, or are overcome with woe. When we do so, we too become God's messengers. We can join the newly redeemed and finally visible *m'vaseret,* so that she no longer stands solitary on the mountain, and we ourselves can become messengers of God's comfort.

הפטרת עקב

Haftarat Ekev

Isaiah 49:14–51:3

*W*here is your mother's bill of divorce
    With which I sent her away?
Asks the Eternal One.
Which of My creditors was it,
To whom I sold you?
You were sold because of your own sins,
For your own transgressions your mother
Was sent away.
Why, when I came, was no one there,
No one to answer, when I called?
(ISAIAH 50:1–2)

O body swayed to music, O brightening glance,
    How can we know the dancer from the dance?
(WILLIAM BUTLER YEATS, FROM "AMONG SCHOOL
CHILDREN")

IN THE HAFTARAH for *Parashat Ekev*, God's search for intimacy is revealed in God's many roles: caring mother, disappointed husband, abandoned lover, admiring groom, admonishing father. God's feelings of angst are played out against a range of archetypal female characters viewed as role models of paradise lost and regained. The haftarah is a portrait of a couple (God and Zion) and their lost children (Israel), lost opportunities, and lost love, shrouded in abandonment and in search of connection. It is a dance of vulnerability and destiny.

Let us look at the female characters that populate our haftarah: caring mothers, negligent mothers, nursing mothers, barren women, bejeweled brides, abandoned wives, queens in the guise of nursemaids, exiled daughters, daughters sold into slavery, daughters who return, and, finally, the matriarch Sarah, the mother of us all. Women without names, known only through the things they do, the way they engage or disengage. This would not be viewed as an unusual way to conceptualize women. According to Rabbi Abba bar Memel, a first-generation Palestinian amora, the way we refer to God is by attribute and deed. "The Holy One, blessed be God, said to Moses: 'What dost thou seek to know? I am called according to My acts'"(*Shmot Rabbah* 3:6). The question is: What is this meant to teach us today about the role women play as individuals doing God's work and as communal spiritual leaders?

There is a story in the Zohar (Vol. 2, *Mishpatim* 99a–b) that goes as follows:

> Like a beautiful woman hidden in the interior of the palace, who, when her friend and beloved passes by, opens for a moment a secret window, and is seen only by him, then again retires and disappears for a long time, so the Tradition shows herself. In the beginning, deeply veiled, she only beckons to one passing. . . . Later, she approaches him somewhat nearer and whispers a few words, but her face is still hidden. After he has accustomed himself to her company, she finally shows herself to him, face-to-face, and entrusts him with the innermost secrets of her heart.

The story depicts God (the Tradition) as an elusive woman whose veiled face is hidden from her beloved as he tries to seduce her. Only when the woman grows accustomed to the lover's presence and learns to trust him are "the innermost secrets of the heart revealed." The haftarah for *Ekev* is that revelation.

For seven weeks after Tisha B'Av, we read the words of the prophet Isaiah—a rich tapestry of consolation. On the surface, the words of this haftarah, also known as the second Week of Consolation, cry out Zion's feeling of insecurity and desperation. Feeling forgotten and abandoned by God during the years of exile in Babylon since the destruction of the Temple in 586 B.C.E., the people wonder if their distinctive relationship with God is also in ruins, and whether they will ever be returned to their homeland. The thrust of the haftarah is God's response to Zion's lament. The haftarah begins with a double declaration of the intimate name of God belonging to the Jews: Adonai. When we refer to God by the name *Adonai*, this signifies God's special relationship with the children of Israel as the Revealer of Torah. Adonai connotes *midat ha rachamim,* or the attribute of a compassionate God, a God who stays close to us and is available; a God of relationship. Zion cries out in pain for fear that their Adonai has forgotten them and that the bond has been broken because of their sins. The parallel structure of what follows reflects back at us like a mirror: a double reference to the woman, as giver of life, sustainer of compassion.

> Can a mother forget her babe,
> Or stop loving the child of her womb?
> Even if these could forget,
> But I could not forget you.
> See, I have engraved you on the palms of My hands,
> Your walls are ever before Me.
>
> (Isa. 49:15–17)

In response to Zion's lament of being forsaken, God is depicted as the most nurturing and loyal of all mothers. The theme of motherhood serves as a metaphor, a universal image encompassing the most basic, steadfast, intimate relationship that exists not only between human beings, but between humans and the Divine as well.

"Can a woman forget her babe / Or stop loving the child of her womb?" The question/metaphor is asked by God, through the prophet. This is not the first time that God has self-referred to feminine aspects. In passages before and after our haftarah, God says: "I have long kept silent, I have been still, I have restrained myself. [But now] I cry out like a woman in childbirth" (Isa. 42:14). Also, in Isaiah 66:13, God says: "Like a man whose mother consoled him, so I will console you, and in Jerusalem you will be consoled."

"Though she might forget, I never could forget you," the prophecy continues. The commentators Ibn Ezra and Radak interpret this to mean that even if there are cruel mothers who desert their young, "the All Merciful God will not forget you" (Isa. 49:15). A kinder, gentler reading is found in the *Tzena U'Rena*, known as the woman's Bible, a Yiddish commentary on the Torah: "Tzion has said: 'The Lord has forsaken me, So says God. The city Tzion thinks: God has abandoned me and forgotten me.' But it is not so. Will a woman forget her infant child, to have mercy upon the child of her womb? It cannot be, that she should forget him. So I, God, do not forget you."

But it is the next proclamation that serves to reveal God's true connection with us: "See, I have engraved you on the palms of My hands, Your walls are ever before Me" (Isa. 49:16). Notice the echo here: In *Parashat Ekev* in the Book of Deuteronomy, the words we recite daily in the *v'ahavta* command us to love God and serve God with all our heart and soul. "Therefore impress these My words upon your very heart: bind them as a sign on your hand . . ." (Deut. 11:18). Here in our haftarah, it is God who has bound Zion on the palms of God's hands as an everlasting reminder of their intimate and special connection and covenant. In Judaism, the hand symbolizes Divine might and protection. Remember, God redeemed the Jews from Egypt in Exodus 6:1, "with a strong hand and an outstretched arm." When we read from the Torah, the object that comes between our fingers and the scroll is the *yad*, the hand serving as a bridge linking God's sacred words and our praying voice. In Shakespeare's *Romeo and Juliet*, Juliet says: "Good pilgrim, you do wrong your hand too much. Which mannerly devotion shows in this; For saints have hands that pilgrims' hands do touch, And palm to palm is holy palmers' kiss." God has engraved Israel on the palm of God's hand, just as we bind God's commandments as a sign upon our hand through the wearing of tefillin. Palm to palm, as it were, a holy kiss.

Relationship imagery is sprinkled throughout the haftarah: "Swiftly, your children are coming . . .You shall don them all like jewels / Deck yourself with them like a bride" (Isa. 49:17–19). Zion is once again God's bride, with Israel as the children with which she drapes herself in order to stand out as more luminous than any other blushing bride. This is the ideal, the time when the marriage will again be good. It is a sign of hope. But this haftarah is the stage where the married couple reveal their hurt, their insecurity, their helplessness. Addressing the children of Israel, God asks: "Where is your mother's bill of divorce, with which I sent her away?" (Isa. 50:1). The question is rhetorical. There has been no divorce, because the parties are still in love with each other. A separation has taken place, certainly, and that separation has hurt both parties. God continues: "Why, when I came, was no one there, no one to answer when I called?" If Zion has felt abandoned and cast aside, so too has God. This touching moment of vulnerability reminds us that our Adonai, our God of relationship, yearns for our affection, and looks toward the female as the ultimate nurturer. Whatever we feel, God feels.

The haftarah for *Ekev* is a well-choreographed, tantalizing dance of seduction between God and Israel. Inside this tiny slice of poetry, any woman searching for clues to establishing an intimate relationship with God can find the seeds of the covenant meant to reflect the unique bond between women and the Divine. Our relationship with God is covenantal and, therefore, reciprocal. Just as we are searching for a way to reach out to God, so too is God striving for a means to reach out and understand us. Clearly, the numerous roles that women play, which are carefully depicted in this haftarah, indicate that God looks toward women as models of strong and intimate relationships.

The struggle for intimacy, whether human or Divine, is an eternal one. We need God's love, understanding, and protection. We ask for it, we plead for it, we even expect it. The haftarah for *Ekev* has given us, as women, a peek into the inner workings of God's world, God's feelings, God's needs. For a brief moment, we are made to realize that God needs and wants a relationship with us, as much as we yearn for a relationship with God.

RABBI JOANNE YOCHEVED HEILIGMAN

הפטרת ראה

Haftarat Re'eh

Isaiah 54:11–55:5

No weapon formed against you shall prevail,
And every tongue that contends with you for
  judgment you shall defeat.
Such is the heritage of the servants of YHVH,
Such is their victory through Me—declares YHVH.
(ISAIAH 54:17)

HAFTARAT RE'EH is the third of the late-summer Haftarot of Comfort. Its overall themes are the rebuilding of the relationship between God and Israel, and God's promise to defend Israel so that no enemy can prevail against it. Closer examination of the Hebrew quickly reveals the subtle richness of this text.

Throughout this haftarah, the nation of Israel is addressed in the feminine, and God, as presented by the prophet Isaiah, speaks in the first-person masculine. Hebrew has no gender neutrality, so each verb must be either male or female. Each image, each noun, conveys something of how the subject is perceived. So in this text, there is a male-female relationship implied, though not openly stated, between God and the Israelites.

God is the all-powerful Creator and Protector and, in verse 17, Master of the Israelites, who are the servants. This is the usual way that traditional patriarchal religion speaks of God: Father, King, Master, who is above and beyond the individual. But there is also potential here to see the relationship in terms of the mystical. Implicit in the

227

language is a love relationship between God and Israel. "He" (God) promises "her" (Israel) precious stones, sapphires, and rubies. Her children will be learned and have great peace. Here, asking nothing of Israel, God demonstrates unconditional love for us. Thus the first part of the haftarah promises absolute love, safety, and physical well-being under God's protection.

In chapter 55, the reading changes tone. The words are no longer directed to Israel collectively, but rather to individuals. In the Hebrew we see a switch to the masculine in addressing the people. This signals a switch in attention to the individual as part of the whole.

The prophet declares, "Ho! All the thirsty, come for water, and the one without money; Come! Buy and eat! Buy without money, Free! Wine and milk! Why do you spend money for what is not bread, your profits for what does not satisfy?" (55:1).

The prophet warns us not to waste our resources on objects of illusory worth. In contrast to the apparently physical riches of the first part of the haftarah, the riches of the second part are spiritual.

These are true delicacies, not distracting material enticements. True food, true knowledge, and true spirituality are not material. They are not "empty calories." God's spiritual bounty here is metaphorically called water, milk, and wine.

Water is the primary life-sustaining substance, the drink that literally flows from the heavens of God. It is essential to all, and it is life's most basic requirement. In our tradition, water is understood to be metaphor for Torah. "The *waters* means nothing else than words of Torah, as it is said, 'Ho, all the thirsty, come for water.'"[1] Torah is essential for life, and God freely gives this life-sustaining Torah to all who want it.

Milk is also a gift from God, but it comes only through the physical body of the female. It is a gift in that no conscious action is required from the woman to produce it. The Torah and Midrash recognize that mother's milk is a Divine blessing. For example, in Genesis 21:7, upon the birth of Isaac, Sarah exclaims, "Who would have said to Abraham that Sarah would give children suck?" The midrash notes that Sarah was exceedingly modest. "Abraham said to her: 'This is not a time for modesty, but uncover your breasts so that all may know that the Holy One, blessed be God, has begun to perform miracles.' She uncovered her breasts and the milk gushed forth as from two fountains . . ."[2]

Milk is a life-bringing gift of God through the mother. It is created in passive partnership of God with the feminine. It is essential to the newborn, but not to the weaned. For the adult, milk is a nourishing food that is a luxury in the sense that one can live without it. Milk is a sign of blessing and abundance; as we are told, the Promised Land flows with milk and honey.

Wine is less essential to life than milk. It is the active creation of humans, male or female, by processing an already edible fruit. Its transformation happens in human hands. Wine is not necessary for life, but it is a powerful symbol of joy in Jewish tradition as it sanctifies the festivals. It gladdens the heart and, properly used, helps us attain an altered consciousness on Shabbat and festivals. God gives us Shabbat and festivals to enhance our spirits. Wine is our gift back to God. When we use it for sacred purposes, we take what God has offered, add our conscious labor to it, and present it back to God as the only drink with its own special blessing.[3] As we need water for life and milk for sustenance, we need wine for pleasure, joy, and gladness.

In the physical world, man, woman, and God are all partners in bringing forth nourishment. In the symbolism of our text, water, milk, and wine are seen as the products of this partnership. Looking again at the haftarah, we see that God is telling us that the best things in life are free. They are not the illusory treasures and toys of materialism. The best that life has to offer is spiritual.

In our own lives, we must mesh these three essential elements— water: the physical; milk: the nourishment of love; and wine: the essence of spiritual joy. In a well-balanced life, our material needs are met, our relationships sustain us, and our spirits soar with joy. Isaiah promises us, as both a people and as individuals, as men and as women, that such balance is possible. If we keep focused on spiritual goals and refuse to be sidetracked by material excess, it is a balance that we can indeed attain, and one in which we may find God.

RABBI CINDY ENGER

הפטרת שפטים
Haftarat Shoftim

Isaiah 51:12–52:12

*Y*ou will not leave in a hurry, and in flight you shall
not go forth . . . (ISAIAH 52:12)

SPEAKING TO THE ANCIENT Israelite community in exile in Babylon,
the prophet Isaiah utters words of consolation, announcing that
change is coming and liberation is near. "Wake up, Israel," the haftarah
repeatedly instructs; it is time to return, time to go home. To those who
suffered the trauma of Jerusalem's destruction in the sixth century
B.C.E. and subsequent exile in Babylon, Isaiah communicated a message
of hope and the nearness of redemption.

Isaiah speaks to us moderns as well. As human beings, we endure
hardships. Some of us suffer trauma. And we, too, sojourn spiritually
in places of discomfort, journeying throughout our lives to return to, or
perhaps for the first time find, a place we can call home. As Jews, we
engage each year in *teshuvah*, a process designed to facilitate the return
from spiritual exile to wholeness. In the Jewish liturgical calendar,
this haftarah contributes to the process of *teshuvah*. It is the fourth of
seven Haftarot of Comfort, one read on each of the seven Shabbatot
following Tisha B'Av and leading up to Rosh Hashanah. In this haftarah, Isaiah reminds us that healing and wholeness are possible, that
redemption and liberation can be part of the human experience.

The haftarah concludes with the words, "You will not leave in a
hurry, and in flight you shall not go forth, because YHVH is walking

before you and the God of Israel gathers you from behind" (Isa. 52:12). *Lo v'hipazon te-tze-u*—"You will not leave in a hurry." The choice of words here is most important.

The word *v'hipazon*, meaning "in a hurry," appears in only two other places in the entire Bible: in Exodus 12:11 and in Deuteronomy 16:3. Exodus 12:11, describing the night before departure from Egypt, instructs that the Pesach offering shall be eaten in a hurry *(b'hipazon)*. Deuteronomy 16:3, outlining the way in which the spring festival of Pesach should be observed throughout the generations, connects the eating of matzah with this hurried departure from Egypt.

The story of the Exodus from Egypt is *the* archetypal model of redemption for the Jewish people. We connect "leaving Egypt" with all sorts of journeys—both physical and spiritual—from slavery to freedom. We sing of it in our daily liturgy, and each week on Shabbat we recall that existential freedom in the Sabbath blessing over the wine. Each year on Pesach we not only remember but retell the story of the Exodus in such a way that we may feel as if we ourselves were redeemed from Egypt.[1] Because the word *v'hipazon* is part of the vocabulary of the epic story of Exodus from Egypt, its appearance in this haftarah draws the reader back to the telling of that Exodus: from the quintessential story of leaving to a new kind of leaving.

"You will not leave in a hurry, and in flight you shall not go forth," Isaiah prepares his exiled community in Babylon. The prophet promises that *this* leaving, *this* experience of redemption, will be different from the Exodus from Egypt. Rabbi W. Gunther Plaut writes, "The parallel to the exodus from Egypt is underscored by the word [*hipazon*], used in the Torah to describe the great event." In addition, explains Plaut, "By invoking the parallel—but saying '*not* in haste'—Isaiah assures his audience that the second exodus will involve fewer hardships than before."[2]

Michael Fishbane also writes of Isaiah's use of *v'hipazon* and its role in effecting an "explicit reversal" of the atmosphere in which the original exodus occurred.[3] In the new exodus, disquietude will be replaced by calm. Fishbane explains that "The new exodus will therefore not simply be a remanifestation of an older prototype, but will have qualitative distinctions of its own."[4]

Isaiah's message—that the exodus for his generation will be different from the previous leaving—is important for us as well. As individuals and as communities, we confront different challenges. As our personal and communal experiences vary, so too will the ways in which we journey from discomfort to freedom. Oppression comes in various forms and so does redemption. Moreover, as Isaiah reminds us, the journey home may not take place in a hurry; the process of liberation often unfolds over time. This is an especially relevant message for women. As we go from generation to generation, we must learn to have patience as well as to press forward to bring about liberating changes.

In addressing his community, Isaiah utilizes the vocabulary of an earlier generation. Yet in drawing upon the tradition that he received, he does more than simply add to it. His teaching causes a shift in the old, a reordering of the relative authority of the tradition that he received.[5] In other words, in his drawing upon the tradition and its epic story of redemption, Isaiah not only recites and transmits that tradition but also effects its reformulation and transformation.[6]

Women rabbis and women in other Jewish leadership roles cause a similar shift. In our teaching, we draw from the tradition we have inherited and the vocabulary of earlier generations. At the same time, we contribute our own voices, which become a new layer in the tradition. Like Isaiah, we not only transmit the tradition but also transform it. In so doing, we journey, slowly but steadily, toward a new promise of redemption.

הפטרת כי תצא

Haftarat Ki Tetze

Isaiah 54:1–10

*R*ejoice O barren one! (ISAIAH 54:1)

"REJOICE O BARREN ONE!—*Roni akara!*" (Isa. 54:1) is a prophecy of utter transformation in the face of hopelessness. "Break out in song, you who have never birthed . . . ," for the unimaginable is about to transpire.

This haftarah is the fifth of seven weekly readings of comfort that bring us from the lowest point in the Jewish year to the highest, from Tisha B'Av to Rosh Hashanah. The prophecy promises the redemption of Israel from the humiliation of exile to the restoration of sovereignty. This turnabout is expressed through poetic images of the abandoned woman, the barren woman, and the widowed woman redeemed through love to become the fertile mother and the desired wife.

Isaiah 54:5 reads: "Your husband is your maker, your redeemer is the Holy One of Israel." In describing the reconciliation between Israel and the Divine, Isaiah likens Israel to a child-bride who has acted in a way that has repulsed her husband. Isaiah 54:8 reads: "In a rush of foaming fury I turned my face away from you for but a moment, and with everlasting love I gather you in . . ." The consolation is in knowing that, in the scheme of things, the furious response (to sin) is but a moment's flash against the backdrop of the everlasting love that God declares more enduring than even the mountains. The hope offered by this prophecy is the possibility of *teshuvah*, repentance, and forgiveness.

Israel is the woman, the wife, and the mother. God the redeemer is the husband and the father of her children. Throughout the metaphor, idolatry is analogous to adultery, the covenant to marriage, exile to divorce or separation, and repentance to marital reconciliation. It is a common image that has served the biblical prophets well in their varied attempts to describe the relationship between Israel and God.

While these images are effective in evoking the utter despair of abandonment and the joyous triumph of love that the prophet wishes to evoke, the underlying assumption in the use of these images is that a woman who is abandoned by her man is the epitome of degradation and loneliness. The assumption in the use of the image of the barren woman is that a woman's worth is measured by her success at childbearing. From a feminist point of view, it may seem ironic and even dissonant to use a sexist metaphor of marital reconciliation to describe a messianic state of wholeness and homecoming. On the other hand, the assumptions of the metaphor within this haftarah reflect a society in which women are indeed dependent upon men for their economic and social status.

Such a society is clearly depicted in the weekly Torah reading, *Ki Tetze*, which corresponds to this haftarah. The very first case of the *parashah*, in Deuteronomy 21:10–14, introduces us to the captive woman taken in war by an Israelite man. The Torah requires the man to let the captive woman grieve for her mother and her father before he may take her as a wife. The Torah also recognizes that after a month's wait, the woman may no longer be as attractive to her would-be husband as she was when she was first captured. The man may decide not to marry her, but is forbidden to sell her and must set her free after having subjected her to disgrace.

This scenario is echoed in the anonymous abandoned woman of our haftarah. Israel taken into exile is like the captive woman of the *parashah*. The image used by the prophet is familiar to the Israelites. Such a woman is the object of the Torah's (and Israel's) compassion, pity, and also distaste.

The very next issue of the *parashah*, in Deuteronomy 21:15–17, deals with inheritance laws as they apply to two different sons from two different wives, "the one beloved and the other one despised" (or "less loved"). This reality is also alluded to in the first verse of our haftarah which sets up the comparison between "the desolate [wife] who will have more children than the husbanded [wife]!" Israel is being told, "You really are my favorite wife. Your children are my favorites and they will fill the earth." Israel's frustration and shame is expressed by the prophet's comparison of Israel to the despised wife. The triumph of the despised wife being reinstated over another wife is a concrete image of redemption. The prophet/poet is comforting Israel through familiar domestic images, which are already a part of the Israelite consciousness.

For us, the scenario of the rejected woman reconciling with her husband may resonate all too well with the familiar domestic reality of battered wives rejoicing in a reunion with their abusers. Such an association strips the prophecy of all redemptive promise. In order for the metaphor to hold its power, its readers must go along with the unspoken assumption of the prophet/poet, which is that, in this scenario, the man is completely righteous in his anger toward his woman; that she has, in fact, betrayed him.

This metaphor reflects the way the Israelites viewed themselves in relation to God. It was *their* sin that caused their exile. Israel, though powerless and exiled, sees itself as the one whose actions drive the situation. There is no other biblical metaphor of dependency that so communicates full responsibility on the part of the dependent as does the metaphor of the husband and wife.

It may seem ironic that the actions of the dependent one (Israel/the woman) have power over the dominant one (God/the man). But in the biblical context, in the world of *Ki Tetze*, we find numerous examples demonstrating that a man's honor is at stake through the women associated with him. In the case in Deuteronomy 25:5–10 of the man who releases his brother's widow, the man must bear shame for the (albeit ritual) abandonment. In the case of the virgin bride, in Deuteronomy 22:13–21, it is the father taking the bridegroom to task for slandering the name of his family. In Deuteronomy 25:10–12, at issue is the woman who, in a scuffle between her husband and another man, grabs the other man by his testicles; in that case, the honor of the assaulted man is considered violated and the woman is penalized.

Throughout the cases in *Ki Tetze*, we see that men and women are entangled in a cultural dance of honor and shame. In a sexist society, the limitations imposed upon one sex necessarily limit the opposite sex as well. The men, whose honor is at stake, are equally constrained by the system that keeps their women dependent upon them.

Sensitivity to this reality may reveal another angle of the domestic image presented in the haftarah. Regardless of his implied righteousness, the husband in this metaphor suffers for not only the (imagined) emotional pain, but from the unavoidable societal shame brought upon him. So, too, God's pride is compromised by Israel's exile. Those whom the prophet is addressing might intuitively sympathize with God's injury, and be deeply moved by the magnanimity of God's forgiveness.

In Deuteronomy 24:1–4, we learn that a woman who is divorced from her husband, or leaves him, and who has subsequently been with another man, can never be reinstated as a wife by her first husband. But in this corresponding haftarah, God does promise to reinstate Israel. Against such a backdrop, God's promise is an act of great compassion. Israel is responsible for the breakup, but God will break the rule and take Israel back.

Forgiveness and liberation comprise the ultimate theme of this haftarah. God's love endures beyond all physical existence. The expression of such love through a sexist metaphor is simply an affirmation that complete redemption is imaginable, describable, if even from a limited perspective. For us, it is comforting to know that we don't have to be able to perfectly envision the fully redeemed world in order to believe that it is possible.

RABBI SHOSHANA DWORSKY

הפטרת כי תבוא

Haftarat Ki Tavo

Isaiah 60:1–22

*A*rise, shine, for your light has come! (ISAIAH 60:1)

FOR A WOMAN reading the opening words of this haftarah in Hebrew, it is hard not to feel as though the prophet were addressing her personally. The phrase *Kumi, ori, ki va oreich!* is usually translated into English as "Arise, shine, for your light has come!" But Hebrew is a gendered language. Lost in translation is the feminine inflection of the address. To recapture it we might render the verse, colloquially, as: "Arise, girl, and shine, for your light has come! *Kvod Adonai alayich zarach*—God's light is shining on you, girl!"

It becomes clear later in the haftarah that Isaiah is addressing Jerusalem, which in his day lay in ruin (cities in Hebrew are feminine). But in these opening words any woman might hear the prophet speaking to her, acknowledging the challenges she faces, goading her with a sense of urgency to optimism and self-actualization. For generations, women have been discouraged from shining in all but limited spheres. Now, centuries after this prophecy was set down in print, we might try listening to the prophet's words afresh, and conclude that God wants women to shine after all, and to shine brightly!

What might it mean for a woman to rise and shine? Different women will hear it differently, at different times in their lives. For the first generation of women rabbis, for example, it might mean overcoming the traditional bias against women whose voices are heard publicly, and choosing to don the mantle of rabbinic authority with confidence and pride. We might hear the prophet assuring us that when women take on positions of leadership in their communities, others will be inspired and drawn to their light, as it is written, "*V'halchu goyim l'oreich, u'mlachim l'nogah zarcheich* / Nations shall walk by your light; kings by your shining radiance!" (60:3).

In context, *Kumi ori* are words spoken by Isaiah to Jerusalem and, by extension, to her inhabitants. The city had been brutally overrun by the Babylonians, her vineyards trampled, her light—her hope, her energy—dimmed, nearly extinguished. The survivors needed to heal and the city needed rebuilding from the ground up. Isaiah envisioned Jerusalem rebuilt and secure, bustling and alive, welcoming caravans from afar, a magnet drawing goodness to her, as it is written, "Your gates will be open day and night, they shall never close" (60:11).

This vision of open gates, of a city breathing freely: Can a woman dare to dream of such ease? We often dim our own light for self-protection. The "Jerusalem" of our own lives as envisioned by Isaiah would be a place—whether a physical place or a state of mind and spirit—in which women could allow their inner and outer beauty to shine without fear.

For a student of Torah, Isaiah's rebuilt Jerusalem might be a modern *beit midrash*—house of study—bursting with creative energy day and night, to which men and women are drawn together to learn. It is written, "*Se'i saviv einayich u'rei* / Raise your eyes and look about, they have all gathered and come to you; your sons shall be brought from afar, your daughters like babes on shoulders!"(60:4). Sons and daughters would be welcomed equally to partake of the treasures of our tradition.

Isaiah envisions Jerusalem rising to a position of political power: Foreign kings will wait upon her (60:10); the nation that does not serve her shall perish (60:12). It is a vision of total security that results in domination of the other. Perhaps we can resist this potential outcome. Our goal, at least, need not be to outshine the other, but rather to become ourselves to the fullest, each of us generating his or her own unique light. This may be the best way to illuminate the darkness for all, and in so doing make our world more secure.

At the end of the haftarah it is written, "*Lo y'hiyeh lach ha'shemesh l'or yomom* / You will not have the sun to light up your day" (60:19). In context Isaiah is not suggesting that there will be no sun, but rather that the sun's light will no longer be *needed*, because light will shine directly from its divine source. Again, the inflection is feminine: You will not need the sun. It can be read as a reminder that light shining on us from without—in the form of attention, approval, acceptance, validation—is not always as important as it may seem in the moment. There is a greater source of light upon which we can count, the prophet assures us, as it is written, "*Lo yavo ode shimshech* / Your light will never got out!" (60:20). No matter what message we might receive about ourselves we must locate the source of light that burns within.

Over time Jerusalem has fallen repeatedly, and she has repeatedly risen like a phoenix from the ashes. From this women can learn a lesson. Even when we feel dark and defeated, when we sense that our light is being resisted, dulled, or compromised, we, like Jerusalem, must locate the source of light within us and resolve to use it to rise and shine again.

RABBI LAURA GELLER

הפטרת נצבים
Haftarat Nitzavim

Isaiah 61:10–63:9

*I*n all their troubles God was troubled . . . (ISAIAH 63:9)

ON THE SHABBAT before Rosh Hashanah, we enter the intense period of preparation for the Days of Awe. For the past seven weeks since Tisha B'Av, the haftarot have focused on consolation. Isaiah is comforting the exiles with the assurance that God had forgiven their sins, and therefore they will return to Jerusalem. The haftarah for *Nitzavim* is the climax of the cycle of the *Sheva de-nechemta*, the seven Haftarot of Comfort. On this Shabbat, as our spiritual work focuses on the challenge of renewal and rebirth, the haftarah gives us not only comfort but also three powerful and somewhat surprising images of beginning again.

The first image is one of new clothes. God is the One who dresses us for a wonderful special occasion: "For God has clothed me in garments of triumph, wrapped me in a robe of victory, like a bridegroom adorned with a turban, like a bride bedecked in her finery" (61:10). It is an image of both power and intimacy. This is "power dressing" at its best, yet with a loving, intimate touch. God is fixing our hair, adjusting our dress, wrapping us in beautiful clothes, and fussing over us to help us look our best. This is not a description of a woman "primping and preening," but rather an evocative image of a bride—Israel—preparing to meet her beloved—God. Later in the haftarah, the image of "power clothing" appears again, this time with God dressed as a warrior, with clothes stained by the blood of Israel's enemies. So not only is God our dresser, but, like God's, our clothes are powerful and protective.

The second image is one of new names:

> And you shall be called by a new name that the mouth of YHVH will bestow. . . . "Forsaken" and "Desolate" give way to "My Delight Is Her" and "Married"; the people Israel will be called "The Holy People, The Redeemed of YHVH" and Jerusalem will be called "Sought Out, a City Not Forsaken." (62:2, 4, 12)

In the Bible, a name change is a signal of a major transformation. Names connote essences and destiny. Changing a name signifies a different future. When God changes the names of Abram and Sarai to Abraham and Sarah in Genesis, God not only adds God's own name to theirs with the addition of the letter *hay*, but God also creates a covenant, an exclusive, intimate relationship. When God changes Jacob's name to *Israel*, God is prescribing an intimate relationship between us—the descendants of this God wrestler—and the God with whom we are close enough to struggle. In our haftarah, the name comes from God's own mouth, like a kiss.

The third image, connected to the other two, is the image of new love and sexual intimacy. The Hebrew root *b-a-l*, which could mean either "marry" or "have sexual intercourse," occurs several times in 62:4–5. One might translate verse 5 to read, "As a young man has intercourse with a young woman, so will your sons [the returning exiles] take possession of you [the land]." Another reading (which depends on a wordplay) renders the verse: "As a young man and woman marry, so will the One who rebuilds you [your Creator] marry you." Either way, the next verse makes the intention of the prophet clear: God loves the people of Israel as a bridegroom loves his bride, an image so powerful that in the sixteenth century it was incorporated into the Friday night *Kabbalat Shabbat* liturgy in the poem *Lecha Dodi*.

All three of these images—new clothes, new names, and new

love—suggest an intense, intimate connection between God and the Jewish people. God is close enough to dress us, as a mother might dress a child; close enough to name us, as parents might name a child; and close enough to rejoice with us, as lovers do when they make love.

No wonder, then, that the end of the haftarah is a puzzle. The Hebrew text in 63:8–9 can be literally translated as: "And [God] said: Surely they are My people, children who will not be false [to me]. So God became their Deliverer. In all their troubles [God was] *not* troubled, and the angel of God's presence delivered them. In God's love and pity God redeemed them, carried them and exalted them in all times past." How could a God so intimately connected to us not be affected by our afflictions?

Rashi rescues the image of a God who is intimate with us by reading the verse in a different way. He reads in Isaiah 63:9 "In all their troubles" as "In all their troubles God did *not* afflict them as much as they deserved." Other commentaries focus on God's power by interpreting 63:9 "God was their deliverer" as "God was their deliverer in all their troubles. There was *no* angel; only God's own Presence saved them."

The tradition is so clear that God is affected by our troubles that the way the Torah is actually read is different from the way it is written. It is read as *l-v* (to Him) instead of *l-a* (not). According to this understanding, the verse reads: "Their troubles were His," or "He was afflicted in their afflictions." In other words, God shares Israel's pain. God feels our anguish.

This is not an image of a powerful God who can fix what is broken. It is instead an image of a God who suffers with us. We see the image occasionally in midrash. One striking example comes from a midrash on Psalm 20. There God is compared to the estranged mother of a pregnant daughter who is struggling through a difficult and painful labor. As the daughter groans with the pain of childbirth, the mother groans as well. The neighbors, hearing the mother, remind her that her own daughter kicked her out of the birthing room and they question the mother's groaning. She responds: "My daughter is in pain. How can

I bear her cries? I am groaning with her because my daughter's pain is also mine."[1]

The analogy employed in this midrash is stunning. The neighbors are understood to be the angels who question God's mourning after the Temple is destroyed. God's response is unequivocal. "My children are in pain; shouldn't I be in anguish? I'm a mother too; I know what my child is experiencing! No matter what she did to me, I'm her mother. I feel her pain." Then God quotes Psalm 91:15: "I will be with [them] in anguish." God might also have quoted our haftarah: "In all their afflictions God was also afflicted."

Haftarot always end in *nechemta,* in comfort. In particular, the special Haftarot of Comfort are meant to offer healing to us as we prepare for the High Holy Days. Certainly there is comfort in the images in this haftarah, which focus on the power of God to restore us to our former glory and avenge our humiliation. But perhaps the real power of this haftarah at this moment in the Jewish year is that it suggests a very specific image of consolation: one of God who is present in our pain.

In our own lives, the lives upon which we reflect as the year draws to an end, there isn't so much victory and renown. Our triumphs are not like flaming torches. The messiah has not yet come. In our own lives, there is pain and anguish, and it is hard to believe that we can change. Our haftarah reminds us that God, like a mother who dresses us, like a parent who names us, like a lover who adores us, can't necessarily take away our hurt. But God loves us, and God is connected with us. God fusses and wraps and hovers and adorns and names and even enters us in the most intimate way imaginable. And therefore, God is with us also in our anguish. And because God is there for us, always, we are not alone. Perhaps that is the source of the courage to trust that we can begin again.

RABBI SUSAN GULACK

הפטרת וילך
Haftarat Vayelech

Isaiah 55:6–56:8

*S*earch for YHVH where God is found,
Call out to God where God is near.
A wicked one will leave that path
and a person filled with sin, those thoughts.
Let these turn to YHVH who will have mercy on them
And to our God who is abundant in forgiveness.
"Because My thoughts are not your thoughts,
and My ways are not your ways," says YHVH.
"As far as the heavens are above the earth
so far are My thoughts above your thoughts."
(ISAIAH 55:6–9)

*I*believe in the sun, even when it is not shining. I
believe in love even when feeling it not. I believe in
God, even when God is not present. (FOUND ON A WALL
IN THE WARSAW GHETTO)

WHAT DOES IT MEAN to search for God where God is found? Isn't God
everywhere? It only appears to us that God is "missing" because our
thoughts are not God's thoughts; our way of seeing is not God's way.

Mark Twain said, "God created man in his own image. Man, being
a gentleman, returned the compliment." How often in the history of

244

religion are things done in God's name, for which, looking back, we are sure that the Holy One would not want the credit. In world religions, these things range from the Inquisition and the terrorist attacks on the World Trade Center and the Pentagon to the idea that there is only one path to salvation.

When we make the effort to align our thoughts with God's, what a change occurs! We cannot always see things from God's perspective, but believing that there is a perspective greater than our own surely changes our view. We can move from understanding the world as a purposeless place, driven by human greed, to seeing ourselves as part of God's plan in a pattern that is beyond our human comprehension.

Those who have "found" religion in prison, for example, wonder if they would have committed their crime had they felt a Divine source in their lives beforehand. Had they seen the work of God earlier on, they wonder, would they have disregarded it?

There is a story in the Talmud (*Berachot* 28b) that illustrates this point well:

> Yochanan ben Zakkai lay ill. His disciples came to visit him. They said, "Master, give us your blessing." He said to them, "May it be the will of the Holy One that your fear of heaven should be as great as your fear of flesh and blood." They said to him, "Only that much?!" He said to them, "If only it could be that much! You know that when a person is about to sin, he says to himself, let no person see me."

Most of us do not commit large sins. Our sins are more ordinary: impatience with our children or our loved ones, acting impetuously in some way, not respecting other people properly. We generally do not commit these sins when we are in the middle of prayer or meditation, or when we are fully aware of God's presence in our lives. We commit them when we are involved in the mundane world. If we were constantly aware of God's presence, we would not do many of the things for which we later repent.

Why then didn't God create a world in which all people would be continuously aware of a Divine presence? Rabbi Isaac Luria, known as the Ari, taught that when God created the world, God realized that people's sins and God's perfection could not exist in the same place. If the earth were full of God's glory at all times, people could never choose to be anything but perfect. In other words, God realized that if we were fully aware of a Divine presence at all times, we would never be able to have free will. To give us this freedom, to "make room" for us to be fully human, God contracted God's full presence. But that results in a vacuum, a place of darkness and sadness. It is our job, then, to fill the darkness with light, to restore God's full presence to the world. We do that each time we make good decisions, bringing God's presence into our lives and the lives of the people around us, and thus we actually repair the world.

When Isaiah calls on us to call upon YHVH when God is near, he is asking us to bring God near by our awareness that God *can* be near. When we are at that level of awareness, we cannot help making the choices that bring God's presence into the world. When we strive to be aware of God's presence in our lives, we cannot help turning from those wicked deeds and thoughts that take us from the proper path.

In *Pirkei Avot* (2:4) Rabban Gamliel says, "Make God's will your will, in order that God should make your will God's will." Rabbi Joseph H. Hertz comments:

> "Obey God readily and joyfully, as if you were carrying out your own desires . . . Strive to do the will of God with a perfect heart and a willing soul; and efface thy will, even if obeying the will of God entail suffering unto thee" (*Machzor Vitry*). We should strive to make our thoughts like those of God—even though they are as far apart as the heavens and the earth.[1]

This is a very difficult thing to do. How do we nullify our own will, setting aside our own wants and desires? Trying to modify our behavior according to God's will is like trying to stick to a diet or give up an addiction. We are, after all "Israel"—the people who wrestle with God. We all make choices about how we incorporate God's will into our lives. Bridging the gap between heaven and earth in order to understand what God's will is, and then nullifying our own wants and desires to make room for God's, is the work of a lifetime.

And the work of clearly hearing God's will for our lives is perhaps even harder for women. We have been trained from childhood to be tuned into other people's needs and desires, and to make meeting those needs more important than meeting our own. We are bombarded with conflicting messages, the social pressure to have careers and put our lives first, and the ticking of our own biological clocks, pressuring us to have and nurture children. The message that we can and must do both at the same time are particularly hard to resist and particularly damaging. No one can make these choices for us as women, and the right choice for each of us, at each moment in our lives, can only be discerned with honest wrestling with who we are and what we hope to become. Ideally, this wrestling will be shaped by our desire to find what God's will is for each of us in our own situation.

This haftarah is read as we enter the season of forgiveness, which marks a period in which we strive to make our thoughts like God's thoughts and to truly forgive. This is the way Rabbi David Kimchi, the Radak, interprets the verse, "My thoughts are not your thoughts":

> Because when a person sins against another and apologizes and the other does not forgive, or even if he forgives, when he sees it again he remembers. . . . But behold, I am abundant in forgiveness, not like them, and when I forgive, I forgive in truth and no trace of the matter remains with me.[2]

God doesn't hold grudges the way we do, even after we seem to "forgive and forget." This is a reminder to treat other people as we hope God will treat us. We want to be completely forgiven. We must remember to extend that same unqualified forgiveness to others.

We cannot see the whole pattern of the universe, or know what part our piece plays in it. But we do fathom what it might mean to be near to God, nearer than we are. By striving to make God's will central to our lives, we increase the possibility of calling God nearer to us, which will nourish us and keep us on the path of righteousness.

RABBI ELIZABETH W. GOLDSTEIN

הפטרת האזינו

Haftarat Ha'azinu

II Samuel 22:1–51

With my God I can leap over a wall.
(II SAMUEL 22:30)

CONTEMPORARY WOMEN have difficulties relating to biblical texts that glorify war. This haftarah, in particular, contains several passages that depict King David truly enjoying aspects of being a warrior and engaging in battle. Although the battle seems to be a defensive one, David nevertheless takes pleasure in annihilating his foes. In reference to his enemies, David says, "I beat them into dust of the earth" (22:43). What also might strike us as excessively exploitative of war is David's pride in turning his enemies into slaves, "a people who I do not know serve me" (22:44). He boasts about causing them utter fear: They are "a people who obey me as soon as they hear of me" (22:45).

The unsettling impact of David's joyous engagement with war is compounded by his fascination with his own achievements. Many modern readers might feel that boastfulness is an inappropriate response to the defeat of one's enemy and, further, do not expect war to be an occasion for self-congratulation. However, despite David's self-promotion, he is careful to attribute his success to YHVH. One of the most positive lessons that can be drawn from this haftarah is David's utter reliance on his relationship with YHVH. The power of this relationship can provide inspiration for our own developing relationships with God. The opening lines express David's feelings toward YHVH.

249

"YHVH, you are my rock, my fortress, my deliverer . . . who saves me from violence" (22:2–3). Ironically, as much as he delights in acts of war, David praises God for saving him from the very thing a professional warrior seeks. In the mind of the writer of David's hymn, God sets the tone for this battle and David is merely following suit.[1] The writer imagines YHVH riding on a cherub with smoke pouring out of His nostrils, flamed with fury, and sending forth lightning (22:7–9). David believes the skills he uses for battle are similar to those used by YHVH. In fact, he attributes his expert abilities to YHVH's teaching, "*melamed yadai lamilchamah*, who has trained my hands for war" (22:35). David also calls YHVH "a lamp" (22:29), the means through which David can leap over a wall (22:30). David finds satisfaction in sharing the victory with YHVH. Though boastful, David is still aware of a personal relationship with God.

Glorifying war in the ancient Near East was not only a product of the male domain. Bloody battles, territory-hungry generals and kings, and tribal warfare were all part of life for both men and women at different periods in the history of the Israelites. The idea that war was initiated by a god was a widespread cultural belief in the ancient Near East. The Song of Deborah (Judg. 5) dates from the premonarchic period, about two hundred years before our complete text was formulated. Although the gender of the actual writer of Judges 5 is unknown, the text itself attributes the hymn, at least partly, to a woman. "And Deborah and Barak the son of Avinoam sang" (Judg. 5:1). By looking at the similarities and differences in the way David and Deborah describe their wartime experiences, lessons emerge about humility, boastfulness, and a relationship with God.

As in David's hymn, the success of Deborah's battle is attributed to YHVH, but unlike David, Deborah does not praise her own skillfulness. One can hardly find language in the first person in the poem. The success of the battle is attributed to several of the tribes: Efraim, Benjamin, Zebulun, and Issachar. It is also attributed to Barak, the army commander, and largely to another woman, Yael, who caused the final victory through her subversive defeat of Sisera, the enemy leader. The one place where Deborah might seem to be praising herself is when she is called "mother in Israel" in Judges 5:7. The verse reads "Until *you* arose a mother in Israel." The grammar of archaic Hebrew shows that this verse is in the second person, which would mean Deborah is not speaking. But, at first glance, *ad sheqamti* appears to be first person, "Until *I* arose as a mother in Israel." The Rabbis of the Talmud read the verse this way and were troubled by Deborah's seemingly boastful words.[2] However, the first interpretation indicates that the phrase is a compliment expressed by someone else.

The starkest contrast between Deborah's song of war and David's is in the treatment of enemies. While the Song of Deborah in no way apologizes for the killing of enemies, the overall nature of the enemy is portrayed differently. Sisera's mother is described in the poem as waiting by the window for her son to return in Judges 5:28–29. Following this description, Sisera's mother is imagined saying, "Why is his chariot ashamed to come, why are the wheels of his chariot late?" In the Song of Deborah, the enemy is acknowledged to have a mother, likely because the poet, writing from a woman's perspective, relates to worrying about the loss of sons in battle. In the hymn, Deborah demonstrates compassion for the other. She shows us the human side of the enemy, an aspect of war David's hymn fails to describe.

Several motifs found in the Song of Deborah can be considered more praiseworthy than those of David's hymn. Certainly, Deborah's accolades for the deeds of others stand out. In addition, the compassion expressed for the mother of the enemy is a much more satisfying image than the picture of David's delight in turning his enemies to dust and subsequently enslaving them. David's expressions of praise for himself are annoyingly self-congratulatory, but we can admire the intensity and strength with which he claims a personal relationship with God. Humility is usually considered an attribute toward which the religious person should strive, but this haftarah encourages women to take a careful look at the pros and cons of humility. Humility can also prompt one to bury her head in the sand, to let someone else take the credit, to let someone else receive love. It is often hard for women to claim honor based on their own worthiness. In promoting others, women forget to promote themselves. Society expects women to be humble, and criticizes them for being "conceited" if they are not. If we do not see our own achievements as praiseworthy, and ourselves as deserving of God's love, we will miss the opportunity to truly connect with ourselves and thus with God. While we should gratefully accept the gifts of humility and compassion bequeathed to us by Deborah, should we not also strive for some of David's pride and self-confidence?

הפטרת וזאת הברכה

Haftarat V'zot Habrachah

Joshua 1:1–18

*A*s I was with Moses, so I will be with you. I will
not fail you or leave you. Be strong and of good
courage, for you shall bring this people to possess the
land that I swore to their ancestors to give them.
(JOSHUA 1:5–6)

A Woman of Strength and Courage

God speaks these words of encouragement to Joshua right after Moses
passes away. Joshua has been groomed for leadership ever since the
Israelites were freed from Egypt. In the Book of Exodus, he leads the
people against the archvillain Amalek and accompanies Moses up on
Mount Sinai. In the Book of Numbers, he gives a good report of the
land as one of the twelve scouts and is only one of two men of his
generation to enter the Promised Land. Such a man is an obvious
choice as Moses' successor, and, therefore, with God's blessing, Moses
lays his hands upon Joshua before all the people and imbues him with
his spirit.

Following Moses' death, Joshua must lead the Israelites to the
Promised Land. God tells Joshua to be strong and to have courage
because by observing the words of the Torah, he will ultimately succeed
in his mission. These words spoken by God are powerful because they
demonstrate that Joshua has Divine support and approval. But is faith

in God enough for Joshua to successfully conquer the Land of Israel? After all, it is ultimately the people and their leader who will have to fight the Canaanites and be willing to endure trials and deprivation during their battles. Fortunately for Joshua, the people are behind him. The tribes of Reuben, Gad, and the half-tribe of Manasseh tell Joshua that they will do everything he commands and go anywhere he sends them. In addition, like God, they also tell him to be strong and have courage.

With God and the people on his side, it will now be up to Joshua to lead the people into the Promised Land. He is going to need to tap into a deep reservoir of inner faith to fulfill God's promise that the descendants of Abraham and Sarah will inherit the land. Aside from the encouragement of God and the people, was there anyone closer to Joshua helping him through the worst of days and the most challenging of battles? The Torah is silent about Joshua's personal life. There is no mention of a wife, children, or family in general. Did Joshua, like other great leaders before and after him, have a personal relationship that enabled him to be as successful as he was?

The Talmud attempts to fill in the gaps left by our haftarah. Boldly, the Talmud tells us that Joshua was not only married but he had children as well.[1] According to the Book of Joshua, chapter 2, Joshua sent out two scouts to check out the region of Jericho. While assessing the land, the two men ended up spending the night at the home of Rahab the harlot. Soon, the news of these two spies reached the king of Jericho, who was immediately concerned and fearful of them. He sent word to Rahab to turn the men over to him. Rahab refused to obey the king's order, courageously hid the men, and then lied to the king's messengers. One can only imagine how Rahab looked. Perhaps she was wearing a revealing dress and had flowers in her hair. Flirtatiously, she tells the king's men that the spies did indeed visit her, but at dawn they left and she has no idea where they are. "Perhaps the king's messengers should quickly go after them before they get too far" we can imagine her suggesting with a wink.

Rahab's ruse worked, of course, for the king's men left completely unsuspecting. As soon as she was alone, though, she went up to the spies and confided her loyalty to God and their cause. After declaring the power of God in heaven and earth, Rahab begs the men to show loyalty to her and her family by sparing them during the invasion of Jericho. In response, the men promise to protect her family as long as she keeps their mission secret. Rahab then gathers her family inside her home, and ties a crimson cord to the same window she allows the scouts to escape from.

When the day arrives for the conquest of Jericho, in chapter 6, Joshua and his men surround the city. Its walls fall with the sounding of the shofar, thus beginning the Israelite invasion of this fortified city. There was massive killing and destruction but Rahab and her family were safely escorted out of the doomed city, and thereafter allowed to live among the Israelites. Accordingly, the Bible tells us how a harlot "changed sides" during Joshua's conquest of the land.

What is even more striking than a prostitute joining the Israelites is that, according to the Talmud, Rahab converts to Judaism and Joshua marries her! A woman of ill repute ultimately becomes the wife of the leader of the Israelites. The Bible is very complimentary of Rahab for her allegiance to God and the Israelites. She is a woman of great courage who risks her life to protect two spies, who are strangers to her. Somehow a woman with a questionable profession turns out to be extremely honorable, brave, independent, and loyal to the Israelites. It is these personal characteristics that undoubtedly drew the later Rabbis to pair Rahab and Joshua.

Ultimately, the story of Rahab teaches that it doesn't matter what one's past is or what one does. What is most important is the present and who we are. Even though Rahab is a harlot, she is a woman of principle and strong character. She recognizes that the king of Jericho is wrong and intuitively accepts the truth of God. Imbued with great courage, which she no doubt passes on to Joshua, she risks personal harm by defecting to the Israelites' side. She is determined to choose the course of her own life and live by her own principles. In making such a radical change, Rahab also disassociates herself from prostitution and the town she serviced. In one small moment, Rahab has altered her life irrevocably. Just as Abraham and Sarah left all they knew to journey to the Promised Land, Rahab also bravely opts for a new beginning, and therefore she must have been a great source of strength for Joshua. To smooth over the last remaining issue of religion, the Rabbis of the Talmud have Rahab convert to Judaism so she can be a compatible bride for Joshua.

But the story does not end here. The Talmud goes on to say that eight prophets who were also priests descended from Rahab: Neriah, Baruch, Serayah, Mahseyah, Jeremiah, Hilkiah, Hanamel, and Shallum. In addition, there is a tradition that Huldah the prophetess also descended from Rahab.[2]

*E*ven in the Face of Uncertainty, Be Strong and Have Courage!

In this haftarah, Joshua is told three times *chazak v'ematz*, to be strong and have courage. He is facing the uncertainty of conquering Israel and battling many people after years in the desert, and he is understandably frightened of what lies ahead. In our own lives we also experience fear and uncertainty. One of the lessons of this portion is to remind us that God and the people we love can be a source of strength for us even during those periods.

Rahab was a good partner for Joshua and an exemplar for the Israelites, and she had a lasting influence on the life of the Jewish people. She was a woman of strength, courage, independence, and justice. Hand in hand, Rahab and Joshua helped bring the Israelites into the Promised Land and also raised up a generation of leaders to bring the Jewish people into the next era. Just as Joshua found love and support from Rahab, we too can find strength and assistance from the people in our lives. God works through people, when we work together for the common good. With good people at our side and a strong faith in God, we will always make it to the Promised Land.

Special Shabbatot

RABBI ILENE SCHNEIDER

הפטרת שבת ראש חדש

Haftarat Shabbat Rosh Chodesh

Isaiah 66:1–24

*F*or as the new heaven and the new earth
  Which I will make
Shall survive by My will
—declares YHVH—
So shall your seed and your name continue.
And new moon after new moon,
And Shabbat after Shabbat,
All flesh shall come to worship Me
—said YHVH.

(ISAIAH 66:22–23)

TRY TO IMAGINE: a pitch-black night, with no light pollution to dim the stars. The Milky Way is a carpet of pinpoint bits of light. Low in the eastern sky is the merest sliver of a crescent moon, the same moon that two weeks earlier had been a glowing disk, bright enough to cast shadows; the same moon that had waned and disappeared, only to appear again, miraculously, as it did in its predictable four-week cycle.

Now, try to imagine how such a phenomenon must have seemed to our ancient ancestors, who had no inkling that the earth was not the center of the universe, or that the surface of the moon was as solid as the earth, or that we would someday walk on it and dream of living there.

The rotation of the moon around the earth, while not understood in the scientific terms we take for granted today, was well observed by ancient peoples. It was a constant in their lives, and a natural focal point for them to use to organize their lives, both ritual and mundane. Most calendars, from the Incan to the Celtic to the Babylonian, were predicated on the lunar cycle. Today, both the Jewish and Muslim religious calendars are still lunar-based. The importance of the new moon can be seen in the Muslim symbol of the crescent moon and in the monthly recitation of the Rosh Chodesh haftarah (Isa. 66:1–24) on the Shabbat before its expected appearance.

At first reading, there is little that Isaiah says that defines Rosh Chodesh as a day special to women. Indeed, there is little, until the end of the haftarah, that even connects his theme with Rosh Chodesh.

At the beginning of the haftarah, Isaiah rails against pride, hypocrisy, and insincerity. He decries those who believe that a human-built Temple is greater than anything God could create:

> YHVH said:
> The heavens are My chair
> And the earth is My footstool:
> Where could you build a house for Me,
> What place could serve as My dwelling?
> My hand made all these things,
> And so it all came into being
> —declares YHVH.
>
> (Isa. 66:1–2)

He continues with a screed against those who bring sacrifices but do not truly repent:

> As for those who slaughter oxen like killing humans,
> Who sacrifice sheep as though they were breaking a dog's
> neck,

Who present the blood of swine as an offering,
Who offer incense but worship false gods—
Just as they have chosen how to act
And take pleasure in their sacrilege
So I will choose to taunt them,
To bring on them the very thing they fear.
For I called and no one replied,
I spoke and no one paid attention.
They did what I deem evil
And chose what I do not want.

(Isa. 66: 3–4)

The connection with Rosh Chodesh is made at the end of the haftarah, in a message of hope for the future:

For as the new heaven and the new earth
Which I will make
Shall survive by My will
—declares YHVH—
So shall your seed and your name continue.
And new moon after new moon,
And Shabbat after Shabbat,
All flesh shall come to worship Me
—said YHVH.

(Isa. 66:22–23)

In between these two sections are passages that ask the people to be patient, and that assure them that all will be well eventually. It is in these passages that we can see a link between women and Rosh Chodesh. Isaiah uses the metaphors of childbirth and maternal comfort to console the Israelites:

Before she went into labor, she was delivered;
Before her pains came, she bore a son.
Who ever heard the like?
Who ever witnessed such events?

Can a land pass through suffering
In a single day?
Or is a nation born
All at once?
Yet Zion went into labor
And immediately bore her children!
Shall I who bring on labor not bring about birth?
—says YHVH.
Shall I who cause birth shut the womb?
—said your God.
Rejoice with Jerusalem and be glad for her,
All you who love her!
Join in her jubilation,
All you who mourned over her—
That you may suck consolation to the full from her breast,
That you may draw glory to your delight from her bosom.

(Isa. 66:7–11)

It is interesting that the images Isaiah chose to assure the Israelites that they had not been abandoned by the Divine, that they would once again be a great nation in a land of their own, are the images of a woman in labor who later nurses her child. It is in these passages that we can glimpse what may be the remnants of earlier fertility rites linking the new moon with a woman's monthly cycle.

The phases of a woman's body were as predictable as the appearance of the phases of the moon. As remarkable and mystical as it seemed to the ancients for the moon to disappear and reappear every month, equally remarkable was the ability of women to bleed without being in mortal danger.

An interesting phenomenon called *synchronous menstruation* has been observed among women who live or work in close proximity. It was first substantiated by researcher Martha McClintock of the University of Chicago in 1971. Women have long noted that female family members, roommates, dorm mates, work colleagues, and cloistered nuns tend to menstruate at the same time. In a tribal society, where proximity was a necessity for safety as well as cohesion, the women would have all menstruated simultaneously, at the same phase of the moon every four weeks, adding to their mystery and mystique. Indeed, the very words themselves—*menses, menstruation, month*—come from the Latin word for *moon.*

In many ancient civilizations, the moon was personified as a goddess. The Aztec moon goddess is shown as cradling in her arms a rabbit, a fertility symbol in many cultures, including Christian. The Greek Selene, who bore fifty mortal daughters to her human lover Endymion, is sometimes identified as Apollo's twin sister Artemis, the goddess of fertility and childbirth, who is often depicted with a crescent moon above her forehead. The Roman Diana is goddess both of the moon and of fertility and childbirth. The Babylonian moon goddess Anunitu later became merged with the Sumerian Ishtar, who, among her many other attributes, was the goddess of love and fertility.

Modern pagans and Wiccans have continued this tradition, with rituals timed according to the phases of the moon. One pagan resource Web site is called Moon Goddess Circles, another the Women's Moon Hut, which describes itself as "a place for women on their moontime to come for rest, reflection, and sisterhood." Many other sites connect fertility and the moon.

In Judaism, too, from our earliest traditions, women have been associated with Rosh Chodesh. According to the Talmud (*Megillah* 22b), women are exempt from work on Rosh Chodesh, just as though it were a Shabbat or Yom Tov. In his commentary on this talmudic passage, Rashi explains that women are exempt from spinning, weaving, and sewing, because these were the activities that women contributed to the building of the *mishkan*. Midrash *Pirkei De Rabbi Eliezer* (chap. 45) explains that women have been rewarded with a special holiday once a month because they refused to contribute their gold jewelry to the building of the golden calf.

Today, Rosh Chodesh celebrations and study groups for women have become part of Jewish expression throughout all facets of our community, from the most traditionally observant to the most devoutly New Age. Most of the groups incorporate prayer, study, and discussion in their celebrations of the new moon. Some are organized by synagogues or other educational institutions and have a curriculum and plan that is followed every year. Others are more spontaneous. In all cases, these Rosh Chodesh groups have reinvented and revitalized the idea of Rosh Chodesh as a women's holiday.

The earliest commandment given to the Israelites in Exodus 12:1–2, even before they left Egypt, was to determine the new moon of the month of Nisan, and to use that date as the beginning of the year. Although we celebrate Rosh Hashanah, the new year, in the fall month of Tishrei, it is the spring month of Nisan that determines our liturgical calendar.

We cannot know if the Sages selected this passage as the one to be read on *Shabbat Rosh Chodesh* in order to remind women that the new moon is a holiday specific to them. One suspects that the choice was made because of the closing passages, and because of the message of optimism it brings along with the returning of the moon.

But as women, we can look at these lines as ones that do celebrate our uniqueness. Even those who have not borne children, through choice or through circumstance, can find resonance in passages that connect us with the natural rhythms of time. Each month we can remember that it is woman alone who has the ability to continue the miracle of creation.

RABBI STACIA DEUTSCH

הפטרת שבת שקלים
Haftarat Shabbat Shekalim

II Kings 12:1–16

*J*ehoash was seven years old when he began his reign. In the seventh year of Jehu's reign, Jehoash began his reign; and he ruled in Jerusalem for forty years. His mother was named Zibiah of Beersheba. . . . And Jehoash said to the priests: Let all the money of the dedicated things which is brought into the House of the Eternal . . . be taken by the priests from the one who is making the gift, and used by them to make repairs in the Temple, wherever it is found that repairs are needed.

(II KINGS 12:1–6)

THERE ARE FOUR special Shabbatot during the year when the regular Torah readings are supplemented by special thematic readings. On *Shabbat Shekalim*, we add the first verses of *Ki Tissa* (Exod. 30:11–16) and follow that reading with this haftarah portion. These texts together are a reminder to the people that the time has come to donate a half-shekel to the Temple maintenance. The story of King Jehoash and the Temple repairs becomes vital to *Shabbat Shekalim* because of the custom that on the first of Adar messengers went to all the Jewish communities to collect this tax.[1]

At age seven, King Jehoash dedicated himself to restoring the Temple to its original glory. Twenty-three years later, nothing had been

265

done; the foundation cracks had widened and more paint had chipped away. Jehoash was incensed. Over the years, money had been collected for the repairs, but none had been used. In a fit of anger, Jehoash stripped the responsibility for tax collection away from his priests and turned the accounts over to the "king's secretary" (12:12).

What's more, the king not only changed the system of *who* collected the money, but he also altered *how* the money would be collected. Calling for a dual system of taxes and voluntary contributions, King Jehoash shifted all fiscal responsibility away from the priests. Knowing that the Temple's restoration would be his legacy, King Jehoash devoted his life to attaining that goal.

Imagine knowing from childhood what would be your legacy. Imagine working your entire life toward one specific goal and the overwhelming fulfillment that must come from having done exactly what you set out to do. King Jehoash's story is an example of devotion and dedication. In our own lives, our paths often diverge from our childhood plans, but Jehoash's story provides for us a model of goal setting and accomplishment, ending in personal fulfillment and a lifelong legacy.

Jehoash's life was not an easy one. He was born in the late ninth century, when there was no peace in the territory of Judah. A succession of kings came and went; most were removed forcibly by the hand of their enemies. Jehoash's grandmother Athalia became queen after her son (his father) was assassinated. To ensure her own rule, Queen Athalia set out to destroy all her descendants, by literally murdering her own grandchildren (II Kings 11:1).

Jehosheba, the wife of the chief priest, rescued Jehoash and secretly raised him behind the Temple walls (II Kings 11:2–3). Though the Bible dwells more on her husband's accomplishments than hers, Jehosheba must have taken great risks to protect the young royal while his grandmother reigned. In the simple act of rescuing this young boy, Jehosheba thwarted Athalia's plans and single-handedly set the groundwork for the restoration of the Davidic line. Jehosheba's story is told in one sentence, but her influence on the child-king cannot be underestimated.

Some commentaries suggest that Jehoash's devotion to the Temple stems from his having grown up there. As a child, Jehosheba showed Jehoash the damage that Queen Athalia had done, and he knew it was his responsibility to make the necessary repairs. The midrash suggests that Athalia was interested in neither the Temple nor in Temple ritual. "Athalia mother of Ahaziah and her sons tore the gold nails out of the Temple."[2] This midrash opens the door to the widespread belief that Athalia worshipped the Canaanite god Ba'al and disregarded the Israelite Temple cult.

As a child, Jehoash lived in the Temple with Jehosheba and the high priest, watching as his grandmother dug holes in the sacred walls and removed valuables for her own nefarious purposes. He watched and waited for his own chance to stem the tide of her destruction.

Turning back to the preceding text, II Kings 11:17–20, gives us a better understanding of Athalia and why Jehoash's life was spent repairing the damage his grandmother had wrought. It is in this prelude to our haftarah that we find the story of Jehoash's grandmother, Athalia, and her short but influential reign.

The text recounts that when Jehoash was seven, the high priest Jehoiada summoned an army to lie in wait while he brought Jehoash to a public place. There they anointed him king and proclaimed loudly, "May the King live!" Queen Athalia heard the commotion and entered the Temple intent on discovering the source of the rejoicing. When she arrived and found that Jehoash had been anointed, she rent her garments and shouted, "Treason! Treason!" She was quickly arrested, removed from the Temple property, and executed (11:9–16).

And so as young Jehoash became king of Judah, he could not disregard the personal impact of Athalia's reign. The text contrasts Athalia's wanton disregard for the Temple with Jehoash's blind dedication to repairing it. It is said that Athalia's murder was "an act of purification. By killing her, Judah showed that she was ready to cleanse herself of the influence of Canaan."[3] All the more, Jehoash's repairs to the Temple reflect his unquestionable legitimacy through his preparedness to renew the people's devotion to the one God of Israel.

Whether King Jehoash's goal was to repair his childhood home, to purge the nation of idolatry, or to establish his own legitimacy, his place in history was secured by the process of the Temple's restoration. We read Jehoash's story in this haftarah every year to effectively link our modern observance of *Shabbat Shekalim* to our historical past.

Yet, while we recount the tale of the savior Jehosheba, and contrast the destructive actions of wicked Queen Athalia with the devoted purity of King Jehoash, we still recognize that Jehoash and Athalia were not as different as we might have thought. Chronicles recounts that after Jehoiada, Jehoash's high priest, died, Jehoash himself turned to idolatry (II Chronicles 24:17). And more, near the end of his life, Jehoash emptied the Temple's treasury, the very one he sought to reform, in order to bribe an opposing ruler (II Kings 12:18–20).

Nevertheless, King Jehoash takes his place in Jewish history as the king who restored the Davidic monarchy and restored the Temple's glory. He overturned the spoils of a corrupt queen and devised an important system of financial reform—a system that remained in effect under King Josiah and King Hezekiah many years later.

It is hard for us to identify with someone who knew his life's destiny at the incredibly young age of seven. We are lucky if at twenty or fifty or seventy-five years of age we can find a single interest to captivate us and propel us to action. As we read this haftarah, we are reminded to set personal goals and make plans. Restoring a dilapidated sacred building is quite a lofty ambition—ours need not be so grand. Even from this very haftarah, we see that Jehosheba helped a child in need and her act of kindness changed history, ultimately leading to the larger context of our *Shabbat Shekalim* commemoration. Finish reading a novel, writing a letter, teaching a child, volunteering time, giving *tzedakah*; little goals lead to larger accomplishments. Though we may never know the full impact of our actions, by setting one goal at a time and striving day by day to complete the tasks we have begun, we will create a world to be proud of—our legacy to the next generation.

RABBI KAREN SORIA

הפטרת שבת זכור
Haftarat Shabbat Zachor

I Samuel 15:1–34

*N*ow go and smite Amalek, and utterly destroy all
that they have . . . (I SAMUEL 15:3)

SAUL'S EXPERIENCE of becoming king, related earlier in I Samuel, sets
the stage for this haftarah as God repeatedly appears as the One Who
willfully and recklessly crosses his path.[1] While Saul seeks his father's
lost livestock, Samuel plucks him out of the holiday crowd to dine with
him, seated in a place of honor. Yet early the following morning, he
sends him away with a surreptitious anointing at the city's edge. When
Samuel convenes the people at Mitzpeh to publicly anoint Saul, Saul
is hidden among the household accoutrements—attempting to conceal
himself, as it were, from God and Samuel's interference in his life. Saul
is the dutiful son, the manly man, the reluctant king who must become
God's own instrument of punishment against the Amalekites (I Sam.
9:2–27; 10:17–24).

Exodus 17:8–16 introduces Amalek as it attacks Israel. Israel pre-
vails by the end of the daylong battle, whereupon God pledges to erad-
icate the memory of Amalek. Deuteronomy provides the rationale for
God's blanket condemnation of Amalek, because "he ambushed your
rearguard—when you were debilitated and utterly exhausted—without
any fear of God" (Deut. 25:18). Yet in Deuteronomy, unlike Exodus,
the responsibility falls upon Israel to punish Amalek. And thus the tension holds, and builds, from Exodus through I Samuel, with a nation

269

marked for destruction; its very memory to be erased, for its opponent is the God Who brought us out of the land of Egypt, and its conscience and executioner is the people of Israel.

I Samuel 15 describes God's command to Saul through Samuel to slaughter everything of Amalek. Saul enters into battle and triumphs, but instead of following God's instruction to the letter, he captures Agag, the Amalekite king, and selectively spares or kills the animals. God informs Samuel of Saul's partial compliance, and regrets the choice of Saul as sovereign. Samuel confronts Saul, who maneuvers around Samuel's words until caught in his own self-deception. Saul acknowledges his sin, and pleads for Samuel's cooperation in a face-saving gesture, but Samuel is finished with Saul. He reiterates God's rejection of Saul following Saul's rejection of God, and then, turning to the captive survivor, Agag, Samuel brutally executes him.

What should Samuel have said upon hearing God's stark command? How should Saul have responded? Jerome Charyn comments, "The first book of Samuel is about the presence and absence of voices, the history of a tribe that has become tone-deaf."[2] No fewer than eight times does the root sh-m-'a—to hear, heed, understand; or to cause to hear, proclaim, summon—occur in the haftarah. The word kol, "voice" or "command," appears six times. Tone-deaf or not, this generation, like ours, is required to listen and respond.

Samuel and Saul, however, play tug-of-war with their words.[3] Samuel calls on Saul to "heed the call of God's words!" but Saul responds by proclaiming to and summoning the people (I Sam. 15:1, 4). When Saul returns, stating that he has fulfilled God's word, Samuel rhetorically asks, "and this sheep-noise in my ears and the sound of cattle I hear are what?" Repeatedly, Saul says, "YHVH," as though mere repetition is proof enough of obedience, but thrice he reveals his spiritual emptiness when he identifies YHVH to Samuel as "your God."

Or perhaps Saul is distancing himself from the seeming murderousness of Samuel's God. The Rabbis are not unanimous in their evaluation of Saul; some view him as too innocent to reign effectively, too pure to grasp political expediencies. It is his simplicity, his naïve but misguided commitment to what he believes to be right, that cause him to fail. His compassion, not his false pride, leads him to spare Agag.[4]

To Samuel, identifying and responding to the Voice is straightforward: God willfully crosses our path to make us follow God's sovereign will. There are no differences of tone or timbre, no shades of meaning to decipher. Samuel's palette of life is black and white. Saul finds nuances and echoes. The Voice is a fugue, with interwoven melodies. God may remember and require Saul to ruthlessly destroy Amalek for its merciless assault on Israel during the Exodus, but Saul remembers and, without thought of God's condemnation of everything associated with Amalek, recklessly rewards the Kenites for their previous kindness to Israel by warning them to withdraw from Amalek. Saul hears the voice of relationship; he cannot ignore the Kenites' need. Interestingly, for this alone Samuel does not condemn him.

But Samuel does condemn Saul for his mercy toward Amalek, and many Rabbis concur. We read in Midrash *Rabbah Esther,* "When you left, you were pure, but you returned guilty for having mercy toward him. . . . So! His offspring will torment you like thorns in your eyes and sharp points in your sides. This is Haman. . . ."[5] Saul's misplaced mercy enables Haman's later persecution of the Jews. Worse than that, Saul's hubris saves Amalek and destroys innocents.

> Be not more righteous than your Creator, as in the case of Saul of whom it is written, "When Saul arrived at the city of Amalek." . . . Whoever shows himself merciful in circumstances where he should be pitiless, in the end becomes pitiless when he should be merciful. . . . As it is said, "So Nov, city of priests, he sliced with sword, from men to women, children to infants, and oxen, asses, and sheep." (I Sam. 22:19)[6]

God willfully and recklessly crossed Saul's path, and Saul recklessly and willfully carried out his own will.

But what happens when mercy is prohibited? When we have

"YHVH God/the Lord God" (*Adonai haElohim*) without "the Merciful One/the Womb-One" (*haRachaman*)? When we are blind to the tie of relationship as Samuel is to Israel's debt to the Kenites? When we cannot see our own vulnerability in the face of another, as Saul recognized his in Agag? What happens when the world turns black and white, turns to extremes, turns to slaughter? When life loses color and nuance, then we are merely surviving—we become diminished in our own eyes, as Samuel notes of Saul. We become incapable, unworthy, "less than" any other. And then the soul that is dead is our own.

Samuel and Saul are both wounded souls. Samuel cannot make his sons follow in righteous ways, but he emphasizes his authority to Saul, "*I am the one YHVH sent to crown you . . .*" (15:1). When God tells Samuel of Saul's disobedience in 15:10–11, Samuel is so distraught that he cries out to God all night with the same pain and passion as the Israelites cried out in Exodus when in bondage to Pharaoh. The Hebrew root *ch-r-h*, which some translate as "distressed" and others as "grieved," means "to burn, be kindled; to become hot, angry, wroth." Surely Samuel is furious—at God, at himself, at Saul. How dare God send this weak-willed man to be sovereign! How stupid and incompetent God makes Samuel appear to the public now! How could God have been so duped by this pretender to kingliness! How could he, Samuel, not have argued with God?

What hopes, what dreams and ambitions Samuel has harbored for Saul. Saul is the replacement son and fearless leader who will convince Samuel of the suitability of a monarchy. Saul is the savior who will conquer Israel's enemies and be living proof of Samuel's worth as a prophet. No wonder Samuel is angry. But the burden is too much for Saul. He has no time to emerge from his small chrysalis—his tribe, the smallest of all; his family, the most junior of the tribe—to the immense responsibility of kingship. His wings have no time to dry and strengthen properly, so he acts precipitously, as in 13:8–14 or 14:26–35. Saul rushes to please God, to pacify the people, to placate Samuel. But Saul is empty inside.

And when Saul, thinking he has done well, reports to Samuel following the battle, the prophet attacks him with all the fury of a betrayed lover. In Samuel's voice we can hear all the rage of pain and betrayal that arises when relationships end. The ebb and flow of Saul's response, as he trips over explanations, show his desperate effort to maintain some control, some semblance of dignity, as he seeks the explanation that will assuage Samuel's anger.

But their pain is too deep, their wills too strong; God has recklessly crossed each of their paths, and neither can find his way back to his old one. Saul asks Samuel to return with him; Samuel refuses and turns to leave. And in the passion of the moment, someone tears his garment.

The Hebrew is ambiguous; either Samuel or Saul could be the subject of "he seized the corner of his cloak . . ." (15:27). Either had reason enough to tear his own garment, or to tear the other's. Rashi explains that some say Saul grabbed Samuel's robe to force Samuel to come with him, while others say Samuel tore Saul's robe as a symbol of God's rejection of Saul. But perhaps Saul, frantic for Samuel's approval and love, lunged for Samuel's robe in a futile attempt to literally keep him in his life. Or Samuel, grief-stricken for his now-shattered dreams and hopes, grasped the hem of his own robe and ripped it in mourning, as Radak notes on verse 27: "for that is the way of the righteous, who ritually tear/perform *k'riah* at the moment their new disciple is no longer praiseworthy." And perhaps Saul, appalled at his new understanding of what this relationship would require of him, ripped his own garment in grief, in horror, and in shame. Here are two men who needed and loved each other much more than either could acknowledge. Their souls are as torn as the cloak.

We wonder: As the garment ripped, did the corner detach completely? Or did it stay, hanging by a few threads, able to be mended? Should Samuel, like Abraham, have argued with God against complete destruction? Should Saul have followed God's command as Samuel delivered it, to destroy every trace of Amalek? Or was it all a horrible mistake? Did God never demand, never desire, the annihilation of all Amalek?

The tearing of the garment is the sound of souls rent in disillusion and despair. It is the sound of Samuel and Saul's shattered relationship. Neither man mends, and they do not meet again in the land of the living. Yet as the saying goes: "The past is not dead. It isn't even past."[7] Nor are relationships finished when someone dies. But there can be healing and comfort. The torn garment may find a new use, and, like the broken bone or the aching heart, become stronger for the mending.

As women and as Jews, we will bring healing across generations when we choose to hear the nuances and recognize the woundedness of another. As women and as Jews, we can understand anew the midrash of the beggars by Jerusalem's gate, cleaning and bandaging their many wounds. We see into the soul of the frayed bandages: The Messiah wears the torn garment of Saul and of Samuel, even, as if one could dare speak it, of God.

הפטרת שבת פרה

Haftarat Shabbat Parah

Ezekiel 36:16–38

*T*he House of Israel dwelling upon their land defiled
it with their ways and doings; like the defilement
of a menstruant woman, so was their way before Me . . .
(EZEKIEL 36:17)

Body and Spirit

What does it mean to live within our bodies, even as we yearn to connect with that which transcends the physical? Do our bodies limit us?
Do they distance us? Do they make us impure? The special haftarah
for *Shabbat Parah* is commonly understood as a spiritual counterpart to
the Torah reading's focus on ritual and the physical. When we take a
closer look at Ezekiel's words about the human body in general, and
about women's bodies in particular, we find that the physical and the
spiritual are not in opposition.

Relating to the Red Heifer

Shabbat Parah, or the Sabbath of the Cow, is the second of four special
Shabbatot preceding Passover. The special *Maftir* reading for the day
is from Numbers 19, and describes an elaborate ritual through which
the priests overcome ritual impurity, which contact with death introduced into the community of Israel. Central to the ritual is the burning

of a red cow, whose ashes, mixed with water, render the impure pure. Most scholars agree that this reading was chosen in anticipation of Passover, because ritual purity was required for the performance of the ancient Passover sacrificial rites.

While the Torah reading from Numbers is a technical legal text, the special haftarah chosen for the day is a poetic passage, Ezekiel 36:16–38 (or 16–36 for Sephardim). Like the *Maftir*, the haftarah is suffused with discussions of purity and impurity, but here the language is evocative, the references ethereal. There are two sources of impurity according to the ritual system laid out in the Torah—contact with the dead and contact with bodily discharges like menstrual blood—and each impurity requires a distinctive ritual of purification. These two kinds of impurity join in the haftarah. While Ezekiel's opening lines compare the people of Israel to a menstruating woman, the process of purification he anticipates for them, a sprinkling of purifying waters (Ezek. 36:25), resembles the ritual of the red cow used for purification from death.

*E*zekiel's Bare Bones

The main thrust of the haftarah reading is clear enough. It begins with Ezekiel's testimony that Israel's dispersion came as punishment for sin, then promises that God will soon restore the people so that they might once again prosper on their land. Ezekiel's central point is that our ancestors deserved the suffering that befell them. The accusation is typical of the prophet, who chastises his listeners again and again. Our discomfort confirms the prophet's role. A call to conscience is never comfortable.

The imagery that Ezekiel uses raises questions that are perhaps unintended. He claims that sinful Israel is impure like a menstruating woman (Ezek. 36:17). Speaking for God, the prophet says of Israel, "I poured my rage upon them, upon the blood that they poured on the land defiled with their idols" (Ezek. 36:18). The menstruating woman still lingers in our mind, and her blood is now associated with the blood poured on the land. Her innocent, natural blood flows into the blood spilled by the idolatrous Israelites. What is this blood, the blood of heathen sacrifice, the blood of murder victims? Why is it connected to menstrual blood?

Negative associations with menstruation might expose Ezekiel's own prejudices, or register the misogyny of his culture and his time. But women are not the overt subjects of his prophecy; our bodies are mentioned as images or symbols, for the sake of what we represent.

$\mathcal{A}$ Marriage Made with Heaven

What does the menstruating woman represent for Ezekiel? Radak suggests that in making the comparison between Israel and a menstruating woman, Ezekiel draws on an allegory that likens the relationship between God and the Jewish people to the relationship between a husband and wife. In traditional Jewish practice, marital relationships ebb and flow according to the cycles of the woman's body. During her menstrual period and for a set time after it, a woman observes a physical separation from her husband. Immersion in a mikveh, or ritual bath, precedes a time of renewed physical intimacy. Radak understands Ezekiel to be explaining to his listeners that their separation from God is temporary: God is keeping Israel at a distance, just as a husband keeps apart from his wife when she menstruates. God will reunite with the people as soon as they purify themselves, just as a husband draws near to his wife after she immerses in the purifying waters of the mikveh.

Radak suggests that hidden amid Ezekiel's stern accusations are hints of consolation for a people aggrieved by God's apparent distance. The prophet comforts his listeners by pointing to an experience they know from their own domestic lives. It is a periodic sadness to separate from one's spouse, Ezekiel acknowledges, but within the broad sweep of a loving marriage, such moments are trifling. With the passage of time, a reunion is assured. Indeed, this is Ezekiel's overt message as the reading continues.

Rashi's reading is similar as he infuses Ezekiel's allegory with emotional content, perhaps drawing on his own intimate experience of marriage: "Scripture compares Israel to a menstruating woman whose husband anticipates when she will immerse, and longs to return to her." For Rashi, Israel's reunion with God is not only inevitable, it is desired. More than this, it is what God longs for. Had Ezekiel's message been one of rejection, he could have described Israel as a spurned wife, or as an adulteress. According to both Rashi and Radak, the key aspect of Ezekiel's menstruating woman is not her impurity, but the temporary separation that her impurity requires.

*I*n the Flesh

As our haftarah continues, Ezekiel foresees God replacing Israel's "heart of stone" with a "heart of flesh" (Ezek. 36:26). Unlike stone, a heart of flesh can pulse, and fill, and even stop. Only a heart of flesh—tender, vulnerable, and feeling—is capable of receiving God's spirit. For Ezekiel, living with God means living in our bodies. Only an embodied existence allows the full range of experience that a complete relationship with God demands. Our bodies grow and change, and so too does our experience of the Divine. Holiness lives beyond our bodies, but we can draw holiness near when we inhabit our humanity, down to the blood, muscle, and bone.

Images of beating hearts and menstruating women convey a relationship between God and Israel that lives and breathes, with cycles and seasons. This comes through in other passages as well, where Ezekiel imagines menstrual blood as an expression of a vital, visceral bond with God: "Then I passed over you and saw you foundering in your blood, and I told you, 'Live in your blood,' and I told you, 'Live in your blood'" (Ezek. 16:6). For Ezekiel, the relationship between God and Israel is no spiritualized platonic relationship, but a connection that is deep and intimate. God the husband is a constant partner who revels in the changeable, fleshly, voluptuous embrace of the espoused.

The idea that God yearns for human attention, body and soul, insists upon the presence of women and our participation. For Ezekiel, the tender, vital, human body is the vessel for God's spirit. A woman's body recommends her as the perfect partner for the Divine.

RABBI HELAINE ETTINGER

הפטרת שבת החדש

Haftarat Shabbat HaChodesh

Ezekiel 45:16–46:18

*T*hus declares the God, Adonai, "In the first
month . . ." (EZEKIEL 15:18)

THE FOURTH OF THE SPECIAL Shabbatot that lead up to Pesach is *Shabbat HaChodesh*. It is the Shabbat that immediately precedes or falls on the first day of the month of Nisan. The *Maftir* reading (Exod. 12:1–20) is the source of the special name, "the Sabbath of the month," for in Exodus 12:2 we read, "This month shall be for you the first month of all the months of the year." God designates the month of Aviv (later known as Nisan) as the first month of the year.[1] In his commentary to Exodus 12:2, Maimonides explains that the designation of Nisan as the first month is God's first commandment to the children of Israel. This designation is to serve as a reminder of the great miracle of the redemption. Thus the Torah does not refer to the months by Hebrew names, but by numbers, that is, the first month, the second month, the third month, and so on, making the Exodus the constant point of reference. With this primary status God elevates this month above all others.

It is easy to speculate why this should be so. Nisan is the month of the Exodus from Egypt. In this month the children of Israel were redeemed from slavery to freedom. We were, in a sense, reborn in Nisan. The themes of spring that permeate the seder ritual are further reminders that during this month, nature itself is renewed. In the physical realm, the dormancy of winter is similar to death and the awakening of spring is like rebirth. In the spiritual realm, slavery is similar to death and freedom is like rebirth. Together, physical and spiritual redemption represent a new beginning, and thus Nisan becomes "the first month of all the months of the year." Hence the first Shabbat of this important month is the Shabbat of the month, *Shabbat HaChodesh*.

The special *Maftir* reading describes in great detail the Israelites' final days in Egypt: the slaughtering of the paschal lamb; the bloody marking of the doorposts; the feasting and special foods of the final night; the preparations for leaving; and the injunction to eat only unleavened bread for seven days. The special haftarah from the Book of Ezekiel creates a parallel to that first historic Pesach and describes in equally great detail the specific rituals of the month of Nisan in the rebuilt Temple. The prophet Ezekiel, although living in exile, imagines the future life of our people when we have returned to our own land and rebuilt the ruined Temple. There, in the new Temple, the *Nasi* (translated as "Prince") will bring forward the sacrifices on behalf of the people.

On the first and the seventh day of Nisan, the *Nasi* shall bring sacrifices to the Temple to make atonement for the whole house of Israel. He shall mark the altar, the doorposts of the gates, and the doorposts of the inner courtyard of the Temple with blood in a ritual reminiscent of the departure from Egypt. Then, on the fourteenth day of the month, the whole community will celebrate the festival of Passover, bringing the appointed sacrifices and offerings, and eating only unleavened bread for seven days.

The Rabbis surely chose these two readings at the beginning of Nisan as a way to immerse us in the story and the details of the holiday of Pesach. Are there other reasons, though, why they might have chosen these two readings? To answer this we must return to the idea of Nisan as the month of redemption.

What is necessary to bring about redemption? First and foremost, Judaism teaches, God is necessary. Humanity cannot bring about its own redemption, although we may participate in it. God must care about our plight on earth and actively intervene to bring us to redemption. Such deliverance is not possible, however, without a second crucial element: the human capacity to *imagine a changed world*. When our ancestors lived as slaves in Egypt, there was not a single Jew who had firsthand experience of freedom aside from Moses. For four hundred years, we had known only slavery and oppression. Then along came a man who proclaimed that the God of Israel would bring us out of Egypt and lead us to freedom in our own land. What an unimaginable and outlandish notion!

Indeed, when Moses first returned to Egypt to fulfill his task of leading the people to freedom, he had to work as hard to convince his fellow Israelites as he did to convince Pharaoh that the people should go free. With God's help, with signs and wonders, and with ten terrible plagues, the slaves began to be able to imagine another life. Perhaps they could not picture it clearly, but the hope that such a life might exist was motivation enough for them to risk their secure enslavement for an uncertain freedom.

How many of us would have had the courage to go forth? After a traumatic night of screams and weeping and death, how many of us would have been ready to set out? And yet, they did. Six hundred thousand, we are told, clung to a vision of a better life, and walked out of Egypt. Surely the audacity to imagine such a change was essential for God to be able to bring about our redemption.

In the first half of the sixth century B.C.E., the prophet Ezekiel witnessed the invasion and surrender of Jerusalem to King Nebuchadnezzar of Babylonia and the destruction of the First Temple. He was sent into exile along with other members of the priestly, royal, and elite classes. There, in Babylonia, he shared God's words with a grief-stricken and disheartened people. In much of his prophecy he castigated the Jews and called for their repentance. He tried to instruct the people, to help them understand the ways in which they had sinned, and the reasons for their terrible punishment and loss. Alongside these harsh messages, Ezekiel consoled and comforted them with God's promise of a return to Jerusalem and a chance to rebuild the Temple. With his prophecy he painted elaborate descriptions of the new Temple, including its measurements and appointments. In our haftarah, he visualized the actual rituals that would be resumed once the Temple was restored. He, too, had the courage to imagine a brighter future.

Ezekiel never doubted that God was with the people. God was the source of their punishment, and God would be the source of their redemption. He died long before King Cyrus of Persia allowed the Jews to return and to begin to rebuild the Second Temple. He had no proof that things would get better; what he did have was the audacity to believe in redemption. We call it prophetic vision, but it is the same radical imagination shared by the Israelite slaves who walked to freedom through the parted Reed Sea. It is also akin to the single-minded belief of Martin Luther King Jr. and the tenacious hope of Nelson Mandela. It is the vision of all great leaders who dare hope that they can lead a group out of oppression.

The month of Nisan, therefore, is the month that inspires all of us to imagine a changed world. We recall the Exodus from Egypt, our first redemption, and relive it through the rituals of the Passover seder. We set our seder table with a special goblet of wine for the prophet Elijah, whose coming will herald the Messiah and our future redemption. And on *Shabbat HaChodesh*, the first Sabbath of the month of Nisan, we also remember our people's experience in exile in Babylonia. We recall their despair and listen to the prophet Ezekiel as he enjoins us to imagine another redemption, the return to our homeland, and the rebuilding of our holy Temple.

From these two examples carefully chosen for *Shabbat HaChodesh*, we see that the survival of the Jewish people is based not only on our shared memory, but also on our shared vision of the future. In *Gates of Prayer*, the Reform prayer book, there is a poetic English interpretation of the Ge'ulah prayer, the redemption prayer, that reads:

> Inspired by prophets and instructed by sages, we have survived oppression and exile, time and again overcoming

the forces that would have destroyed us. Our failings are many—our faults are great—yet it has been our glory to bear witness to our God, and to keep alive in dark ages the vision of a world redeemed.[2]

The tenacity of that vision, the boldness to imagine a changed world even in the midst of oppression, exile, and discrimination, has enabled us to go forward and work to make that changed world a reality.

How fitting that in many communities it is now customary to hold a women's seder during the month of Nisan. A women's seder, like a traditional Pesach seder, recalls the history of our people, and draws on the radical capacity of our imagination to envision a redeemed world. In the women's seder, however, redemption is conceptualized as an egalitarian world where both men and women have equal opportunities to develop as human beings and to contribute their unique gifts to the world. At these new celebrations women participate in and lead the discussion and the rituals, whereas in many generations and in other contemporary settings the women facilitate the men's participation in the seder. Thousands of women take part in women's seders each year,[3] fashioning the commemoration to include new perspectives, new rituals, and new questions along with the familiar traditional ones. For example, in *The Ma'yan Passover Haggadah*, each of the four cups of wine are linked both to God's four promises to Israel found in Exodus 6:6–7 and also to "historical and living Jewish women, who in their own eras have acted as God's partners in fulfilling the divine promises of redemption and freedom."[4] Many now set the seder table with two cups—one the customary cup for the prophet Elijah, and the other a new cup for the prophetess Miriam. Women, we can see, use their experience to transform and perpetuate the Passover messages of freedom and redemption in fresh ways that simultaneously illuminate the particular and the universal.[5]

Some question the need for a women's seder. Others question the appropriateness of such a seder. *Shabbat HaChodesh* shows us that a women's seder is another inspired moment in our history. We learn from the story of Moses and the slaves, and from the example of Ezekiel and the exiles, that it is essential to put forward a vision of a better world. No matter how far our present circumstances may be from that for which we yearn, if we are to move from slavery to freedom, from exile to return, or from inequity to equality, we must set before ourselves a vision of a changed world. The women's seder is just such a vehicle for our imagination, a way to harness that same audacity that has enabled our people to survive for millennia—in partnership with a God who cares and redeems.

RABBI MICHELLE MISSAGHIEH

הפטרת שבת הגדול

Haftarat Shabbat HaGadol

Malachi 3:4–24

*B*ehold, I will send Elijah the prophet to you, before
the coming of the great and awesome day of YHVH,
to return the heart of fathers toward their sons and the
heart of sons toward their fathers. (MALACHI 3:23–24)

MALACHI'S VISION IS undoubtedly messianic. Read on *Shabbat HaGadol*, the Shabbat before Passover, when we recall the ultimate example of a destructive father-son relationship between Pharaoh and Moses, the question arises: What does it mean to be a parent in the twenty-first century? How are we to translate the principles of the Jewish tradition, along with feminist and egalitarian values of modernity, into one cohesive and consistent philosophy of child rearing?

Some families have a mother and father; others two mothers or two fathers. Some are blended families, others are headed by single parents. Some families grow through adoption and others through surrogacy. At times grandparents raise their grandchildren; still other times an aunt, uncle, or close friend may have to step in to fulfill this responsibility. Given these different models, the goal of family cohesion is complex and dynamic.

Though this may seem to be a contemporary challenge, Malachi, known as the last prophet of Israel according to the Talmud in *Yoma* 9b, understood the challenge inherent in parent-child relationships. He lived during a time of spiritual instability, when people doubted

God and Divine justice, and when divorce and intermarriage rates were rising. He also experienced a time of renewed hope, when the Temple in Jerusalem was rebuilt after its first destruction around 515 B.C.E. A combination of these two forces—destruction and repair, chaos and the hope of renewed stability—affected family relationships. Malachi in 3:24 knew that in the real world parents and children can become estranged, old wounds may never heal, and that it is a messianic concept to ask God to help us "return the heart of fathers toward their sons and the heart of sons toward their fathers."

For Malachi, as for us, honoring parents is a heavy responsibility. Even the Hebrew word for *honor, kavod,* comes from the same three letter Hebrew root *k-v-d* as the word *heavy.* This commandment is not always easy to perform, and perhaps even burdensome. How do we honor our parents if they abused us as children? What if they fail to live up to our moral expectations, or engage in extramarital affairs? What if they abuse drugs, alcohol, or food? How do we honor our parents if we feel unsafe sharing our feelings with them? What happens if they are no longer living and we are left with unresolved issues? In addition, the word *kavod* might also characterize the weightiness or significance of the parent-child relationship, as if to remind us that we carry both the blessings and burdens of our early parent-child relationship patterns into our marriages, friendships, work environments, and with our own children.

The Talmud in *Kiddushin* 30b tries to guide us on this difficult path by teaching that "There are three partners in a person: The Holy One, the father, and the mother. When a person honors his or her father and mother, God says 'It is as though I had dwelt among them and they had honored Me.'" When we strive to honor our parents, God as ultimate parent is honored.

How can we work toward achieving Malachi's messianic parent-child relationship in our own lives? The prophet hints at a direction with his use of the word *shuv,* meaning "return" or "turn." He urges us to return to the past as a model of redemptive parent-child relationships. The haftarah begins in Malachi 3:4 with God asking Israel to give offerings "as they were in days of old, like years long past." God continues in 3:7 by begging Israel to "return to Me and I will return to you." And as a result, in 3:17–18 when we "turn back" we will be able to "see the difference between the righteous and the wicked, between the one who serves God and the one who does not serve God."

This romantic and simplistic notion of returning assumes an ancient time of mythical family bliss. However, when we look to our past, this is not the way things really were. For example, after Terach's death, Abraham did not return to his father's birthplace or stay by his father's grave in Haran; he simply moved on (Gen. 11:31–12:4). Rebekah had to use her child Jacob as a pawn in her uncommunicative relationship with her husband Isaac (Gen. 27:5–13). Laben shattered his daughters' bond of sisterhood when he chose to marry Rachel and Leah off to the same man (Gen. 29:16–30). And during Passover we read about how Moses rejected and ran from the values of his step-father, the Pharaoh, in order to free the Israelites.

Malachi's desire to return to the good old days is natural but misguided. Holding on to an idealized past is often preferable to change, because the known is ironically comfortable, even if it is unhealthy. In addition, change involves reflection, recognition of dysfunction, and a re-visioning of what the future might hold. Simply put, it's easier to continue in a damaging parent-child relationship of self-denial, miscommunication, or hurt than to do the emotional soul searching necessary to confront one's own responsibility in causing another's pain and ultimately change oneself and one's relationship.

Malachi clings to a troubled past and condemns the present, but misses the opportunity to explore the historical and interpersonal dynamics of alienation between parents and children. Malachi does not help the Israelites change. Instead he hopes for it to happen, without a hint at how hard the road may be and what it will take to occur.

In truth, deep change between parents and children requires not a turning back but a leap of faith forward toward a new future. We have to ask ourselves, What does it mean to be in a loving adult-child relationship with one's parent? What does it mean to raise one's own family and enjoy a loving sexual partnership with a spouse alongside one's relationship with one's parents? In order to heal we must work through our reactions of rejection, separation, and independence, while at the same time building new, different, and more satisfying bonds of appreciation, understanding, and deep love with our patents. This is not always possible. Both parties may not be receptive to doing what is necessary in the process, namely being willing to emotionally expose oneself to the other. It's commendable if one is able to travel through this journey by oneself or with a spouse. But to add the complicated layers of authority and hierarchy that inevitably enter the parent-child relationship makes it almost messianic.

Malachi promises a turn in "the heart of fathers." It is peculiar that the word *heart* here is in the singular. One would expect the Hebrew to read in the "hearts of fathers," reflecting the notion that each parent and each child will one day draw closer to his or her own parent. Perhaps the singular *heart* is found here to remind us of Pharaoh's singular all-consuming "heart" in the Book of Exodus. Not only did Pharaoh's heart harden because he was unable to see beyond his own selfish behavior and insecurities, but also because he was unwilling to change his relationship with his "children." His one stubborn, hard heart affected all the people of the land—the Egyptians and the Israelites alike. When Malachi teaches that the singular "heart of fathers" will one day return to their sons, he is teaching that just as one heart can cause suffering and death, a single heart can bring peace and wholeness. Just as one person's heart was able to negatively affect the history of the world, so too can one heart, one individual, be the catalyst for positive, loving change in the future.

In addition to the singular heart that changes, Malachi subtly points to another type of transformation in 3:17, one of traditional gender roles. God says that on Redemption Day, Israel will be God's precious possession and "I will be compassionate toward them, as a father is compassionate toward his son who serves him." The Hebrew verb for *being compassionate* is *yachmol*. Compassion is often associated in the Torah with the feminine. For example, at the beginning of the Passover story in Exodus 2:6, we read how Pharaoh's daughter took in baby Moses because she noticed a basket floating in the Nile, opened it, saw the baby boy crying, and "took compassion on him." Yet Malachi uses the verb "being compassionate toward" as if to tell us that this messianic time will demand a change of expected social norms; a time when men will feel comfortable showing tenderness, compassion, and empathy toward their sons. Parents and children will turn toward one another because they will feel the freedom to discover their true God-given emotional potential, and, perhaps as a result, even the meaning of *masculine* and *feminine* will change.

Malachi asks us to redefine who we can be by reworking the first and most primary significant relationship in our lives, that of a parent to a child, and a child to a parent. In doing so, he offers us a messianic vision of unimaginable magnitude.

Haftarot for
Days of Awe

RABBI SERENA RAZIEL EISENBERG

הפטרת ראש השנה א'

Haftarah for the First Day of Rosh Hashanah

I Samuel 1:1–2:10

*W*hen she had weaned him, she took him up with her, along with a three-year-old bull, one ephah of flour, and a jar of wine. And the weaned one was dedicated when she brought him to the House of God at Shiloh. (I SAMUEL 1:24)

THIS HAFTARAH PORTION, the story of Hannah's miraculous conception and dedication of Samuel, introduces an emphasis on weaning. Hannah prays desperately to bear a child, vowing that if she does give birth to a son, she will offer him to God "all the days of his life" (I Sam. 1:11). Yet after Samuel's birth, she does not bring him immediately up to the Temple at Shiloh, but rather keeps him home until he is weaned.[1]

The verse cited above describes the weaning transition with a curious repetition of the Hebrew word *na'ar*. Why is the word *na'ar* repeated? *Na'ar* is generally translated as "child," though the word appears frequently in the Tanakh with a range of meanings, including "older lad" and "servant." In the Hannah story, most translations interpret the phrase as "When she had weaned him, she took him up with her . . . though the child was still a young child." *Metzudat David* explains that the repetition glorifies Hannah's sacrifice, in that she

293

brought Samuel to the house of God while he was still at such a ten-der age. Rashi, on the other hand, explains that the repetition indi-cates that Samuel was still nursing. But that doesn't make any sense, given that the verse has just told us that Hannah weaned him. Mod-ern biblical scholars posit that the line is corrupt, unintelligible, and/or a scribal mistake.[2]

These commentators have missed a subtle but noteworthy empha-sis that recurs throughout biblical birth stories. The use of the word *na'ar* suggests a shift in status from one who is nursing to a weaned child dedicated to the Deity. According to this reading, the text would be translated: "And the weaned one was dedicated."

In Hebrew, two words are often translated interchangeably for *child*: *yeled* and *na'ar*. There are differences, however. The word *yeled* is rooted in the verb for giving birth, *yalad*. The word *na'ar*, by con-trast, has an ancient connotation of shaking off and bringing forth.[3] Modern biblical scholars conjecture that a *na'ar* is one who was "forced out of his mother's womb." A more plausible reading relates to wean-ing, as in one who has been shaken off the mother's breast, and then brought forth for dedication.

Similar language and themes of nursing, dedication, and weaning also appear in the parallel stories of Sarah and Hagar, read together with the haftarah of Hannah on the first day of Rosh Hashanah. The Torah story begins with God's remembrance of barren Sarah and the miraculous birth of Isaac. In Sarah's story, in Genesis 21:7, we hear her laughter, her amazement at motherhood and her ability to nurse, and we hear her own words, "Who would have said to Abraham that Sarah would suckle sons?!" Here, again, there is a textual puzzle: Sarah only had one son, Isaac. So why would the verse say that she nursed sons? A later midrash explains,

> Our mother Sarah was exceedingly modest, so that our
> father Abraham had to say to her, "This is not a time for
> modesty. To hallow God's Name, uncover your breast,
> that all may be aware of the miracles the Holy One has

begun to perform." Sarah uncovered her breast, and her nipples poured out milk like two jets of water. Noble ladies came forward to have their children suckled by Sarah . . ."[4]

Why would our Sages imagine Sarah uncovering her breasts to bring forth fountains of mother's milk? Perhaps they were influenced by the prevalent images of nursing Mother Goddesses from surrounding Near Eastern civilizations. During the biblical era, the Egyptian goddess Isis was described as nursing the pharaohs at birth, at enthronement, and at rebirth after death. The nursing mother icon spread from Egypt to mystery cults through Greece and Rome during the early centuries of the Common Era. In some Christian iconography, Mary is explicitly represented as a nursing mother.[5]

The rabbinic Sages drew upon similar imagery to interpret Sarah's story: Sarah is our matriarch who overflowed with Divine abundance. Though Sarah bore only one son, through him she nurtured all the future generations of children of Israel.

In this imagery, we see all mothers as vessels of Divine sustenance. Like us, the biblical characters are humans filled with a wellspring of God's love. As humans, we have limits; we cannot sustain a growing child alone. Sarah nursed Isaac, and then she weaned him. What meaning can we make of the weaning transition, emphasized so clearly in these biblical texts?

We don't know from the biblical text how Sarah felt about her experience; we know only from Genesis 21:8 that "Abraham made a great feast on the day that Isaac was weaned." Perhaps the feast was the joyful celebration, even relief, of a child growing to independence and maturity. But close reading of the text suggests that the feast was a sacrificial ceremony, similar to the food offerings brought by Hannah (meat, flour, wine) when Samuel was weaned. Until his weaning, Isaac is referred to as a son *(ben)* and as a *yeled*. The very next time we encounter Isaac he is referred to with the special status of a *na'ar*—when Abraham brings him as a sacrifice to God at Mount Moriah. The shift in language and status, from *yeled* to *na'ar*, occurs at weaning, and is marked by sacrifice.

We hear the echo of Abraham's sacrifice of Isaac in Hannah's story. There is a sacrifice inherent in Hannah's prayer to bear a child with the knowledge that she will not raise him to adulthood. Why does the Torah portray a weaned child as a sacrifice? Weaning somehow captures the painful paradox of parenthood: there is abandonment and dedication. Nurturing a child culminates, ultimately, in letting go as the child moves toward independence. Progeny provide a promise of immortality entangled with grief, all in the service of God.

These themes of weaning and sacrifice are subtly explored in the parallel story of Hagar and Ishma'el, also read as the Torah portion on Rosh Hashanah. When Hagar and Ishma'el are cast out of Abraham's household, the word *na'ar* appears curiously, and breast-feeding/weaning imagery is an important metaphor. At first reading, it seems that Ishma'el is called both *yeled* and *na'ar*, interchangeably. But there is a clear difference. Every time Abraham and Hagar refer to their child, they call him *yeled*. Abraham gave a skin of water to Hagar and the *yeled*. Hagar and the *yeled* wandered in the wilderness until Hagar's skin of water ran dry. She is figuratively an empty breast, even though Ishma'el is fourteen years old at the time. Hagar then placed Ishma'el, the *yeled*, a bow's distance away from her, so as not to hear his cry. At this point in the story, the language and perspective shift. As Ishma'el is now seen from God's perspective, he is not a *yeled*, but a *na'ar*. God heard the cry of a *na'ar*. God revealed to Hagar a well of water with which she could "water" the *na'ar*. This is a story of weaning and replenishment. It is God who ultimately provides redemption by nursing Ishma'el at the fountain of compassionate encounter.

We reach the climactic implication of weaning: When the mother reaches the limits of her strength, her patience, and her nourishment, God overflows with compassion and sustenance. In these stories of Hannah, Sarah, and Hagar, weaning marks the dangerous threshold when the mother alone can no longer sustain the child. Hannah reminds us that when our ability to nurture runs dry, there is a greater source of replenishment.

The Torah overflows with imagery of a nursing God. One of the names of God is *El-Shaddai*, which is related to the Hebrew word for *breast*, *shad*. God sustained the Israelites as they wandered through the wilderness with manna that had the taste of breast oil—*l'shad hashemen*.[6] In the JPS translation, this expression is rendered as "rich cream" or "cream of oil." In midrashim, manna is described in terms remarkably similar to breast milk: It was a milky white substance that tasted like milk to children, while to the old people it tasted like honey.[7] Manna exuded a fragrant odor, and the amount of manna gathered by each family corresponded to the exact need of that family, just as the mother's supply of milk typically accommodates the need of the child. In our Torah stories, God sustained the Israelites in the desert with manna, formed a river of melted manna from which the righteous will drink in the hereafter,[8] and then led the children of Israel to the land of "milk and honey."

Hannah's story provides us with the comforting metaphor of God as our Divine Nurse, a powerful contrast to the predominant images of God as King and Judge in the Rosh Hashanah liturgy. When we turn to God during times of despair, as did Hannah who prayed in her bitterness, it is comforting to find a God who will salve our suffering with wellsprings of compassion. Hannah's story helps us to discover the Divine well within ourselves, the source from which we overflow and nurture others.

הפטרת ראש השנה ב'

Haftarah for the Second Day of Rosh Hashanah

Jeremiah 31:1–20

*T*hus said YHVH: A voice in Ramah is heard— lamentation, bitter weeping. Rachel is weeping for her children, refusing to be comforted for her children, for they are no more. (JEREMIAH 31:15)

THE HAFTARAH FOR the second day of Rosh Hashanah comes as a liturgical embrace to those whose introspection has brought them to an awareness of their own estrangement from God and their need for *teshuvah*, "return." It is a prophetic poem promising return, originally addressed to a people who had already seen their Northern kin swept out of the land of Israel into exile, and who awaited their own imminent exile. The prophet Jeremiah insisted that the people's physical exile was caused by their self-estrangement from God through sin. Nevertheless, Jeremiah reassured the people that God's compassion would eventually cause God to reverse the severe decree and allow the people to return.

What was to stir God's compassion so greatly that God would reverse Divine judgment? Traditional commentators often assume that it is Israel's repentance, symbolized by the male figure of Ephraim engaging in an emotional confession.[1] However, the text strongly suggests that it was not Ephraim's confession alone that triggered God's response.

God's consoling promises are addressed to, and come in immediate response to, the female figure of Rachel. In the text, we encounter mother Rachel lamenting, weeping, and crying bitterly because her children "are no more." God immediately begins to console her, urging Rachel to refrain from further weeping and crying. In urging Rachel to stop her mourning, God reverses Jeremiah's earlier prophetic demand calling upon the professional mourning women to engage in lamentation and crying in order to mourn the coming destruction and exile (Jer. 9:16–17).

Rachel initially "refuses" to be comforted, suggesting another reversal of prophetic judgment. Earlier in his prophecy, Jeremiah repeatedly used the word *refuse (ma-ein)* in reproving accusation. The people *refused* to be ashamed (Jer. 3:3), they *refused* to receive correction (Jer. 5:3), and they *refused* to return (Jer. 5:3; 8:5). Rachel's refusal to be comforted, unlike these earlier refusals, is clearly meritorious. God consoles her with a promised reversal of those very judgments: Ephraim will indeed be ashamed, accept correction, and ask to be returned, and God will indeed cause Rachel's children to return.

God's comforting message goes on to reverse Rachel's lament itself. Rachel weeps because her children "are no more" *(einenu)*, but God counters the lament of nonexistence with two messages of existence: "there is" *(yesh)* reward for Rachel's work, and "there is" *(yesh)* hope for her future.

God's response to Rachel makes it clear that God has indeed already heard Ephraim's confession of sin and his plea, "Return me that I may return." The plea itself suggests that *teshuvah* is not only a human action, but also a Divine gift. God is now prepared to grant Ephraim's request for *teshuvah*, in response to Rachel's tears.

God describes to Rachel the process God is prepared to undertake in order to reverse the decree of exile. God will progress from judgment against Ephraim ("I speak against him") to impartial remembrance ("I surely remember him") to passionate but passive emotion ("My innards churn for him") and finally to active compassion ("I will surely show compassion to him").

This third step, the idea of God's innards churning, is astonishingly anthropomorphic, yet our passage is not without parallel in the *Tanakh*. Both Hosea and Isaiah present the metaphor of God as a corporeal being, whose inner parts are churning with anxiety on behalf of the peoples who are God's creatures.[2] The nature of God's *innards* is not clear. This word has a broad range of meanings in biblical texts, from gender-neutral organs of the intestinal system to the gendered organs of procreation. *Innards* refers to the womb in the following three instances of poetic parallelism: "Two nations are in your womb, and two peoples shall be separated from your innards" (Gen. 25:23); "YHVH has called me from birth, from the innards of my mother" (Isa. 49:1); "By you have I been sustained from the womb; you are the one who took me out of my mother's innards" (Ps. 71:6).

That *innards* is also a womb metaphor here is supported by the fourth step of the process, God's promise "I will surely show compassion to him" *(rachem arachamenu)*. The verb root *r-ch-m* (have compassion) in singular noun form is *rechem*, or womb. *Compassion*, in Hebrew, is thus etymologically related to the loving care and concern a mother would naturally show to the children of her own womb. To comfort the grieving mother Rachel, God assures her that God too will show maternal compassion. God responds, in effect, Mother to mother. This prophetic poem stays in the realm of mother-love, moving from the maternal sorrow of the weeping Rachel to the redemptive maternal compassion of God.

Further support for the idea that God's promise of compassion points to a feminine, maternal aspect of God is found in the structure of the four-step process of reversal of God's judgment. The second and fourth steps of the process are emphasized through the emphatic grammatical construct of doubled verbs (otherwise known as the infinite absolute construct). Translated here as "I surely remember" and "I will surely show compassion," the Hebrew is more literally "remember—I will remember!" *(zakhor ezk'renu)* and "show compassion—I will show compassion!" *(rachem arachamenu)*. The roots of both of these emphatically stated verbs point to gender. Not only is the verb for showing compassion *(rachem)* "female" in that it shares its root with the word for *womb (rechem)*, but the verb for remembering *(zakhor)* is "male" in that it actually shares its root with the adjective *male (zakhar)*. The process of reversing judgment in order to show compassion can trace a path from "masculine" to "feminine" attributes of God.

This reading is also supported by Jeremiah 31:22, which is part of the same poetic unit as our text, although it was excluded from the haftarah portion. It concludes Jeremiah's prophetic poem with the line: "YHVH has created a new thing in the land; female will encircle male." The "female" aspect of God's compassion will encircle the "male" aspect of God's remembrance, allowing God to overcome and reverse judgment and compassionately bring about return.

It is no accident, then, that the figure that calls forth God's compassion is the feminine, maternal figure of Rachel. Mother Rachel's mourning for the lost children calls forth God's own yearning for the children of Israel. Rachel's deep compassion for the exiled children awakens God's compassion for them.

But what is so exceptional about Rachel's compassion to stir such an exceptional response? Would not any mother weep for her missing children? One answer is suggested by a midrash to the Book of Lamentations that pictures the patriarchs and Moses unsuccessfully pleading on behalf of the captive children of Israel.[3] Abraham and Isaac argue that their obedience to God shown through the Akeidah, the binding of Isaac, merits the reward of letting their descendants go free, but God is not moved. Moses argues that God should let the children of Israel go free for his sake, because he dedicated his entire life to God's work, but, again, God is not moved. Finally, Rachel goes to speak with God. She argues that if she was able to overcome her human jealousy of her sister and rival, Leah, and have enough compassion not to expose her to shame and contempt by disclosing her ruse to marry Jacob, then the God of compassion should surely be able to overcome the Divine jealousy of idolatry and have enough compassion not to leave the children of Israel in exile. Through Rachel's plea, God is moved, and promises to return the exiled children of Israel.

This midrash not only suggests that God's compassion is a response to Rachel's, but it also reminds us that Rachel was the mother of only some of the tribes of Israel; Leah was the mother of more tribes than Rachel. When Rachel weeps for the exiled children, she weeps not only for her own children, but also those of her rival sister. Her compassion exceeds the natural feelings of a mother, extending maternal compassion to all the exiled children, not merely her own.

And it is this abundance of compassion that calls forth God's compassion, perhaps even against God's own will. This is a new kind of ancestral merit, different from the traditional *z'chut avot* ("merit of the fathers") exemplified by Abraham and his willingness to suppress his parental compassion and sacrifice his son. Rachel's merit is a good antidote for those troubled by the Rosh Hashanah message, in Torah reading and liturgy, that Abraham's act of sacrificial obedience was an act of extraordinary merit, allowing God to grant a favorable judgment for us today. The haftarah also offers us the option to draw upon the merit of Rachel's overflowing compassion, allowing us a favorable judgment today through *her* merit.

Thus this haftarah gives us two tremendous gifts on the second day of the High Holy Days. First, it offers us an optimistic picture of the potential for human merit to affect, even transform, God. Here Rachel's compassionate sorrow stirs God to contemplation and action, impels God to undergo a process of transformation, and ultimately wrests compassion from God. Our own compassion for one another, even those not of our own "tribe," can bring about a more compassionate Divine response to all.

This haftarah also gives us an optimistic view of the process of *teshuvah*. It suggests that if we engage ourselves in the process of *teshuvah*, we will not be alone. God supports and aids our efforts to make *teshuvah*, for God is like a compassionate mother, whose inner essence yearns for the wayward child to return, whose very innards are agitated, churning with anxiety for the child. Just as a runaway child can be confident that a call home will bring her mother rushing to meet her wherever she is and bring her home, so too can we call upon God's compassion to help us return.

As we go though our own process of *teshuvah*, we can be comforted by the dual images of God as our loving Mother, yearning for us, ready to greet us whenever we are willing to return, willing to help us to return; and Rachel, overflowing with compassion, a compassion we can emulate in our own lives.

הפטרת שבת שובה

Haftarah for Shabbat Shuva

Hosea 14:2–10; Joel 2:15–27; Michah 7:18–20

*T*urn, O Israel, toward the Eternal, your God, that you may confess to your transgressions. Take with you words and turn to God saying, Sweep away in forgiveness all that is sinful, and in taking what is good let us become whole through the wealth of our lips.

(HOSEA 14:2–3)

THESE WORDS FROM HOSEA are read as the haftarah portion on the Shabbat that falls during the High Holy Days. It is called *Shabbat Shuva* because of the first words of this section: *Shuva Yisrael* ("Turn, O Israel"). The theme of Hosea's words is fitting for the *Aseret Yemei Teshuvah*, the period between Rosh Hashanah and Yom Kippur known as the Ten Days of Repentance. By urging Israel to turn toward God, Hosea reminds us to take seriously the task of reflection and introspection, as we strive for repentance during this holy time.

Hosea's words are as timely as they are motivating. There is a sense of urgency in his voice as he pleads and cajoles a stubborn Israel to change, to make amends, and to repair its relationship with God. His message is important, yet to whom does he speak? Hosea addresses Israel, but it is unclear who exactly has gathered to hear Hosea's words. It is often assumed that *Israel* refers to the entire community, the men and women of every age. There are times, however, when the text of the Bible is much more explicit.

In Deuteronomy, Moses says: "You stand this day, all of you, before the Eternal, your God—the heads of your tribes, your elders, your officials—every man of Israel; your young ones, your women . . ." (Deut. 29:9–10). In that passage it is clear that Moses is speaking to the entire community. He mentions each kind of participant, not only to note their presence, but also to make certain that they are included among the audience for the words he is about to utter.

In the words of our haftarah portion, however, women are not mentioned. But once we determine the essence of the first few verses of Hosea's message, in particular 14:3, it will become clear that women *were* a part of the community of Israel that day.

Hosea gathers the people and declares, "Take with you *devarim* and turn to God . . ." *Devarim* can mean "words," yet this is only one of many possibilities of what Israel was expected to bring to God. For *devarim* is understood not only as words, but also as commandments (Ps. 107:20), matters (I Chron. 26.32), events (Gen. 22:1), and things (Gen. 22:16). So Hosea's direction to us can mean more than "take with you *words* and turn to God."

The key to this verse lies in understanding the meaning of another word in the verse: *farim*. *Farim* can mean "wealth," but it can also mean "cattle." If we look through the lens of our biblical ancestors, we understand that cattle and wealth amounted to the same thing.[1] If one was wealthy, it meant that one had acquired a large herd.

Hosea encourages us to turn to God in order to "become whole through the *farim* of our lips." If *farim* is translated as "cattle," then how can cattle be "of our lips?" It is possible to understand this metaphorically. Our material possessions become "of our lips" when we speak of them. They do make us rich, but not necessarily in the way that Hosea suggests. The *farim* of which Hosea speaks are riches of a different sort. The words we bring to God represent the "wealth of our lips." This is what helps us to become whole. Radak confirms this: "Take with you words . . . In your returning to God, God does not require of you material wealth or animal sacrifices, but words of sincere confession coming from a contrite heart."[2] Our wealth, then, comes not from our figurative cattle, our possessions, but rather from our words. Words are what God wants of us. Our voice, our most valuable possession, is the true wealth of our lips, and thus the true gift we can give to God.

How do we know—or imagine—that women were there to hear Hosea's words? Women who have struggled to be heard could understand how wealthy we become with the power that voice gives us. Women forbidden to speak could interpret the prophetic message of *devarim* and *farim* in this way. Women who felt powerless could understand that "to have a voice is to be human."[3] Women could convince Israel to bring words to God, thereby offering the greatest of all possible human gifts.

The ability to give voice to words is uniquely human. It is what distinguishes us from the rest of God's creatures and one of the ways in which we were created *b'tzelem Elohim*—in God's image. With words, God creates. With words, we too create, and sustain the world around us. Words are powerful forces that give meaning to our communications, whether it is in the context of turning to God seeking repentance or expressing ourselves to loved ones.

As women, there is no doubt that speech empowers. It gives us the opportunity to make ourselves heard. As Jewish women, having a voice restores us to our rightful place in the ongoing dialogue of passing on our traditions. Oral communication has always been the favored medium of Jewish instruction—handing down information from person to person, teacher to student, parent to child.[4] The resurgence of women's voices has restored previously weakened links in the chain of tradition. Even the phrase *kol isha*—the voice of a woman—has been redefined. Traditionally, it represented the talmudic prohibition against hearing a woman's voice.[5] Now, however, *kol isha* is a term used proudly by women's groups whose voices ring out loud and clear.

Hosea's words call on all of us to find and use our voices. Imagine that our ancestors, the women who heard Hosea's message, understood that this was the meaning of his instruction—that the words our voices speak are what matters most to God. So it is with us as well. Nothing is more precious to us than the wealth our voice affords us.

On *Shabbat Shuva* we heed Hosea and turn to God. With words we speak of transgressions, and with words we ask for forgiveness. With words we seek atonement. Our words become a gift of indeterminable value—a wealth of connection to God and relationship with those around us. When we turn to each other to speak and to listen, we will become whole.

הפטרת יום כפור (שחרית)

Haftarah for
Yom Kippur Morning

Isaiah 57:14–59:4

*L*ift up your voice like a shofar . . . (ISAIAH 58:1)

EACH YEAR, ON YOM KIPPUR, we are forced to ask one question of ourselves. What does God want? This piercing question haunts the Yom Kippur morning haftarah like a shofar call. In Isaiah 58, God shows the prophet that the people are fulfilling ritual precepts while neglecting our tradition's moral foundation. "They seek Me daily and they search to know My ways, as if they were a people who acts justly and has not abandoned the way of its God." In conclusion, God asserts that prayers and sacrifice are meaningless "because on your fast day you pursue your own affairs and you oppress your workers" (58:2–3). The people have failed to "share your bread with the hungry and bring the homeless into your home" (58:7). Such moral lapses call into question the whole religious enterprise. God tells Isaiah to "raise your voice like a shofar's blast" (58:1) and articulate the central question: "Is this the fast that I [God] have chosen?" If rituals are followed in the absence of moral precepts, is God satisfied?

This query is the essential question of Yom Kippur. While fasting and praying, we are commanded to examine whether our ethical behavior lives up to the powerful rituals of the *Yamim Noraim*, the Days of Awe.

What does God really want of women? Does God want something different or special from us? This question is also at the core of Jewish feminism and must be addressed, like Isaiah's question, as one of morality. For generations, women looked on, as study and most ritual practice was reserved for men. Powerful mourning rituals were established, yet women were prevented from saying Kaddish for loved ones. The doors to leadership—leadership that could have lifted the people—were closed. Like the prophet Isaiah, contemporary women raise their voices and ask: "Is this the fast that God has chosen?" A fast of the spirit of half of the Jewish people? Does God want to have a glorious and scrupulously maintained tradition that excludes half its members?

Bava Batra 10a poses the existential question: Why is the world so flawed now? Turneous Rufous (the Roman governor of Judea) asked Rabbi Akiva: "If your God loves the poor, why does God not support them?" Rabbi Akiva replied that God created an imperfect world so people could earn merit by repairing it. Turneous replied that, on the contrary, people lose merit by failing to repair it. Then he offered a parable:

> [Let's say that an] earthly king was angry with his servant and imprisoned him, and ordered that no food or drink should be given to him. If someone went ahead and gave [the prisoner] food and drink, when the king heard about what happened, wouldn't the king become angry?

Rabbi Akiva responded with another parable:

> [Let's say that] an earthly king was angry with his son, and imprisoned him, and ordered that no food and drink should be given to him. If someone went ahead and gave him food and drink, when the king heard about what happened, wouldn't the king reward the person [who saved the son's life]? We are all called sons, as it is written. "Sons are you to the Lord your God."

Rabbi Akiva reversed Turneous Rufous's parable to highlight the fact that the Almighty wants us to care for the poor because we are all

God's children. Even though there is injustice in the world, God wants us—in fact expects us—to rectify the situation. This is the Divine-human partnership. So the feminist revolution can be seen in this light; as the correcting of wrongs, as *tikkun olam*.

But Isaiah's question can also be read as a critique of ritual. As W. Gunther Plaut explained:

> During the 19th Century when reformatory zeal gripped German and North-American Jews, these and similar such prophetic passages were taken as clear proof that Isaiah was concerned with the deeds of his people rather than with ritual exercises like fasting . . . Such interpretation encouraged disregard for ritual in general, which was replaced by devotion to social justice.[1]

Isaiah's question "Is this the fast that God has chosen?" seemed to reject practices like fasting altogether. It called into question, and discredited, much of the religious enterprise. Likewise, feminist critiques of Judaism have led some people to replace religious observance with social activism. This haftarah calls on us to reach a balance.

After Isaiah criticizes the people, he offers hope that if Jews act justly, God will answer their prayers with redemption (58:7–12). Isaiah then abruptly shifts his focus from his original critique of "empty rituals" to stress the importance of keeping the Sabbath (58:13–14). This juxtaposition is striking to commentators. As Plaut writes: "Seeing the prophet's disdain for spurious fasting and praying, the mention of strict Sabbath observance comes as a surprise."[2] Isaiah's focus on the Sabbath sheds new light on his earlier message. The prophet is arguing in favor of powerful ritual, coupled with equally compelling moral action. Isaiah maintains that ethical conduct is the essence of what fasting represents. Actions create "the fast that God has chosen."

This is what God requires of women as well—a Jewish feminism ready for action but steeped in the traditions of Judaism itself. Women should not give up their Jewish ritual practices in the pursuit of social action, no matter how exclusionary those rituals may have been in the past. Isaiah's message is not to repudiate ritual but to prompt everyone to fulfill those principles upon which Jewish customs are built. One of those principles is that both male and female were created in God's image, as we learn from Genesis 1:27 when God brought people into existence: "God created humanity in God's image . . . male and female God created them." As feminists, we have sometimes undermined our own position by losing touch with its religious core. But it takes a long time to learn what God wants.

When we hear the haftarah on Yom Kippur, we can see ourselves as bearers of Isaiah's legacy, asking tough questions and calling for moral actions. Recognizing injustice, we can take upon ourselves the work of repair, *tikkun*. Then, indeed, we can embark upon the "fast that God has chosen."

הפטרת יום כפור (ספר יונה)

Haftarah for Yom Kippur Afternoon

The Book of Jonah

*G*od appointed a great big fish to swallow up Jonah, and Jonah was in the belly of the fish for three days and three nights; and Jonah prayed to God, his God, from the bowels of the fish . . . (JONAH 2:1–2)

AS WE ENTER the afternoon service of Yom Kippur, our bodies are weary from fasting and our minds and hearts are focused on the intensive *teshuvah* process. We divest our thoughts, words, or deeds that have caused harm to others or ourselves; repent for our mistakes; and seek a renewed, revitalized relationship with ourselves and God. At this time of day when our bodies are weakened and our intellectual faculties are fragile, we turn our attention to the haftarah reading from the Book of Jonah. Of all the many haftarot from which we might glean meaning, inspiration, and insight, why is this story of the reluctant prophet, the fish, and the people of Nineveh's fantastic repentance chosen to be read at the most vulnerable time on this most holy day? The Book of Jonah offers a view of the power of Divine femininity, the power to vastly, oceanically contain the potential for new life, to gestate it, and to forge a most terrific birthing, sometimes even in spite of deep resistance. As we seek our own spiritual rebirth and renewal on Yom Kippur, Jonah's journey and God's compassionate actions compel our attention.

Jonah's adventure is potent as a counterpoint to and an echo of the priestly journey into the mysterious inner sanctum, the Holy of Holies, which has been recounted dramatically in the morning *Avodah* service. When we reflect on both these narratives together we come to a fuller, more balanced sense of self, and perhaps of God, which we might read into the narratives of each dramatic near-death and rebirth experience. In each case, the protagonist must surrender himself to the Divinely ordained, Divinely feminine enclosure and only there undergo the dangerous, mysterious processes of death and birth and profound *teshuvah*, "returning."

*J*onah: Swallowed Whole, Emerging Anew

Jonah is a most reluctant prophet. He is called by God to go to Nineveh and to cry out to the Ninevites to repent and come before God. However, Jonah utterly resists his calling to speak Divine truth to these strangers. He literally runs "from the face of" (*mi'lifnay*) God, away from dry land—the solid structures of his known terrain—and into the vast waters of the sea. He does not think God will find him in the oceanic chaos, but he is mistaken. Jonah first finds a boat en route to Tarshish, pays his fare, and "descends" into this boat, again, *mi'lifnay*, away from the face of God, or so he thinks. Jonah sleeps in the lower parts of this ship, while a great storm causes it to heave and creak and the sailors, terrified, finally wake Jonah up to ask if it is his God Who is causing such trouble. Jonah admits to them that it must indeed be his fault that this storm is raging. He asks them to throw him overboard, so they might survive, rather than perishing on his account. The men do not want to do so at first, but as the storm grows worse, they comply, praying for Jonah's safety as they throw him overboard. Immediately, the surface of the waters grow still and calm, and the sailors feel unprecedented awe for Jonah's God, and they make offerings to God and make vows.

As the narrative continues, the implication that these waters are cosmically amniotic and life-giving, in all of their natural, terrific unpredictability, is made more specific and clear. Jonah does not go to his death in this ocean, though he might easily have. Instead, we read in 2:1: "God appointed a great big fish to swallow Jonah, and Jonah was in the belly of the fish three days and three nights." It is here, within the belly of this fish, a fish whose natural home is these waters, that a transformation happens to this reluctant prophet. As James Ackerman points out, the fish's belly is a safe enclosure of containment and protection, even as it is fraught with uncertainty and danger.[1] Within the dark mysterious innards of this creature, Jonah cannot run away. Jonah is not descending from before the face of God, nor is he sleeping to avoid consciousness, as he did in the boat. The text says that instead Jonah turns, and prays to Adonai, his God, from the "bowels of the fish" (2:2).

Something mysterious happens to Jonah as he lies in the belly of this huge fish in the midst of an oceanic wilderness. The fish seems to represent the face of God, which is womblike, prestructural, a most primal force capable of creating life from within its own essence. The text itself is silent as to what exactly Jonah experiences inside the belly as the fish churns in the ocean. Yet the implication is that the fish's belly is an enclosure for generativity and birth—a womblike container within which Jonah might be symbolically gestated for a period of time, and born anew. Since it is clearly God's doing that the fish appears and swallows Jonah whole in this manner, we are to understand that God seeks to be known through the powerful vessel of the fish's womb, swimming amid the vastness of an ocean, just as the amniotic fluids surround a fetus as it swims and floats in the container of the mother's womb.

Magical Encounters in the Belly

Rabbinic commentaries reflect on Jonah's mysterious period in this dark, deep place. They ascribe to this time a flurry of activity in which Jonah's perceptions and powers are created anew. They suggest in a magical and fanciful way echoes of what a fetus might experience in his or her mother's womb, apprehending the deepest secrets of creation. While in this inner sanctum, Jonah discovers new capacities for literal and metaphorical vision and ability. In a sense, Jonah is being "knit together" afresh in this womblike place (Ps. 139:13), as he is given new ways of understanding the nature of existence, of God, and of himself that shape his future decisions and actions.

The fish—that was created during the six days of creation for just this purpose—provides Jonah with physical light and the ability to see, even in the depths of the darkness surrounding him. The two eyes of the fish, which never close, are like windows, and there is a large diamond or pearl that hangs from the inside of the fish. Both provide light for Jonah so that, even amid this deepest darkness, Jonah can see all around him into the sea and "into the depths."[2] Further, this sight has a psychic dimension. Jonah convinced the leviathan, the giant mythical fish whose privilege it is to eat all fish in the sea in good time, not to consume his host. In gratitude, the fish shows Jonah everything in the sea, piercing the mysteries of creation with his gaze.

Jonah and the fish are in intimate communication and activity, just as a pregnant woman is in frequent and active touch with the life growing inside her. Yet there comes a time when the belly is too small for the fetus, when it has developed to such an extent that it must leave the safe container of the womb and be born into its human journey. Another midrashic legend gives us this piece of Jonah's story as well. It is said that Jonah "felt so comfortable that he did not think of imploring God to change his condition," to let him leave the fish's belly, after the three days. He was comfortable not being fully born. Yet God knows it is Jonah's time to emerge. So, God sends "a female fish big with 365,000 little fish" inside of her and requires Jonah to transfer to this new abode. Reluctantly he does so, and is far from comfortable. It is only now that Jonah calls out to God in prayer for release, and is spit out onto dry land to begin the next chapter of his life, going to Nineveh to carry out God's command after all.[3] Just as there comes a time when the womb can no longer sustain the growing life, and it is time for the baby to emerge and begin to fulfill its purpose on earth, so too must Jonah be born again into the world to fulfill a Divine purpose. The rabbinic commentaries suggest that Jonah is growing too large—in psychic and physical awareness—to stay in the place of enclosure. He is ready to be born.

In another midrash, the fish shows Jonah God's Temple, saying: "'Look, you now stand near the Temple of the Lord. Pray, and you will be answered.' Jonah said to the fish: 'Remain still where you are, fish, because I do wish to pray.'"[4] Self-possessed, able now to turn and face God rather than skulking away, Jonah articulates the urgings of his heart, as we find in 2:2–10. He prays to God for release, and he is answered as "God spoke to the fish, who spit Jonah out onto the dry land," in 2:11.

The High Priest: An Eager Servant Awaiting Rebirth

The narrative of Jonah's journey thus provides us with a poetic and intuitive model for the *teshuvah* process, in all of its subconscious drama and weightiness. Although we pray with full hearts on Yom Kippur, Jonah's story reminds us that we are more often reluctant and flawed. We are in some respects like the Jonah who resists being awake and alert and who must be led by God's hand into the very belly of God's creative center in order for the dark mysteries of the transformative powers of this day to take effect and cleanse. God's power to assist the human being in this process is humbling. The *teshuvah* process is represented by the potent raging and dark, mysterious, oceanic, womblike, primal forces of God's nature. It is in these waters that our antihero journeys to his own transformation and growth.

But unlike Jonah, who ran from God when God began calling to him, the high priest is the model of one whose being is oriented fully and authentically toward serving the Divine. There is no sleeping nor floating for the high priest. Rather, in preparation for his Yom Kippur journey, he has been purifying himself actively for seven days, and is not permitted to sleep at all the night before, lest his lapse in consciousness cause him to inadvertently become impure in any way. While Jonah's mystical encounter of God happens in the dark, in the waters, in dreamlike liminality, the high priest is on dry land, known terrain, and the high priest's journey is undertaken with the watchful eye of someone for whom the dream world is, at this time, off limits.

In the Holy Temple, the high priest emerges to perform a most holy action, in the innard of innards, the Holy of Holies. He performs a series of actions, including uttering the Divine name—which is done only on this day, at this time—and which enables the Israelites to experience cleansing and rebirth. This place, this innermost point of holiness and intimate connection with the Divine, says Bonna Haberman, represents none other than the sacred female enclosure. She argues that the priest's entering and performing holy actions, which include the appearance of blood as well as words, represents a heterosexual, mystical coupling of the male and female on a cosmic, life-giving level.[5]

Jonah and The High Priest: A Beloved Coupling

Jonah and the high priest stand in sharp contrast to one another in terms of their readiness, their understanding of the nature of their missions, and the ways in which they enact their entrance and time spent in the innermost realms of the female enclosure spaces. Yet both indeed do so, and the coupling of these two very different narratives on this most holy day gives us a particular insight into the complexity of the *teshuvah* process.

The high priest serves as a model for total concentration and devotion to a practice of serving God; a willingness to risk even one's life in order to "get it right" on behalf of self and others. There is an expectation that, when we seek to reach God in such a clearly explicit manner, we will in some way make that connection point that provides for us the seeds of our regeneration.

By structuring the Yom Kippur readings to include the Jonah

narrative, the Rabbis suggest that there are elements in the human psyche that are neither linear nor clear. We see ourselves both in Jonah's reluctance to surrender and serve the Divine and in the high priest's alacrity and functionality. It is the two of these images together that swim in the fertile birthing waters of our own psyches, as we move through the Divine enclosure of the day of Yom Kippur itself.

The Jonah narrative provides a visceral, magical, gritty possibility that God's power—and God's mercy—are raw, deep, and vast as the ocean. These powers have the ability to enclose, to surround, and to create, just as a fertile female body reflects the Divine by creating. The reading of Jonah can help us to hear the sounds of God's waters surrounding us, holding us, and helping to gestate us anew, as the sound of the waves rages inside every seashell, if only we stop to listen.

Holiday Haftarot

RABBI CHANA THOMPSON SHOR

הפטרת חג הסוכות

Haftarah for the First Day of Sukkot

Zechariah 14:1–21

*F*or I will gather all the nations to Jerusalem for war:
The city shall be captured, the houses plundered,
and the women raped . . .
Then YHVH will come forth and make war on those
nations, as when He made war on a day of battle. On
that day, He will set His feet on the Mount of Olives, by
Jerusalem on the east; and the Mount of Olives will split
across from east to west . . .
On that day, live waters will flow from Jerusalem, part to
the Eastern Sea, and part to the Western sea, [even]
throughout the summer and the winter.

(ZECHARIAH 14: 2, 3–4, 8)

THE GRAPHIC VIOLENCE of God's punishment of the nations (Zech.
14:12), and the extreme anthropomorphism of this haftarah's depiction of God, cry out to be addressed. What is most noticeable is the
overwhelming "masculinity" of the imagery. In visually powerful
descriptions, warrior God appears, with the heavenly army not far
behind, and sets God's feet on the Mount of Olives, splitting it in two,
so that each half crashes down, a cataclysm unlike anything seen since
the earthquake in the days of King Uzziah in the time of the First

Temple. Water gushes out of Jerusalem, half to the Mediterranean and half to the Dead Sea, while the lands surrounding Jerusalem are flattened, leaving the city to tower over them. God does battle against Judah's enemies, flesh melting from their bodies and eyes melting from their sockets; their animals are also stricken, while we gather in the wealth of the nations. In the meantime, the normal pattern of day and night has ceased, and all is now continuously light. God is hailed as universal King, over all the earth and all the nations, and everyone, including the survivors among the nations, is enjoined to come and celebrate Sukkot, or be dried up through lack of rain.

Most striking is the image of the Warrior standing on the mountain. There is no more intensely male image in the Bible than that of God as the Divine Warrior. While other ancient Near Eastern traditions have warrior goddesses, the Bible is insistent that the character of the Divine Warrior is masculine. God as King, the other dominant "persona" of God in this haftarah, also has an implied martial component, given that kings were conceived as the heads of their armies, even if they didn't literally lead the troops themselves. Warrior and king were the primary images of temporal power of the day, so anthropomorphizing language about God—the Power above all others—is likely to take one of these forms as its model.

In the context of war and other violence in the Bible, one may often find a female image in the depiction of Jerusalem as *Bat-Tzion*, Maiden Zion, as in Lamentations 2:1:

> Alas!
> The Lord in His Anger
> Has shamed Maiden Zion,
> Has cast down from heaven to earth
> the glory of Israel.
> He did not remember His Footstool
> On His day of wrath.

In texts like this one, she (the city) evokes tender feelings in her lover, or her father. However, while Jerusalem is certainly the focus of attention of our haftarah, the city is curiously not referred to as *Bat-Tzion*. The only overt reference to women (or to anything obviously female) in this haftarah is at the very beginning of the passage, where Judah is defeated prior to its subsequent redemption.

> For I will gather all the nations to Jerusalem for war:
> The city shall be captured,
> the houses plundered, and the women *raped*.
>
> (Zech. 14:2)

The Hebrew word in the text for *raped* (*tishagalnah*) was deemed too raw or obscene by the Masoretes to be read out loud, necessitating a euphemism (*tishakhavnah*), which translates most accurately as the bland "lain with." A similar phrase, with the same Masoretic emendation, occurs in Isaiah 13:15–16, this time in reference to the destruction of Babylon:

> all who are captured shall fall by the sword.
> And their babes shall be dashed into pieces in their sight,
> their houses plundered, and their women *raped*.

It appears that this expression is part of a set of stock images of the destruction of a city in biblical texts and, generally, in the Near East of biblical times.[1] Thus, the women may be seen as representing the entire city, and their fate, their violent rape, stands for the unspeakable destruction of Jerusalem that will occur immediately prior to its ultimate redemption. In that case, even without the presence of the title *Bat-Tzion*, we may plausibly read Jerusalem as appearing in a female persona.

Yet there is a subtle shift to another female aspect that becomes more evident beginning in 14:3. Here, the Divine Warrior towers over the text, both literally and figuratively. The might of God as Warrior, in defeating the enemies of Israel, is unleashed in the form of a preeminent power over nature: God splits a mountain in two, as God dramatically enters the scene of Jerusalem's ultimate liberation. These events should evoke memories of the Exodus; the first time we encountered

God in this guise was at the Reed Sea, when God parted the waters for us, so that we could pass through on dry land, while the pursuing Egyptians were drowned. There in Exodus 15:3, God is called *Ish Milkhamah*, "Man of War," and the same verb, *b-k-j*, is used to describe both the splitting of the sea (Exod. 14:21) and the splitting of the mountain (Zech. 14:4). In fact, Rashi interprets the line "as on a day of battle" in Zechariah 14:3 as meaning, "as the day he waged war on the Reed Sea."

From an eschatological or messianic viewpoint, this parallel comes as no surprise, for the initiation of the eschatological future age of a people generally repeats, in some form, the story of its origins. For example, prophets from the period of the Babylonian exile describe the anticipated triumphant return to the land in terms of a second Exodus, this time in the form of a lush green pathway for the people, through an inhospitable desert.[2]

The Exodus, in turn, parallels Creation; much of the same language is used in Exodus as in Genesis. The main point of the plagues appears to be the recognition, by Israel and the world in general, of God as Master of Creation. Waters, with both their creative associations and chaotic nature, are featured in both Genesis and Exodus. If Genesis is the birth of the world, Exodus is the birth of the nation, a fact emphasized by the language of the story. Exodus itself has a multitude of images connected with birth, of coming from a confined place to a place of liberation, through water, aided by midwives, and facilitated by other female characters. If crossing the Reed Sea represented parturition and the birth of the people, then certainly the recapitulation of the Exodus at the end of time must be a rebirth—both of Israel and of all Creation—with the same sense that God, for all the armor and weaponry, is really a sort of midwife.

It is one thing to be born through the splitting of the sea to allow the birth of the people, which parallels the breaking of the amniotic fluids and the birth of the child; but how is one born through the splitting of mountains? It seems that rebirth into a world where the rules of nature no longer apply would have to be different in some way from the birth of a nation in a world ruled by the natural laws set in place by God at Creation. One clue that a discontinuity in the "nature of nature" must be the case after the Day of the Lord, is the removal of distinctions set in place at the time of Creation. The very first division that God made—between Light and Darkness—has been transformed into perpetual light. It is into this new world, where the old laws of nature no longer apply, that a splitting-of-something will this time result in a rebirth of Israel that leaves nothing to chance; Jerusalem should not be threatened ever again, by drought, by war, by darkness, by sickness, by death. How, then, does this "birth" correspond with this new condition?

The Mount of Olives, which is a famous and ancient burial site, is split. This may represent, in a sense, the "death of death."[3] And the valleys are filled with rubble,[4] so that they effectively disappear; there is no more high and low. All is level, apart from Jerusalem itself. Distinctions of night and day are removed, not dissolving into chaotic darkness as before Creation, but rather distilled into perpetual light. And then as if it were Eden, the primeval source of all waters, Jerusalem flows forth with a perpetual spring that is divided into eastern and western streams. Zion is heir to a cosmological view much older than herself, in which she is seen as a cosmic mountain,[5] the center of the universe, and, as developed by rabbinic tradition, the capstone of the primordial waters of chaos,[6] a holy mountain akin to—or even identical with—the holy mountain in the original paradise of Eden.[7]

A fuller description of what results when this spring opens up in Jerusalem is included in a passage in Ezekiel's vision of the Temple in 47:1–12:

> He led me back to the entrance of the Temple, and I found that water was issuing from below the platform of the Temple . . . I saw trees in great profusion on both banks of the stream. "This water," he told me, "runs out to the eastern region, and flows into the Aravah; and when it comes into the sea, into the sea of foul waters [the Dead Sea], the water will become wholesome. Every living

creature that swarms will be able to live wherever this stream goes; the fish will be very abundant once these waters have reached there. . . . All kinds of trees for food will grow up on both banks of the stream. Their leaves will not wither nor their fruit fail; they will yield new fruit every month, because the water for them flows from the Temple. Their fruit will serve for food and their leaves for healing."

Here is our water of rebirth; the primordial waters of the deep do not burst out chaotically and engulf the world in this new scheme; they flow out as orderly streams, to water the land regularly, much as the Nile dependably floods and waters Egypt. With the perpetual waters as its irrigation, Israel will no longer need to depend on the seasonal rains, or suffer from famine when they do not come. This eliminates, for Judah, the Deuteronomic connection[8] between divine wrath and drought, even as it is emphasized for the nations in Zechariah 14:16–17. And this water saves us not through its chaotic nature, as God does by releasing it at the Reed Sea, but precisely because final control has been achieved over chaotic water. It serves and feeds us, and therefore we are saved, once and for all. Once God has set the scene, it is a more gentle birth than at the Reed Sea.

The imagery of the flowing waters from Eden (and Jerusalem as God's garden) can be seen as explicitly female when compared with the description of the female lover in the Song of Songs, 4:12–16:

> A garden locked, is my sister-bride,
> a reservoir locked up, a fountain sealed.
> Your sluices are a paradise of pomegranates,
> with bountiful fruits,
> of henna shrubs with spikenards
> of nard and saffron, fragrant cane and cinnamon,
> with every tree of frankincense, myrrh, and aloes,
> with every chief balm.
> A fountain of gardens, a well of live waters

and flowing streams from Lebanon.
Arise, O Zaphon, and come, O Teman
Breathe upon my garden. Let its balms stream out . . .[9]

The description of the woman as a walled garden with a fountain flowing from inside it is intended to compare her to the primeval Paradise of delights, for this is a description of Eden. Given the connection between Jerusalem and Eden, it could also serve as a description of Jerusalem, or *Bat-Tzion*, if you will, after the Day of the Lord, as envisioned by Zechariah. The image of Eden, used for whatever purpose, is meant to convey a deeply female association, and one that casts God's role as quite different from that of Warrior. In addition, while the emphasis in the passages in Song of Songs is on the love and attraction connected with sexual union, it is not difficult to see the outflowing of the waters as bringing about the desired conclusion of that act, that is, birth.

God, in Zechariah, has bidden that the hidden spring beneath his beloved Jerusalem flow out, gently, and water the land, which will then become a paradise for its people. Through this gentle water, they are reborn. The towering image of the giant Deity on the mountain and the King on the throne represent power over nature, but not, crucially, what that power is there to accomplish: birth and rebirth. God, though dressed as a Warrior, is also a midwife.

RABBI SHARYN H. HENRY

הפטרת שבת חנוכה

Haftarah for Shabbat Chanukah

Zechariah 2:14–4:7

*N*ot by might nor by power, but by My spirit,
said YHVH, the God of heavenly hosts.
(ZECHARIAH 4:6)

THIS WELL-KNOWN PHRASE appears at the tail end of the haftarah portion for the first Shabbat of Chanukah, and has inspired Jewish souls
for millennia, transforming in one line the entire Chanukah story.
These ten words remind us that Chanukah's message is not about
power; it is about God's spirit in our lives.

The haftarah portion for Chanukah comes from the prophecies of
Zechariah. Zechariah was one of the last prophets, living and teaching during the time of the rebuilding of the Temple in Jerusalem, some-
time after 538 B.C.E. The principal builders were the high priest Joshua
ben Yehozadak, and the governor Zerubbabel. Zechariah sought to
encourage the people of Judah in their work as their enthusiasm
waned. Objections from outsiders to the rebuilding effort, no doubt,
had a negative influence on the people's commitment to the project.

The portion contains three main sections. The first contains God's
promise to dwell in the midst of the people once again. Radak believes
the passage has messianic overtones and was likely meant to give the
builders hope for their own redemption. In the second part, Zechariah

describes his vision of the high priest Joshua ben Yehozadak standing before the Accuser (known in Hebrew as *ha-satan*). Joshua's filthy clothes represent the sinfulness of the people, and their impoverished spiritual state without the Temple. After his acquittal in the "trial," Joshua receives new, clean clothing, a symbol of his purification, and is presented with a stone with seven facets (*aynayim*, literally "eyes").[1] The last section contains the clearest link to Chanukah. Zechariah awakens from his sleep to a vision of a golden menorah with seven branches for seven lights. Two olive trees, one on each side of the bowl, stand next to the menorah. Zechariah does not understand the message of the vision, and so the angel explains: "This is the word of YHVH to Zerubbabel: not by might nor by power, but by My spirit, said YHVH, the God of heavenly hosts."

Was it the description of the menorah that led our Sages to choose this passage as the haftarah for Chanukah?

The Hasmoneans, a small band of Jewish resistance fighters, fought and defeated the great Syrian-Greek army and thereby returned the Temple in Jerusalem to the Jewish people. The Jews restored the desecrated Temple to its glory, and held an eight-day rededication to its sacred purpose. The Talmud, in *Shabbat* 21b, makes no mention of the military defeat. Rather, we read that when the Hasmoneans retook the Temple, they found only one day's supply of consecrated oil. Faced with the reality of an unlit menorah, and not enough oil to light it and keep it lit, the Jews had to make a decision. They could have waited to relight the menorah until they had a full supply of consecrated oil, or, knowing it was a three-day journey in each direction, could have waited until one day before it was expected and then relit the menorah. The choice they made, interestingly, was the least logical: They kindled the menorah anyway, having only the one container of oil. The talmudic legend tells us that a miracle happened and the oil lasted for eight days, until the new oil was ready. The Hasmoneans made an illogical, but faithful—and miraculous—choice.

We might imagine that in its day, the "front page" story about Chanukah would be about the spectacular military victory. Vivid pictures of soldiers triumphant in their defeat over their enemy would accompany the article. The related story, the one about the resolute faith of the people, would be relegated to the "Style" section or maybe the "Religion" page. The Haftarah reflects the essential, hidden-away story—the story of God's presence.

In a commentary about the menorah, flanked by two olive trees, Rashi teaches that just as the olive trees fed the menorah without any human intervention, Zerubbabel would not rebuild the Temple with his own physical strength or power, but with God's spirit.[2] Likewise, the Hasmoneans' victory was not their own—it belonged to God: not by might, nor by power, but by My spirit. And then, the most miraculous part of Chanukah was not about the war at all; it was about the steadfastness of the people who rededicated the Temple to God's purpose. With that act they not only affirmed their own faith, but publicized that faith to the rest of the world. Our victories are not a result of our own strength or power; they are a gift of God's spirit. *Lo v'chayil*, the text tells us—not by *chayil*.

And here, in this word *chayil*, there is a special relevance for women. *Chayil* is usually translated as "might." There are, however, a multitude of other meanings. In Psalm 76:6 *chayil* is "bravery." In Proverbs 12:4 it means "capability." *Chayil* is also understood to mean "triumph" and "wealth" (or worth), as in Psalms 118:15 and Proverbs 13:22, respectively. In contemporary Hebrew, a soldier is a *chayal*. And, in Proverbs 31, known as *Eshet Chayil*, the word appears again. This time it refers to a woman.

In many homes, the husband recites *Eshet Chayil*, commonly known as Woman of Valor, at the Shabbat dinner table to show respect and honor to his wife. The passage extols, in acrostic form, a wife and mother whose "worth is far beyond that of rubies." This text is of particular interest to us, because *chayil* is used in such a positive way. Is it then in contradiction to the haftarah text that implores *Lo v'chayil*— not with *chayil*? What can it teach us about the nature of *chayil*? When, where, and how is the use of *chayil* appropriate?

Even a quick read of the text from Proverbs suggests that this *chayil* is not the *chayil* in the conventional sense, that of "masculine" strength and power, or military prowess. A more careful analysis reveals the nature and purpose of the woman's *chayil*. There are phrases from *Eshet Chayil* with direct parallels to the Chanukah haftarah that may inform us.

Amid the many references to clothes in *Eshet Chayil*, we find two rather striking descriptions of the woman's garments: "She girds herself with strength" and "She is clothed with strength and splendor." In both cases the Hebrew word for strength is *oz*, a word used elsewhere to connote strength from God, as in Psalm 29, where we read, "*YHVH oz l'amo yitayn* . . . YHVH gives strength to our people." Near the end of *Eshet Chayil* we read, "A woman who fears YHVH is to be praised." The *Eshet Chayil* is undeniably strong—she is the backbone of the family and exemplary in her acts of *chesed*. She reaches out to others in generosity and kindness with the kind of humility that makes what she does more important than who she is. Her strength is God-given and God-inspired.

In *Eshet Chayil*, Proverbs 31:18 we read: "Her *ner* [lamp, light, candle] never goes out at night." The *ner* here mirrors the *ner* in the haftarah portion. Her *ner* never goes out; neither does the one in the menorah in the Temple.

Like the Temple's light, which illuminated the Jewish world in antiquity, the Shabbat candles, so closely associated with women, light the Jewish home and the Jewish world today. When a woman kindles Shabbat candles, she brings light, and with that light, all that it symbolizes—understanding, clarity, and hope—into her home. She kindles flames that remind us that we are in God's presence, just as the priests did when they kindled the menorah in the Temple.

Light displaces "darkness," or evil, and light allows us to see what is hidden. Light is the way we visualize truth. Light is the way we recognize God's eternal presence and spirit in our lives. It is the essence of our existence as Jews to help bring light and peace into the world. It is our "power." *Lo v'chayil*—not by might nor by power, but by My spirit: The Hasmoneans, with their physical strength did not possess this kind of power, but the *ner* of the menorah in the Temple did.

We have strength when we harness not might and power, but light and clarity and God's spirit. We have strength when we choose to use our *chayil* for good, when we choose to use our *chayil* to make a difference in the lives of others, and when we choose to reflect God's spirit.

RABBI LINDA JOSEPH

הפטרת חג הפסח

Haftarah for the First Day of Pesach

Joshua 3:5–7; 5:2–6:1; 6:27

W hen they had purified all the people through circumcision, they returned to their places in the
camp until they were healed. . . . The children of Israel
camped in Gilgal, and made the Passover sacrifice on the
fourteenth day of the month, in the evening, on the
plains of Jericho. (JOSHUA 5:8, 10)

JOSHUA 5 BEGINS WITH the mass circumcision of the Israelite men in
preparation for warfare (verses 2–9), and then continues with the first
Passover in the land of Canaan (verses 10–12). One could imagine
from a modern feminist perspective that having the menfolk in recovery from a circumcision that occurs three days before Passover, given
the cleaning and cooking preparations this particular festival entails, is
not the most convenient of timing! Yet such a feminist interpretation
would be projecting our elaborate Passover preparation rituals onto a
different historical period. There are deeper feminist issues that we can
glean from the connection of circumcision and Passover in this haftarah, issues that have their basis in traditional Jewish text as well as
in symbolism.

In Exodus 12:43–49, God instructs Moses and Aaron to tell the
people that only family, servants, and strangers who are circumcised are

333

permitted to partake of the Passover sacrifice. In the Babylonian Talmud there are also several linkages made between circumcision and the Passover ritual. In *Yevamot* 71a, Rabbi Zera questions whether a father from a priestly family may partake of the Passover sacrifice if he has a son who is uncircumcised. In *Pesachim* 4a, it is told that the zealous show their eagerness to fulfill mitzvot by searching for leaven early in the morning on the fourteenth day of Nisan, just as they perform circumcision early in the morning on the eighth day. Further, in *Shabbat* 132a, we learn that both the Passover sacrifice and circumcision are mitzvot that override the Sabbath.

These constant connections in tradition suggest a symbolic connection between the Passover preparation and circumcision. The connection is apparent if we understand both circumcision and the paschal sacrifice as symbols of the feminine, and then seek to reconcile the connection of these symbols in our Joshua narrative.

Circumcision as Feminine Symbol

Howard Eilberg-Schwartz proposes that when a male is placed in an intimate position with God, he is taking on a feminine role. God is portrayed in the biblical text as male in gender and in action. For example, God is the impregnator of fertility as illustrated in the matriarch's lives—God remembers Sarah in her elder years and God opens up the wombs of Rebekah, Leah, and Rachel. If God is imagined as male, for men to have the most intimate of relationships with God—symbolized by sexual union—there need to be either homoerotic tendencies between the male Israelite and the male God or a feminization of man to create a heterosexual relationship. Since God is definitively male in the Bible, for men to have an intimate relationship with God they need to be "unmanned," since biblical mores will only sanction an intimate male-female relationship.

Thus Moses, the human in the Bible who gains the greatest intimacy with God, has his face transfigured through his encounter with

God on the mountain, and is required to be veiled, a form of dress usually associated with women. In Numbers, Moses protests with a denial of his femininity when the children of Israel complain about their lack of meat. He retorts to God, "Have I conceived all of this people? . . . Carry them at your breast as a nurse carries a baby . . ." (Num. 11:12). Further, Eilberg-Schwartz suggests that the reason Miriam was punished with leprosy and Aaron wasn't when they both protested Moses' marriage to a Cushite woman in Numbers 12 was that Miriam's authentic feminine nature provided a greater threat to Moses, whose femininity was contrived so that he could be an intimate of God.[1]

If the biblical author knew intuitively that to become an intimate with God men must be "unmanned," then circumcision can be seen as a feminization of manhood through removal of the foreskin to expose the genitals, analogous to the exposed vagina in a woman. Abraham and his male children undergo circumcision/feminization to bring them into a covenant, an intimate relationship with God. In Exodus 12, the enslaved children of Israel, uncircumcised due to Pharaoh's repression, are circumcised/feminized prior to leaving Egypt so they are readied for intimacy with God in the wilderness. Similarly, members of the new generation preparing to enter the Promised Land in our haftarah are required to be circumcised/feminized, so that they too can be intimate with God.

This theory is strengthened by a comparison made in the Zohar between the young women of Zion who need to be perfected in order to gaze upon King Solomon in Song of Songs 3:11. The circumcision of the people in Joshua 5 is a purification ritual readying the men for an encounter with God.[2] This midrashic parallel portrays the men as young women who require appropriate preparation to be intimate with God. It also understands the circumcision in the Joshua 5 text as a means through which men are suitably readied for an intimate exposure to God. The men are "unmanned" by the analogy just as men are "unmanned" through circumcision.

The Passover Sacrifice as Feminine Symbol

In Exodus 12, God commands the Passover sacrifice prior to the destruction of the firstborn of Egypt. In Joshua 5, forty years later to the day, the same ritual is performed in the same way—this time as a preparation for the people's entrance into the Land of Israel. The Israelites are directed in the Exodus passage to take a lamb of the flock without blemish, and to slaughter it on the fourteenth day of the month. The fourteenth day is the eve of the fullest moon, a symbol of womanhood in its most fertile manifestation. In Judaism, women's cyclical physiology is associated with the cycles of the moon as well, as evidenced by their special connection to Rosh Chodesh.

The lamb is a symbol of the pure and innocent, akin to a young virgin girl.[3] Its slaughter involves the penetration of a knife, reminiscent of penile penetration of a virgin, and the subsequent breaking of the hymen. Blood is the result: In the case of our paschal lamb it is smeared on the doorposts of the house as a protective amulet against the execution of the firstborn and a sign of the home's fidelity to God. In the case of the virgin in ancient Near Eastern cultures, blood was likewise smeared on a blanket as evidence of a girl's virginity, and would be displayed as a sign of her fidelity in case of slander by her husband.[4]

The Pairing of Feminine Symbols

With this in mind, we return to our question of the link between circumcision and the Passover preparation that is found in Joshua 5. We must understand the symbols of circumcision and paschal sacrifice in light of the first generation that left Egypt, before progressing to the second generation depicted in Joshua, for there is a connection between the accounts.

In the Book of Exodus, God courts the Israelites enslaved in Egypt. The Israelites are not at first convinced. Moses cajoles them into trusting God, and into believing in God's power to redeem them. Once they have been courted, members of the first generation are purified and readied for a sexual union with God—the men's genitals are exposed/feminized through circumcision, for only as females can they have a legitimate sexual union with a male God in the biblical world-view. The eve of the consummation of the relationship between God and the Israelites is then symbolized by the paschal sacrifice that can only be eaten by a circumcised/feminized male.

The blood of the paschal sacrifice smeared on the doorposts is evidence of the sexual union and marriage of God and the Israelite people. Freedom is the currency through which the wife is procured. And later in the wilderness the relationship is further cemented by the giving of Torah, symbolic of a marriage contract between them. We have here symbolic elements comparable to those the Rabbis of the Talmud require for a valid marriage—*biah*, sexual connection (paschal lamb); *kesef*, money (freedom); and *shtar*, document (Torah).[5]

This initial marriage, as we read in the narratives of Exodus, Numbers, and Deuteronomy, is not idyllic. In the wilderness the children of Israel are wistful for the luxuries of Egypt, and are full of complaints about their symbolic husband. So God waits forty years for a new generation to arise so that God may recourt and thus be rejoined to the children of Israel once more in a remarriage.

Only after all these events do we arrive at our haftarah. Joshua 5:5 explains that for forty years in the wilderness the Israelites had not practiced circumcision, and thus they would not be able to partake in eating the paschal lamb. The menfolk are circumcised en masse for the second time. Their feminization is given a masculine rationale: Circumcision is a requisite preparation for warfare. Yet symbolically they are feminized, and readied for a second unification ceremony with God.

The symbolic "unmanning" is once more followed by the paschal sacrifice, symbolic of penetration and sexual union with the female virgin; that is, the new unsullied Israelite generation. This time, the Israelites' entrance into the Promised Land, a place symbolic of the marital home of God and Israel, serves as a confirmation of the sexual union.

The Mystical Union of Male and Female

This feminine understanding of circumcision and paschal sacrifice is the reverse of the image in mystical Judaism in which men cleave to a female God, *Shekhinah*, in a spiritual/sexual union. As women who have no need to be "unmanned," this reading of Joshua 5 provides us with a new paradigm. As females we are natural spiritual/sexual partners of a male God. We need no circumcision to prepare us to be God's intimate partner. We need no paschal sacrifice to symbolize our loss of virginity.

We can view the constant male imagery of God in our tradition in a new way, opening us up to the possibility of mystical union with God's maleness. We can affirm our own femaleness with a male God, not as subjugated women but as partners, wives, or even lovers. Perhaps through an understanding of the power of these symbols, we can learn to conceive of our own mystical union with God, and to cleave to and embrace the male God of tradition in a new and exciting way.

RABBI SHAINA BACHARACH

הפטרת חג השבועות

Haftarah for the First Day of Shavuot

Ezekiel 1:1–28; 3:12

*A*nd it happened in the thirtieth year in the fourth month in the fifth day of the month, and I was in the midst of the exile on the Kevar River, and the heavens were opened—and I saw a vision of God. . . . And I saw, and behold, a storm wind came from the north, a great wind and fire flashing, and brightness around it, and in its midst was the appearance of bright metal in the midst of the fire! And in its midst, the likeness of four creatures, and this was their appearance—they were the likeness of a human! (EZEKIEL 1:1, 4–5)

AN ORDINARY PERSON, seeing that the heavens "were open" with storm clouds gathering, is not likely to stand on a riverbank and watch. A normal person would immediately seek shelter. However, Ezekiel ben Buzi, an Israelite priest living in exile in Babylonia, modern Iraq, did just the opposite. He remained in place and watched. Did he stay because he sensed—or hoped for—God's presence? Or was his world already so spiritually and emotionally dark that no storm could have made things worse?

Rashi, on Ezekiel 1:4, describes the storm coming from the north as a Divinely given prediction of the soon-to-come destruction of Jerusalem and the Holy Temple. Just as Ezekiel's storm comes from the north, so will the Babylonian hordes come from that direction and raze the Temple. While the symbolism no doubt holds, summer storms of wind and sand are common in Babylonia, modern Iraq. According to the *Encyclopaedia Britannica*, the harsh, northerly winds of the *shamal* cover huge areas with dust and sand. Even the most courageous observer would understand the impending lack of visibility and grasp the futility of sitting outside and trying to see.

For those of us on earth, dust storms can make visibility nearly impossible. Pictures of Iraqi dust storms taken from the space shuttle, however, give a very different perspective on this phenomenon. Colors range from amber to white to gold, and the various hues swirl around, forming different shapes.[1] From the vantage point of space and of heaven, a sandstorm is beautiful and majestic, an awesome sight.

Perhaps for Ezekiel, the blackness, the obscured vision imposed by the *shamal*, was no worse than the spiritual darkness of exile. Whatever the reason, because he braved the darkness and the fierce winds, he had an awe-inspiring vision. Even more remarkable, this happened while in exile from Israel and from the *Shekhinah*—God's presence, God's feminine aspect—for the ancient Israelites believed that the *Shekhinah* could only be experienced in the Holy Land.

In the Bible, God often appears in the midst of storms. These storms are not merely physical; they also serve as metaphors for spiritual states related to emotional upheaval, great stress, or overwhelming moments in general. We often characterize our emotions the same way. Just as we take shelter during a storm, we often try to hide from our emotions. For women, emotional reactions can become "proof" of weakness no matter how appropriate the response may be. We may be struggling with generic stressors such as school or work, or more gender-specific issues—spousal abuse, unwanted pregnancy, menopause, or rape. Regardless of the cause, it all too often feeds the stereotype of the "hysterical female." But if Ezekiel had sought shelter from the storm/emotions, he would not have experienced God's presence. If we accept the canard that strong emotional reactions show weakness, we risk fragmenting our psyches even further. Rather, we must learn from Ezekiel how to face the storm directly and brave its ferocity.

Ezekiel 1:3 ends by stating: "The hand of YHVH was upon him there." According to Rashi, "The prophecy seizes him against his will, like a person going mad." It is as if the storm's darkness and chaotic winds had thrown a cloak over his rational mind, and opened him up to the deeper recesses of his psyche. He had not expected to encounter the Presence, but the storm has caught him off guard. So often, when we are caught by surprise, we are at our most vulnerable. In this manner, Ezekiel experienced one of the most stunning visions ever recorded by a prophet.

In the midst of the worsening sandstorm, with normal vision obscured, Ezekiel "saw" wind and fire swirling, brightness and flashing lights. If one could picture this scene—the storm as viewed from the space shuttle—it isn't too hard to imagine the shapes and the colors shifting into these images. Ezekiel glimpsed another world, another side of the storm—from the viewpoint of heaven, not mortal humans. And then suddenly, in the midst of the chaos, he saw four living creatures, and he realized that they had the "likeness of a human."

This vision occurs during the summer month of Tammuz, five years after Ezekiel's arrival in Babylonia. He was there because of a failed revolt in the fifth century B.C.E. when King Jehoiakhin of Judah rebelled against the kingdom's Babylonian overlords.

During those first five years of exile, Ezekiel did not experience the Divine presence, nor did he expect it. So, too, in our day, because of stress and low expectations, we often fail to notice even the most obvious things in our environment. Our preconceived notions of reality blind us to new ideas and approaches. When Ezekiel was caught off guard, and perhaps frightened by a fierce storm, he saw one of the most profound mystical visions ever recorded.

We learn from Ezekiel's experience that we, too, must sometimes fight the reflexive instinct of seeking an emotional hiding place or relying on old patterns to deal with new scenarios. When spiritual, emotional, or intellectual storms gather, we must summon the courage to weather that storm, and not to fear moving to another stage of life, for that is what storms generally do—move us to new phase.

After the text tells us that the beings looked human (implying that they weren't), it describes the creatures and how their wings touched one another. In 1:9, Ezekiel says, "Their wings were joined a woman to her sister." This reads awkwardly even in the Hebrew text. For that reason, translators generally handle this as "their wings were joined one to another." But we should not discount the fact that the prophet went out of his way to personify the wings and the humanlike characteristics—the life essence—that he saw in every aspect of these strange creatures.

The Hebrew word used for *human* is *adam*. We generally associate the word *adam* with man, since Adam was the first man. But *adam* here is not gender specific; it is rooted in the Torah's first mention of the creation of people in Genesis 1:27: "And God created the human in God's image; in God's image did God create 'him'; male and female God created them." God created the first human as a unified whole. Differentiation into male and female gender identities came only as the last step of creation. The original human being was neither male nor female and assigned no specific role besides serving God; this is the brilliant vision of Ezekiel. The human soul transcends gender.

A few verses later, Ezekiel realized that each face actually consisted of four, and each one contained three other countenances: an eagle, an ox, and a lion. In other words, when Ezekiel experienced the *Shekhinah*, the Divine presence, his awareness widened to include the essence of life itself, the transcendent root of being. The Talmud considers the ox, the eagle, and the lion rulers of their own domains with humanity exalted above them all.[2] Through this vision, Ezekiel experienced both the unity of life and humanity's unique role as the epitome of creation. If these animals reign in their own spheres, and humanity stands above them, how much more so are humans able to master their own domains!

Women—not just men—have an inner power through which we can make reasoned, moral choices and not be buffeted about as helpless victims of fate. We have the ability—the duty—to rise to our full potential as human beings. It is interesting to note the particularly feminine imagery of the lion and the eagle with this concept in mind.

While folklore describes the lion as "king" of beasts, the female is actually the dominant animal. She protects both her young and her mate. She does the bulk of the hunting and feeds not just her young, but also her mate. The survival of lions depends on both male and female lions acting together as a team. Traditional gender roles do not pertain here.

What of the eagle? When we see a picture of the bald eagle, the American symbol, don't we generally picture it as a male? In Exodus 19:4, God brought us out of Egyptian slavery and carried us as if we were "on the wings of eagles." Rashi explains that this is because the eagle not only flies higher than other birds, but does so with her young on her back. In this way, he says, she shields her youngsters from the arrows of hunters. The eagle thus becomes the epitome of maternal loyalty as well as protection.

Ezekiel's vision of God's chariot, borne aloft by these multifaced creatures, teaches that we must grow and reach beyond our preconceived ideas. We can and should avoid the snare of thinking that we must base our lives and goals on traditional gender roles, whether male or female. Some of us will find that the more traditional roles suit us better, but that should be a free choice, informed by the sure knowledge that we humans are terribly complex, a composite of many faces. Ultimately, those different "faces" have a common root—the soul.

Ezekiel learned this by not hiding from the storm or from swirling, troubling emotions. Had he merely gone into a building for shelter, he might never have learned that even during the despair of exile, one could encounter God. Ezekiel might have continued seeing God through a narrow lens that limited God to geographical borders. Because he braved a storm and faced Truth, he soared to spiritual heights. He grasped the unity of life, the core of humanness. Ezekiel the prophet learned, and taught us, that the Divine presence is not limited by arbitrary definitions and boundaries.

Above all, the God of the Hebrew Bible is most often found during storms—of weather, of emotions. In our own lives, this means that we must summon the courage to face our churning emotions, no matter how troubling. When we do that, we *can* spiritually soar, no longer fettered by partial truths about who we really are. We can be a little more like Ezekiel, who was able to see the storm from the standpoint of heaven.

Five Megillot

RABBI RACHEL SABATH-BEIT HALACHMI

מגילת שיר השירים

Shir HaShirim

The Song of Songs

*H*is left hand should be under my head,
his right hand should be embracing me!
(SONG OF SONGS 2:6)

AMONG ALL THE CANONIZED TEXTS of the Jewish tradition, the Song of Songs is the most erotic. No other text describes female desire in such vivid terms, with an urgency that immediately pulls us into its passionate search for sexual fulfillment. Is it possible that female sexual desire is not only acceptable but also even glorified in a sacred Jewish text? Traditionally read in the synagogue on the Sabbath of Passover, the Song of Songs is a poetic and potent tale of male-female sexual desire. Some scholars understand the text to be a collection of ancient love songs, while others are certain that it is a unified composition. Regardless, one is struck by this sacred Jewish text in which a woman's desire is the central subject and force of the text. How does our tradition handle such a text? Like the female protagonist of the Song of Songs, might we understand our own sexuality as a natural part of what it means to be human and whole?

While other biblical texts speak of sexual encounters and even of love to the point of tears, only the Song of Songs speaks the language of passionate love and desire for the body of the beloved. Sexually charged images and dialogue flow from nearly every verse. The opening verse itself proclaims: "That he will kiss me with the kisses of his mouth, for your love is better than wine" (1:2). In the majority of such verses, the woman is the main actor: It is she who speaks, acts, responds, and turns repeatedly to the chorus of the daughters of Jerusalem, saying: "I adjure you, O daughters of Jerusalem; do not stir up, nor awake my love, until it please" (3:5). And it is she who turns over and over again toward her beloved, seeking him out both in dreams and while awake (chapters 3 and 5). This is not a model of a passive or hidden woman. Unique to this book is the fact that the woman does not hide her sexual desire. She proclaims to her lover, without shame: "If I met you outside, I would kiss you, and no one would despise me" (8:1). She is willing to seek out her lover all through the night and against all odds:

> At night while on my bed I searched for the one whom my soul loves; I searched for him, but I did not find him. I will rise now, and go about in the city; in the markets and in the wide streets will I look for the one whom my soul loves; I searched for him, but I found him not. The watchmen who go about in the city found me and I asked them: 'Have you seen him whom my soul loves?' I had just passed them when I found the one whom my soul loves; I held him, and would not let him go, until I took him to my mother's house, and into the chamber of her that conceived me (3:1–4).

Throughout the text the woman's sexual desire is laid bare, and she speaks of it freely in graphic details: "Your two breasts are like two fawns, twins of a gazelle" (7:4). Or consider these verses: "Your stature is like a palm tree, and your breasts are like clusters of grapes. I will go up to the palm tree, I will take hold of its boughs; may your breasts be like clusters of the vines" (7:8–9). While the woman of this love story ultimately never reaches fulfillment, it is impossible to ignore the intensity of the longing and the power of the desire itself.

How do we as women read such an erotic text? How do we understand its portrayals of female desire and sexuality? During different periods of Jewish history, the Rabbis attempted to restrict female sexuality and to limit it through rules of modesty. But depending on how we read the text, it can teach us about the experience of our own bodies, about desire, and about our attitude toward the forces that stand between us and our desire's fulfillment.

*T*raditional Allegorical Interpretations and the Denial of Sexuality

Many ancient and medieval rabbinic scholars avoided a literal reading of the text, reinterpreting the entire scroll as an allegory of love between God and the people of Israel. When the text has the woman describing the legs of her lover as "pillars of marble" (5:15), the authors of the midrash convert the human imagery into other terms altogether. They write: "*His legs* alludes to the world, which is 'as pillars of marble [*shesh*] because its foundation is based upon the days of creation; as it is written, For in six (*sheshet*) days the Lord made heaven and earth . . ." (Exod. 20:11).[1]

Another example of the ancient rabbinic interpretive stance toward the Song of Songs can be found in the following midrashic text:

> Rabbi Berekiah said: In these ten places in Scripture God refers to Israel as a bride: Come with Me from Lebanon, my bride (4:8); I am come into my garden, my sister, my bride (5:1); You have ravished my heart, my sister, my bride (4:9); How fair is your love, my sister, my bride (4:10); Your lips, O my bride, are dripping with honey (4:11).[2]

In the eyes of the ancient interpreters, such lush imagery could only be used between Israel and God. The woman described here is Israel, the bride, and the groom, the man, is God. The Rabbis transformed the lusty love poetry of the Song of Songs into a spiritual text in which the desire of the woman is that of Israel seeking out her beloved God. Not only were the Rabbis uncomfortable with such clearly sexual imagery, but in order to understand the significance of the Song of Songs and its place in the canon of Jewish texts, they were forced to reinterpret it as an allegory, as a spiritual text. Afraid that the Bible would appear to have a lowly love song about sexual desire worthy only of base people, they, in turn, elevated the Song of Songs above human lust and reframed it as a metaphor for the longing of the human heart for a passionate relationship with God.

Nonetheless, the Sages of the Mishnah in *Yadayyim* 3:5 recognized the problematic nature of the text, and disputed whether or not it should be considered a sacred text like the rest of the Jewish Bible. They even debated whether it should be included in the canon of holy writings *at all*. Yet, while some Sages questioned whether or not it should be included in the canon, others argued that it is in fact uniquely sacred: "Rabbi Akiva said: Far be it from anyone in Israel to dispute that the Song of Songs renders the hands unclean,[3] for the whole world only existed, so to speak, for the day on which the Song of Songs was given to it. Why so? Because all the Writings are holy, and this is holy of holies."[4] Clearly, the opinion of Rabbi Akiva demonstrates the awareness of the power of the text; and recasts it as the "inner chamber" of all Jewish texts.

*F*eminist Interpretations: Toward an Ethical Judaism

Unfettered by the limitations of the ancient rabbinic commentators, we can read and interpret the text more explicitly, and thus learn about our own search for fulfillment on all levels, and the role that search plays in our lives as Jewish women. The text, by its very language, challenges us as women to understand our own desire on both physical and spiritual levels. How does it lead us closer to fulfillment and how, when our desire is frustrated, does it prevent us from finding fulfillment? What can we learn about desire, about human disappointment, and about love from this text? To begin to answer these questions, each person who reads the text must not only accept the sheer power of the experience of sexual desire in human life, but also consider how gender, power, and culture allow for or prevent its fulfillment, and thus our own fulfillment as human beings.

The Song of Songs is particularly important for Jewish women and men who seek to understand the relationship between the religious and the sexual, the erotic and the holy. Here, after all, is a sacred text, one that is read aloud in the synagogue, that does not deny sexuality but rather celebrates it as a sacred element of human experience. Is female sexuality to be celebrated or is its public display a source of shame? In fact, toward the end of the Song of Songs, the female protagonist is not only frustrated by the evasion of her lover, but in her dream she is *mitrapeket* (8:5), meaning either that she falls apart onto her lover, shattered, or that she is stretched out over her lover. Each possible interpretation carries with it implications either of self-destruction or the hope of sexual fulfillment.

Feminist biblical scholars such as Marcia Falk, among others, believe that this text can teach us something about the redemption of sexuality and love in a world that is broken and far from its ideal wholeness.[5] The notion that the separation between lovers can be bridged and that brokenness and loneliness can ultimately be repaired carries with it the possibility that all that is broken and unjust in our world can be restored to a state of perfection.

The feminist reader, male or female, might read this text in a variety of ways. While ancient readers are not alone in interpreting the imagery of heterosexual love as an analogy for the relationship between God and Israel, the modern and postmodern feminist reader might see within the text the foundations of the immediate experience of the sacred in the human experience of sexual love. The search for and encounter with God are not unlike the search for and fulfilled encounter with the "significant other" of one's sexual desire, which is available and desired by men and women alike. Nothing about gender, one learns from the Song, distances or prevents one from an equally passionate search for a relationship with the holy, or the Holy One. As Alicia Ostriker writes, "Reading the Song as an image of human passion leads us to the possibility of a mutually delighting love-relationship with God, which is not contingent upon obedience or subordination."[6]

The possibility of human sexual relationships devoid of power struggles or manipulation is certainly a central element of feminism as well as of modern ethics. While the woman in the Song of Songs is repeatedly hindered in her search for her beloved by a variety of factors—watchmen and foxes, for instance—the very fact of her search and passion is not denied. This woman is never thwarted because of her gender; she is neither shamed by others because of the force of her passion, nor is she ashamed of it herself. The intensity and importance of a woman's quest for fulfillment are equal to those of a man. For Jewish feminists, this awareness allows for the creation of a religious system and spiritual community in which men and women are allowed equal expression of their full selves, intellectually, religiously, and physically.

The world we seek to create is one in which both female and male desire to seek full union with the beloved, both human and Godly, unhindered by the law, or by the other gender.

Ultimately, among many lessons, the text teaches us that as human beings we are by nature dependent on each other in order to find fulfillment. We need the love of another human being, and we will be frustrated without a sense of his or her complete love and support. The woman of our text calls out: "His left hand should be under my head, his right hand should be embracing me!" (2:6) She is aware of the interdependence of humanity in every realm and is aware that to be denied such fulfillment is not only unhealthy, but signals the lack of wholeness in the world itself. Such a conclusion necessarily means that the repair of the world is dependent on the establishment of equally supportive and fulfilling relationships among men and women.

RABBI BARBARA ROSMAN PENZNER

מגילת רות
Megillat Ruth

The Book of Ruth

Where you go, I will go; where you lodge, I will lodge; your people shall be my people; and your God shall be my God . . . (RUTH 1:16)

NOT MERELY A BOOK about two women, the Book of Ruth contains an important message affirming women's leadership and women's experience. Read on Shavuot, the book is placed prominently in the readings of the Jewish year. Standing side by side with the revelation at Sinai, the Book of Ruth can inspire us to celebrate Jewish women and women's contributions to Torah. It stands in stark juxtaposition to the Shavuot Torah reading, with its admonition in Exodus 19:15 to the Israelites at the foot of Mount Sinai, "[D]o not go near a woman." The Sages who determined the weekly and holiday scriptural readings chose Ruth as a counterpart to the Sinai Revelation, thereby affirming the centrality of women's experience in Jewish history and theology.

Ruth is a symbol of the outsider in the biblical context: A woman who "marries in," she is a Moabite, and thus a non-Israelite and a foreigner. While the Torah and prophets do not condemn intermarriage outright, Deuteronomy 23:4 specifically prohibits marriage to Moabite women. In addition, when Ruth and Naomi return to Bethlehem, they are poor widows, two of the biblical categories demanding charity from the community (strangers, orphans, widows, and the poor are frequently cited as those requiring special support). The Book of Ruth

353

champions Ruth and Naomi throughout, culminating in the genealogy at the end of chapter 4, in which Ruth is celebrated as the great-
grandmother of King David, one of the Bible's most revered figures.
The book's author, and those who admitted it to the biblical canon,
cannot emphasize Ruth's goodness enough, with Naomi's women
friends in 4:15 enthusiastically proclaiming, "She is better to you than
seven sons," and Boaz's praise of her in 2:12, "May YHVH give you
compensation for all you have done, and may you receive full reward
from YHVH the God of Israel, as you have found shelter under the
Divine wings."

This celebration of Ruth is hardly surprising, since she fits the traditional model of life-giving mother. Indeed, her exalted place as the
ancestor of King David underscores her value as the bearer of children. Yet, in this literary masterpiece and in the rabbinic midrash, the
worth of both Ruth and Naomi derives from qualities of character,
virtuous action, and demonstrations of deep faith, rather than from
fecundity. Few books of the Bible or narratives in the Torah develop a
character of such complexity, and with such overwhelming approval of
the protagonist, woman or man. Ruth stands out in so many remarkable ways. Why?

A Book About *Chesed*

The standard rabbinic explanation for the inclusion of this book in our
Hebrew Scriptures is that it is a book that teaches about *chesed*.[1] *Chesed*
is a positive quality that many have translated as "loving-kindness."
However, as used throughout the Bible, *chesed* is more accurately
defined as "covenantal loyalty," that is, love arising out of loyalty. As
opposed to "random acts of kindness," *chesed* implies consistency: an
act arising out of an enduring bond, whether between God and human
beings, or between parties to a treaty, or simply between people as creatures created in the Divine image. Ruth and Naomi stand out, according to the midrash, because of the loving acts that each performs out
of devotion to the other, and to God. Their story also illustrates a fem-

inist appreciation of the power of relationships. As Jewish feminist Judith Plaskow has written, "The sacred is met or experienced through the power of relation."[2] As we shall see, *chesed,* the backbone of the story of Naomi and Ruth, reveals the feminine aspect of God's presence in the world.

The most outstanding example of an act of *chesed* in the book is Ruth's decision to accompany her mother-in-law back to Bethlehem, thereby leaving her own home, family, and culture behind. The men of the story, Naomi's husband and two sons, are erased from the tale within the first five verses of the book. Naomi determines that she wants to leave Moab and return home. Her two daughters-in-law, Ruth and Orpah, begin the long, lonely journey by her side. Ruth's famous words in chapter 1, written in stunning Hebrew poetry, speak of undying loyalty, as she promises to follow Naomi until death separates them:

> And Ruth said, do not urge me to leave you, or to turn
> away from following you, for wherever you go, I will go,
> and wherever you stay, I will stay with you. Your people
> shall be my people and your God my God. Where you die,
> I will die and there will I be buried. Thus will YHVH do
> for me, this and more, for only death will separate me
> from you. (1:16–17)

Not only does Ruth pledge herself to Naomi, but to her people, her God, and her way of life as well. Often described as Ruth's "conversion," this speech emphasizes that Ruth loves Naomi's values and faith, and desires to emulate her mother-in-law's devotion to her God and her people. Ruth's devotion is therefore grounded in a sense of the holy and transcendent, which augments their emotional bond.

Ruth is in a partnership with Naomi; they share a mutual bond of *chesed.* Prior to Ruth's speech, Naomi cites the goodness of both daughters-in-law, Orpah and Ruth, in 1:8. As she urges them to return to their mother's houses, Naomi prays, "May God bring you *chesed* in return for the *chesed* you have shown to the dead and to me." This verse underscores the deep commitment, love, and respect between these women. Naomi acknowledges their acts of devotion to her, as their mother-in-law, as well as to their dead husbands, but releases Ruth and Orpah from any obligation to her. Naomi then prays that they find peace and the security of marriage, upon returning to their ancestral homes, having left home ten years earlier to marry foreigners. This separation will not be easy for any of them. Knowing that she will have to risk traveling alone, and admitting that she has nothing to give these women, Naomi also understands the challenge that they will face if they remain in Moab. When Orpah decides to obey Naomi's request, turning her back on her mother-in-law and choosing the Moabite way of life, neither Naomi nor the book's author criticizes Orpah's decision. Devotion can take different forms; for Ruth it entails rebellion and closeness, while for Orpah it means both obedience and separation.

Upon returning to Bethlehem, Ruth and Naomi each demonstrate their devotion to God, and their commitment to each other when they are most needy. Naomi uses prayer and praise, while Ruth is a woman of action. They work as a team, combining Naomi's wisdom with Ruth's energy. The younger woman heads to the fields to collect the fallen grain of the harvest. There she is introduced to Boaz, a distant relation, who insists that she be treated with hospitality and respect, another act of *chesed*. Upon returning home to Naomi at the end of a full day of gathering barley, Ruth surprises her mother-in-law with her provisions. Naomi responds with thanks to God in 2:20, noting that Divine *chesed* has brought them good fortune: "Blessed is this man [Boaz] before YHVH, Who has not stopped showing *chesed* to the living or the dead." Again, Naomi recalls how Ruth, and God, supported her following the deaths of her husband and sons, and marvels that Divine providence does not flag. In essence, she is blessed that the relationships with those she has lost continue in those she has gained. Naomi can envision the unfolding of the tale, as she realizes that Boaz, a distant relative, might marry Ruth. This relationship promises lifelong support and security for both women.

Unlike the majority of biblical men, Boaz is not the initiator of action. While the historical context demands that Boaz become the financial support for these two widows, the storyteller feels no need to disguise the behind-the-scenes manipulation of events by both Ruth and Naomi. Boaz becomes a willing partner to the two women in carrying out the scheme they have devised. The bonds of human compassion and loyalty, *chesed*, outweigh any of his other possible concerns. Indeed, Boaz seems to have no objection to Ruth, and works quickly and deliberately to fulfill his destiny to marry this pious stranger. He, too, cites the acts of *chesed* that he has heard about Ruth in 3:10: "May you be blessed before YHVH, my daughter. This last act of *chesed* is greater than the first, because you have not sought out other men, either poor or rich." Since she has reached out to him so honorably, he honors her by accepting her proposal. Once again, the story teaches us the power of relationships and their godly quality.

A Model *Eshet Chayil*

Boaz also praises Ruth at this point, calling her an *eshet chayil*. This phrase is best known from the Book of Proverbs, 31:10–31, in a lengthy poem that portrays the ideal woman. This passage has taken its place in the traditional Friday night array of blessings for the family. The notion of an *eshet chayil* calls forth an image of a hard-working, generous, and devoted wife and mother. But the Hebrew word *chayil*, which appears in the Book of Ruth three times, connotes more than the traditional depiction of "a woman of valor." Alternate translations include "a fine woman," "a woman of substance," or "a virtuous woman." What does Boaz mean in this context?

Modern Hebrew uses the word *chayal* to mean "a soldier." The Hebrew root encompasses strength, energy, wealth, and courage. Not surprisingly, the text also refers to Boaz in 2:1 as *ish gibor chayil*, translated as a man of wealth as well as might. Thus, Ruth and Boaz are well suited for each other. Ruth's strength, both physical and emotional, and her perseverance and integrity, can all fall under the description of *chayil*, a word denoting heroism. Both Ruth and Boaz are wealthy in the sense

taught by Ben Zoma in *Pirkei Avot* 4:1: "Who is rich? One who is con-
tented with one's lot." Boaz praises Ruth for all these noble qualities.
Similarly, at the tale's conclusion, the leaders of the town use this same
term to celebrate the union of Boaz and Ruth in 4:11:

> All the people assembled in the gate, and the elders pro-
> claimed, "We are witnesses! May YHVH make this
> woman who enters your household like Leah and Rachel,
> who built up the household of Israel. May you create
> strength [*chayil*] in Efrata and bring a good name to Beth-
> lehem."

The term *chayil* stands in sharp contrast to Ruth's status as a weak
and dependent alien. Whether she draws her strength from a Divine
source, or from her partnership with Naomi, or from some innate qualities, Ruth the outsider has become not only an insider but an exemplar
for the entire community.

Ruth and Naomi: A Model Partnership

The Talmud teaches that acts of *chesed* are greater than giving *tzedakah*
(righteous giving) in three ways. *Tzedakah* is only with money, while
acts of *chesed* can be accomplished with money or by action. *Tzedakah*
is only for the poor, while acts of *chesed* are for rich or poor. *Tzedakah*
is only for the living, while acts of *chesed* are for the living and the
dead.[3] *Chesed* is a value that equalizes human experience, allowing us
to participate in weaving the web of human life no matter what our
social or economic position. With the purposeful placement of the
Book of Ruth side by side with the central Sinai revelation, women's
experience moves from the margins of Jewish life to the center. The
celebration of Shavuot demands attention to both texts. The loving
relationship between Naomi and Ruth, succeeding as partners in a
world dominated by men, teaches that God works through human
interactions as well as through Divine inspiration. The power of *chesed*
cannot be underestimated.

It is important to note that we can read between the lines of the Book of Ruth a model of a more intimate relationship between Ruth and Naomi. Rabbi Rebecca Alpert documents how Ruth and Naomi's love "resonates powerfully with Jewish lesbians in search of role models."[4] Whether we view Ruth and Naomi as loving companions or devoted kin, they can teach us that those who appear marginal, even invisible, make valuable contributions to our community. They serve as models of compassion and cooperation, as well as strength and integrity. They also teach us the power of female bonding—that, indeed, "sisterhood is powerful."

On the whole, the depth of character portrayed in this book provides us with an astonishing vision. Not only does this story encourage Jewish women to take a more prominent place in Jewish life, but it also promotes qualities of partnership and peaceful coexistence: between women and men, between wealthy and poor, between strong and weak, and between "insiders" and "outsiders." Strength is derived from inner conviction rather than physical power. The Book of Ruth presents a model of cooperation, even while presaging the ultimate monarch, King David, with the hope that he will inherit some of the *chesed* so ever-present in his great-great-grandmother Naomi and his great-grandmother Ruth.

RABBI MELINDA PANKEN

מגילת איכה
Eicha

The Book of Lamentations

*H*ow can she sit alone? The city once great with people has become like a widow. Great among the nations, a princess among provinces has become a tributary. She weeps bitterly in the night and her tears are on her cheek. She has no comfort from among her lovers, all her friends have turned against her—they have become her enemies. (LAMENTATIONS 1:1–2)

THE BOOK OF LAMENTATIONS chronicles the destruction of Jerusalem and the First Temple at the hands of King Nebuchadnezzar. In great sorrow, its author (traditionally believed to be the prophet Jeremiah) asks the theological and emotional questions that are raised at a time of national, religious, and political tragedy. How could God have allowed the Temple—the Divine dwelling place—to fall? The writer poignantly draws out many themes: the question of national isolation, the role of God in destruction, the meaning of suffering, and the distress of those left to rebuild their lives. The reader of Lamentations cannot but be moved by the powerful language and imagery used to express the author's sense of emotional loss and turmoil. The author of the book personifies this tragic moment of destruction so that we may better feel and appreciate its implications for Jewish history. It is women's experience thus personified that plays a large role in defining our understanding of ourselves at difficult moments.

360

Lamentations is rich with female imagery and experience. Within the first sentence, Jerusalem is personified as a woman. "How can she sit alone? The city once great with people has become like a widow. Great among the nations, a princess among provinces has become a tributary" (1:1). The image evokes the sadness of what has happened. Jerusalem is the widow. She who once had joy, intimacy, and companionship in her life is now alone and mourning. Jerusalem is the fallen princess, once sustained by her people and now forced to pay tribute to others. Jerusalem is the woman who has been humiliated and forsaken: "All who honored her despise her, for they have seen her shame. Moreover, she moans and turns away. Her uncleanness was exposed . . . she fell astonishingly with no one to comfort her" (1:8–9). These images evoke a kind of sadness and empathy for the city and its people. She is a ruined woman, but still we want to reach out to her in compassion.

Yet the text goes beyond merely personifying the city. It gives voice to the tragedy of those who experienced the destruction firsthand. The narrator is moved to weeping when he witnesses what has happened to the women around him: "The elders of the daughters of Zion sit on the ground in silence, they laid dust on their heads, put on sackcloth; the maidens of Jerusalem have bowed their heads to the ground. My eyes are empty of tears, my spirit is troubled. My heart is poured out in grief because of the destruction of the daughter of my people" (2:10–11). In these images we see not only weeping women as the symbol of all mourning, but we are given a sense of the historical as well. The author paints a picture of the aftermath of this destruction and how it must have been the city's women who first publicly grieved.

The description of the humiliation continues: "They clapped their hands at you, those who passed along the road. They hissed and wagged their heads at the daughter of Jerusalem" (2:15). It is not only smooth stones and sturdy city walls that are demolished, but people, and, as a result, the survivors of this tragedy will be transformed in radical ways. The narrator is astonished to see this devastation and how "the hands of compassionate women cooked their children, they became their food during the destruction of the daughter of my people" (4:10). Life-givers forced to take life in order to sustain themselves—can we imagine any greater horror? This reminds us that often during destruction it is not only the physical that is shattered but morality as well.

There are no fewer than nine different female images drawn upon to personify and explore this moment of destruction. We read of the *almanah* (widow), the *sarti* (princess), the *betulah* (virgin/young maiden), *emotam* (mothers), *nashim* (women), *b'not* (daughters), *bat-Tzion* (Daughter of Zion), *bat-Yerushalayim* (daughter of Jerusalem), and *bat-ami* (daughter of my people). Who are these women? They are reflections of their time. They are wives and mothers, daughters and sisters. They are women whose sexuality and status are both determined and controlled by their relationships to men. Widows were granted special protection in biblical times because they lacked a husband to provide for them. Daughters lived according to the will and determination of their fathers. Virgins were chattel, transferred as property between father and husband. These women did not have control over their own lives and destinies. Perhaps they best represented the experience of the Jewish people who had lost control over their lives and destinies during this tragic moment in history.

Lamentations challenges us to identify with the victims of devastation. It moves us to understand their pain in a human way and their loss in human terms. It takes us from the anonymous victim to the personal one: We are the mothers and daughters, we are the sisters and wives. The feminization of this tragedy personalizes history, and thus connects us all in very human ways.

Most important, Lamentations reminds us that the destruction of Jerusalem happened to the entire Jewish people. Not only was the destruction of the Temple a tragedy for the Jewish men who were its priests and keepers, but it also devastated Jewish women and children, young and old alike. *Woman* here represents the common folk. Abandoned in the ruins of the city, we felt that God was far away from us all. The challenge is for us, as women, who first symbolized the grief of mourning, to be the first to reconnect with God, and thus lead the community to joy. Women abandoned—Jerusalem destroyed—is no more. Woman as Israel restored is our new role.

RABBI LAURA M. RAPPAPORT

מגילת קהלת

Kohelet

Ecclesiastes

*V*anity of vanities, says Kohelet; vanity of vanities,
all is vanity. (ECCLESIASTES 1:2)

IT IS NOT EASY to get human beings to change. Once we start on a life track, no matter how misguided, it takes a bulldozer, an army, or, perhaps, very harsh prose to make us change direction.

The author of the Book of Kohelet (according to tradition, an aged King Solomon) chooses prose to prod us from our complacent stroll along an unprofitable path. Affluence, wine, fame, even wisdom and good deeds, Kohelet claims, ultimately bring us no joy, no promise of satisfaction.

In the Torah account of Abraham's binding of his son Isaac, God must call out Abraham's name twice in order to break Abraham's trance and gain his full attention. Here, too, *vanity* is repeated to catch the reader. *Hevel*, the Hebrew word for vanity or futility, appears no less than seven times (tradition counts each plural as two) in this, his first utterance! Why does Kohelet resort to repetition of this magnitude? Because we are so intensely focused on pursuits that will prove worthless.

Kohelet speaks to us from a unique perspective that many would find enviable. He has been king over Israel in Jerusalem (1:12). As a man of great power, status, intellect, and wealth, he has seen it all, thought it all, and done it all. His list of achievements includes making great works, building houses, planting vineyards, acquiring servants, gathering silver and gold, possessing herds and flocks, and acquiring great luxuries (2:4–8).

From Kohelet's vantage point, he informs us that the fulfillment of many of humanity's desires is vastly overrated. Kohelet instructs us that these traditionally coveted trophies will not benefit our souls.

For centuries, material wealth and social status have defined success within male-dominated social systems. The philosophy that "more is better" has permeated the worldview of cultures around the globe. Women have only relatively recently been able to attain this type of material prosperity and recognition (and only in the Western/developed world), and many have jumped at the chance to enter the fray. This ancient text, however, authored many centuries before the modern women's movement, urges us to cover different territory in our search for lasting meaning. Women searching for their own path in a new millennium should not follow the well-trodden, conventional trail, but should look instead to values that run counter to normative social pressures. Thus, perhaps surprisingly, Kohelet offers contemporary women a refreshing, maybe even radical, message of great relevance.

Kohelet's first lesson concerns humanity's futile drive to consume and acquire possessions. The root of the Hebrew word *kohelet* is "gather." The primary message behind this biblical title is that a lifetime spent gathering goods is the highest of vanities.

"All rivers run into the sea, yet it is never filled" (1:7). In the race for material success, we can never reach a finish line. "The one who loves silver shall not be satisfied with silver; nor the one who loves abundance, with increase; this also is vanity. . . . What advantage is there to the owner except the beholding of them with their eyes?" (5:9–10).

Since society measures success by one's material possessions, women may choose to prove themselves equal to men through the accumulation of valuables. But the spiritual and emotional emptiness of this drive to acquire material things will manifest itself in women just as it has in men for so many centuries. The never-ending drive to acquire is a trap that will prove as dangerous today as it did in the time of Kohelet. As he teaches, "A person to whom God gives riches, wealth, and honor so that nothing is wanting, does not receive from God the power to enjoy it" (6:2).

The thirst for "more" is never quenched, and the competition to possess "the most" is never won. Both men and women who narrowly focus on acquisition will find themselves permanently discontent.

Kohelet addresses another human drive that seems to have become a modern obsession: the desire to find happiness. If we often find this desire unfulfilled within ourselves, we can console ourselves with this insight from the Rabbis: Joy eludes even God. In a midrash on Psalms 104:31, we read: "God will rejoice . . ." The Rabbis conclude that this use of the future tense teaches us that even the Eternal struggles to rejoice in the present moment! If God has such difficulty, perhaps we can be excused for failing to maintain a constant state of happiness. Yet we continue in this futile quest.

"All one's days are pains and one's occupation vexation, even in the night one's heart takes no rest" (2:23). Life so often weighs heavily on our hearts and souls. The widespread popularity of self-help books and brain chemistry–altering medications indicates that our society is willing to pour much of our resources into finding happiness, even after this goal proves beyond our reach.

Women seem especially prone to seeking a constant state of happiness. Socialized to remain pleasant, to offer cheer and warmth through all life's circumstances, to project a gracious smile through good times and bad, women who exhibit sadness and anger call into question their sexual identity. But striving for perpetual happiness is no way to live, counsels Kohelet. In fact, it is futile to pursue an emotion that no one can sustain.

A third theme of Kohelet also concerns us in the modern day—how often it seems that credit is not given where credit is due, and given liberally where it is not.

Time and time again we are both hurt and infuriated when our efforts and talents go unrecognized. Yet this reality was articulated most eloquently centuries ago when Kohelet observed, "The race is not to the swift, nor the battle to the strong nor yet bread to the wise, nor yet riches to those of understanding nor yet favor to those of skill. Time and chance happen to them all" (9:11).

If we expect to receive our fair share of recognition from the outside world, chances are excellent that we will be sorely disappointed. Injustice is woven into the human condition. "There are the righteous who perish in their righteousness and the wicked who lengthen their lives in their evildoing" (7:15).

Does it seem as if one's influence is based primarily on the people one knows? This is not a new state of affairs. "The wisdom of the poor is despised," Kohelet observes, "and their words are not heard" (9:16).

The Rabbis acknowledge this reality in a midrash on Proverbs 22:22, "Rob not the poor because they are poor." Why this repetition of the word *poor*? Because, teach the Sages, the poor are poor on two levels: They have no possessions and no one listens to their words of wisdom.

All too often, society judges words and works not on their inherent merits, but on the clout, fame, power, or wealth of the one who forms them. How relevant this message seems to many women who often feel invisible and unheard amid a strong "old boys' network." Many women strive to break into the "right" circles, only to be frustrated in the attempt, rather than stepping back to see the big picture that Kohelet paints for us as his biblical book nears its end.

Much of Kohelet reads like a bleak and often hopeless litany of life's inevitable disappointments and broken dreams. Yet this harsh style is necessary to break our focus on fruitless endeavors. We need to question society's well-entrenched expectations. And women, who now struggle to craft their own definition of success, need to consider his radical message.

Even though deep frustration dominates Kohelet's lament, subtle rays of hope peek through the fog of despair. These positive messages can help orient us in our quest for a life of meaning and gratification.

Tradition teaches that the lens through which the Book of Kohelet should be viewed is its final lines:

> The end of the matter, all having been heard: Fear God and keep God's mitzvot; for this is the whole human being. For God shall bring every deed into the judgment concerning every hidden thing, whether it be good or whether it be evil. (12:13–14)

When all is said and done, teaches Kohelet, success is judged by something much larger than an individual existence, much greater than a short-term perspective. Our fulfillment derives from our active participation in a broad Divine scheme.

Kohelet's final words emphasize the act of performing mitzvot, the work that truly matters to God. This focus relates to an earlier insight: "I saw that nothing is better than that people should be satisfied in what they are doing, for that is their portion" (3:22).

While many have chosen to focus on finding happiness through power and wealth, Kohelet urges a different strategy. Work is not the means toward the end of stuff and status; the work *is* the end. The mishnaic Rabbis further this theme in *Pirkei Avot:* "Who are truly rich? Those who are content with their lot" (4:1). Only work that is meaningful, that serves to advance the Divine cause, will bring a sense of inner wholeness.

"There is a time for every purpose and every work" (3:17). This teaching speaks especially to women, whose life trajectories seldom follow a simple upward line from the bottom to the top of the career ladder. Many women start on one path, take another with the arrival of children, perhaps take a side road to pursue additional schooling or training, and end up working in an area completely unforeseen in younger years.

Whether one's energy is devoted to the family or the outside world, to volunteer or paid work, to a part- or full-time vocation, one's deeds must be inherently meaningful. They must play some role in bringing holiness to the world.

Every experience, every moment holds the possibility of touching our souls. "In the day of bounty be pleased, and in the day of adversity consider" (7:14).

Women are often accused of not playing the success game by the proper, male-constructed rules. This may be a result of women choosing alternative ways of attaining and defining success or women's general discomfort with the power plays required by corporate life. Yet each female participant can find satisfaction in "playing like a girl." This involves, as Kohelet radically advocates, eschewing established routes to success and happiness in favor of a more fulfilling life of holiness and mitzvot. As women create their own unique life journeys in this age of expanded freedoms and options, they would do well to incorporate Kohelet's ancient wisdom.

RABBI KAREN L. FOX

מגילת אסתר
Megillat Esther

The Book of Esther

*E*sther was brought into the king's house . . . and the girl pleased him. (ESTHER 2:8–9)

*I*nscribe this . . . for a memorial . . . in a book!
(BT MEGILLAH 7A)

THE BOOK OF ESTHER commemorates a victory of the Jews over their enemies. Esther might be perceived as unique for that reason alone, and therefore worthy of inclusion in the Jewish canon. However, this text also illuminates the ways in which women obtain and maintain leadership within the context of the ancient world. Two women, Esther and Vashti, acquire personal and political power against the backdrop of an ancient Persian cultural setting. The text reveals a psychological and political savoir faire that women need in order to maintain leadership, and perhaps that is why it is so important to analyze it from a feminist viewpoint.

The Power of Vashti

The Book of Esther begins with a lavish description of a seven-day banquet given by King Ahashuerus. No restrictions were imposed at this party, and the wine flowed with abandon. The text notes that each man could eat and drink what he desired and he was free to affirm his will (Esther 1:7–8). The text seems to suggest that this event reeked of excess. As an aside the text notes, "Queen Vashti presented a lavish party for the women" (1:9). The reader knows nothing else about the queen except that she provided a social opportunity for the women, an opulent gathering, separate from the men's banquet. It was probably a chance for conversation, for women to observe and influence the elite in the kingdom.

However, Queen Vashti's party for the women was interrupted by the demand of the king, who insisted that she display her beauty at the men's banquet, wearing her royal tiara. Commentators suggest that Vashti danced nude[1] and that Ahashuerus wanted her there to entertain the voyeuristic and inebriated crowd. Such a performance by his wife would certainly prove his authority and sexual prowess. However, Vashti refused the king's command.

Vashti's refusal upset the balance of power between king and queen and therefore, according to the king's advisors, between all men and women in society. The text asserts that because one prominent woman dared to oppose her husband, all women throughout the kingdom would feel free to follow her example. There would be no end to disgrace, to scorn, to embarrassment of men by women. Therefore, the king's advisors banned Queen Vashti and decreed: "All wives will treat their husbands with respect, high and low alike . . . every man will rule his own home and hearth, every man will be king in his own castle" (1:20–22).

Vashti's influence, symbolic of all women's power, served as a frightening reality check for the king and his advisors. Her example of independence might endanger each and every Persian household. After Vashti defied the king, clear boundaries needed to be established to maintain the hierarchy in which men's authority was secure.

Laws that regulate psychosocial dynamics are written when the reality does not match the ideal. Perhaps even more women were gaining a prominent role in Persian society; perhaps Vashti was not alone in asserting her will in the social and political sphere. The king's legislation (1:20–22) attempted to reestablish a social order in which women were subservient to men. In so doing, the biblical text reveals not only a fear of women's independence but of their psychosocial-political influence in the ancient world as well. Vashti is portrayed as a woman with the power to influence all other women in the king-dom and endanger each man. She serves as a model of the assertive woman, one whom women admire and men fear.

The Power of Esther

After these events, Esther enters the scene to fill a void. In the ancient world, every king needed a beautiful, young queen: Certainly, Ahashuerus needed a new queen who would publicly obey him. All those who were selected as potential wives were treated to a year of the finest in "spa treatments." Mordecai, Esther's uncle and guardian, encouraged his niece to enter the contest, and it appears that he sug-gested that Esther be lovely, quiet, and subservient in the selection process. Esther entered the harem with a secret: She was instructed by Mordecai not to reveal her faith, her culture, or her people (2:10). Even the name *Esther* means the "hidden one."

Esther was selected to be the next queen, and she was presented with a royal tiara and a lavish banquet in her honor. But Queen Esther did not actually speak until potential danger for the Jews emerged. A decree was issued in the king's name, directed by Haman, the enemy of the Jews. The decree ordered, "Destroy, massacre, and exterminate the Jewish people, young and old throughout the land" (3:13).

Queen Esther became agitated, but she was afraid to approach the king without being summoned. However, Mordecai reminded her that her own life was in danger along with the whole Jewish community: "Do not imagine that you, of all the Jews, will escape with your life remaining in the king's palace. You will die, however, and the other Jews will receive help from Above. You have achieved your status as queen for exactly this purpose, a crisis of Jewish survival" (4:13–14). With Mordecai's words in her ears, Esther used her beauty to convince the king to pay attention to her words and deeds (5:2). When the king asked what she wanted, she requested that her life and the lives of the Jewish people be spared (7:2–3). She then set a clever and believable trap for Haman: The king found Haman in a compromising position that indicated that he might have raped the queen (7:8). The king was enraged; he ordered Haman's death and the death of his descendants (7:10). The Jews survived.

Esther used whatever means available to ensure her people's survival. Her cunning use of beauty, relationship, and authority enabled her to acquire, maintain, and enhance her influence within the structure of Persian society. She understood that her access to power came through the king, and, after securing that relationship, she could direct action and resources to benefit her nation. Collaboration with the king served as a successful leadership strategy.

Women and Leadership

In a unique way, this book acknowledges the difficulty that women may experience in leadership roles. Through the character of Vashti, the gaps between political power and psychosocial influence are highlighted. Fear of women who challenge men is acknowledged, even as Vashti is whisked off the stage. Vashti's anger and rebellion reveal one way to protest authority; her influence is experienced and feared by leadership throughout the kingdom.

In the character of Esther, a woman achieves power through association. The encouragement and support of her uncle Mordecai and her husband, King Ahashuerus, give her access to authority. Esther understands the subtleties of relationship that are needed to maintain authority. Maintaining an ongoing conversation with her husband allows Esther access to power and influence with her husband and society as a whole. Esther makes the transition from the young, frightened girl into the assertive, confident woman who masterminds the rescue of the Jews. Her subtle but strong range of influence indicates directions by which a mature, confident woman can enhance herself, her family, and community.

Esther serves as a catalyst to widen the model for women in religious/cultural life. Israeli professor Alice Shalvi recognizes that "Esther is a marvelous role model for women everywhere. Knowledge and perceptiveness can empower women to bring about betterment of family, community, and society as a whole."[2]

While Vashti and Esther serve as models of women in ancient times, modern women can learn much from their vulnerabilities and their strengths. Women in political, social, scientific, and religious roles understand that asserting power is a balancing act, one in which motivation, vision, and collaboration can lead to endless possible outcomes. In some settings, fear of women's psychosocial influence is still expressed. Women in leadership roles are necessarily cognizant of this fear. In addition, the Book of Esther demonstrates how relationship building and association can lead to greater possibilities in leadership for women and for men.

When the Rabbis of the Talmud established the holiday of Purim and instituted the reading of *Megillat Esther* for future generations, they wanted to retain a book that affirmed Jewish survival despite its enemies.[3] Most likely they never imagined the Book of Esther as a model of power and influence for women. When the Rabbis in the Talmud proclaimed this book for all times, they projected its legacy of women in leadership for the future.

Special Additional Selections

בת-שבע

Bathsheba

II Samuel 11

*A*nd it was near evening when David got up from his couch and went for a walk on the roof of the palace. And from the roof he saw a woman bathing and the woman was very beautiful. (II SAMUEL 11:2)

ON A VISIT TO THE City of Jerusalem, it is possible to stand on the Southern Steps that led up to the site of the *Beit HaMikdash*, the Holy Temple. Standing on these steps, looking south, one faces *Ir David*, the City of David. The City of David is the name given for the part of Jerusalem that was established during the time of King David. It lies outside the wall of the Old City of Jerusalem because David was not permitted to build the Temple, in part because he had blood on his hands and in part because of his relationship with Bathsheba, the woman he falls in love with on that rooftop. Standing on the Southern Steps in the Old City of Jerusalem, facing south toward the City of David, one can almost imagine the setting of the story that unfolds.

Many of the stories of King David's reign are set during battles fought by the king. This time, instead of David going off with the rest of his troops to fight, he remains in Jerusalem. Walking on the roof of his palace, he sees a woman bathing on another roof. Curious about the identity of this beautiful woman, David sends a messenger to find out more about her. He learns that she is Bathsheba, wife of Uriah the Hittite. Uriah the Hittite just happens to be one of the soldiers in his army, and the irony is not lost on the reader when David, who has remained in Jerusalem, sends for Bathsheba to come to his bed while her husband is out fighting battles for him. The only words that Bathsheba utters in this chapter come after she has been sent for and lies with David. She sends David the message, "I have become pregnant" (II Sam. 11:5).

David reacts to the news by sending for Uriah the Hittite. When Uriah appears before David, David urges him to return home to his wife, no doubt with the hope that Uriah will lie with his wife, throwing a veil over the probability of David's paternity. Three times David attempts to get Uriah to return home to his wife, but Uriah does not follow David's wishes. He says to David, "Your Majesty's men are camped out in the field, and I should return to my house to eat and to drink and to be with my wife? This I will not do, as I live" (II Sam. 11:11). The third time David even gets Uriah drunk, but Uriah still returns to sleep with his solders rather than going home to Bathsheba.

After this third attempt, David writes a letter to Joab, the commander of David's army, ordering him to place Uriah in the fiercest fighting and withdraw the rest of the troops, guaranteeing his demise. Joab does as ordered, but, as a result, other officers also die in battle. David is told the details of the battle, including the death of Uriah. Finally, the action turns again to Bathsheba, the woman around whom the story revolves. The text says that Bathsheba mourns the loss of her husband and then in the final verse of the chapter, Bathsheba becomes David's wife and bears him a son.

Although Bathsheba lies at the center of the action, the textual evidence points to her passivity. She says very little and seems to have little control over the course of events that will change her life. Instead, the two characters pitted against one another are David and Uriah. This chapter is seen as a turning point in the life of David, whose actions seem all the worse when compared with the decent actions of Uriah.[1] David, home from battle, which the text suggests is unusual, lies with a woman who he knows is married.[2] So rather than fighting with his troops, David is having sexual relations with the wife of one of his soldiers. By contrast, when Uriah comes home, Uriah's words demonstrate that he, unlike David, is dedicated to his fellow soldiers.

With the chapter playing Uriah and David against each other, Bathsheba's actions seem like an extension of Uriah's. She conducts herself like Uriah in light of the circumstances into which she has been thrust. Like Uriah, who makes decisions that seem right and noble, she also does right thing. For example, II Samuel 11:4 states that Bathsheba had purified herself from her uncleanness. This means that she has carried out the laws of family purity incumbent upon a woman. She has gone to the mikveh in the requisite period of time, as Jewish law instructs a woman to do. And because the text makes mention that she has just purified herself after menstruation, and then lies with David, while her husband is away at battle, this clarifies that David is the father of the child. This information portrays Bathsheba as an innocent character practicing what Judaism commands.[3] In contrast to a woman following Jewish law, David had broken it by committing adultery. Later, when Bathsheba receives the news that her husband has been killed in battle in II Samuel 11:26, she mourns for him for the appropriate period of time (11:27), as Jewish law prescribes, until David sends for her. Ironically, the message of her husband's death is sent by the one messenger in the chapter who does not come from David.

In the worst of circumstances, it is inspiring to see Bathsheba maintain a sense self-preservation and control over the events in the chapter that pertain to life cycle. Like her husband, she carries her responsibilities out to the best of her abilities. But it is impossible to ignore the events that Bathsheba is unable to control. Through a series of passive verbs, there is an assembly-line–like sequence of events, with David in the active role and Bathsheba in the passive.[4] Her interactions with David, both at the beginning and the end of the chapter, exhibit this passive style. In II Samuel 11:4, David sends messengers for her, he takes her and lies with her, but when Bathsheba acts by sending messengers to inform David that she is pregnant, he does not interact with her. Instead he sends for her husband, Uriah (11:6).

Bathsheba's passivity extends beyond the actions of this chapter and into the life she establishes with David, once he sends for her at the end of the chapter. There are many cases where biblical women name their own children. The naming of children by women is one of the few places where we hear a woman's words in the Bible, and gain further understanding of her sentiments. In Genesis, for example, Rachel and Leah name the sons of Jacob in a way that demonstrates their feelings toward Jacob, their praise of God, or their hopes to have more children.[5] Hannah names her son Samuel in I Samuel 1:20, in gratitude that her prayers to God have been answered. And in Ruth, women have a role in the naming of the son of the union of Ruth and Boaz. Bathsheba has no such role in the naming of her children. In II Samuel 12:15–18, the child of the adulterous union between David and Bathsheba dies and is not named at all. Solomon, the second child they have later, is named by David, and not by Bathsheba (12:24).

There must be more to the woman Bathsheba than just as an extension of her husband's behavior, or as a passive participant in the interactions with David. There is a certain power that lies in Bathsheba, and the effect she has on both David and Uriah.[6] After all, up until the Bathsheba incident, David is successful in both deceiving others and overcoming others' attempts to deceive him, but, "after the Bathsheba incident . . . his fortunes in this area change." Among the negative events that happen after the Bathsheba incident are the rape of his daughter by one of his sons, the killing of that son by another son, and a rebellion led by that second son.[7] As happens in other biblical stories, the ultimate reversal of fortunes and eventual downfall of a king are caused by a woman. The strongest parallel is found in the story of Abimelech in Judges, a king whose life is literally ended by a woman who smashes his skull.[8]

But Bathsheba's greatest influence will not come until later in I Kings 1 when she takes an active role in influencing her own future and that of her family and the Jewish people. Wanting to ensure that the future of the sovereignty will lie with her son Solomon, she goes to David, on the urging of the prophet Nathan, asking David to make sure that Solomon will become his successor.[9] Bathsheba, together with her cohorts who work to guarantee Solomon's succession, undertakes a great task. Solomon is David's tenth son, but his fourth son, Adonijah, is the "surviving, eldest prince" at the time.[10] Bathsheba speaks loudly and clearly to David, telling him, "My lord, you swore by Adonai your God to your maidservant that Solomon, your son, 'He will rule after me and sit on my throne'" (I Kings 1:17). This Bathsheba, who succeeds in ensuring Solomon's rule, is different from the Bathsheba of II Samuel 11. For at this moment, Bathsheba has secured the succession of her son Solomon and guaranteed her role in the annals of Jewish history as the mother of the king. It is our last memory of her, overtaking our associations with the adulterous liaison with King David that led to the death of Uriah.

The concept of Bathsheba's legacy is an uplifting element in a feminist examination of this story. Bathsheba, a victim of David's deception, is no doubt hurt by his actions; but she gains strength over time and eventually becomes an advocate for her son's future.[11] Bathsheba's life was forever changed from the moment David spotted her, bathing on a rooftop, but she always remains an honorable woman whose goodness only accentuates the disgraceful actions going on around her. Like the multiple midrashim that forgive King David for his actions in the Bathsheba affair and other acts of deception in his life, Bathsheba's power lies beyond the pages of the Bible.[12] It lies in her ability to retain her integrity and nobility at all times while ensuring what is best for her family and her people.

RABBI BETH L. SCHWARTZ

מיכל
Michal

I Samuel 18:17–29; I Samuel 25:44; II Samuel 3:13; II Samuel 6:20–23

*A*nd Michal, Saul's daughter, loved David . . .
(I SAMUEL 18:20)

MICHAL, DAUGHTER OF SAUL and first wife of David, appears in only a few episodes of the First and Second Books of Samuel. When these episodes are taken together, they reveal how her relationship with her husband changes over time. They also show how she herself grows.

In I Samuel 18:20, we learn: *Va-te'ehav Michal bat Shaul et David*—Michal, the daughter of Saul, loved David. Of all of David's wives, it is only Michal who is described as loving him. Even more significant is that her love for David was a cause for her father to be afraid: "When Saul realized that the Lord was with David and that Michal daughter of Saul loved him, Saul grew still more afraid of David; and Saul was David's enemy ever after" (I Sam. 18:28–29). Her love was what emphasized to Saul his own loss of God's favor.

Descriptions of emotions are rare in the Bible, and the emotions of women even rarer, so we must pay attention to Michal, whose love is mentioned twice. No explanation is given for her love, but we can glean a few hints from the text. Michal must have been attracted not only by David's ruddy good looks (I Sam. 16:12), but also by the accomplishments that she would have seen in her father's house, namely, David the poet and harpist. He was a brave young warrior, but he also had a softer, more cultured side. David was a favorite in Saul's service, both as an arms-bearer and as a soother of Saul's troubled spirit (I Sam. 16:21–23). One can imagine her easily falling in love as a young girl, seeing how her father favored David for his musical talents and for his budding reputation as a fighter. One can also imagine the father, Saul, seeing this love as more than he bargained for when he brought David into his service. And yet David and Michal prevail, and the marriage takes place.

The second encounter with Michal shows us how she has transferred her loyalties from her father to her husband. Michal helps David to escape before he can be captured by Saul's men; she lies to her father to protect David and gives him time to get away (I Sam. 19:11–17). Michal's actions show us that she understands the situation between her father and her husband, but also that she knows where she stands. She has grown from an infatuated girl into a politically aware wife. Women have been the object of manipulation by fathers and husbands throughout history: Michal demonstrates that she can hold her own and protect herself; she can play the same game.

The relationship between Michal and David is never a reciprocal or equal partnership. David refers to Michal both as "Saul's daughter" and as "my wife," depending on his political motivation (II Sam. 3:13–14). Michal must submit to her father taking her back and marrying her to someone else, Palti, who loves her enough to weep when David reclaims her. One must wonder how she felt about this marriage, both its beginning and its end. She spoke up for love once, but she is silent now. Surely she was a pawn of royal politics, yet the protest comes not from her but from Palti (I Sam. 25:44). It is possible that Palti was an inferior match in terms of social status, or perhaps Michal still loves David.

Michal can transfer her loyalty from her father to her husband, but her sense of her marriage is very different from David's. This is only in part because of the position and status of women in ancient Israelite culture. Where David sees his ultimate loyalty being to God, Michal see hers as being to the nation.

Michal is disdainful of David's dancing half-naked in the streets when the Ark is brought into Jerusalem, and she criticizes David severely. His response is clearly about his relationship with God, and his right and obligation to express his joy; if that involves dancing with women in the streets, so be it. David's populism is as clear to him as his devotion to God. The Mishnah teaches us that a king may wash and anoint himself on Yom Kippur (Mishnah *Yoma* 8:1); there are things that are appropriate and necessary for a king to do for the sake of his position. Michal is a first-generation princess, and she understands the requirements of royalty. Like many women, Michal's identity is strongly connected to her social position, and her choice is to use her position selfishly or for a larger purpose. Her criticism may sound prudish or snobbish, but it shows us that Michal understands the need for dignity and order in the kingship.

As Saul's daughter, Michal brings a sense of legitimacy to David's leadership. Although David is God's choice for king, the kingship itself is a result of the people's insistence: "We must have a king over us, that we may be like all the other nations" (I Sam. 8:19–20). Marriage to the king's daughter brings David into the royal house. The union of Michal and David provides for the continuity of kingship, at least potentially, and the appearance of stability at the top.

Yet this continuity is not to be. II Samuel 6:23 informs us that Michal, although twice married, remains childless. The implication is that her barrenness is her punishment for her criticism of David. The continuity of the kingship will not depend on Saul's children, after all. It is truly God's love for David that is most important.

The Rabbis are not harsh in their judgment of Michal, and we need not be, either. The Rabbis give her credit for raising the five children of her sister, Merab, and she is held up as an exemplar of an adoptive parent.[1] The Rabbis further attribute the nickname of *Eglah* to Michal; according to them, it is a term of endearment that David used to refer to her.[2] Why was she dear to him? Because she arranged for his escape from Saul, and saved his life. The midrash tells us that this act demonstrated that Michal's love for David was greater than that of Jonathan, since she saved his life from inside the royal house (Midrash *Psalms* 59:1). Michal is also associated in the midrash with the Woman of Valor of Proverbs,[3] having a great capacity to love and to give of herself, and earning our esteem by these actions.

She was pious as well. Those who taught that the wearing of tefillin was not a time-bound commandment understood this from the teaching that Michal wore tefillin, and was not prevented by the Sages from doing so.[4] Since, as a woman, Michal was exempt from those mitzvot that must be done at certain times of the day, her wearing of tefillin must be voluntary and thus praiseworthy.

One can see that our tradition is not content with a one-dimensional Michal. Her loyalty to David must come from more than girlish love, so tradition gives us a multifaceted woman. She has an understanding of politics and a sense of history. Because she supports David's cause, she supports God's cause as well, and so she rises above her personal unhappiness to be esteemed for piety, and for generosity of heart.

Michal grows from an infatuated girl, a lucky princess who gets her heart's desire, into a mature woman who must live by the rules of politics. Her choices are not her own, and her dignity and position are not her own to defend. And yet Michal always has the strength to maintain her own opinions. She is not afraid to stand up to her father the king, nor to her husband the king. She is also a reflection of the growing national identity of her people under these two kings. Early on, her father is properly humble and respectful of his need to grow into his position, and of the needs of the people to be led.

Michal absorbs this lesson well, and by the time she is married to David, she understands the dynamics of power and her own role in power politics. She plays that role skillfully and successfully, advancing David's cause. But her understanding of royal power and position force a clash with David, whose self-confidence as God's choice allows him to flout the social conventions that should govern a king's behavior. Michal's scolding is not snobbery; rather, it comes from her sense that the people want, and should have, a king who is kingly.

Although David has rejected her, there is not a hint that Michal herself is anything but unbowed. Her criticism remains in the text, like an alternative opinion that is let stand. Her ability to give her husband children is not as important as that ability is for other women in the Bible. Tradition teaches that good deeds are like children.[5] Michal's good deeds and dignity are her progeny, and her legacy to us. Jewish tradition teaches us that she acted in the public realm, as daughter and wife of kings, for the sake of her country; in the private realm, as a pious woman and adoptive mother. Thus, Michal comes down to us as a woman of strength and purpose, of dignity and intelligence.

RABBI KARYN D. KEDAR

חולדה הנביאה
The Prophetess Huldah
II Kings 22; II Chronicles 34

*A*nd the King commanded Hilkiah the priest . . .
saying, "Go inquire of the Lord for me, and for the
people, and for all of Judah concerning the words of this
book that is found. . . . So Hilkiah the priest and
Achikam, Achbor, Shaphan, and Asaya went to Huldah
the Prophetess . . . (II KINGS 22:12–14)

THE HILLS OF JERUSALEM contain the secrets and mystery of our people. To uncover the secrets, we dig and penetrate the surface, looking
for buried treasures. On the southern exposure of the walls of the
ancient city, there are three gates that are sealed. These gates are
known as the Huldah gates. The answer to the question "Who is Huldah?" is one of the secrets buried in the antiquity of Jerusalem. The
uncovering of these gates is the work of archeologists, historians, students of wonder and curiosity, and construction workers. When roads
are built, buildings erected, and renovations designed in Jerusalem,
inevitably an ancient artifact is unearthed, all construction is stopped,
and the archeologists take over to excavate the area. The treasure is
examined, tested, dated, and scrutinized, and a piece of our puzzling
ancient story is put in its place.

Astonishingly, this procedure took place in the seventh century
B.C.E., when King Josiah ordered that the First Temple be renovated.
Josiah had ordered the renovations either to simply make repairs or to

institute reforms. At the time, there was a foreign influence pressing upon the people, and idol worship was being practiced. Perhaps the king was hoping to rid the Temple of these foreign influences.

The Temple was the central place of worship for the Jews. It was the place they came together to offer sacrifices to God. It was the place where the Jews of the world came three times a year as a pilgrimage, to gather as a community and to celebrate the three pilgrimage holidays of Passover, Sukkot, and Shavuot.

Josiah, who was crowned when he was merely eight years old, reigned in the Kingdom of Judah for thirty-one years. In the eighteenth year of his reign, which was the year of these renovations, the king sent his scribe Shaphan to Hilkiah, the high priest, who was essentially the supervisor in charge of the work being performed on the Temple. Shaphan was charged with delivering the money levied as taxes against the people in order to pay the workers at the Temple.

Hilkiah, upon receiving the money, informed Shaphan that "I have found a scroll of teaching in the House of the Lord." He gave the scroll to Shaphan and Shaphan read it, but he does not appear to have been particularly impressed by it, because he then returned to the king and said, "Your servants have melted down all the silver and delivered it to the overseers of the work, who are then going to pay the workers." He then told the king, almost as an afterthought, "the high priest has given me a scroll." Shaphan then read the scroll to the king. Upon hearing it, the king tore his clothes, a symbolic act of mourning and repentance. In doing so, the king showed his dismay at not having followed the teaching of the Law, and he then intensified his efforts to purge Judah and Jerusalem of foreign shrines, idols, and altars.

King Josiah ordered the high priest, his scribe, and several others to go to the prophet to find out if this was indeed an authentic scroll. This was the time of the prophet Jeremiah, considered one of the major prophets. But the group is not sent to Jeremiah, who lived in a town outside Jerusalem called Annatot, but rather they were sent to the prophetess Huldah. Huldah lived in the Mishneh, a special quarter in the city of Jerusalem where the people came to seek counsel from the wise—apparently, Huldah among them.

When the group presented her with the scroll, she read it and said:

> Thus saith the Lord, the God of Israel, "Say to the man who sent you to me, 'Thus saith the Lord: I am going to bring disaster upon this place and its inhabitants, in accordance with all the words of the scroll which the king of Judah has read, because they have forsaken me and have made offerings to other gods and vexed me with all their deeds. My wrath is kindled against this place and it shall not be quenched.' But say this to the king who sent you to inquire of the Lord, 'Thus saith the Lord, the God of Israel: As for the words which you have heard, because your heart was softened and you humbled yourself before the Lord when you heard what I decreed against this place and its inhabitants, that it will become a desolation and a curse, because you rent your clothes and wept before me, I, for my part, have listened,' declares the Lord. 'Assuredly, I will gather you to your fathers and you shall be laid to your tomb in peace. Your eyes shall not see all the disaster which I will bring upon this place.'" (II Kings 22:15–20)

Huldah the prophet reported, in other words, that because King Josiah was a good king, dedicated to the one God, the disaster that would befall the Kingdom of Judah would only occur after his death. She then predicted, accurately, the destruction of the First Temple, which occurred in 586 B.C.E. That is all we know of Huldah.

Huldah's prophecy exists in two very similar accounts, one in the Book of Kings, one in the Book of Chronicles. No other details are given, no other prophecy relayed. Her contemporary, Jeremiah, on the other hand, is allotted an entire book of his prophecy in the Tanakh.

Clearly, Huldah was a prominent prophet of the time, and yet her voice was nearly silenced, except for the precious strands of this one story. In the biblical text, her lineage is traced through her husband's family and not her own. She is called "Huldah, the wife of Shallum, son of Tikvah, son of Harhas, the keeper of the wardrobe" (II Kings 22:14). Her husband's important position in the royal palace confers status upon her, rather than her own wisdom or prophecies.

Even the Rabbis, several centuries later, are perplexed about the character of Huldah, yet there is only one discussion of her in the Talmud (BT *Megillah* 14b). The question raised there is twofold: Who is the mysterious female prophet, and why is her male contemporary, Jeremiah, not consulted about the authenticity of the scroll? Rav surmises that she must have been a relative of Jeremiah's, for no woman would have prophesied instead of the great Jeremiah, without some connection and without his permission. Rabbi Johanan on the other hand claims that Jeremiah was out of town on more important business: He was searching for the ten lost tribes. Rabbi Nahman offers yet another explanation. Huldah, he teaches, was one of the two haughty women of the Bible, both of whose names are "hateful." The first is Deborah, whose name means "hornet," and the second is Huldah, whose name means "weasel." The proof that Huldah was "a hateful weasel" is that, in the biblical account, she refers to Josiah as a "man" rather than as "the king." Rabbi Judah simply calls her the daughter of a harlot, for only a whore would be so bold as to presume to prophesy in Jeremiah's place.

Clearly, the rabbinic literature struggles with the mystery of Huldah, and the Rabbis' male bias does not allow them to conceive of a woman who would be great in stature and wise in her counsel. But she must have been, for several centuries later, when Herod rebuilt the Temple, three gates on the southern exposure were named for the prophetess Huldah. These were the gates through which the pilgrims entered the Temple to pay homage to the one God. In the seventh century C.E., the gates were sealed, and today we can see the arches, filled in with Jerusalem stone. As those gates were sealed, so were the details of the life and teachings of the prophetess Huldah. So often in our history, women's voices are silenced or forgotten or simply lost. As students of the mystery of our people, we try to uncover what has been buried and bring to light the great teachings of our prophets. As we walk the streets of Jerusalem and hear the sound of the cranes rebuilding the ancient city and at the same time unearthing its secrets, let us also hear the echo of all the voices, the ones recorded and the ones omitted, the ones named, and the ones whose names have been forgotten. Let us tell the stories of the women who were our teachers and guides, even if their legacy is but a fragment, and the details of their lives sealed in the past.

RABBI SHOSHANA BOYD GELFAND

יהודית

Judith and the Story of Chanukah

*T*he essence of the miracle was at [women's] hands.
(TOSAFOT, MEGILLAH 4A)

*S*he was greatly renowned among all, because she feared God, neither was there anyone who spoke ill of her. (JUDITH 8:8)

WHEN THE RABBIS of the Talmud decided how to canonize the Bible, there were huge debates about which books should be included. Some controversial books, like Esther and the Song of Songs, were eventually included. Others, like Judith, were not. However, some of those that were omitted were later compiled into a collection called the Apocrypha. To this day, the tale of Judith, one of the great heroines of Jewish literature, can be found in the Apocrypha, along with other books that were left out of the Tanakh.

The story of Judith opens with the Assyrian army laying siege to the Jewish town of Bethulia, where a wealthy and pious widow named Judith resides. Bethulia is the only town blocking the Assyrians' way before they capture Jerusalem in their campaign to conquer the Land of Israel. When the Assyrians cut off their water supply, the elders of Bethulia decide to surrender to General Holofernes, but Judith chastises them for their lack of faith and volunteers to take matters into her own hands to save the town. She literally "dresses to kill" and—as a living "Trojan horse" of sorts—enters the enemy camp. The general, struck by her beauty, becomes enamored of her and takes her into his tent, ostensibly to seduce her. She charms him into drinking heavily, and when he falls asleep, she seizes his sword and cuts off his head. Without their leader, the army is easily defeated, and the Jews of Bethulia (and therefore Jerusalem) are saved.

While the story of Judith does not appear in the Tanakh itself, we nevertheless hear in her story resonances of various biblical stories and personalities, both male and female. For example, in chapter 5 of the Book of Judges, Yael also beguiles an enemy general and wins his trust for the sole purpose of assassinating him as he sleeps in his tent. While the plot line of this story is similar to that of the Judith story, Yael's character is quite different from Judith's. In contrast to Judith, the Book of Judges depicts Yael strictly in warrior terms, without mention of her feminine qualities. While Yael is identified as a woman and a wife, the stereotypically feminine characteristics of beauty or piety are not applied to her. Rather, she is depicted primarily in masculine language, ignoring her identity as a woman (except to mention that she is married). The language associated with Judith, on the other hand, embraces both stereotypically masculine and feminine terms. She is alternately referred to as a pious widow, a fierce fighter, and a stunning display of feminine allure. Judith, unlike Yael, does not need to sacrifice her feminine qualities in order to function in a man's world.

In fact, the narrator of the Book of Judith repeatedly emphasizes her beauty, introducing her as "very beautiful and fair to see" (Jth. 8:7) and later describing how all the soldiers in the Assyrian camp "wondered at her beauty" (Jth. 10:19). In this sense, Judith reminds us of Esther, also known for her beauty and for saving her people from physical annihilation by an enemy. Like Esther, Judith uses her "feminine wiles" to save her people. Yet, unlike Esther, Judith is not limited to the indirect power of seduction and raising suspicions of jealousy. To be sure, Judith makes full use of her femininity and sexuality to disarm the enemy, but she does not hesitate to attack directly as well, even using the general's own sword to behead him! She is thus, a sort of combination of Yael (warrior) and Esther (beautiful seductress).

Judith not only combines characteristics of female biblical characters, however. She also embodies major male figures from the Bible. Judith's physical warrior aspect, for example, is reminiscent of David in his famous battle against Goliath in the Book of Samuel. In both cases, the seemingly weak character overcomes the strong enemy through cunning, courage, and faith in God. In both stories, the "weak" and humble character beheads the champion with the victim's own sword and then dedicates the disembodied head as a trophy.[1]

Judith can thus be seen as a combination of the characters of Esther, Yael, and David. In addition, she mirrors the leadership of Deborah, who also announces that the enemy will be delivered into "the hand of a woman."[2] Ruth is another character who finds resonance with Judith, as both of them share the attributes of widowhood and "lying at the foot of a man."[3] Her character thus conflates David's "weak beheading the strong," Esther's feminine wiles, Yael's seduction of a general, Ruth's pious widowhood, and Deborah's outshining and shaming her male counterpart. In addition, Judith adds her own sense of piety and religiosity, expressed through her fasting, prayer, and a seeming commitment to keeping kosher even while in the enemy camp. She even brings her own dishes with her for the journey![4]

Judith is indeed a strong and multifaceted character. She floats in a seemingly effortless fashion from role to role, regardless of its stereotypically masculine or feminine qualities. She begins the story as a pious and humble widow, yet when the situation calls for outspokenness in the town council, she summons the elders (and they come to her!) and berates them for their lack of faith. When they refuse to take action, she transforms herself into a vision of feminine beauty and courageously travels behind enemy lines armed only with her ingenuity, her attractiveness, and her faith in God. She uses her feminine charms to seduce the general in his tent, but when he falls asleep, she draws on her physical strength and warrior instincts to chop off his head. Judith is indeed a rich and complex character, capable of moving between many layers of personality: humble widow, valued town advisor, beautiful seductress, and fierce warrior. She is not easily pegged into a single role, but rather bursts forth as a nuanced and fully developed character.

Perhaps it is the very richness of Judith's character that kept her story from being canonized as part of the Tanakh itself. While we do not have a record of the Rabbis' discussion, one can hypothesize that they did not have a category for a woman so flexible and nuanced in those days. Perhaps at the time, it was inconceivable for a woman to contain both masculine and feminine traits and, therefore, the Rabbis preferred the Books of Ruth and Esther, whose female heroines appear far more one-dimensional (and therefore more "containable") than Judith. One could also speculate that another reason the Book of Judith was not canonized was the sheer power and threatening independence of her character. Her ability to identify herself completely as a woman, while functioning without a man, makes her unique in all of biblical literature.

Another possible reason for the exclusion of Judith from the Tanakh is that a minor character, Achior, "converts" to Judaism during the course of the story. Since Achior is an Ammonite, and therefore prohibited from ever becoming part of the people of Israel, the story may have been deemed inappropriate. The counterargument for this is, of course, the story of the "conversion" of Ruth the Moabite (Moabites and Ammonites alike are forbidden to convert to Judaism), which was included in the Tanakh.

Luckily for women today, the Apocrypha preserved her story. Along with other stories from the late biblical period (including Maccabees I and II, Susanna, Tobit, and Ben Sirah), the Book of Judith was codified by the Catholic Church and kept alive in Greek translation in the Apocrypha. She also became a central female character in medieval Christian art and iconography. Although Jewish tradition did not embrace her fully by including her story in the Tanakh, there appears to have been at least an oral or folk tradition that continued to tell the story throughout the generations. For this reason, we find allusions to Judith in medieval commentaries like the Tosafot: "Rashbam interprets that the essence of the miracle was in [women's] hands. On Purim—in the hands of Esther. On Chanukah—in the hands of Judith. On Pesach—it was on account of the merit of the righteous women that that generation was redeemed."[5]

Already in medieval times, Judith's story was closely connected with the holiday of Chanukah. Numerous Hebrew midrashim tell of the daughter of Yohanan the high priest who fed the Greek king a salty cheese in order to get him to drink large quantities of wine.[6] The *Shulchan Arukh* even codifies the tradition of eating cheese on Chanukah, and attributes its origin to Judith.[7]

Why is Judith associated with Chanukah? While the origin of the connection remains unclear, definite literary parallels exist between the Books of Judith and Maccabees. For example, both were written during the Hellenistic Period. (Despite the Assyrian setting of the Book of Judith, the linguistic and stylistic cues identify it as being written during the Hasmonean Period.) In terms of plot, both Judah Maccabee and Judith behead a general, and are celebrated by their people as heroes. And both stories are military tales, complete with strategic language and similar Greek words. For example, the word *hyperkerao*, "to outflank," appears only twice in the entire Greek Bible—once in the Book of Judith and once in the First Book of Maccabees.[8] And there is, of course, the name of the main character: Yehudah (Judah) [Maccabee] and Yehudit (Judith), which are the exact same Hebrew name in masculine and feminine form, and which literally mean "Jew."

We may therefore speculate that in the Middle Ages, Judith became the feminized version of Judah Maccabee, the well-known hero of the story of Chanukah. In medieval *Chanukiot* (Chanukah candelabra), she makes frequent appearances. Sometimes she is even depicted side by side with the Maccabee brothers. Her story is also told in medieval midrashim as a sequel to the story of the daughter of Mattityahu (Judah Maccabee's father), who refused to defile herself and sleep with the Greek governor on her wedding night. Judith's story is even immortalized into the medieval liturgy as a *yotzer* (a *piyyut*, or liturgical poem) for *Shabbat Chanukah*, where the "miracle of Chanukah" becomes the defeat of the Greek army, beginning with Judith's beheading of their general! (See the end of this chapter for an excerpt from the text.)

Judith became a folk heroine of Chanukah, in stark contrast to Hannah, the other woman usually associated with the holiday. Unlike the famous story of Hannah and her seven sons from the Book of Maccabees, Judith is not a martyr. She expresses her piety through prayer, fasting, and action, as opposed to sacrificing herself and her children as martyrs. Judith's active expression of strength fits well with her character of a powerful heroine who uses not only her physical strength, but also her femininity to save her people. This ability to embrace both the masculine and feminine aspects of her personality continues to make her a powerful role model for all of us, male and female, today.

I encourage us to reclaim the tradition of celebrating Judith on *Shabbat Chanukah*, in much the same way that we celebrate Esther on Purim and Miriam on Pesach. This could be done by reviving the medieval custom of telling her story at Shabbat services during Chanukah. We could read the traditional words of the medieval *yotzer* for *Shabbat Chanukah* during prayer services as a way of celebrating this forgotten heroine:

> She [Judith] was protected during the night,
>
> . . . .
> He [the King] fell into a deep sleep.
> They called the girl to be with him.
> He rested his forehead on her and appeared to be sleeping.
> They [soldiers] got up and went their way, swiftly they left
>   the king alone
> And returned to their tents of protection.
> She [Judith] called upon her fear of God and wisdom.
> She cut off his neck like the top of wheat.
> She took it and brought it to benefit her people's hope . . .
> When morning came, they cried out loudly,

"Hear, O Israel, the Lord gives light!"
When the enemies heard the noises of the crowd,
they hurried to awaken the king and protect him.
They saw him lying in his palace.
Their noises became subdued and their spirit left them.
They were depressed and filled with fear.
Their captives pursued them and smote them to pieces.
 They finished them off, killing them by the heap.
Then the elected [Israel] sang songs and praises.
The power of the miracle was permanently established
by the wise [Rabbis] to conclude Hallel for eight days,
to kindle lights in joy always, year after year.
Today is both Shabbat and Chanukah.
God is praised by the occasions and the refined people.
We will be your eternal witness—to you belongs
sovereignty.[9]

Our ancestors celebrated the story of Judith each Chanukah. Let us do the same by reciting her story in our synagogues and at our Shabbat tables during the holiday of Chanukah. This way, she can continue to serve as a role model for all of us, and inspire us to embrace our masculine and feminine attributes fully. That way, we can each reflect all aspects of the Divine that exist in each of us.

RABBI DEBRA ORENSTEIN

דלילה
Delilah

Judges 16:4–31

*A*nd it happened afterward, that he loved a
woman in Wadi Sorek whose name was Delilah.
(JUDGES 16:4)

THE STORY OF SAMSON and Delilah has entered our culture through movies and books. It is widely known, often without even being read, as an archetypal tale of women betraying men. Everyone knows that Delilah betrays Samson. But maybe "everyone" is wrong.

In chapter 16 of Judges, Samson meets and falls in love with Delilah. She is approached by Philistine leaders, who tell her to entice him in order to learn the secret of his strength. They inform her of their intention to capture, torture, and humiliate Samson as payback for his attacks. The Philistine lords also promise her eleven hundred pieces of silver each, in exchange for her cooperation.

Delilah asks Samson: "Tell me [*hagida*], please, in what is your great strength? And with what can you be restrained for your torture [*teiaser le'anotecha*]?" He tells her that seven fresh bowstrings can fell him—a lie (16:6–7). Philistines are lying in wait. Delilah ties Samson up, trapping him according to his instructions. Then she cries out: "The Philistines are upon you, Samson!" Of course, he breaks free easily, and "his strength is not known" (16:9).

We then go through the cycle again. Delilah complains that Samson has mocked and lied to her. "Now tell me [*hagida*] with what can you be restrained?" Samson says that new ropes can weaken him—another lie. Philistines, again, are lying in wait. Delilah ties Samson up, trapping him according to his instructions. She cries out: "The Philistines are upon you, Samson!" He breaks free a second time, escaping his would-be captors (16:13–14).

Again, the story repeats. Delilah demands: "Tell me [*hagida li*] with what can you be restrained?" Samson tells her that braiding his hair with the web of the loom will make him vulnerable—yet another lie. She braids his hair and fastens it with the weaving pin, trapping Samson according to his instructions. Crying out, "The Philistines are upon you," Delilah wakes Samson, who walks away with full strength, carrying pin and loom (16:13–14). She protests: "How can you say you love me when your heart is not with me? You have mocked me three times, and not told me [*higadeta li*] in what is your strength" (16:15).

The narrator tells us: "And it came to pass when she tormented him (*heitzika lo*) every day with her words, and urged him until he was sick to death, that he told her his whole heart." Samson finally reveals the true secret of his strength: namely, his uncut hair, "for I am a Nazirite of God from my mother's womb" (16:16–17). Delilah calls back those who want to capture him. This time, the men lying in wait have turned into a single man. Some scholars propose that Delilah is calling to Samson to see if he has been lulled into sleep yet.[1] In any case, she "puts Samson to sleep in her lap, cuts his hair,[2] and "begins to torture him [*le'anoto*]. His strength left him" (16:19). For the fourth time Delilah says: "The Philistines are upon you, Samson." He awakens and says, "'I will leave as I have every other time, and shake myself.' But he did not know [*lo yada*] that God had departed from him." The Philistines gouge out Samson's eyes and take him to prison, where his hair slowly grows back (16:20–22). He eventually destroys their Temple in a massive murder-suicide.

This can be—and has been—superficially understood as a story of Woman using her sexual wiles against Man. Yet sex is all but absent. We know that Samson loves Delilah, and we have a symbolic suggestion of sex when he finally puts his head in her lap. But the "temptress" gets her way by cajoling and acting hurt. She resorts to nagging and making Samson feel guilty.

It is hard to make sense of this story at face value. To understand it literally, we must believe both that Delilah is the world's worst spy and that Samson is the world's most moronic dupe. Their game is more cruel than playful. Delilah is transparent in her attempts to harm Samson, even the first time. What kind of temptress uses the same failed tactic over and over again? What kind of victim escapes a scam the first time, stays around to watch it attempted twice more, and finally gets "fooled" on the fourth try?

To understand why Samson behaves as he does with Delilah, and who Delilah is to him and to the narrator, it is helpful to look back at three women who have shaped Samson's destiny until now: his mother, his betrothed, and the prostitute he visits. In reviewing their stories, we will see how the themes and key words of the Samson and Delilah narrative are part of a larger context.

The themes of gender, trust, and secret knowledge are at play even before Samson's birth. The scene in which an angel predicts Samson's birth portrays his unnamed mother as knowing and trustworthy. She quickly understands that this visitor is no ordinary person: "a man of God came to me and his appearance was like an angel [or messenger] from God." She conveys her trust in him by accepting his instructions unquestioningly. "I asked him not from whence he came, nor did he tell me [*higid*] his name." She also conveys trust in her husband, Manoah, by passing along the vital instructions for Samson's care: "[The angel] said to me, 'Behold, you shall conceive and give birth to a son, and now drink no wine nor strong drink, nor eat an unclean thing, [nor cut his hair] for he shall be a Nazirite of God from the womb until his dying day'"(13:6–7).[3]

By contrast, Manoah's response conveys a lack of confidence in his wife: "Let the man of God . . . come and teach us what to do with the boy who is to be born" (13:8). Of course, this is precisely what she has already told him. The angel does come back, but again to her, and not to "us." She tells Manoah that the same man has arrived. Dismissing her word, he asks the angel if he is indeed the same man. The angel answers as tersely as possible: "I [*ani*]." When Manoah requests instructions concerning the boy, the angel refers him back to his wife and validates her authority: "Of all that I told the woman, let her take heed" (13:13). From the Divine messenger's perspective, though not her husband's, her stewardship is trustworthy.

Mistaking the angel for a man, Manoah foolishly offers him food. He boorishly asks questions about the visitor's name, whose mystery his wife has respected. He misinterprets the angel's flight up to heaven as dangerous rather than miraculous. Thus, Manoah is portrayed as ignorant, and even foolishly comical. He is *lo yada* (not knowing—verse 16) for most of the chapter and finally *az yada* (then knowing—verse 21) once it is all quite obvious. Along the way, he doesn't seem to *know* or appreciate his wife's character any more than he *knows* who the angel is or how to treat him properly. Moreover, it is Divine intervention—not Manoah's biblical *knowing* of his wife—that ensures her pregnancy.

The characteristics that make Manoah a buffoon become dangerous in the next generation. Samson's crises are precipitated by failing to trust women, offending elder or higher-ranking males, and not understanding women. While Samson is busy making sure that no one knows his secrets, his own ignorance becomes as noxious as his father's was obnoxious.

Perhaps having learned distrust from his father, Samson does not confide the secret of his strength to either parent (*lo higid*—14:6), any more than he does to Delilah (*lo higadeta*—16:15). He distances himself from them, declaring his attraction to, and intention to marry, a Philistine woman. She is not named, but we do know that she comes from Timnah, the place where Tamar used her sexuality—the only means at her disposal—to trick her father-in-law, Judah.[4] Tamar's dishonesty was a response to men betraying her first. The same can be said of Samson's betrothed, and possibly even of Delilah. Yet, Tamar is praised, while the women in Judges are ignored, condemned, and killed.

Samson poses a riddle to his future in-laws during a feast preceding the wedding. He bets against the men with whom he should be bonding, asking a question to which they could not possibly know the answer, since it is based on an experience he kept secret. Samson should be seeking guidance and favor before his marriage. Instead, he is posing as the "know-it-all" about sweet things in the belly and the food that comes out of the eater—the content of his secret and euphemisms for orgasm. The Philistine men threaten their relative, the bride-to-be, with burning "you and your father's house." The nameless woman of Timnah is thus pitted between her aggressive, insensitive fiancé and her threatening, disloyal relatives. She argues with Samson exactly as Delilah does: "You only hate me and do not love me." To this Samson gives an answer as revealing as it is wounding: "Look, I haven't told my father or my mother; would I tell [my secret] to you?" (14:16). Again, the woman from Timnah uses the same strategy as Delilah, perhaps because both women have such limited options.[5] Samson's betrothed "cried upon him [or because of him] the seven days that their feast lasted; and it was on the seventh day that he told her (*vayaged la*) the riddle, for she tormented him (*heitzikathu*)" (14:17). She gives her relatives the answer, but her crying is more than a ploy. She cried for all seven days of the feast, although her relatives only threatened her on the last day (14:15, 17).[6]

When the relatives answer the riddle correctly, Samson condemns and objectifies his betrothed, comparing her to a virgin cow: "If you had not plowed with my heifer, you would not have found out my riddle." He kills thirty Philistines and collects their clothing to make good on the bet. Then he leaves in anger without marriage or its consummation. For all his bravado and innuendo, Samson is apparently still a virgin. By the time he cools off and returns, his intended has been married off, presumably without being consulted, to the best man. Oblivious to his own part in the matter, Samson considers the marriage a betrayal against him that justifies revenge (15:3). In an attempt at conciliation, the father of Samson's betrothed speaks disloyally about his own daughter: "I [thought] you utterly hated her . . . isn't her younger sister better than she? Let her be yours instead" (15:2). Once the woman Samson scorned is not his to scorn any longer, he avenges that insult by burning the Philistines' crops. Holding her responsible, her relatives burn her and her father's house after all.

Now it becomes clear how little choice or bargaining power his betrothed ever had. How could she have trusted Samson enough to tell him about threats made against her when he had already betrayed her by posing the riddle in the first place? The fiancée suffered both when Samson abandoned her and when he exacted vengeance over the consequences of that abandonment. Had she withheld the answer to the riddle, her male relatives would have burned her and her father's house. She therefore revealed it, but was condemned to die the same fiery death. Damned if she did, and damned if she didn't.

Samson's fiancée is purely innocent, and completely violated, in ways that Delilah is not. But the two women have more in common than it might first appear: Both are caught between Samson and Philistine men, both are being tested by the man to whom they are bonded, and neither has much power. Imagine if Delilah had refused the Philistine men who approached her. What would her fate have been? Surely, she would not have been any better off than Samson's betrothed.

After leaving Timnah the second time, Samson finds another woman—this time, a prostitute. When a man visits a prostitute, the sexual roles and expectations are clear, and the sexual favors presumably guaranteed. Even in this case, Samson doesn't seem to connect easily or completely with a woman. He "comes to her." But then his enemies realize "Samson has come [to the city]," and so his encounter is interrupted. He leaves in the middle of the night. Has he had sex, or not? Do the Philistines find out that he has been with her, or not? Did she tip them off, betraying him? Or did Samson mark the prostitute as a traitor and then leave her behind, betraying her and possibly signing her death warrant?

Samson's relationships with women are literally unresolved. It's not just that he is ambivalent, or that gaps in the text leave us wondering about many details. Samson doesn't finish with women: He doesn't finish getting married, or consummating his marriage, or spending the night with the prostitute. The text never states explicitly that he has sex with Delilah. Perhaps he never knows a woman in the "biblical sense." The Talmud suggests as much: "What does it mean [that Delilah] tormented him? Rabbi Isaac of the School of Rabbi Ammi said: At the time of the consummation, she detached herself from him."[7] Samson's life is marked by his encounters with women, but from his mother to his betrothed to the prostitute to Delilah, he never fully knows, or connects with, any of them. Nor do we, as readers. Except for Delilah, we don't even know their names. We never learn whether Delilah returns Samson's love. We do not know if she is a widow or a prostitute, a Philistine or a Jew.[8]

When the role of women is taken into account, we can no longer read these chapters as "Samson's betrayal by evil women." Rather, we uncover a more complex narrative of betrayal. The story of Samson and Delilah—and all the other women in his life—becomes a tale about men's failure to trust, and about *mutual* betrayal and miscommunication.

It is certainly possible to read Delilah as a vicious traitor. But this hardly proves that *women* are Samson's betrayers. After all, it is males who threaten and bribe women into harming Samson. Moreover, the fact that the Philistine lords promise not to kill Samson is interpreted by some rabbinic commentators as a sign of Delilah's reluctance to cooperate. She wanted to be sure, at least, that his life would be spared.[9] Whatever one thinks of Delilah, Samson clearly fails to trust three women whom he has no reason to doubt. Withholding trust is costly to him. Perhaps he longs to share "his whole heart." Like many people who hesitate to trust, he finally confides his deepest secrets injudiciously, to exactly the wrong person. This "proves" once again what he—and his father—feared all along: Women can't be trusted.

The surface story is that Samson loses his strength when he loses his hair. But the reverse is a deeper truth: Samson loses his hair because he has already lost his strength. He is physically strong enough to lead and defend Israel, but he has no command of himself. Repeatedly, he gives in to whim and fury, to lust and an immature version of love. He cannot properly decide whom to trust or distrust because he does not trust his own instincts. Thus, he gives up his power, and his clear thinking, to Delilah. Samson spends the better part of three chapters defending his honor and strength as a "man." Yet he is weak in love, mistrusting and untrustworthy as a son, a son-in-law, and a husband-to-be. From the time he first discovers his true self, he hides it (14:6). Trust requires vulnerability, and Samson avoids both.

Upon his capture, Samson is consigned to a degraded and feminized position—doing women's work, being tortured and humiliated [*onato*] in language that alludes to sexual submission or rape.[10] As his hair grows, his strength returns. He eventually reclaims a stereotypically masculine role, dominating and killing the Philistines.

Notwithstanding all the gendered images, the ultimate questions posed by the story of Samson and Delilah transcend gender: Whom do we trust and distrust? Whom do we end up betraying, and why? How can we bridge the chasm between self and other without losing ourselves? What is that elusive brand of strength that yields the love and victory that Samson longed for, instead of the revenge and death that he settled for? In the end, the story of Samson and Delilah teaches us to long for and cultivate trust, and to fear the diminished humanity that men and women will suffer without it.

RABBI GEELA RAYZEL RAPHAEL

אשת בעלת-אוב
The Witch of Endor

I Samuel 28:3–28

*A*nd Saul had put aside the mediums and the wizards . . . (I SAMUEL 28:3)

IN CHAPTER 28 of the Book of Samuel, we encounter a remarkable woman, able to help King Saul by speaking to the dead. Indeed, King Saul had already banished all mediums, necromancers, witches, and other dabblers in the occult and the underworld, when he seeks out the "Witch/Medium" of Endor to conjure up the prophet Samuel from his grave. Here we see the themes of power and powerlessness, hospitality, mystery, and ritual arts, as they relate to women's role in biblical society and beyond.

The context for this portion is the transition from Saul's kingship to the Davidic dynasty. Samuel the prophet has just died, and King Saul has banished the mediums, those who communicate with the dead, from the land. The Philistines are encamped at Gilboa, and Saul is afraid of their pending invasion.

Saul tries to consult the "traditional" oracles of the *Urim-tumim,* a prophetic device worn by the priests, but it gives him no guidance. He also wants to receive instruction from his dreams, and the prophets, about the military situation. But God seems silent, so he turns to the very practitioners he has banned.

Who are these seers? In Leviticus 20:27, we read: "A man or woman who is a [medium] or spiritist with you must be put to death.

407

You are to stone them; their blood will be on their heads." In Deuteronomy 18:10–11, we read "There may not be found among you anyone who makes his son or daughter to pass through fire or casts spells, or who is a [medium] or spiritist, or who consults the dead." The message is clear: To consult one who has contact with the spirit world is forbidden. This was an attempt to limit the contact of the Israelites with Canaanite pagan practices, so they would only hear the voice of YHVH as the one true God. This injunction was intended to keep the Israelites from intermingling with "the locals," and adopting their religious beliefs and traditions. However, the fact that this is stated not once but twice in the Torah suggests that it must have been a serious concern, and may have been common practice, and thus a strong temptation for the Israelite community. Why would anyone need to listen to the leadership of Moses, or the priest, if they could consult an oracle and find their own guidance? Yet the Witch of Endor is still practicing after the ban. This woman has defied the decree against calling the dead and is still adept at her trade. This story sets the stage for centuries of Jewish women's spiritual arts that were banished underground but somehow managed to survive.

There are others, even before the Witch of Endor, who consulted oracles. Rebekah goes to inquire of the Lord (Gen. 25:22). Rachel's mysterious capture of the teraphim in Genesis (31:34) opens the possibility that she was using them as oracular agents. Talking directly to God, the spirit world, the dead, and angels bypasses the traditional authority structure. It is a rebellious act. It circumvents the authority of the king, the priests, and the institutional prophets. It is a special threat when it comes from women, traditionally expected to follow the rules of societal order.

Let us examine our story, I Samuel 28:7. Saul said to his attendants, "Find me a woman who is a [medium], so I may go and inquire of her." "There is one in Endor," they said. What does it say about Saul's character and situation that in his hour of desperation he seeks out the very thing he abhors? We are struck by his hypocrisy. He is consulting the witch at this time for guidance on the battlefield. Except for Deborah, we can assume that in biblical times women were not usually military experts, yet at a time of impending war, a woman's authority is being sought out to influence the general's strategic plans.

At their first encounter, although Saul is disguised, the woman does not let her guard down. She is well aware of the ban that has been decreed against magical arts and is reluctant to consult the dead as he has asked. She knows it carries the death penalty. When the text refers to her she is called in Hebrew *Ba'alat ob*. An *ob* is defined as a necromancer or wizard. An *ob* is also a "skin bottle," and there may be some association between rattling, or making noise, chirping, or muttering as the dead are called.[1] It is usually paired in the Levitical phrase with *Y'doni*, "one who knows," a wise one who knows the spirit world, or a knowing one. Know the truth, know God's will, who knows?

We also notice that she is *ba'alat*, a master, a professional at her craft. This is unusual for women in the biblical narrative. We do find professional harlots, and women who served at the entrance to the Tent of Meeting, acting perhaps as professionals.[2] However, most of our images of "professional women" are not public performers of ritual but rather water-carrying women; singers (I Sam. 18:7); mourners (II Sam. 1:24); and perfumers, bakers, and cooks (I Sam. 8:13).[3] Professions were reserved for men. The fact that this woman has maintained her practices, and is not only noted for it but not punished, is astounding.

Mystery is also her forte. Her name is not mentioned, and all names are highly significant in the biblical text. However, just as Saul disguises himself, so she is robed in mystery by being nameless.[4] Perhaps she chooses to be unnamed to ensure her protection. She is famous enough to be known by where she lives, and perhaps that is enough for her. "Biblical stories contain a variety of unnamed characters whose individuality is expressed through their roles." As Adele Reinhartz writes: "Anonymity [in this story] contributes to the theme of stealth and deception."[5]

The woman "calls" up Samuel, and the story peaks with excitement as the medium exclaims at a pivotal moment, "Why have you deceived me? You are Saul!" Something is revealed to her in her vision so that she knows it is Saul who is before her. The text says: "*Elohim rah-i-ty olim*," which means, "I saw God," or some Divine being, come up out of the ground. Like Hagar in the desert (Gen. 16:7–14), this woman has some direct encounter with the Divine, and it was for her an epiphany. To this day, we will never know exactly what she saw. The Rabbis wonder what it was that revealed Saul's identity to her. "In necromancy the peculiar rule holds true that, unless it is summoned by a king, a spirit raised from the dead appears head downward and feet in the air. Accordingly, when the figure of Samuel stood upright, the witch knew that the king was with her." Other midrashim explain that while only the medium could see the vision, only the one who summons him hears it. This would explain her excitedly crying out when she sees her vision, and Saul asking, "What do you see?"[6]

When the witch proclaims that she sees an old man wearing a robe, Saul knows it is Samuel and he bows. Samuel was robed in his "upper garment," the garment worn at death. According to the midrash, she also perceived a number of spirits with Samuel, including Moses. Because of the presence of others, Samuel thought he was being summoned for the judgment day, and the resurrection of the dead.[7]

Saul then goes on to explain that he has called Samuel because of his need for help with the war. Samuel confirms that God has abandoned him, will call him and his sons into the underworld, and will give his kingdom to David. Saul is overcome, and falls to the floor. The medium now reenters the action, and asks Saul to eat something. She uses her power of negotiation to convince him: She listened to him, and now he must listen to her. She put her life in his hands, and then she offered him food to sustain his life. She recognizes that she may be offering him his last meal, if indeed Samuel's prediction is correct.

The medium then slaughters a fattened calf and bakes bread, both reminiscent of Abraham's hospitality in Genesis 18. The men eat and leave. This is her last appearance in the story. We do not know if she is offering him a meal out of compassion, or if the text intentionally likened her to Abraham to elevate her status with the readers. It is unlikely, however, that a female medium would be compared with the main patriarch of the Jewish people, no matter how much we would have liked that. Most likely, she is taking the ritual of invoking the dead to its logical conclusion, as most ceremonies of this sort conclude with a sacred meal. With this meal, she symbolically becomes the midwife for Saul's transition to the other world, and a new era for the Jewish people.[8]

How ironic that an unnamed woman, practicing an illegal craft, becomes advisor to the king! Like Queen Esther, our unassuming heroine is elevated to a higher status as the story unfolds. Like Hannah, whose story of the birth of Samuel alludes to a reversal of fortunes in her prophecy, we see how power can be transformed in an instant. As feminists, we must hold on to the vision that simple actions, such as feeding the downtrodden, become symbols of hope and of a new era— corrupt power overthrown, justice done.

The medium's story is also important to us as it opens the door for ages of explorations about life after death in Jewish tradition. The story of the witch and her encounter with the world beyond death embodies the idea that human beings are able to communicate with the dead. Her direct communication is something that most of us wish we were able to achieve. Countless stories and visions about the afterlife throughout history have been mere speculation, but our heroine is a professional. There may have even been a "thriving guild of Endor-type practitioners of the condemned art of spiritualistic mediumship,"[9] something that has been lost in our modern day. Just as Circe serves as Odysseus's guide to the underworld, our witch guides us to a belief in the afterlife.[10]

Finally and most significantly, this story is a template for centuries of women with direct connections to Divine guidance, practicing their art outside a centralized authority. The medium is our archetype of women's spiritual and psychic abilities. She precedes the women of the Talmud who used their magical arts to heal.[11] She predates the women of the Middle Ages, such as So—adora, Rachel Aberlin, and Francesa

Sarah, recorded in the writings of noted kabbalist Chaim Vital in his *Sefer Ha-Hezyonot* around 1570, who were "prominent diviners and ecstatic prophets precisely because these were areas beyond rabbinic control where women could come into their own, unencumbered."[12]

For centuries, women were persecuted and killed as witches, as we read in our own Talmud,[13] because they were older, wise women operating without patriarchal approval. Their skills came naturally, rather than through academic training. Although this persecution has ended, we must continue to rebel against societal structures that limit the power of women, or do not hearken to the wise words and spiritual teachings of women. We look to the Sorcerer of Endor to find inspiration in seeking our own spiritual paths, and in developing our own psychic abilities. We give tribute to the women of old who leave us remnants of a craft as reminders of our potential, and a wisdom both ancient and new.

RABBI DIANNE COHLER-ESSES AND
RACHEL JACOBY ROSENFIELD

ירושלים

Jerusalem as Woman in the Book of Ezekiel

O n the day you were born, you were cast out on the open field, utterly rejected. When I passed by you and saw you wallowing in your blood, I said to you: In your blood live! In your blood live! I let you grow like the plants of the field and you continued to grow up until you attained full womanhood, until your breasts became firm and your hair sprouted. You were naked and bare. I passed by you and, here, I saw it was your time for love. I spread My robe over you and covered your nakedness, and I swore to you, and entered into a covenant with you, declares the Lord God; and you became Mine.

(EZEKIEL 16:4–8)

Beloved of God

Here, in Ezekiel 16, painted with loving strokes, is a portrait of an abandoned baby girl, adopted, comforted, and nurtured by God. She is raised by this Divine figure to womanhood. When she is ready for love, God covers her with His robe,[1] enters into a covenant with her, and claims this young woman as His own. He bathes this young woman, washes the blood from her, anoints her with oil, and dresses her in elaborate embroidered clothes and fine leather sandals.

(Note: Using male God language here may seem strange to the reader. However, we specifically chose to do so; we believed it was crucial to the reader's understanding of the sexually charged heterosexual relationship between God and the female subject of the passage.)

The union is a kind of spiritual romance, a marriage, perhaps an adoption, or all of the above. In any case, in Ezekiel it is this abandoned infant, this reclaimed daughter, this nubile young lover who represents Jerusalem and the people of Israel. She embodies the ideal of an intimate and loving relationship, a model of covenant between Israel and God.

God's Grammar

Our biblical corpus is replete with the masculine gender. Men are commanded to stand at Sinai; to love God, to know God, and to tell the story of the Exodus to their male children. Not so with our passage from Ezekiel, which has an entirely different sound, especially to the Hebrew reader. God's words are explicitly addressed to a female. This passage practically sprouts second-person-singular feminine like a new and exotic flower, grown wild. Words strange to the ear, but pleasing. A cause for celebration.

Divine Seduction and Betrayal

Just a few verses later, the reader is jolted awake from this dream of Divine love. God's words of rage also use the female form:

> You believed in your own beauty and used your reputation to prostitute yourself. You poured your harlotry on every passerby; they were for him. You took some of your garments and made for yourself colored platforms and fornicated on them. Such things shall not come about, neither shall they continue. You took your glorious gold and silver ornaments that I gave you and you made yourself phallic images and fornicated with them. . . . And in all your abominations and harlotries, you did not remember the

days of your youth, when you were naked and bare, and
lay wallowing in your blood. (Ezek. 16:15–17, 22)

God, betrayed by His lover, is wrathful. He wants revenge. The
gentle caring strokes creating the portrait of our beloved, covenantal
young woman have become violent. The idyllic model of female union
and intimacy with God is replaced by sullied, perverted imagery. The
reader feels betrayed. The text turns on her. Does this betrayal in fact
delegitimize the powerfully positive and intimate image of a female
relationship with God? Or can we still reclaim this text despite the
lethal turn this relationship takes?[2]

Rabbinic Arts: Ancient Cutting and Pasting

As we continue in this chapter, we find that the tone becomes even
more pornographic and violent. After the loving quality of the previous passage, it will most likely feel brutal to the reader. Yet, even in its
graphic portrayal, Ezekiel 16 offers women a unique opportunity to
explore the nature and meaning of our covenantal relationship with
God. This text is still worth claiming and using for our own religious
lives.

The ancient rabbinic art of interpretation offers us a guide in our
quest for reclamation. The ancient Rabbis used biblical texts freely, lifting texts out of contexts, creating radically new meanings, and expanding original meanings. Our passage in Ezekiel itself is a prime example
of a text to which the Rabbis applied their arts of interpretation. In
fact, carefully chosen words from Ezekiel 16 have been used to create
liturgy and ritual. These words, now part of a new text, are recited
during two pivotal moments of Jewish life: birth and menstruation.

The Blood of Birth and Menstruation

"In your blood you shall live, in your blood you shall live": The community recites these words from our passage in Ezekiel (16:6) to an

infant boy upon his circumcision. God's words, originally to an aban-doned baby girl (a girl representing the body of Israel) covered with the blood of birth, are now addressed to a newborn boy bleeding from his circumcision. Irony abounds. The Rabbis appropriate the rare Divine address explicitly to a woman concerning her covenantal develop-ment, and use it to refer to the blood of circumcision. In this blood the baby boy is reborn as a member of the covenant.

The rabbinic appropriation of these words for a boy's covenantal ritual exemplifies a split in Jewish thought: Men are constructed as his-torical, covenantal beings, while women are creatures of nature. Men's bleeding is the result of an intentional cut, of fulfilling a command-ment, signifying a relationship to God. Women's bleeding, whether it be a result of birth or menstruation, is "nature's" bleeding, unrelated to history and unacknowledged in Jewish life as it relates to covenant.[3]

The male blood of covenant and the female blood of birth are con-strued by Jewish tradition as representing two discrete realms: history and nature.[4] But, concerning the relegation of men to history and covenant and females to nature, the traditional Jewish legal system is more complex than it first appears. A woman's body is the necessary vessel for conferring the status of Jew on a child. Without the womb of a Jewish mother, tradition requires conversion, immersion in a mikveh. A mikveh, a natural pool of water used in physical and spiri-tual purification, recalls the womb.[5] In other words, without a Jewish womb (or womb substitute), a child is simply not Jewish. A woman thereby *embodies* covenant. In fact, not only does passing through her body bestow covenant, but the Talmud also considers females as if they were already "circumcised"[6]—their genitalia being open to a relation-ship with God. Male genitalia need a cut to fully admit, so to speak, the covenant, to admit a relationship with God.[7] Thus, what emerges is the notion that a female body is both covenanted and covenanting. Sadly, neither status is marked by Jewish ritual.

Another rabbinic take on our text implies a radically different understanding of Ezekiel 16. In a midrash[8] cited by the Haggadah, 16:6 and 7 are inverted. The result is startling:

And populous [Deut. 26:5]. As it is said . . . Your breasts were formed, and your hair was grown; yet you were naked and bare. And when I passed by you and saw you wallowing in your blood, I said to you: In your blood live, In your blood live. (Ezek. 16:7, 6)

The child first reaches nubile womanhood, and only then is the salient image of her weltering in her blood invoked. This flip changes what was the blood of birth to menstrual blood. Though this inversion represents a radical shift in the meaning of the blood, it leads us much closer to the simple meaning of our text. It insists on the womanhood of the subject and her inherent power—a power that the text treats as both alluring and dangerous.

The key to this mysterious flip lies in the juxtaposition of Ezekiel's depiction of a relationship between our young woman and God, with our national liberation story. Israelite survival during their four hundred years of slavery depended on their willingness and ability to reproduce. According to midrashic understanding, the Israelites managed to survive and witness their own redemption through the blossoming *(revavah)* of Israelite girls into alluring young women whose sexuality and reproductive power ensured that the Israelites would remain populous *(rav)*.[9] Their success was not merely a result of their physical womanhood, but also of their astounding courage to continue to bear children under the most harsh and dangerous conditions.[10] In this new context, *In your blood live!* is amplified to historic significance, as the bleeding, procreative bodies of women are elevated to vehicles of hope, courage, and ultimately freedom. If the blood of birth is the sign of the covenant, then the blood of menstruation is a harbinger of redemption.

Unlike our young woman from Ezekiel, this midrashic rabbinic rendering of Ezekiel's story ends with hope, revelation, and a romance with God. That intimacy, that covenant, is her turning point: from abandonment to covenantal love, from *wallowing* in her blood to *living* in her blood.

New Ritual Possibilities

What emerges from our reading of Ezekiel's prophecy and rabbinic responses is this: The very blood of birth and the blood of menstruation may be construed as covenantal moments—moments in which women are addressed, encountered, and encounter the Divine.[11] Returning to the *peshat*, to the simple meaning of our text, we find two merging subtexts: One describes the physical maturation of a young woman and the other refers to the unfolding covenant between God and this young woman. However, the Jewish life cycle offers no such amalgam. No such integration of the physical and spiritual development exists for girls and women in ritual form.

Ezekiel 16 offers us the raw material for developing such liturgical and ritual traditions—traditions that will link covenant with the female body and its development. This text, and its rabbinic flip, can be used to affirm, acknowledge, and articulate the covenantal status of a baby girl, or it can be used by a Bat Mitzvah. A Bat Mitzvah at once accepts the yoke of the mitzvot at the same time that her body is blossoming just as our text describes!

Jewish communities have celebrated the covenantal status of the male child, signified by public circumcision, for generations. Throughout history they have acknowledged male obligation. In recent times the greater portion of the Jewish community has come to acknowledge and celebrate a girl's status of Bat Mitzvah. Our text opens the door for the Jewish community to celebrate the covenantal status of girls, beyond a simple "naming ceremony." Girls and women need more than a name. We need communities that acknowledge and celebrate our standing in history, our standing before God. We need community affirmation of the potential for an unfolding, maturing relationship with God. We need communities that declare to their women: "In your blood you shall live! In your blood you shall live!"

RABBI WENDY SPEARS

אשת חיל
The Woman of Valor

Proverbs 31:10–31

*A*woman of valor—who can find? Her worth is far above rubies. (PROVERBS 31:10)

THE WOMAN OF VALOR leaps out of this timeless biblical poem, her compelling qualities of wisdom, leadership, and compassion arising from the extraordinary accomplishments of an ordinary woman, a wife and mother, as well as a businesswoman. As Rabbi Elyse Goldstein notes in her book *ReVisions: Seeing Torah through a Feminist Lens* (Jewish Lights), feminists have seen this poem in both a positive and negative light in its portrait of "ideal womanhood."[1] The simplest way to interpret the poem is praise of an industrious woman's daily life. But moving beyond the simple list of someone's mundane activities gives us a more compelling and complex picture: a tribute to a long life lived wisely and well, a testimony to all a woman can accomplish through years of diligent work, study, and human interaction. Neither a classical heroine nor a classical matriarch, the Woman of Valor has nevertheless become a role model and motherly presence across the ages. Like the battle commander Deborah in Judges 5:7, she leads and inspires. In that respect, she is hailed as an *em b'Yisrael* (a Mother in Israel) who parents her own and subsequent generations.

The poem can be seen as presenting an impossible paradox. A reader might ask herself, "Who could work this hard, achieve so much, and still have time to study, pray, and treat others with understanding

419

and kindness?" We see in our own world those who are ruthless in commerce, stepping over the less fortunate to get ahead, racing off to many meetings instead of making time to enrich relationships with friends and family. At first glance, the Woman of Valor could be seen as an overly idealized picture pieced together from a zealous daily to-do list of accomplishments. Many women today in the paid workforce come home to a second shift of housework, and some to the additional job of child care. They are overwhelmed, exhausted, overextended, with little time or energy for their own intellectual or spiritual pursuits. It could be disheartening to hear about the Woman of Valor each week, as it is traditionally recited on a Friday evening around the Shabbat table, about that long-ago woman who did so much so well. We fear that it is all but impossible to achieve this ideal in a real person's ordinary life.

Instead, our deeper reading of the poem reveals a reflection on the long span of a woman's life, her achievements over many years. No person should attempt to do everything at once, but rather, given time, grow through a variety of experiences that can lead to wisdom. The Woman of Valor teaches us the rewards of a life well lived, by simultaneously making a living for one's family and making time for oneself. Even an ordinary woman can accomplish much, cultivate wisdom, and be deemed valorous.

If one reads the poem as biography, the woman is at first accorded a measure of trust at the beginning of her married life; she later justifies and reinforces this trust. She works hard as a weaver, expanding her skills and expertise into a business; she seeks wool and flax, holds the distaff and works the spindle; she makes coverlets, garments, and girdles and sells them (Prov. 31:13, 19, 24). As she continues to prosper, she shares her good fortune through philanthropy and becomes a role model in her community, sought out for advice. Her prosperity allows her to attire herself beautifully, a healthy measure of self-indulgence she has earned. Her good reputation reflects well on her husband and family. As she matures, she delegates responsibilities to others, helping them grow and allowing herself more time for study and spiritual pursuits. She leaves a precious legacy, more precious than her material assets: the example that a woman can achieve any goal she sets for herself through hard work, perseverance, and kindness. In that respect, she is a protofeminist, not confined by societal stereotypes; able to dream and set goals that benefit her, as well as her family and community.

For a woman who is so busy with commerce and family obligations, it is interesting that the Woman of Valor, like many modern women today, also carves out some time for her personal pursuits, including study. Rabbi Johanan said, "The full crop of the Torah is garnered only at night, for so it says, 'She rises while it is still night.'"[2] This recognizes that if one works during the day, study must take place at night. While Rabbi Johanan intended his message to be that men were permitted to study Torah at night as well as during the day, he uses our woman as a proof text. This reflects again on the theme that all spheres of activity are open to both women and men, dissolving the misconception that a woman's world should be limited to the privacy of the home. The Woman of Valor strives for balance in her personal and professional life, rooted at home, yet taking advantage of what the world has to offer. She juggles the responsibilities of work and family with aplomb. She is intelligent for she "speaks with wisdom" (Prov. 31:26). She is spiritual: "It is for her fear of God that a woman is to be praised" (Prov. 31:30). She is loved and fulfilled in her life. Jewish women continue to strive to be like her: happy, fulfilled, successful, loved.

The Woman of Valor is not what the reader has come to expect in female biblical characters, like Sarah, Abraham's wife, or Miriam, Moses' sister, or even Michal, King Saul's daughter and King David's wife. These women are most often cast in supporting roles to their husbands, brothers, and fathers. By contrast, the Woman of Valor is the central figure in her family and community. Her heroic character is woven together from a series of very human accomplishments. This is one reason it has become a custom for much of Jewish history that a Jewish husband recites this particular poem to his wife at the Shabbat table, as praise for the very real Woman of Valor before him.

Similarities exist between the Woman of Valor, the *eshet chayil*, and Deborah the prophetess. In Judges 4:4, Deborah is identified as *eshet lappidot*, the torch woman (or perhaps torch bearer) who leads and inspires the Jewish people to military victory from the heights of Mount Tabor. In modern Hebrew usage, a *chayal* is a soldier. A woman who is *chayil* is brave enough and capable enough to venture out into the world and effect positive change. It is possible to see a parallel between the military influence of Deborah, and the familial and commercial influence exercised by the Woman of Valor. Deborah the tribal leader draws forth her troops with her war cry (Judg. 5:12) and organizes the battle plan. The Woman of Valor makes a business plan and inspires her employees. She is a paradigm of effective and compassionate communication; she speaks with wisdom, and kindness is on her tongue (Prov. 31:26). The Woman of Valor leads in a more mundane arena than Deborah, without the mythical heroic glory ascribed to military battle. Her story resonates strongly with people in our time because she provides an example of power that seems attainable: an inspiration to achieve greatness through human activity rather than heroic activity.

Jewish tradition has downplayed the importance of a woman's public role. *Genesis Rabbah* interprets the concept *michra*, "her worth" (Prov. 31:10), as her ability to get pregnant.[3] Although children are mentioned near the end, the poem focuses on the accomplishments, industriousness, and wisdom of this woman herself. She plays the role of protector and provider for her family, a circle cast wide to include her employees. In Proverbs 2:2, a mother teaches her son to "call to understanding and cry aloud to discernment." It is this quality of motherly instruction that is embodied by the Woman of Valor. Deborah is described in Judges 5:7 as *em b'Yisrael*, a Mother in Israel, though there is no mention that Deborah has her own children. Rather, as the tribal leader, she protects her troops much as a mother would protect her children. The biblical scholar Susan Ackerman explains Deborah's attribute as a Mother in Israel by suggesting that the term is applied to a woman who is willing to step forward as a commander to lead those under her protection.[4] Ackerman says: "'A mother in Israel' must be a good and effective counselor."[5] Deborah provides good and effective counsel in the decisions she renders for the Israelites who come to her for advice (Judg. 4:5). The Woman of Valor provides good counsel as "she speaks with wisdom" and "the law of kindness is on her lips" (Prov. 31:26).

Biblical scholars date the story of Deborah among the earliest of the biblical texts, presenting a rather ancient archetype of an Israelite woman. The Woman of Valor in Proverbs, recognized as having been written centuries later than the story of Deborah, draws on this archetype of a Mother in Israel who protects and provides for her "family" not on the field of battle or in a tribal council, but in the marketplace community that has its own rules, which are ideally based on honest dealing, integrity, and compassion. So when Proverbs 31:28 declares that "her children declare her happy," the reference may not only be to biological children but also to all those people who depend on her, and who follow her example.

The central theme of the book of Proverbs revolves around how to gain wisdom in life. Proverbs 3:14 declares that wisdom is more precious than rubies; this phrase is repeated in relation to the Woman of Valor. The person who gains wisdom will prosper financially, personally, and spiritually. Throughout Proverbs, the quality of wisdom is personified as a woman. Beginning in Proverbs 1:33, Lady Wisdom first speaks and entreats the reader to seek wisdom and thus prosper in life, for "whoever listens to me will dwell in safety, untroubled by the terror of misfortune." Wisdom is depicted as a precious treasure. The poem about the Woman of Valor comprises the closing lines of the Book of Proverbs. It is its culmination, and draws together all the book's combined teaching: The Woman of Valor, a person who has attained knowledge and understanding, a person whose actions are guided by wisdom, is *more* precious than treasure.

Like Lady Wisdom in chapter 8 of Proverbs, the Woman of Valor is personified wisdom. She speaks clearly, and her voice is heard in the marketplace and at the city gates, the public place of study and

423

arbitration (Prov. 1:20–21). She courageously goes out into the world, and inspires others with her words and her deeds. Proverbs teaches what a wise person should know and do. The Woman of Valor's wisdom is demonstrated in her work, in her conduct as a mother, in her acumen as a businesswoman, and through the trials and blessings of a productive life. Thus she is extolled and praised (Prov. 31:31).

RABBI DEVORAH JACOBSON

מזמור לדוד (תהילים כ״ג)

Psalm 23

*A*donai is My Shepherd, I do not lack for any-thing . . . helping me lie down in green pastures, leading me beside the still waters, restoring my soul, and guiding me on the paths of justice. And though I walk through the valley of deep darkness, I fear no harm, for You are with me. Your rod and your staff comfort me. You set a table before me in the presence of my enemies. You anoint my head with oil. My cup overflows. Surely goodness and mercy shall follow me all the days of my life, and I shall dwell in God's presence forever. (PSALM 23: 1–6)[1]

PSALM 23 ENDURES as a spiritual masterpiece, possessing a place all its own among the classics of religious literature. With its elegant sim-plicity, its honest recognition of life's vicissitudes, as well as its reas-surances of God's trustworthy love, it has served as a spiritual oasis to many of life's pilgrims. It continues to be a source of inspiration, cen-tering, and hope.

For many Jews, this psalm is associated with death, its words heard in the context of the funeral or graveside service. When we find our-selves walking in the valley of deep darkness, experiencing the grief and loss that follow in death's wake, we take in these words, seeking comfort and the courage to keep going.

But Chofetz Chayim, author of the *Mishna Berurah*, tells us about another use of this psalm. He teaches that there is a custom among some Jews to recite Psalm 23 before saying the *motzi* and eating a meal.[2] As we prepare to nurture our bodies, we pause to acknowledge God's boundless generosity as the Ultimate Source of nurture. Like an extended *berachah*, Psalm 23 becomes a daily expression of our gratitude.

From a feminist perspective, it is specifically the image of God as Shepherd that is of most interest. Many women and men have been engaged in rereading our sacred texts and traditions for images and metaphors that speak to us and capture more honestly our experiences with the Divine while not violating our sense of dignity and selfhood. We are seeking alternatives to the dominant maleness of the God of Judaism and its metaphors of Divine power such as lord, king, and judge.

We find the image of God as a *ro'eh*/shepherd several times in the Tanakh. More commonly, we find the use of *roeh* to describe a human ruler/teacher who guides the people. King David, traditionally understood as the author of the Book of Psalms, is described as a shepherd of Israel in texts such as II Samuel 5:2 and Psalm 78:71. God imaged as *ro'eh Yisrael* is extensively described in this classic passage from Ezekiel 34:12–16:

> As a shepherd goes in search of his sheep when his flock is dispersed all around him, so I will go in search of my sheep and rescue them, no matter where they were scattered in dark and cloudy days. . . . I will graze them on the mountains of Israel, by her streams and in all her green fields. . . . I will search for the lost, recover the straggler, bandage the hurt, strengthen the sick, and leave the healthy and strong to play and give them their proper food.

This is a significant description of the *ro'eh*, a description that will help us in our reading of Psalm 23: provider, leader, caregiver, and nurse who is deeply devoted to each member of the flock; attentive in different and appropriate ways to the diverse needs they manifest. Some need more help; others less. All efforts seem to be on supporting them, helping them stay strong, and maintaining their dignity.

In light of this passage, what can we say about the shepherd image used in Psalm 23? How do we hear it and how might we hear it?

Despite the comfort that many experience from the traditional recitation of the psalm, the image of the shepherd is troubling. If God is the shepherd, then we humans obviously are the sheep. Though softer than *king* or *lord*, because it also projects a sense of nurturer and nourisher, the image of God is still one of dominance, with the all-knowing shepherd in control, and the sheep as ignorant, weak, and dependent. While this pastoral image provides us with an important sense of connection to the natural world, it still upholds the notion of Divine power that dominates and controls us, and of a Deity that seeks our obedience and constantly reminds us of our smallness and power-lessness.

But read in a different way, and read especially in light of the shepherd image described in Ezekiel 34, this important metaphor of God can be read more in the spirit of Divine-human partnership. In this way, it does not have to foster a lack of human responsibility or submissiveness and it can promote a sense of mutual respect and concern that the covenantal relationship with God would seem to suggest.

For example, when we read, "YHVH helps me lie down in green pastures, leads me beside still waters, and restores my soul," we might reinterpret the language to mean the following: Our journey with God the Shepherd will take us to important, life-giving, and restorative moments and places we might not go to ourselves, in our hectic routine existence. Life with the Shepherd can also reconnect us to the natural world, where so many of us experience divinity most profoundly. It is in nature, surrounded by the majesty and mystery of creation, that our sense of awe and wonder is reawakened and our sense of being part of something so much greater than ourselves is deepened.

Or when we read, "YHVH leads me in the paths of justice," we can hear this truth: Our journey with God will include hearkening to the cries of the world and responding daily with mitzvot/acts of justice and loving-kindness. Living life with the Faithful Shepherd will mean committing ourselves to a life of service.

When we read, "And though I walk through the valley of the shadow of death, I fear no harm, for You are with me. Your rod and Your staff comfort me," how shall we think about God? Has the shepherd led us here to the valley of suffering? For what purpose? It is a critical theological question, one of the most important of all. But it is not, I believe, the question the psalm is ultimately asking. Instead, it is asking: Where is God when life can be so painful and we find ourselves in the valley of deep darkness? Where is God when we experience profound loss, our own physical diminishment, and a world in such moral disarray?

Ki atah imadi, the psalmist affirms, "You are with me." It is exactly at this point in the text that the psalmist speaks to God in a more direct and intimate way, and the Hebrew pronoun changes from third person to second person. It is exactly now, in the experience of deepest darkness, that we sense that we are not alone. Like the consummate pastoral caregiver, God offers the fullness of Presence.

Pastoral counselor Henry Close writes, "Deeper than our grief, deeper than our hopelessness and anguish, deeper even than our doubts, there we experience God. The psalmist does not say that the Shepherd lifts us out of the valley of deep darkness. Rather, the psalmist affirms that God walks with us through those valleys."[3] Precisely when we feel our vulnerability, when we experience the dark and painful places of our lives, the psalmist affirms that God is with us. Perhaps only then, when we know that we are not alone, when we feel reassured and protected, can we begin to feel our own strength and confidence again and begin to lift ourselves out of those valleys. Then we can even come face to face with our "enemies." In light of the presence of a caring, attentive, and guiding force, we might know courage again, and the ability to take risks.

This way of reading the text includes our experiences when we are not "at the top of our game." It includes the times when we feel most vulnerable and least confident. When life brings us to the valley of deep darkness, the psalmist is saying, whatever anyone else might think about us, or however we might feel about ourselves, we are not small in God's eyes. And we are not alone. Bolstered by a Presence that is wholly present and abiding, we know more about our goodness and our strength. In time, we can be inspired to courageous living again.

The image of shepherd, here as in Ezekiel 34, can offer an array of attributes that may speak to us in a contemporary reimagining of God that would include gentleness, abiding presence, and generosity. We can also discover another deeply resonant image of God by doing what the classical rabbinic commentators did all the time with our sacred text: playing with the individual words, letters, and vowels and exploring them for new meanings. In this way, with a slight change of the vowels, the word *Ro'ee,* translated as "my Shepherd," becomes *Ray'ee,* "my Beloved Friend." Now we can call out to God my Shepherd or God my Beloved Friend. This is what the Rabbis had in mind when they commented on Psalm 23:1: "I said to God, Thou are my well-beloved friend [*Ray'ee*]. Let Thy kindness never be wanting, as it says, '*Adonai Ray'ee* I shall not want.'"[4] The image of Beloved Friend, an image of human-Divine friendship, allows us to connect deeply to the wellsprings of kindness and trust within us, and also to a profound acceptance of who we are and how we are in the world.

Psalm 23 thus offers two rich ways of imaging God that may help us move away, at least somewhat, from traditional models of the Divine-human partnership where power and dominance is so emphasized, toward a Divine-human partnership that is rooted in the soil of attentiveness, presence, and love.[5]

Notes

Bereshit / Genesis

Haftarat Bereshit · *Rabbi Amy Joy Small*

1   Solomon Grayzel, *A History of the Jews* (Philadelphia: Jewish Publication Society, 1969), p. 13.
2. Compare with Isaiah 61:1. Michael Fishbane, *The JPS Bible Commentary: Haftarot* (Philadelphia: Jewish Publication Society, 2002), p. 6.
3. From midrash from *Tanna de Bei Eliyahu*, chap. 18, as quoted by W. Gunther Plaut, *Haftarah Commentary* (New York: UAHC Press, 1996), p. 8.
4. Mayer Gruber, in "The Motherhood of God . . ." surmises that Isaiah may have made deliberate use of both masculine and feminine similes for God as a way to make his message more appealing to women. Gruber notes the participation of Jewish women in "cults of femaleness" in pre-exilic Judea, which may have resulted from the way in which women were kept at a distance from the official Israelite cult. Another factor could have been the way major prophets like Jeremiah and Ezekiel spoke of God—as a husband to Israel, the wife, while they also never used feminine expressions for God. From Mayer J. Gruber, as quoted by W. Gunther Plaut, *Haftarah Commentary* (New York: UAHC Press, 1998), p. 10.
5. Fishbane, *The JPS Bible Commentary*, p. 10.
6. From Safer Deuteronomy, as quoted by Fishbane, *The JPS Bible Commentary*, p. 10.

Haftarat Noach · *Rabbi Jill Hammer*

1. *Genesis Rabbah* 31:12.
2. *Genesis Rabbah* 23:4; *Exodus Rabbah* 1:13.
3. *Genesis Rabbah* 23:3.

4. Sandy Eisenberg Sasso, Bethanne Andersen, illus., *Noah's Wife: The Story of Naamah* (Woodstock, Vt.: Jewish Lights Publishing, 1996).
5. BT, *Taanit* 7a

Haftarat Lech Lecha · *Rabbi Sue Levi Elwell*

1. "*Lech Lecha:* What's in a Name?" in Elyse Goldstein, ed. *The Women's Torah Commentary: New Insights from Women Rabbis on the 54 Weekly Torah Portions* (Woodstock, Vt.: Jewish Lights, 2000), p. 57.
2. Cantor Sarah Sager, in a speech to the Women of Reform Judaism National Biennial, San Francisco, November 1993.

Haftarat Chaye Sarah · *Rabbi Beth Janus*

1. Adele Berlin, *Poetics and Interpretation of Biblical Narrative* (Sheffield, U.K.: The Almond Press, 1983), p. 27.
2. Randall C. Bailey, *David in Love and War* (Sheffield, U.K.: JSOT Press, 1990). Bailey argues that Bathsheba, in fact, is an equal partner in this story.
3. *Midrash Rabbah Ecclesiastes*, translated by A. Cohen (London: Soncino, 1939), p. 121.

Haftarat Vayeitze · *Rabbi Kathy Cohen*

1. Hayyim Nahman Bialik and Yehoshua Hana Ravnitsky, eds., *The Book of Legends, Sefer Ha-Aggadah* (New York: Schocken Books, 1992), p. 343.

Haftarat Vayishlach · *Rabbi Nina Beth Cardin*

1. Louis Newman, ed., *The Hasidic Anthology: Tales and Teachings of the Hasidim* (New York: Schocken Books, 1963), p. 508.

Haftarat Vayashev · *Rabbi Hara E. Person*

1. BT *Ketubot* 111a.

Haftarat Vayigash · *Rabbi Marsha J. Pik-Nathan*

1. The state of affairs Ezekiel is looking to rectify in this prophecy began in 722 B.C.E. At that time, Israel fell to the Assyrians, and the Northern Kingdom, consisting of ten of the twelve tribes of Israel, essentially disappeared from the stage of history, and remains nothing but a memory to this day; these tribes are referred to as the "ten lost tribes" of Israel. The Southern Kingdom, comprising the other two tribes, and known as Judah, remained the only viable and continuing locus of the people.
2. *Exodus Rabbah* 5:9.

3. Adrienne Rich, "Notes Toward a Politics of Location" in *Blood, Bread, Poetry* (New York: W. W. Norton, 1986), p. 224.

Haftarat Vayechi · *Rabbi Amber Powers*

1. See Deut. 31:7–8 and Josh. 1:6–9.
2. See Gen. 49:29, 50:12 and II Sam. 17:23.
3. A. Cohen, ed., *The Soncino Chumash* (New York: Soncino Press, 1950), p. 315.
4. W. Gunther Plaut, *The Haftarah Commentary* (New York: UAHC Press, 1998), pp. 119–120.

Shmot / Exodus

Haftarat Shmot · *Rabbi Sharon Brous*

1. R. Shalom Noah Barzovski, *Netivot Shalom* 2:12 (Jerusalem: Yeshivat Beit Avraham Slonim, 1991). My translation (emphasis added).
2. Ibid.

Haftarat Va-era · *Rabbi Andrea Carol Steinberger*

1. Michael Fishbane, *Etz Chayim Torah and Commentary* (New York: The Rabbinical Assembly, 2001), p. 369.
2. Karen Propp, "The Path to Loving Relationships," *Lilith: The Independent Jewish Women's Magazine* (Summer 2003): 21.

Haftarat Bo · *Rabbi Denise L. Eger*

1. Lewis Spence, *Ancient Egyptian Myths and Legends* (New York: Dover, 1990).
2. J. H. Hertz, *The Pentateuch and Haftarahs* (London: Soncino, 1961) p. 264.

Haftarat Beshalach · *Rabbi Deborah J. Schloss*

1. Sondra Henry and Emily Taitz, *Written Out of History: Our Jewish Foremothers* (New York: Biblio Press, 1990), p. 1.
2. BT, *Megillah* 14a.
3. Henry and Taitz, *Written Out of History*, p. xiv.
4. Ibid.
5. Leila Leah Bronner, *From Eve to Esther: Rabbinic Reconstructions of Biblical Women* (Louisville, Ky.: Westminster/John Knox Press, 1994), p. 173, based on *Tosafot Niddah* 50a.

6. BT, *Megillah* 14b.
7. Bronner, *From Eve to Esther*, p. 172.
8. BT, *Megillah* 14b.
9. BT, *Pesachim* 66b.
10. Ibid.
11. Bronner, *From Eve to Esther*, p. 173.
12. Joseph Telushkin, *Jewish Literacy* (New York: William Morrow and Company, 1991), p. 71.
13. *The Living Nach: Early Prophets* (Brooklyn: Moznaim Publishing Corporation, 1994), p. 116, note 6:1.
14. Ibid.

Haftarat Yitro · *Rabbi Shira Stern*

1. The tradition of the well predates Miriam: Abraham, Hagar, Isaac, and succeeding patriarchs and matriarchs all possess the ability to find it. See references in Gen. 21:19, Gen. 21:24–25, Gen. 26:18–23. Further, in *Shir HaShirim Rabbah* 1:2, there is a reference to link Torah to water. Miriam is given credit for being the keeper of the well because she was responsible for reuniting her parents, who then bore Moses, for bringing him to and watching over him in the water. See Louis Ginzberg, *Legends of the Jews*, Vol. II (Philadelphia: Jewish Publication Society, 1968), p. 262–265.
2. E. M. Broner, *The Women's Haggadah*. (San Francisco: HarperCollins, 1993), p. 19.

Haftarat Mishpatim · *Rabbi Lori Cohen*

1. Boaz Cohen, *Jewish and Roman Law—A Comparative Study* (New York: Jewish Theological Seminary of America, 1966), p. 176.
2. Francis Brown, S. R. Driver, and Charles A. Briggs, *A Hebrew and English Lexicon of the Old Testament* (New York: Oxford University Press, 1959), p. 204
דרר—a. Flow abundantly, of milk, tears, rain; b. Be abundant, luxuriant; c. Run easily like a horse; d. Give light, shine; דרור—flowing, free run, liberty, proclaim liberty.

Haftarat Terumah · *Rabbi Elisa Koppel*

1. BT, *Gittin* 68a.
2. BT, *Sotah* 48b.
3. Exod. 28:20–21
4. BT, *Sotah* 48b.
5. BT, *Gittin* 68a–b.

Notes

Haftarat Tetzaveh · *Rabbi Alison B. Kobey*

1. BT, *Berachot* 12b.
2. Rabbi Abraham J. Twerski, *The Shame Borne in Silence* (Pittsburgh: Mirkov Publications, 1996), p. 41.
3. BT, *Eruvin* 100b.
4. Ezek. 43:27.

Haftarat Ki Tissa · *Rabbi Valerie Lieber*

1. Phyllis Trible, "The Odd Couple: Elijah and Jezebel," in *Out of the Garden: Women Writers on the Bible*, ed. Christina Buchman and Celina Spiegel (New York: Fawcett Columbine, 1994), p. 170.
2. Ibid.
3. Louis Ginzberg, *The Legends of the Jews*, Vol. IV (Baltimore and London: Johns Hopkins University Press, 1941), p. 189. JT *Sanhedrin* 10, 28b.
4. JT *Esther Rabbah* 1:9.
5. *Webster's Third New International Dictionary* includes the following definition and proof text: "an impudent, shameless, or abandoned woman <painted, screaming *jezebels* hauled away by the raiding constables—Albert Parry.>" *Webster's Third New International Dictionary* (Springfield, Mass.: Merriam-Webster, Inc., 1986), p. 1215.
6. Peter Ackroyd, "Goddesses, Women and Jezebel," in *Images of Women in Antiquity*, ed. Averil Cameron and Amelie Kuhrt (Detroit: Wayne State University Press, 1993), p. 246.

Vayikra / Leviticus

Haftarat Vayikra · *Rabbi Tina Grimberg*

1. Mayer I. Gruber, *The Motherhood of God and Other Studies* (Atlanta: Scholars Press, 1992), pp. 3–15.
2. Frank McConnell, *Storytelling and Mythmaking: Images from Film and Literature* (New York: Oxford University Press, 1979).
3. Yitzhak Buxbaum, *Storytelling and Spirituality in Judaism* (Northvale, N.J.: Jason Aronson, 1994), p. 12.
4. Ibid., p 11.

Haftarat Tzav · *Rabbi Elaine Rose Glickman*

1. Louis Ginzberg, *The Legends of the Jews*, Vol. IV (Philadelphia: Jewish Publication Society, 1947), p. 294.

2. Ibid, p. 296.
3. This idea is inspired in part by Aristophanes' play *Lysistrata,* in which the women of Greece refuse to engage in sexual intercourse until their husbands cease making war.

Haftarat Shimini · *Rabbi Julie Wolkoff*

1. According to BT *Sanhedrin* 19b, Michal and this second husband, Palti or Paltiel, did not have sexual relations, since she remained "David's wife."
2. BT *Eruvin* 96a. There is a parallel text in *Mekilta Bo* 17, which states that Michal wore tefillin.
3. I am indebted to my friend and colleague Ebn Leader for this question.
4. Louis Ginzberg, in a note in *The Legends of the Jews,* Vol. I (Philadelphia: Jewish Publication Society, 1968), p. 274, speaks of the midrashic texts that link Michal to this mitzvah. The identification of Michal with Proverbs 31:25, "Strength and splendor are her clothing," provides the direct link to tefillin.

Haftarat Tazri'a · *Rabbi Mary Lande Zamore*

1. *Tzara'at* is commonly translated as "leprosy." It is not clear if Naaman truly had leprosy or another type of skin disease.
2. BT *Sanhedrin* 96b.
3. The text emphasizes the joy of this moment by describing Naaman's skin becoming like a young boy's. This reminds the reader of the change in Moses' appearance after encountering God (Exod. 34:29).

Haftarat Metzorah · *Rabbi Rochelle Robins*

1. Leibowitz, Nehama, *New Studies in Vayikra* (Jerusalem: World Zionist Organization, 1993), p. 195.
2. BT *Masechet Sanhedrin* 107b.
3. BT *Masechet Sanhedrin* 90a.

Haftarat Acharei Mot · *Rabbi Nina H. Mandel*

1. In 1990, Judith Plaskow spoke to this issue: "[Thus] Jewish feminists might agree that it is a matter of simple justice for Jewish women to have full access to the riches of Jewish life. But when a woman stands in the pulpit . . . she participates in a profound contradiction between the message of her presence and the content of what she learns and teaches. It is this contradiction that feminists must address, not simply 'adding' women to a tradition that remains basically unaltered, but transforming Judaism into a religion that women as well as men

have a role in shaping." (*Standing Again at Sinai* [San Francisco: HarperCollins, 1990], p. xvi.)

Haftarat Emor · *Rabbi Rachel Esserman*

1. The laws of forbidden marriages are also called the incest laws. They forbid both men and women from marrying close relatives by either blood or marriage.
2. Lev. 21.
3. Rachel Biale, *Women and Jewish Law* (New York: Schocken Books, 1984), p. 71.

Haftarat Behar · *Rabbi Nancy Wechsler-Azen*

1. See II Kings 22:14–20.
2. *Pesikta Rabbati: Discourses for Feasts, Fasts and Special Sabbaths*, trans. William G. Braude (New Haven, Conn.: Yale University Press, 1968).
3. JT *Middot* 1:3.
4. Louis Ginzberg, *The Legends of the Jews*, Vol. V (Philadelphia: Jewish Publication Society, 1946), p. 33.
5. Ginzberg, *The Legends of the Jews*, Vol. IV (Philadelphia: Jewish Publication Society, 1946), p. 246.
6. Rabbi Samuel Eliezer Halevi Edels (1555–1631).
7. Francis Brown, S. R. Driver, Charles A. Briggs, *Hebrew and English Lexicon of the Old Testament* (New York: Oxford University Press, 1959), p. 317.
8. Ibid.

Haftarat Bechukotai · *Rabbi Hanna Gracia Yerushalmi*

1. Solomon Freehof, *Jeremiah: A Commentary* (Philadelphia: Jewish Publication Society, 1977), p. 116.
2. Isa. 2:3; Mic. 4:2.
3. Adapted for communal worship, the singular pronoun ("heal me" and "save me") was changed to the collective plural ("heal us" and "save us").
4. The Jeremiah text is an echo of other verses in the Bible, for example, the famous phrase in Deuteronomy 30:19, which is read in most Reform congregations during Yom Kippur: "See this day, I set before you the blessing and the curse."
5. Adoption has its own set of "blessings" and "curses," some similar to those of birth parents; others, completely different.
6. Naomi Wolf, *Misconceptions: Truth, Lies and the Unexpected on the Journey to Motherhood* (New York: Doubleday, 2001), p. 2.
7. Lauren Slater, *Love Works Like This: Moving From One Kind of Life to Another* (New York: Random House, 2002), p. 148.

Bamidbar / Numbers

Haftarat Behalotecha · *Rabbi Margot Stein*

1. Although *roni vesimchi* is most simply translated as "sing and rejoice," Brown, Driver, Briggs, *Hebrew and English Lexicon* (Oxford: Clarendon Press, 1957) defines *roni* as "to give a ringing cry in joy or exultation, especially in praise of God" (p. 943), noting a related meaning of "rattle," as in shake a musical instrument or, presumably, one's own body. *Simchi* is defined as "to rejoice religiously" (p. 970); the two together reinforce the meaning of vibrant, bodily celebration in a religious context.

2. Scholars have argued that Miriam, rather than Moses, composed the initial verses of *Shirat HaYam* / Song of the Sea, even though the placement of her poem in Exodus 15 gives the impression that she was merely repeating these lines from Moses' longer poem, which appears just before hers. See, for example, S. D. Goitein, "Women as Creators of Biblical Genres," *Prooftexts* 81 (1988): 7.

3. See, for example, 1 Kings 22:6ff.

4. S. D. Goitein asserts, "Poetry was the original form of female prophecy. . . . The poetry of the prophetess was felt to have a power as real as that of the military activity of the commander of the battalions of Israel." ("Women as Creators of Biblical Genres," p. 13.)

5. Mieke Bal, "Displacement of Mother," *Anti-Covenant: Counter-Reading Women's Lives in the Hebrew Bible* (Decatur, Ga.: The Almond Press, 1989), p. 209.

6. Barnabas Lindars, *Deborah's Song: Women in the Old Testament* (Manchester, U.K.: John Rylands University Press, 1982), p. 166.

Haftarat Shelach Lecha · *Rabbi Pamela Wax*

1. Some commentators do see this story as comic, perhaps as a parody of the *Shelach Lecha* version of the scout story. Robert G. Boling in *The Anchor Bible: Joshua* (Garden City, N.Y.: Doubleday, 1982), pp. 144–145, for instance, contrasts the story of Jephthah, a son of a prostitute, and his reconnaissance missions in Judges 11, with Joshua 2. Boling concludes, "If the Jephthah story in Judges 11 has a tragic ending, the genre here in Joshua 2 is more like comedy."

2. Rashi on Joshua 2:1, based on the Targum and Josephus, *Antiquities*, Vol. 1.2.

3. BT *Zevachim* 116b. "There was no prince or ruler who had not possessed Rahab the harlot."

4. BT *Megillah* 14b. This illustrious genealogy rivals that of Christian tradition. In an apparent Christian "midrash" on the concluding genealogy found in the Book of Ruth, Rahab is the mother of Boaz, and therefore an ancestress of David, as well

as Jesus (New Testament, Matthew 1). Christian tradition also characterizes her as a person living by faith (New Testament, Hebrews 11:31; New Testament, James 2:25). In Jewish midrashic tradition, too, "Legend paints Rahab in very black colors to bring out the effect of repentance" (Louis Ginzberg, *The Legends of the Jews*, Vol. VI [Philadelphia: Jewish Publication Society, 1954], p. 171, note 12).

5. See, for example, Exod. 34:15–16, Num. 25:1–2, and Hosea 1:2. For more virulent examples of misogyny interwoven with the admonitions against idolatry, see for example, Jer. 3:1–3, Ezek. 16:25–38, and Hosea 4:10–19.

6. *Midrash HaGadol*, cited in Ginzberg, *The Legends of the Jews*, Vol. II, pp. 36–37.

7. Interestingly, L. Daniel Hawk notes that Rahab's name "links her implicitly to the land; the adjective [*rahab*] occurs within the larger narrative (Gen. through II Kings) only in connection with the land of Canaan, where it signifies its goodness and abundance" (*Joshua* [Collegeville, Minn.: Michael Glazier, 2000], p. 41).

Haftarat Korach · *Rabbi Barbara Borts*

1. Women need to make inroads both theologically and sociologically. In the book *On Being a Jewish Feminist: A Reader*, Cynthia Ozick contended that the most important inroad feminists could make would be changing the social and cultural patterns of Jewish communal life. In reply, Judith Plaskow argued that until the language and the images we Jews used to conceive of and describe God were altered, women would never be completely accepted as whole Jews. In classical Jewish tradition, one could say that they are both right, and that the efforts have to be made and are being made in both realms. See Cynthia Ozick, "Notes Toward Finding the Right Question," and Judith Plaskow, "The Right Question Is Theological," in *On Being a Jewish Feminist: A Reader*, ed. S. Heschel (New York: Schocken Books, 1983), pp. 120ff and 223ff.

Haftarat Chukkat · *Rabbi Vicki Lieberman*

1. See, for example, Miriam leading the women in song in Exodus 15:20; and women rejoicing upon David's return from warring with the Philistines in I Samuel 18:6.

2. For example, the custom of *keriya*, the rending of one's garment before a funeral, or the tearing of a black ribbon pinned to one's clothes. The falling to the knees or being low is represented by mourners sitting on low stools or benches during the customary mourning period of Shiva.

3. *Midrash Rabbah* on *Chaye Sarah* includes a few midrashim stating that Jephthah should have gone to the High Priest and offered a monetary sacrifice. However, each midrash clearly states that Jephthah did not avail himself of this option and

did take his daughter's life. To date, this author has not found a traditional midrash contending that Jephthah did not actually kill his own daughter.

Haftarat Balak · *Rabbi Jane Kanarek*

1. *Genesis Rabbah* 88:5.
2. Exod. 15:20–21; Num. 12:1; Num. 20:1; Num. 26:59; Deut. 24:9; Micah 6:4; I Chron. 5:29.
3. Michael Fishbane, *The JPS Bible Commentary: Haftarot* (Philadelphia: Jewish Publication Society, 2002), p. 248.
4. BT *Sotah* 11b.
5. *Exodus Rabbah* 1:13.
6. *Yalkut Shimoni Numbers* 683.
7. *Song of Songs Rabbah* 4:12.
8. *Rashi Numbers* 12:1.
9. *Sifrei* to *Deuteronomy Piska* 275.

Haftarat Pinchas · *Rabbi Susan P. Fendrick*

1. See, for example, the Torah commentaries of Rabbi Baruch Epstein (the *Torah Temimah*), who explains that under normal circumstances it is impossible to know whether such an actor is prompted by righteous or base motives, and of Rabbi Abraham Isaac Kook (Rav Kook), the first Chief Rabbi of pre-state Israel, who says that all who act in the way that Pinchas did must first be sure that they have eliminated all hatred from their own heart.

Haftarat Mattot · *Rabbi Rachel R. Bovitz*

1. Robert P. Carroll, *Jeremiah: A Commentary* (Philadelphia: Westminster Press, 1986), p. 94.
2. Formal Jewish term for *rabbi*, which appears on certificates of ordination.
3. Carolyn Duff, *Learning from Other Women: How to Benefit from the Knowledge, Wisdom, and Experience of Female Mentors* (New York: American Management Association, 1999), pp. 36–37.
4. Angela Bauer, *Gender in the Book of Jeremiah: A Feminist-Literary Reading* (New York: Peter Lang Publishing, 1999), p. 14.
5. BT *Niddah* 30b.

Haftarat Ma'asei · *Rabbi Jennifer Elkin Gorman*

1. *Mishnah Mikvaot* 1:8.
2. Tikva Frymer Kensky, "A Ritual for Affirming and Accepting Pregnancy," in

Daughters of the King, ed. Susan Grossman and Rivka Haut (Philadelphia: Jewish Publication Society, 1992), p. 292.

3. Diana Stevens, "Coming of Age: The Growth of the Conservative Mikveh Movement," *United Synagogue Review* (Fall 2001): p. 18.

4. Rahel R. Wasserfall, ed., *Women and Water* (Hanover, N.H.: Brandeis University Press, 1999), p. 237.

Devarim / Deuteronomy

Haftarat Devarim · *Rabbi Analia Bortz*

1. Midrash *Rabbah*, *Bereshit* 56:16.
2. BT *Sukkah* 51b.
3. Shulchan Arukh, *Orah Hayyim* 560:1–2.
4. JT *Bava Kama* 7:10; *Hagigah* 3:6.

Haftarat Va'etchanan · *Rabbi Sheryl Nosan-Blank*

1. *Nachamu* is a verb stated in the second person, imperative plural. Thus, the opening phrase may be more precisely translated "All-of-you comfort, all-of-you comfort My people!"

2. For an excellent treatment of Jerusalem personified as mother of the Jews, see Mary Callaway, *Sing O Barren One: A Study in Comparative Midrash* (Atlanta: Scholars Press, 1986), pp. 73–90.

3. *V'daber 'al lev*, literally meaning "speak to the heart," is more often used to indicate the speaker's wholehearted intention than the speaker's tenderness or the listener's receptiveness; see Gen. 50:21, II Sam. 19:8, II Chron. 30:22, and Ruth 2:13. Of special feminist interest is the use of the phrase before acts of violence against women in Genesis 34:3, 50:21; and Judges 19:3.

4. Mark E. Biddle, "Lady Zion's Alter Ego," in *New Visions of Isaiah*, ed. Roy F. Melugin and Marvin A. Sweeney (Sheffield, U.K.: Sheffield Academic Press, 1996), p. 137.

5. The Aramaic reads *n'veeyahyah de m'vaserien l'tzieyon*; the key word, *n'veeyahyah*, is translated as "prophets" and is in the masculine plural.

6. Moreover, Ibn Ezra, along with most other commentators, simply ignores the five feminine verbs that accompany the feminine noun in verse 9.

7. Michael Fishbane, *The JPS Bible Commentary: Haftarot* (Philadelphia: Jewish Publication Society, 2002), p. 281.

Haftarat Re'eh · *Rabbi Joanne Yocheved Heiligman*

1. *Ecclesiastes Rabbah* 11.
2. *Genesis Rabbah* 53:9.
3. *Borei p'ri hagafen*—Blessed is God, Ruler of the Universe, who created the fruit of the vine.

Haftarat Shoftim · *Rabbi Cindy Enger*

1. See, e.g., Michael Strassfeld, *The Jewish Holidays: A Guide & Commentary* (New York: Harper & Row, 1985), p. 7; Noam Zion and David Dishon, *A Different Night: The Family Participation Haggadah* (Jerusalem: Shalom Hartman Institute, 1997), p. 114.
2. W. Gunther Plaut, *The Haftarah Commentary* (New York: UAHC Press, 1996), p. 476.
3. Michael Fishbane, *Biblical Interpretation in Ancient Israel* (Oxford: Clarendon Press, 1985), p. 364.
4. Ibid.
5. Ibid., p. 440.
6. Ibid., p. 543.

Haftarat Nitzavim · *Rabbi Laura Geller*

1. *Pesikta Rabbati* 31.

Haftarat Vayelech · *Rabbi Susan Gulack*

1. Joseph H. Hertz, *The Authorized Daily Prayer Book* (New York: Bloch Publishing, 1974), p. 631.
2. *Mikraot G'dolot* on Isaiah, translated by the author.

Haftarat Ha'azinu · *Rabbi Elizabeth W. Goldstein*

1. Although this hymn is attributed to David, it was not necessarily written by him. Literary evidence suggests that some parts of the hymn may have been written during David's lifetime, about 1000 B.C.E. See F. M. Cross and D. N. Freedman, "A Royal Song of Thanksgiving: II Samuel 22 = Psalm 18," in *Journal of Biblical Literature* 72 (1953): 15–34. It is likely that the hymn underwent an editing process in the seventh century and needs to be examined as a complete unit in this context. See *The Anchor Bible, II Samuel: A New Translation with Introduction, Notes and Commentary* by P. Kyle McCarter, Jr. (New York: Doubleday, 1984), pp. 474–475.
2. BT *Pesachim* 66b. I am grateful to Allison Cook for pointing me to this reference.

Haftarat V'zot Habrachah · *Rabbi Nancy Rita Myers*

1. BT *Megillah* 14b.
2. Ibid.

Special Shabbatot

Haftarat Shabbat Shekalim · *Rabbi Stacia Deutsch*

1. "Sabbath," *Encyclopedia Judaica* (Jerusalem: Keter Publishing House, 1972), 14:574.
2. *Exodus Rabbah* 40:3.
3. J. Robinson, *The Second Book of Kings* (Cambridge: Cambridge University Press, 1976), p. 109.

Haftarat Shabbat Zachor · *Rabbi Karen Soria*

1. I am indebted to Dr. Kim Nielsen for this concept of God. I also wish to thank Rabbi Dr. Michael Panitz of Temple Israel, Norfolk, Virginia; and Chaplain Heather Smith, Canadian Forces, for their questions, reflections, and study time.
2. Jerome Charyn, "I Samuel: Meditations on the First Book of Samuel and King Saul," in *Congregation: Contemporary Writers Read the Bible*, ed. David Rosenberg (New York: Harcourt, Brace, and Jovanovich, 1987), p. 98.
3. For a detailed analysis of their conversation, see Meir Sternberg, *The Poetics of Biblical Narrative: Ideological Literature and the Drama of Reading* (Bloomington: Indiana University Press, 1987), pp. 482–515.
4. Louis Ginzberg, *The Legends of the Jews*, Vol. IV (Philadelphia: Jewish Publication Society, 1936), pp. 65–66. For narratives on Saul's conflicted character, see Adin Steinsaltz, *Biblical Images: Men and Women of the Book* (New York: Basic Books, 1984), pp. 137–143; and Elie Wiesel, *Five Biblical Portraits* (South Bend, Ind.: University of Notre Dame Press, 1981), pp. 61–95. Compare *Pesikta Rabbati* 15:3.
5. Midrash *Rabbah Esther Pesikta* 7; cf. Ginzberg, *Legends of the Jews*, p. 67.
6. Midrash *Ecclesiastes* VII:33; cf. BT *Yoma* 22b.
7. I have heard this attributed to William Faulkner.

Haftarat Shabbat HaChodesh · *Rabbi Helaine Ettinger*

1. We learn from the Mishnah that there are four different new years (*Rosh Hashanah* 1:1). Nisan, although it is the first month, is not the start of the religious new year. Tishrei, the seventh month, is the month of Rosh Hashanah, the religious new

year. Nisan is the month of redemption, one form of renewal, while Tishrei is the month of judgment and repentance, another form of renewal.

2. *Gates of Prayer: The New Union Prayerbook* (New York: Central Conference of American Rabbis, 1975/ 5735), pp. 149 and 324. The English is a revision by Rabbi Chaim Stern of a prayer on the theme of redemption by Rabbi Chaim Stern and John Rayner, first published in the 1967 British prayer book *Service of the Heart.*

3. This is the figure suggested by Rabbi Sharon Cohen Anisfeld, Tara Mohr, and Catherine Spector, eds. in their introduction to *The Women's Passover Companion* (Woodstock, Vt.: Jewish Lights, 2003), p. xxvi.

4. Tamara Cohen, ed., *The Journey Continues: The Ma'yan Passover Haggadah* (New York: Ma'yan, The Jewish Women's Project, 2000), p. 35.

5. For other examples of new liturgical and ritual adaptations of the Passover seder that explore women's experience, see Rabbi Sharon Cohen Anisfeld, Tara Mohr, and Catherine Spector, eds. *The Women's Seder Sourcebook: Rituals & Readings for Use at the Passover Seder* (Woodstock, Vt.: Jewish Lights, 2003); *The San Diego Women's Haggadah*, 2nd ed. (San Diego: Women's Institute for Continuing Jewish Education, 1986); E. M. Broner with Naomi Nimrod, *The Women's Haggadah* (San Francisco: HarperCollins, 1994); or, in Hebrew, Karni Goldschmidt, ed. *Bat-Chorin Seder Nashim* (Jerusalem: The Masorti Movement, Schechter Institute for Jewish Studies, Knesset HaRabbanim b'Yisrael, 2000).

Haftarot for Days of Awe

Haftarah for the First Day of Rosh Hashanah · *Rabbi Serena Raziel Eisenberg*

1. Traditional commentators question whether Hannah fulfilled her vow if she promised to dedicate Samuel "all the days of his life," but then kept him home until he was weaned. Rashi reconciled the discrepancy with a proof text from the Book of Numbers 8:24 that prescribes the length of priestly service from ages twenty-five to fifty. Rashi then calculated that Hannah's vow was fulfilled because Samuel served in the priesthood for a full fifty years (which corresponds to *ad olam*—permanently) after he was weaned and presented to the Temple.

The text does not state explicitly how long the nursing continues, yet rabbinic commentators read into Hannah's story the later codifications of "normal" breast-feeding durations. Kimhi cites a talmudic passage that places a two-year limit on nursing. "A child nurses continuously for twenty-four months. From

that age onward [he is regarded as one who sucks an abominable thing]. These
are the words of R. Eliezer." The talmudic passage continues with the dissenting
voice of R. Joshua, who says that a child (male) may be breast-fed even for five
years continuously. (BT *Ketubot* 60a). Three years is also sometimes cited as the
ideal duration for breast-feeding, based on verse 7:27 from the Second Book of
Maccabees. The mother of seven martyred sons, also named Hannah, exclaims, "I
carried you nine months in my womb, and I nursed you for three years." These cal-
culations generally refer to nursing a son. It is possible that daughters were weaned
earlier, so that the mother might try to conceive a son. If so, perhaps the curious
stipulation of Leviticus 12:1–5 (that a mother is impure/unavailable for intercourse twice as long after the birth of a daughter as she is after the birth of a son)
provides an extra margin of time for mother and daughter to establish bonding
through breast-feeding. See Mayer Gruber, "Breast-Feeding Practices in Biblical
Israel and in Old Mesopotamia," *The Motherhood of God and Other Studies*
(Atlanta: Scholars Press, 1992), p. 78.

2. Stanley Walters, "Hannah and Anna: The Greek and Hebrew Texts of I Samuel
1," *Journal of Biblical Literature* (September 1988): 403.
3. "Na'ar," *Theological Dictionary of the Old Testament*, Vol. IX, ed. Johannes Botter-
weck, Helmer Ringgren, and Heinz Josef Fabry, trans. David Green (Grand
Rapids, Mich.: William B. Eerdmans Publishing Company, 1988), p. 475.
4. *Genesis Rabbah* 53:9, as cited in Hayyim Nahman Bialik and Yehoshua Hana
Ravnitzky, eds., *The Book of Legends: Sefer Ha-Aggadah: Legends from the Talmud
and Midrash*, trans. William G. Braude (New York: Schocken Books, 1992),
p. 38.
5. Gail P. Corrington, "The Milk of Salvation: Redemption by the Mother in Late
Antiquity and Early Christianity," *Harvard Theological Review* 82 (1989): 406.
6. Num. 11:8.
7. *Exodus Rabbah* 5:9.
8. Tanhuma. BT. *Exodus* 67, cited in "Manna," in *Encyclopaedia Judaica*, 11:883.

Haftarah for the Second Day of Rosh Hashanah · *Rabbi Linda Bertenthal*

1. See, e.g., Jeremiah Unterman, *From Repentance to Redemption: Jeremiah's Thought
in Transition* (Sheffield, U.K.: Sheffield Academic Press, 1987), JSOT Supp. Series
54, pp. 51–52.
2. Hosea 11:8; Isa. 16:11.
3. *Eikha Rabbah Pesikta, Midrash Rabbah* (New York: Soncino Press, 1983), 7:49.

Haftarah for Shabbat Shuva · *Rabbi Jessica Locketz*

1. Job 42:10ff.
2. Radak, commentary on Hosea 14:3.
3. Carol Gilligan, *In a Different Voice: Psychological Theory and Women's Development* (Cambridge, Mass.: Harvard University Press, 1993), p. xvi.
4. Tamar Frankiel, *The Voice of Sarah: Feminine Spirituality and Traditional Judaism* (New York: HarperCollins, 1990), p. 120.
5. BT *Berachot* 24a

Haftarah for Yom Kippur Morning · *Rabbi Ilana Berenbaum Grinblat*

1. W. Gunther Plaut, *The Haftarah Commentary* (New York: UAHC Press, 1996), p. 45.
2. Ibid., p. 44.

Haftarah for Yom Kippur Afternoon · *Rabbi Myriam Klotz*

1. James S. Ackerman, "Jonah," in *The Literary Guide to the Bible*, ed. by Robert Alter and Frank Kermode (Cambridge, Mass.: Belknap Press, 1987), p. 242.
2. Hayyim Nahman Bialik and Yehoshua Hana Ravnitsky, eds., *The Book of Legends: Sefer Ha-Aggadah*, trans. William G. Braude (New York: Schocken Books, 1992), p. 134; and Louis Ginzberg, *The Legends of the Bible* (Philadelphia: Jewish Publication Society, 1956), p. 606.
3. Ginzberg, *Legends of the Bible*, p. 606.
4. Bialik and Ravnitsky, *Book of Legends*, p. 134.
5. Bonna Haberman, "The Yom Kippur *Avoda* Within the Female Enclosure," in *Beginning Anew: A Woman's Companion to the High Holy Days*, ed. Gail Twersky Reimer and Judith A. Kates (New York: Touchstone, 1997), pp. 243–257.

Holiday Haftarot

Haftarah for the First Day of Sukkot · *Rabbi Chana Thompson Shor*

1. Carol L. Meyers and Eric M. Meyers, *The Anchor Bible* v. 25c; Zechariah 9–14 (New York: Doubleday, 1993), p. 415.
2. Isaiah 43:16–19 is one such passage.
3. It is generally assumed that the Mount of Olives became a cemetery because of

its earlier associations with eschatological passages such as those found in Zechariah 14. However, there were First Temple memorials at the site since before Zechariah's time.

4. Using, as the JPS translation does, the vocalization *v'nistam*, "stopped up," following the Targum, the Septuagint, and one ancient Hebrew manuscript; rather than *v'nastem*, "you shall flee," as appears in most printed editions of the Bible.

5. Jon D. Levenson, *Sinai and Zion: An Entry into the Jewish Bible* (Minneapolis: Winston Press, 1985), p. 133. Those interested in the biblical cosmology of Zion will find a clear discussion of it in Part 2, chap. 4, "Zion as the Cosmic Mountain," pp. 111–137.

6. BT *Sukkah* 53a.

7. Ezek. 28:13–16 describes Eden as a mountain.

8. Deut. 28:12, 23–24.

9. Translation by Jennifer Parkhurst, used with permission. The names Zaphon and Teman are left untranslated, because in addition to being the names of winds, they have other associations. It is significant that *Zaphon*, in addition to meaning "north," is used as an epithet for Zion in the Bible (e.g., Ps. 48:3) when Zion appears in its role as cosmic mountain.

Haftarah for Shabbat Chanukah · *Rabbi Sharyn H. Henry*

1. Radak suggests that the restoration of the Temple would be strictly guarded; watched over by God to protect against the evil designs of those who would thwart Israel's attempt to rebuild it.

2. *Numbers Rabbah* 14:3.

Haftarah for the First Day of Pesach · *Rabbi Linda Joseph*

1. Howard Eilberg-Schwartz, *God's Phallus and Other Problems for Men and Monotheism* (Boston: Beacon Press, 1994), pp. 137–152.

2. Zohar 1:90a–b.

3. "Sheep" in *Encyclopedia Judaica*, Vol. 14, col. 1333–1334.

4. Roland de Vaux, *Ancient Israel: Its Life and Institutions*, trans. John McHugh (London: Darton, Longman and Todd, 1961; reprinted 1973), p. 34.

5. BT *Kiddushin* 1:1.

Haftarah for the First Day of Shavuot · *Rabbi Shaina Bacharach*

1. NASA'S Visible Earth: http://visibleearth.nasa.gov/Countries/Iran/index_2.html.

2. BT *Hagigah* 13b.

Five Megillot

Shir HaShirim: The Song of Songs · *Rabbi Rachel Sabath-Beit Halachmi*

1. *Leviticus Rabbah* 25:8.
2. *Deuteronomy Rabbah* 2:37.
3. The Rabbis ordained that scrolls of the Pentateuch and other holy works make the hands unclean, so as to prevent the holy texts from being handled disrespectfully. With regard to the Song of Songs, however, some hold that there was a dispute, which implies that its canonicity, too, was in doubt.
4. *The Song of Songs Rabbah* 1:11.
5. Marcia Falk, *The Song of Songs: A New Translation and Interpretation* (San Francisco: HarperCollins, 1990), p. 135.
6. Alicia Ostriker, "A Holy of Holies: The Song of Songs as Countertext," in *The Song of Songs: A Feminist Companion to the Bible*, ed. Athalya Brenner and Carole R. Fontaine (Sheffield, U.K.: Sheffield Academic Press, 2000), p. 37.

Megillat Ruth: The Book of Ruth · *Rabbi Barbara Rosman Penzner*

1. "Rabbi Zeira teaches: This book carries no impurity or purity, and contains no prohibitions or permissions. Why was it written? To teach the reward of those who perform acts of *chesed*." *Ruth Rabbah* 2:14.
2. Judith Plaskow, *Standing Again at Sinai* (San Francisco: Harper & Row, 1990), p. 68.
3. BT *Sukkah* 49b.
4. Rebecca Alpert, *Like Bread on the Seder Plate: Jewish Lesbians on the Transformation of Tradition (Between Men—Between Women)* (New York: Columbia University Press, 1998), p. 48.

Megillat Esther: The Book of Esther · *Rabbi Karen L. Fox*

1. Rashi 1:12.
2. Etta Prince-Gibson, Interview with Alice Shalvi, *Jerusalem Post*, March 17, 2002.
3. BT *Megillah* 7a.

Special Additional Selections

Bathsheba · *Rabbi Jessica Spitalnic Brockman*

1. David Marcus, "David the Deceiver and David the Dupe," *Prooftexts* 6 (May 1986): 167.
2. Meir Sternberg, *The Poetics of Biblical Narrative* (Bloomington: Indiana University Press, 1985), p. 198.
3. Adele Berlin, "Bathsheba," in *Women in Scripture*, ed. Carol Meyers (Boston: Houghton Mifflin, 2000), p. 58.
4. Sternberg, *The Poetics of Biblical Narrative*, p. 198.
5. Gen. 29:32–35, 30:6–13, 30:18–21, 30:23–24.
6. Sternberg, *The Poetics of Biblical Narrative*, p. 221.
7. Marcus, "David the Deceiver and David the Dupe," p. 164.
8. Sternberg, *The Poetics of Biblical Narrative*, p. 221.
9. I Kings 1:11–21.
10. Tomoo Ishida, "Solomon," in *The Anchor Bible Dictionary*, Vol. 6, ed. David Noel Freedman (New York: Doubleday, 1992), p. 106.
11. Marcus, "David the Deceiver and David the Dupe," p. 167.
12. The Rabbis are forgiving of King David. BT *Shabbat* 30a implies that the goodness that God did for King David reflects a forgiveness of David for the sin of the Bathsheba incident. There, King Solomon is unable to open the gates to the Holy of Holies of the Temple until he praises David. This incident, the text goes on, can be seen as evidence of Gods' forgiveness of David. In BT *Shabbat* 56a, it is implied there was no sin in the David and Bathsheba story, because Uriah had given Bathsheba a *get* (bill of divorce), as was customary for soldiers going out to battle.

Michal · *Rabbi Beth L. Schwartz*

1. BT *Sanhedrin* 19b.
2. BT *Sanhedrin* 21a.
3. Louis Ginzberg, *The Legends of the Jews* (Philadelphia: Jewish Publication Society, 1956), p. 258.
4. BT *Eruvin* 96a.
5. *Akedat Yitzchak*, cited in Nechama Leibowitz, *Studies in Bereishit* (Jerusalem: Joint Authority for Jewish Zionist Education, 1995), pp. 334–335.

Judith and the Story of Chanukah · *Rabbi Shoshana Boyd Gelfand*

1. The similarity between the two even prompted the Italian sculptor Donatello to create twin statues of David and Judith. To this day, one can go to the Piazza

della Signoria in Florence and see both David and Judith in a parallel stance, with a sword in hand and an enemy head at their feet.

2. Compare Jth. 8:33 and Judg. 4:7.

3. Compare Jth. 12:15–16 and Ruth 3:7–8

4. Jth. 10:5: "She filled a bag with parched grain and figs and pure bread, and she packed all her dishes and had her [maid] carry them."

5. Tosafot *Megillah* 4a, *she'af*.

6. For the full text of the midrash, see A. Jellinek, *Midrash Ma'aseh Yehudit* in *Bet HaMidrash*, part 2 (Leipzig, 5613), p. 19, or J. D. Eisenstein, *Otzar Midrashim*, Vol. 1 (New York, 1915), p. 207. A complete English translation of a version of the midrash can be found in Bernard H. Mehlman and Daniel F. Polish, "A Midrash for Hanukkah," *Conservative Judaism* 36, no. 2 (Winter 1982): 26–35.

7. *Shulchan Arukh*, *Orah Hayyim* 670:2; See Rema's comment.

8. Jth. 15:5 and I Macc. 7:46.

9. Ashkenazic siddur, *yotzer* for Shabbat Chanukah I. The *piyyut* is authored by Rabbi Yosef bar Shlomo and cited by Rashi in his commentary to Yechezkel 21:18. I am grateful to Rabbi Rudolf Adler for this translation.

Delilah · *Rabbi Debra Orenstein*

1. See J. Cheryl Exum, *Fragmented Women: Feminist (Sub)versions of Biblical Narratives* (Valley Forge, Pa.: Trinity, 1993), p. 88, and Jack M. Sasson, "Who Cut Samson's Hair? (And Other Trifling Issues Raised by Judges 16)," *Prooftexts* 8: 333–339.

2. Many translations state, "called a man to cut his hair." The Hebrew, however, is third-person feminine singular, pointing to Delilah as the one who cuts Samson's hair.

3. Manoah's wife neglects to tell her husband about Samson's destiny to "begin to deliver the people of Israel from the hand of the Philistines" (13:5). One can legitimately view her as withholding crucial information. However, her decision is validated when the angel later speaks to Manoah and withholds the same information (13:13–14). Though there is a degree of mutual betrayal, Samson's mother is a paragon of trust and mutuality compared with his father. See Exum, 66.

4. See Gen. 38.

5. Compare to Judg. 16:16.

6. Samson poses the riddle on day 1 (14:12–14). The Philistines cannot figure it out for three days (14:14). They threaten Samson's wife-to-be on the seventh day (14:15). She wept for seven days of the feast (14:17). Some modern scholars conclude that inconsistencies in this chronology prove that variant texts have been woven together. Traditional commentators, including Rashi, have said that

it was on the seventh day *of the week,* but the fourth day *of the feasting,* that the Philistines approached the betrothed. Accepting the chronology as presented in the text makes the betrothed a more poignant and sympathetic character.

7. *Sotah* 9b. The word translated as *tormented* or *pressed (vatealtzeihu)* appears only once in the Bible and is understood by its context.

8. Delilah's homeownership, and the fact that the Philistines negotiate with her and not a husband, suggest that she is either a widow or a prostitute. Readers often assume that Delilah is a Philistine, but the phrase "The Philistines are upon you" undercuts that assumption. The name might be Hebrew.

9. *Malbim* and *Da'at Sofrim.* See Rabbi Abrohom Fishelis and Rabbi Shmuel Fishelis, eds., *The Book of Judges: A New English Translation* (New York: Judaica Press, 1979), p. 128.

10. See Gen. 34:2; Deut. 21:14, 22:24, 29; Judg. 19:24, 20:5; II Sam. 13:12ff; Ezek. 22:10, 11; Lam. 5:11.

The Witch of Endor · *Rabbi Geela Rayzel Raphael*

1. *ob* in Frances Brown, S. R. Driver, Charles Briggs, *Hebrew English Lexicon* (Clarendon, U.K.: Oxford University Press, 1968) p. 15.

2. I Sam. 2:22; Exod. 38:8.

3. Article by Jo Ann Hacket, Carol Newsom, and Sharon H. Ringe, *The Women's Bible Commentary* (Louisville, Ky.: Westminster/John Knox Press 1992), p. 873.

4. She is named Zephaniah, mother of Abner, in the Midrash. See *Pirkei de Rabbi Eliezer* (New York: Sepher Hermon Press, 1981), p. 244.

5. Adele Reinhartz, *Why Ask My Name? Anonymity and Identity in Biblical Narrative* (New York: Oxford University Press, 1998), p. 68.

6. Louis Ginzberg, *The Legends of the Jews*, Vol. IV (Philadelphia: Jewish Publication Society, 1968), p. 70.

7. Ibid.

8. Tikveh Frymer Kensky, *Reading the Women of the Bible* (New York: Schocken Books, 2002), p. 314.

9. Simcha Paull Raphael, *Jewish Views of the Afterlife* (Northvale, N.J.: Jason Aronson, 1994), pp. 50–51.

10. Jean Houston, *The Hero and the Goddess: The Odyssey as Mystery and Initiation* (New York: Ballantine Books, 1992), pp. 181–192.

11. For example, Abaye's mother was a Babylonian who lived from approximately 320 C.E. to 350 C.E. She is mentioned in the Talmud in reference to her healing remedies.

12. See J. H. Chajes, "Women Leading Women (and Attentive Men): Early Modern

Jewish Models of Pietistic Female Authority," forthcoming in a volume on the history of Jewish leadership, edited by Jack Wertheimer, from the writings of Chaim Vital, *Sefer Ha-Hezyonot*.

13. Simon ben Shetach had eighty women hanged as witches (see JT *Hagigah* 2:2).

Jerusalem as Woman in the Book of Ezekiel · *Rabbi Dianne Cohler-Esses and Rachel Jacoby Rosenfield*

1. Reminiscent of the Book of Ruth, Ruth asks Boaz to "spread your wings over your handmaiden, because you are a redeemer"—a symbol of protection and redemption through marriage. See Ruth 3:9.

2. For further discussion of this text and other prophetic texts that use women to embody God's relationship with Israel, see Atalya Brenner, *A Feminist Companion to the Latter Prophets* (Sheffield, U.K.: Sheffield Academic Press, 1995); Renita J. Weems, *Battered Love: Marriage, Sex and Violence in the Hebrew Prophets* (Minneapolis: Fortress,1995); and Tikva Frymer-Kensky, *In the Wake of the Goddess: Women, Culture and the Biblical Transformation of Pagan Myth* (New York: Fawcett Columbine, 1993).

3. While there is a traditional naming ceremony for girls, *Zeved habat*, a rite of the Sephardic Jews, there is no traditional covenant ceremony.

4. Howard Eilberg-Schwartz has written extensively on this notion. See, for example, *People of the Body: Jews and Judaism from an Embodied Perspective* (Syracuse: SUNY Press, 1992) or *God's Phallus and Other Problems for Men and Monotheism* (Boston: Beacon Press, 2002).

5. For a discussion of the concept of *Brit Leyda*, the covenant of birth, see Gary Shapiro, "Sealed in Our Flesh—Women as Members of the Brit," in *The Pardes Reader 1997* (Jerusalem: The Pardes Institute, 1997), esp. p. 94.

6. See BT *Avodah Zarah* 27a. Shapiro cites this in his article. Cohler-Esses used this notion as the basis for a covenant ceremony for her daughters, along with the Ezekiel text and other texts.

7. Examination of the concept of *orlah*, "foreskin," in the Bible illustrates that it stands as a barrier. For example, see the following verses that refer to "foreskinned" lips, heart, and ears: Exod. 6:30; Jer. 6:10 and 9:30. Thus, circumcision removes a barrier to a relationship with God, allowing covenant to occur.

8. Sifre: *Ki Tavo*, Piska 301.

9. The word in this passage that interests the Rabbis is *rav* (populous). They cite Ezekiel 16:7 because it begins with the word *revavah* (increase, in this context meaning coming into physical womanhood), which shares a common root and similar meaning with *rav*.

Notes

10. See BT *Sotah* 11b. The Talmud tells the story of the *nashim tzidkaniyot* (righteous women) who went out into the fields and magically nourished and seduced their exhausted husbands. Under the conditions of slavery, the ability of these women to arouse the erotic interest of their husbands is an act of radical heroism: believing in the power of the body to nurture, to love, to create, even as one suffers unspeakable hardship.

11. While there have been no covenantal rituals for women at moments of birth and menstruation, bodily events that, by their very nature, excluded men, it is interesting to note that traditionally it was precisely these two moments that occasioned the communal events females were excluded from: circumcision and Bar Mitzvah.

The Woman of Valor · *Rabbi Wendy Spears*

1. Elyse Goldstein, *ReVisions: Seeing Torah through a Feminist Lens* (Woodstock, Vt.: Jewish Lights, 1998), p. 38.
2. *Song of Songs Rabbah* 11:1 on Proverbs 31:15.
3. *Genesis Rabbah* 45:1.
4. Susan Ackerman, *Warrior, Dancer, Seductress, Queen* (New York: Doubleday, 1998), p. 42.
5. Ibid.

Psalm 23 · *Rabbi Devorah Jacobson*

1. Translating a well-known psalm, recited so often in a communal context, is a difficult task. I have observed in my work with the aged, non-Jewish, and even Jewish that it is the King James version of Psalm 23 that is "inscribed" in people's hearts and memories. I have also observed that even those with various kinds of dementia are often able to recite this psalm by heart, and always in the King James version. Thus, when officiating at a service, for example, on the dementia unit of the nursing home, when this psalm is used in translation, I am torn about which translation to use. While I obviously prefer a gender-neutral version, I find that that version affects the way in which people participate, especially because it lacks the well-known cadences of the King James version. I have not yet found a solution to this problem.
2. Rabbi Avrohom Feuer, *The Artscroll Tehillim*, Vol. 1 (New York: Mesorah Publications, 1977), p. 287.
3. Henry T. Close, "A Ceremony for Grieving," *Journal of Pastoral Care and Counseling* (Spring 2002): 68.
4. *Shir HaShirim Rabbah II*, 16:1.

5. I am grateful to the following people, including some of the members of Chavurat ha-Emek, of which I am a member, for their thoughtful and wonderfully engaging discussion of Psalm 23: Martha Ackelsberg, Joyce Galaski, Philippe Galaski, Larry Goldbaum, Jane Gronau, Margaret Mastrangelo, Regina Mooney, Saul Perlmutter, Judith Plaskow, Zvi Rozen, Amy Leos-Urbel, Anna Leos-Urbel, and Shoshana Zonderman.

Glossary

Adonai: The accepted pronunciation of YHVH, the four-letter name of God. It is not clear how those four letters were originally pronounced, since they are not vocalized in the Torah scroll. See *YHVH*.

Alenu: Prayer said at the end of the morning, afternoon, and evening services, recalling the Jews' special relationship to God and to the world at large.

Amidah: Eighteen prayers of benediction said at morning, afternoon, and evening services, often recited silently and then repeated by the service leader.

Ashkenazim: Jews who trace their lineage to the Eastern European countries.

Bar Mitzvah: A boy child's coming of age at thirteen, at which time he is permitted to count in the *minyan*. Bar Mitzvah also refers to the ceremony which acknowledges this milestone, as in "I had a Bar Mitzvah." Bat Mitzvah is a girl child's coming of age, traditionally at twelve, but acknowledged in the liberal communities at thirteen. Bat Mitzvah ceremonies began in the 1920s and exist now in almost all denominations in one form or another.

Beit HaMikdash: The Hebrew term for the Temple that stood in Jerusalem, first destroyed in 586 B.C.E., rebuilt, and then destroyed for the last time in 70 C.E.

Bimah: The platform in the synagogue from where services are led; usually the rabbi and cantor stand on the bimah, as well as others who have service honors.

B'nei Yisrael: Hebrew term for the children of Israel, today known as the Jews.

Bris: The Ashkenazic pronunciation of *brit*.

Brit: Literally means "covenant." God makes a *brit* with many biblical characters. Today we usually associate this word with the covenant of circumcision.

Challah: Braided bread used on the Sabbath.

Chesed: The quality of compassion and loving-kindness.

Haftarah: A selection of the Prophets read as an adjunct to the Saturday Torah reading. The haftarah of each week corresponds in theme to the weekly Torah reading. Plural is *haftarot*.

Haggadah: The prayer book used for the home ritual of the Passover seder service.

Halachah: The overall term for Jewish law, codified through the ages, since the Torah. Halachah is still evolving in all the denominations.

Halachists: Experts in halachah.

Kabbalah: Jewish mysticism, developed throughout the ages but mostly associated with the system popularized in the thirteenth century C.E. in Safed.

Kabbalists: Those who practice Kabbalah.

Kashrut: The system of permitted and prohibited animals for eating. Presented in different sections of the Torah first, it was later refined and further defined by the Talmud.

Keriya: The tearing of a garment or a black ribbon put on a garment to symbolize mourning a relative. Done at a Jewish funeral and worn throughout the mourning period.

Lashon ha'ra: Literally "evil tongue" or speech that harms both the listener and the talker. Often translated as "gossip," but any form of slander, talking behind someone's back, or harmful talk.

Levites: Assistants to the priests, they were honored servants of the sacred rites in the desert Tabernacle and then in the Temple in Jerusalem.

Maftir: The last section or *aliyah* of a Torah portion read.

Megillah: A one-handled scroll read on specific holidays. Plural is *megillot*.

Menorah: The seven-branched candelabrum used in the ancient biblical sanctuary and then later in the Temple in Jerusalem. This seven-branched menorah was adapted into a nine-branched menorah used only and specifically for the winter holiday of Chanukah.

Mensch: Yiddish word for "a good person," a person of fine ethical and moral standing.

Midrash: A rabbinic story, parable, or interpretation of biblical text, coming from the root *d-r-sh*, which means "to examine." These midrashim (pl.) help fill in gaps in the text, supply missing details or dialogue, and enliven the text with personal anecdotes. Early midrashim can be found in the Talmud, from the second century, but the first actual compendium was edited in the fifth and sixth centuries C.E. Modern midrashim are still being written today.

Midrashists: Those involved in the writing or creating of midrashim.

Mikveh: A pool of water used for ritual immersions. Composed of natural rainwater plus tap water, built and filled to exact legal specifications, mikvaot (pl.) are used traditionally to immerse new dishes, brides (and, in some cases, grooms), converts to Judaism, and women after their monthly menstrual period. Separate mikvaot are used to immerse corpses for final purification before burial. Sometimes spelled *mikvah*.

Minyan: A quorum of ten needed for public prayers. In Orthodox services, only men are counted in the ten. In liberal services, either women or men or both together are counted in the ten.

Mishkan: The desert Tabernacle erected by the Israelites after they left Egyptian slavery. The details of the building of the *mishkan* are in Exodus 25.

Mishnah: The first written summary of Jewish law, compiled in the Land of Israel about the year 200 C.E., and therefore the first overall written evidence for the state of Jewish prayer in the early centuries.

Mitzvah: A commandment from the Torah or later enacted by the Rabbis. Plural is *mitzvot*.

Nechemta: A "happy ending" or note of comfort on which all public readings or sermons are supposed to end.

Parashah: The weekly Torah portion. The Torah is divided into fifty-four portions, one to be read each week in the synagogue, on Mondays, Thursdays, and Saturdays. Plural is *parshiot*.

Pesach: Hebrew name for the spring holiday of Passover, commemorating the liberation from Egyptian slavery.

Peshat: The simplest or most literal understanding of a text.

Purim: The spring holiday commemorating the victory of the Jews of Persia over Haman, the anti-Semitic advisor to the king. The story is recounted in *Megillat Esther*.

Rosh Chodesh: The new moon, celebrated monthly on the first day of the new Hebrew month.

Rosh Hashanah: The Jewish new year.

Seder: The ritualized service and dinner celebrated on the first two nights of Passover.

Sephardim: Jews who trace their lineage to Spanish countries.

Shabbat: The Jewish Sabbath, beginning Friday at sundown and lasting until Saturday at sundown. Also known in the Ashkenazic pronunciation as *Shabbos*.

Shavuot: The spring holiday celebrating the receiving of the Torah.

Shekhinah: One of the names of God (though not found in the Torah) that has a feminine connotation, from the mystics. *Shekhinah* is understood to be God's indwelling presence as opposed to a more transcendent presence.

Shiva: The intense seven-day mourning period immediately after the death of a close relative.

Sukkot: The fall Festival of Booths, during which Jews eat—and sometimes sleep—in fragile huts for eight or seven days, depending on the community. The huts are reminders of the booths the Jews lived in during the forty years of wandering in the desert.

Tallis: Ashkenazic pronunciation of *tallit*.

Tallit: A prayer shawl worn during daytime services and once a year at night on Yom Kippur. Women have begun making and wearing the *tallit* in recent times.

Talmud: The compilation of rabbinic law which includes the Mishnah (legal decisions edited in the third century C.E.) and the *Gemara* (rabbinic discussions of those laws, edited in the sixth century C.E.). In the traditional community, the Talmud is authoritative on matters of daily life.

Tanakh: The Hebrew acronym for the three sections that make the full Jewish Bible: Torah, Neviim (Prophets), *Khetuvim* (Writings).

Tefillin: Phylacteries, or small leather boxes attached with straps that are worn on the head and arm each weekday morning as part of the worship. Though they are traditionally only worn by men, many women are now taking on the donning of tefillin.

Tikkun Olam: The notion of improving or bettering the world; acts that help make one's society more civilized.

Tisha B'Av: The summer fast day in commemoration of the destruction of the two Temples.

Tzadikkim: Righteous men and women.

Tzedakah: Alms for the poor, though literally translated as "righteousness." It is incumbent upon every Jew to give regular and cyclical *tzedakah*.

Yamim Noraim: Hebrew term for the High Holidays or High Holiday period.

Yeshiva: A full-time house of study of traditional texts. Plural is *yeshivot*.

YHVH: The four-letter Hebrew name of God, commonly pronounced "Adonai."

Yisrael: Israelites, the third "caste" in the hierarchy of priests and commoners. Also a general designation for any member of the people of Israel.

Yom Kippur: The Day of Atonement, the most holy day of the Jewish calendar.

Bibliography and Suggested Further Reading

Torah Commentaries

Englemayer, Shammai; Ozarowski, Joseph S.; Sofian, David M. *Common Ground: The Weekly Torah Portion Through the Eyes of a Conservative, Orthodox, and Reform Rabbi.* Northvale, N.J.: Jason Aronson, 1998.

Fields, Harvey J. *A Torah Commentary for Our Times.* New York: UAHC Press, 1998.

Fox, Everett, ed. *The Five Books of Moses: Genesis, Exodus, Leviticus, Numbers, Deuteronomy: A New Translation With Introductions, Commentary, and Notes.* New York: Schocken Books, 1995.

Goldstein, Elyse, ed. *The Women's Torah Commentary: New Insights from Women Rabbis on the 54 Weekly Torah Portions.* Woodstock, Vt.: Jewish Lights Publishing, 2000.

Grishaver, Joel Lurie. *Learning Torah: A Self-Guided Journey through the Layers of Jewish Learning.* New York: UAHC Press, 1998.

Kushner, Lawrence S., and Olitzky, Kerry M. *Sparks Beneath the Surface: A Spiritual Commentary on the Torah.* Northvale, N.J.: Jason Aronson, 1995.

Leibowitz, Nechama. *Studies in Bereshit, Shmot, Vayikra, Bamidbar, Devarim.* Jerusalem: World Zionist Organization, 1980.

Lieber, David L., ed. *Etz Hayim: A Torah Commentary.* Philadelphia: Jewish Publication Society, 2003.

Moyers, Bill D. *Genesis: A Living Conversation* (PBS Series). New York: Doubleday, 1997.

Peli, Pinchas. *Torah Today: A Renewed Encounter with Scripture.* Washington, D.C.: B'nai Brith Books, 1987.

Plaut, W. Gunther, ed. *The Torah: A Modern Commentary*. New York: UAHC Press, 1981.

Sarna, Nahum M. *Exploring Exodus*. New York: Schocken Books, 1987.

———. General Editor. *The JPS Torah Commentary*. Philadelphia: Jewish Publication Society, 1991.

———. *Understanding Genesis*. New York: Schocken Books, 1970.

Steinsaltz, Adin. *Biblical Images*. Trans. Yehudit Keshet. Northvale, N.J.: Jason Aronson, 1994.

Zakon, Miriam Stark, trans. *Tzenah U'Renah: The Classic Anthology of Torah Lore and Midrashic Comment*. Jerusalem: Mesorah Publications, Inc., 1983.

Zornberg, Aviva. *Genesis: The Beginning of Desire*. Philadelphia: Jewish Publication Society, 1995.

Midrash

Bialik, Hayyim Nahman, and Ravnitzky, Yehoshua Hana, eds. *The Book of Legends Sefer Ha-Aggadah: Legends from the Talmud and Midrash*. Trans. William G. Braude. New York: Schocken Books, 1992.

Ginzberg, Louis. *The Legends of the Jews*. Philadelphia: Jewish Publication Society, 1909.

Women as Rabbis

Greenberg, Simon, ed. *The Ordination of Women as Rabbis: Studies and Responsa*. Moreshet Series: Studies in Jewish History, Literature, and Thought, Vol. XIV. New York: Jewish Theological Seminary, 1988.

Nadell, Pamela Susan. *Women Who Would Be Rabbis: A History of Women's Ordination, 1889–1985*. Boston: Beacon Press, 1998.

Zola, Gary Phillip, ed. *Women Rabbis: Exploration & Celebration: Papers Delivered at an Academic Conference Honoring Twenty Years of Women in the Rabbinate, 1972–1992*. Cincinnati: Hebrew Union College Press, 1996.

Women, Feminism, and Judaism

Adler, Rachel. *Engendering Judaism: An Inclusive Theology and Ethics*. Philadelphia: Jewish Publication Society, 1998.

Alpert, Rebecca. *Like Bread on the Seder Plate: Jewish Lesbians and the Transformation of Tradition (Between Men—Between Women)*. New York: Columbia University Press, 1998.

Berrin, Susan, ed. *Celebrating the New Moon: A Rosh Chodesh Anthology*. Northvale, N.J.: Jason Aronson, 1996.

Cantor, Aviva. *Jewish Women, Jewish Men: The Legacy of Patriarchy in Jewish Life*. San Francisco: Harper & Row, 1995.

Davidman, Lynn, and Tenenbaum, Shelly, eds. *Feminist Perspectives on Jewish Studies*. New Haven, Conn., and London: Yale University Press, 1994.

Diament, Carol, Ph.D. *Moonbeams: A Hadassah Rosh Hodesh Guide*. Woodstock, Vt.: Jewish Lights Publishing, 2000.

Frankiel, Tamar. *The Voice of Sarah: Feminine Spirituality and Traditional Judaism*. San Francisco: Harper & Row, 1990.

Greenberg, Blu. *On Women and Judaism: A View from Tradition*. Philadelphia: Jewish Publication Society, 1981.

Heschel, Susannah, ed. *On Being a Jewish Feminist*. New York: Schocken Books, 1995.

Orenstein, Debra. *Lifecycles Vol. 1: Jewish Women on Life Passages and Personal Milestones*. Woodstock, Vt.: Jewish Lights Publishing, 1994.

Peskowitz, Miriam, and Levitt, Laura, eds. *Judaism Since Gender*. New York: Routledge, 1997.

Plaskow, Judith. *Standing Again at Sinai*. San Francisco: HarperSanFrancisco, 1990.

Plaskow, Judith, and Christ, Carole. *Weaving the Visions: New Patterns in Feminist Spirituality*. San Francisco: HarperCollins, 1989.

Umansky, Ellen, and Ashton, Diane, eds. *Four Centuries of Jewish Women's Spirituality: A Sourcebook*. Boston: Beacon Press, 1992.

Zolty, Shoshana Pantel. *And All Your Children Shall Be Learned: Women and the Study of Torah in Jewish Law and History*. Northvale, N.J.: Jason Aronson, 1997.

Feminist Biblical Interpretation

Adler, Rachel. "In Your Blood, Live: Re-Visions of a Theology of Purity." *Tikkun* 8, no.1 (January/February 1993).

Antonelli, Judith S. *In the Image of God: A Feminist Commentary on the Torah*. Northvale, N.J.: Jason Aronson, 1997.

Bellis, Alice Ogden. *Helpmates, Harlots, and Heroes: Women's Stories in the Hebrew Bible*. (Louisville, Ky.: Westminster/John Knox Press, 1994.

Bird, Phyllis A. *Missing Persons and Mistaken Identities: Women and Gender in Ancient Israel*. Philadelphia: Fortress Press, 1997.

Brenner, Athalya, ed. *Feminist Companion to Reading the Bible: Approaches, Methods & Strategies*. Ithaca, N.Y.: Cornell University Press, 1997.

Buchmann, Christina, and Spiegel, Celina, eds. *Out of the Garden: Women Writers on the Bible*. New York: Fawcett Columbine, 1994.

Exum, J. Cheryl. *Fragmented Women: Feminist Subversions of Biblical Narratives*. Harrisburg, Pa.: Trinity Press International, 1993.

Feigenson, Emily, ed. *Beginning the Journey*. New York: Women of Reform Judaism, 1997.

Frankel, Ellen. *The Five Books of Miriam*. New York: G. P. Putnam's Sons, 1996.

Goldstein, Elyse. *ReVisions: Seeing Torah through a Feminist Lens*. Woodstock, Vt.: Jewish Lights Publishing, 1998.

Meyers, Carol. *Discovering Eve: Ancient Israelite Women in Context*. New York: Oxford University Press, 1991.

Newsom, Carol A., and Ringe, Sharon H., eds. *The Women's Bible Commentary*. Louisville, Ky.: Westminster/John Knox Press, 1992.

Orenstein, Debra, and Litman, Jane Rachel, eds. *Lifecycles Vol. 2: Jewish Women on Biblical Themes in Contemporary Life*. Woodstock, Vt.: Jewish Lights Publishing, 1997.

Pardes, Ilana. *Countertraditions in the Bible*. Cambridge, Mass.: Harvard University Press, 1992.

Schussler Fiorenza, Elisabeth. *Bread Not Stone: The Challenge of Feminist Biblical Interpretation*. Boston: Beacon Press, 1995.

Trible, Phyllis. *Texts of Terror: Literary-Feminist Readings of Biblical Narratives*. Philadelphia: Fortress Press, 1984.

Female Biblical Characters

Bach, Alice, ed. *Women in the Hebrew Bible: A Reader*. New York: Routledge Press, 1998.

Bronner, Leila Leah. *From Eve to Esther*. Louisville, Ky.: Westminster/John Knox Press, 1994.

Burns, Rita J. *Has the Lord Indeed Spoken Only Through Moses?* Atlanta: Scholars Press (Dissertation Series), 1987.

Dame, Enid; Rivlin, Lilly; Wenkart, Henny; and Wolf, Naomi, eds. *Which Lilith?: Feminist Writers Re-Create the World's First Woman*. Northvale, N.J.: Jason Aronson, 1998.

Diamant, Anita. *The Red Tent*. New York: St. Martin's Press, 1997.

Hyman, Naomi Mara. *Biblical Women in the Midrash: A Sourcebook*. Northvale, N.J.: Jason Aronson, 1998.

Jeansonne, Sharon Pace. *The Women of Genesis*. Minneapolis: Fortress Press, 1990.

Koltuv, Barbara Black. *The Book of Lilith*. York Beach, Maine: Nicolas-Hays, Inc., 1987.

Labowitz, Shoni, *God, Sex and Women of the Bible: Discovering Our Sensual, Spiritual Selves*. New York: Simon & Schuster, 1998.

Phillips, J. A. *Eve: The History of an Idea*. San Francisco: Harper & Row, 1984.

Rosen, Norma. *Biblical Women Unbound*. Philadelphia: Jewish Publication Society, 1996.

Teubal, Savina J. *Ancient Sisterhood: The Lost Traditions of Hagar and Sarah*. Columbus: Ohio University Press, 1997.

Thaw Ronson, Barbara L. *The Women of the Torah: Commentaries from the Talmud, Midrash, and Kabbalah*. Northvale, N.J.: Jason Aronson, 1998.

Zones, Jane Sprague, ed. *Taking the Fruit: Modern Women's Tales of the Bible*. Chico, Calif.: Women's Institute for Continuing Jewish Education, 1981.

On God, God Language, and the Goddess

Campbell, Joseph, and Muses, Charles, eds. *In All Her Names*. San Francisco: HarperSanFrancisco, 1991.

Falk, Marcia. *The Book of Blessings*. San Francisco: HarperCollins, 1996.

Frymer-Kensky, Tikva. *In the Wake of the Goddess*. New York: Macmillan, Inc., 1992.

Goldenberg, Naomi R. *Changing of the Gods*. Boston: Beacon Press, 1979.

Gottlieb, Lynn. *She Who Dwells Within*. San Francisco: HarperSanFrancisco, 1995.

Graves, Robert, *The White Goddess*. London: Faber and Faber, 1961.

Graves, Robert, and Patai, Raphael. *Hebrew Myths*. Garden City, N.Y.: Doubleday, 1964.

"If God Is God She Is Not Nice." *Journal of Feminist Studies in Religion* 5 no. 1 (Spring 1989): 103–117.

Patai, Raphael. *The Hebrew Goddess*. Detroit: Wayne State University Press, 1990.

Plaskow, Judith. "Facing the Ambiguity of God." *Tikkun* 6, no. 5.

Stone, Merlin. *When God Was a Woman*. New York: Dial Press, 1976.

Weaver, Mary Jo. "Who Is the Goddess and Where Does She Get Us?" and "Can a Sexist Model Liberate Us? Ancient Near Eastern 'Fertility' Goddesses." *Journal of Feminist Studies in Religion* 5, no. 1 (Spring 1989).

About the Contributors

Rabbi Judith Z. Abrams was ordained by the Hebrew Union College–Jewish Institute of Religion in Cincinnati in 1985. Her main inspiration for becoming a rabbi was Rabbi Jason Z. Edelstein, who has been her rabbi since she was born. She received her Ph.D. in rabbinic literature from Baltimore Hebrew University in 1993. She is the author of many books for adults and children. She founded and is the director of Maqom: A School for Adult Talmud Study (www.maqom.com), a place where everyone, with any background, can learn Talmud via the Internet and classes held in Houston. She is married and has three children.

"I decided to become a rabbi after confirmation. My rabbi, who'd been there my whole life, Rabbi Jason Edelstein, was and continues to be my mentor. He has such authenticity and integrity that showed that this was an honorable calling. Developing a relationship with God and with the Sages of rabbinic literature have been two of the building stones upon which my life has rested."

Rabbi Shaina Bacharach was ordained by the Jewish Theological Seminary in 1999 and is the spiritual leader of Congregation Cnesses Israel in Green Bay, Wisconsin. Her congregation, while small, maintains a high level of activity and, despite the cold winters, a great deal of personal warmth. Her duties vary and include administrative, educational, pastoral, and spiritual aspects—the full range of Jewish life. Before entering rabbinical school, she worked first as a registered nurse and later taught Judaica in the Solomon Schechter Academy in Oklahoma City. She is married to Robert Dick. Between them, they have four children and a grandson.

"I wanted to be a rabbi from the time I started Hebrew school as a child. I can't put my finger on what motivated me. Part of it was the warmth of our congregation and the dedication of the rabbi. However, at that time, none of the movements accepted women for ordination. I ran into a religious closed door. I spiritually drifted. Following the birth of my children, a deep spiritual hunger drove me to study Eastern religions. That didn't work for me, but as I got more and more in touch with myself, my Jewish roots surfaced. More important, I understood that my own relationship with God could only take place in a Jewish context. This of course includes Torah and study, but also an ethos of love and respect for others, and a passion for God."

Rabbi Y. L. bat Joseph was born in Birmingham, England, immigrated to Canada at the age of three and became affiliated with Temple Anshe Shalom in Hamilton. She graduated from the University of Calgary with a B.Ed. in secondary social studies and a B.A. in religious studies and applied ethics and was ordained by the Hebrew Union College–Jewish Institute of Religion in Cincinnati in 1996. She currently serves Temple Beth Ora in Edmonton, Alberta.

"Rabbi Bernard Baskin was my childhood rabbi. He and the temple were among my earliest Jewish influences. My daughters, Jessica and Elizabeth, were ages eight and six, respectively, when I began my studies in Jerusalem. My daughters are now nineteen and seventeen."

Rabbi Linda Bertenthal was ordained by the Hebrew Union College–Jewish Institute of Religion in 2001. She also holds a bachelor of arts in sociology from Stanford University and a juris doctor from Boalt Hall School of Law. Prior to entering rabbinical school, she practiced law for thirteen years, clerking for a federal judge and serving low-income people at a Legal Aid office. She is currently the associate director of the Pacific Southwest Council of the Union for Reform Judaism in Los Angeles, where she lives with her attorney husband, Philip Bertenthal, and their two children, Jacob and Sarah.

"I found Judaism as an adult, after many years of having only a personal theology, not a religious community. When I completed my conversion studies, I couldn't bear to give up studying, so I studied for an adult Bat Mitzvah ceremony, and then continued to study with my cantor in order to be able to serve my congregation as a volunteer cantorial soloist. It was leading services as a soloist that drew me to the rabbinate. One person after another told me that though they usually had trouble praying, they could pray when I was leading a prayer. I decided that if my love of God and Judaism could help other Jews recover their lost connection, that was a gift that I could not ignore."

Rabbi Barbara Borts received *smichah* from the Leo Baeck College in 1981 and became the third female rabbi in Europe. She was the first woman to become the sole rabbi of an RSGB (Reform Synagogues of Great Britain) synagogue. She founded and chaired the Social Issues Group of the RSGB and was a founding member of both JONAH (Jews Organized for a Nuclear Arms Halt) and JSH (Jewish Support for the Homeless). Her areas of interest are women in Judaism, social issues, construction of identity and other postmodernist critiques of Jewish dualisms, conversion, and Yiddish. She has worked in pulpits, as a chaplain, as

465

an adult Jewish educator, and as a lecturer at Colgate University. Rabbi Borts has published three essays in books and has written articles for journals and newspapers. Currently she works at Temple Adath Yeshurun in Manchester, New Hampshire.

"The idea of becoming a rabbi came to me after a casual glance at a career booklet describing the profession of rabbi, which stated that the Reform movement had just begun to ordain women. The idea stuck and tantalized me from the age of sixteen until I entered rabbinical college at the age of twenty-two."

Rabbi Analia Bortz, M.D., Ph.D., studied at the Seminario Rabinico Latinoamericano in Buenos Aires and finished her studies at the Beit Midrash LeLimudei Yahadut, where she was ordained as a Conservative rabbi. She is married to Rabbi Mario Karpuj and has two daughters, Tamar and Adina. She is the first female rabbi ordained by the Seminario in Jerusalem. She is also a physician (University of Buenos Aires, with a postgraduate degree in Radiology) with a Ph.D. in bioethics from the Catholic University in Chile. She works as a full-time rabbi at Congregation Or Hadash in Atlanta, Georgia, and as a member of the Bioethics Committee at the Scottish Rite Pediatric Hospital/Egleston Hospital–Emory University in Atlanta.

"I decided to become a rabbi when I was eighteen years old, at the time I started to study medicine; I felt that I wanted to help people physically but also take care of their souls and spirits. To heal with love was my main goal. I thought about what it would mean to be a woman rabbi, so as to participate in this vocation with another vision. I do believe that if God gave the Torah to men and women, all standing at the edge of Mount Sinai, we, as women, have something different to express. We can complete the task by being partners of God with different perspectives. I value, as the aim of my life, the words of Rabbi Abraham Joshua Heschel (*z"l*): Medicine is Religion in acts, and Religion is Medicine in prayers."

Rabbi Rachel R. Bovitz was ordained by the Ziegler School of Rabbinic Studies at the University of Judaism in 2001 with distinction in Talmud. She earned her B.A. in Jewish Studies, Phi Beta Kappa, from the University of California–Los Angeles. She currently serves as the second rabbi of Temple Aliyah in Woodland Hills, California. Her portfolio focuses on adult education, *bikkur cholim*, and the synagogue's Center for Spirituality.

"For eight summers, growing up in the warm and spirited Jewish mecca of a Chabad summer camp, I experienced a vital, meaningful, and passionate Judaism. Ever since, I have been seeking to live out an adult egalitarian version of this reality. Working at the University of Judaism after college—and with the aid of several mentors there—my eyes were opened to the possibility of the rabbinate. What a joy to discover that my professional life could be both intellectually stimulating and spiritually compelling!"

Rabbi Jessica Spitalnic Brockman is associate rabbi at Temple Beth El in Boca Raton, Florida. She formerly served as assistant rabbi at Temple Beth El in Charlotte, North Carolina, where she was active in raising community awareness on issues from gun violence and battered women to the separation of church and state. She received rabbinic ordination from the Hebrew Union College–Jewish Institute of Religion in New York in 1999. She sits on the Reform Movement's Commission for Social Action. Rabbi Brockman is a native New Yorker who has worked in Jewish communities in New York, Chicago, London, and Jerusalem. In Israel, she served as a tour educator for the North American Federation of Temple Youth (NFTY) summer program, guiding Jewish teenagers through the historical sites of the Land of Israel.

"After college, I worked in the Jewish community in London. England has an amazing Progressive Jewish population, and I worked with the Reform and Liberal movement's Jewish university students on campuses throughout England, and at the Sternberg Center for Judaism in London. It was through my work that I met many rabbis, including several female rabbis who are leaders of that community. It was with the influence of my boss, Rabbi Tony Bayfield, the head of the Reform movement in England, that I first started to think about the rabbinate as a career. I am always amazed at how a simple conversation with someone who said, 'You should really think about the rabbinate as a career' changed the path of my life."

Rabbi Sharon Brous was ordained by the Jewish Theological Seminary in New York in 2001. While in rabbinical school she received her master's degree in religion and human rights from Columbia University. After ordination, Sharon served as Marshall T. Meyer rabbinic fellow at Congregation B'nai Jeshurun in New York City, a synagogue known for its spiritual depth and vitality. Rabbi Brous and her husband David Light, a comedy writer, currently live in Los Angeles, where Rabbi Brous serves as rabbi-in-residence and director of advanced Jewish studies at Milken Community High School. She is working to build a passionate, spiritually challenging, creative Jewish community in Los Angeles, and actively working to engage Jews in interfaith human rights work, conflict resolution, and faith-based activism.

"I decided to become a rabbi after developing a deep passion for the study of traditional Jewish texts, which I felt offered a foundation for my lifelong commitment to the *tikkun* of our deeply broken world. As an educator, I have had the privilege of witnessing the absolutely transformative effect that serious engagement with the foundational claims of our tradition can have on people's lives. Through helping teenagers and adults fall in love with Torah and engage earnestly in their own spiritual journeys, I believe we are creating a more responsible community—awake to the pain of the other, and prepared to respond by garnering our emotional, intellectual, and spiritual resources in the active pursuit of justice in the world."

About the Contributors

Rabbi Nina Beth Cardin was ordained by the Jewish Theological Seminary of America in 1988, as part of the first class of Conservative women rabbis. She is the director of Jewish life at the JCC of Greater Baltimore. In the years following graduation, she held several positions at JTS, including assistant to the vice-chancellor for administration and advisor to rabbinical students in the rabbinical school office. She served as editor of *Sh'ma*, and as associate director of the National Center for Jewish Healing. Her books include *Out of the Depths I Call to You: A Book of Prayers for the Married Jewish Woman* (a translation and annotation of Italian Jewish women's prayers from the 1700s), *Tears of Sorrow, Seeds of Hope: A Jewish Spiritual Companion for Infertility and Pregnancy Loss* (Jewish Lights), and *The Tapestry of Jewish Time: A Spiritual Guide to Holidays and Life-Cycle Events*.

"I was trained as a Conservative rabbi, but my pulpit is the JCC. I am far from unique. More than 50 percent of students in rabbinical schools these days will assume positions outside the congregation. This is a welcome redefinition of the rabbinate for the twenty-first century, for it takes rabbis beyond the walls of the synagogue, into the places where Jews work and play, and into pan-denominational settings. But it is a challenge for rabbis as well, for we are almost all denominationally trained. Clearly, our seminaries will once again have to redesign the rabbinical curriculum to better meet the new needs of the rabbinate and *amkha*. And each rabbi will have to answer the most personal of questions: How do I pursue an allegiance to a particular denomination or set of beliefs while authentically serving the diversity of my entire community?"

Rabbi Kathy Cohen was ordained by the Hebrew Union College–Jewish Institute of Religion in Cincinnati in 1988. She served congregations in Cincinnati and Westport, Connecticut, before becoming the rabbi of Temple Emanuel in Roanoke, Virginia. She is active in local schools, enjoys coaching softball, and occasionally teaches at local universities.

"After a trip to Israel in 1978 with high school in Israel, I was sure that I wanted to become a rabbi. It never occurred to me that there were very few female rabbis at that time. Judaism was such an important part of my life and I yearned to professionally share that interest with others. It has been an honor to serve the Jewish community for the past fifteen years."

Rabbi Lori Cohen was ordained by the Hebrew Union College–Jewish Institute of Religion in Cincinnati in 2000. She is currently the assistant rabbi at Temple Sinai Congregation of Toronto. Prior to attending HUC, Rabbi Cohen was the founder of Congregation Or Hadash in Newmarket, Ontario. During her years at HUC, she worked with the Jewish elderly at Cedar Village—A Home for Jewish Living. After ordination Rabbi Cohen spent a year doing advanced clinical and pastoral education in chaplaincy at the Cincinnati Children's Hospital and Medical Center. Rabbi Cohen is the mother of three teenage boys, Aaron, Joshua, and Daniel.

"As the founder of Or Hadash synagogue, as well as president, Hebrew school principal, and cleaning lady, I tried to stay one week ahead of the congregation in terms of Torah study. I loved the role and dreamed of being able to do it full time—that is, more than 40 hours a week! I decided that it was not worthwhile to have a dream if you don't at least try for it. After being accepted, I packed up my three boys and eight duffel bags, and headed to Jerusalem; before that time I was just enjoying *Torah lishma*. The past two years have been everything that I dreamed it could be. I enjoy the privilege and honor of being with people at the most intense and intimate times in their lives and bringing a touch of the sacred to those moments."

Rabbi Dianne Cohler-Esses is the first woman from the Syrian Jewish community to become a rabbi, ordained by the Jewish Theological Seminary in 1995. After graduating, she received a yearlong fellowship to study with Rabbi Yitz Greenberg, teach, and design curriculum at CLAL, the Center for Leadership and Learning. Subsequently, she did advanced academic work in Midrash at the Jewish Theological Seminary and served as educational director for Mishpacha, an online education and support program for alienated Jewish families across America; director of a feminist retreat for Maayan (which included creating a feminist Shabbat liturgy with Maayan staff); and a faculty member for the HUC–JIR Kollel, the JTS Hevrutah program, and the Bronfman Youth Fellowship (BYF). In 1998 she became the co-director of the Bronfman Youth Fellowship and served as such until the fall of 2002. She is currently BYF's senior educator and is beginning a new job as Rav Beit Midrash (the rabbi of the study hall) at a new Jewish high school. She also teaches, lectures, and writes. She is the mother three young children, ages four and two-year-old twins. She lives with her husband and children (and Eno!) in New York City.

"Why did I become a rabbi? For some conscious reasons and other mysterious ones. I grew up in a very traditional community of Syrian Jews where it is expected that women be married at age eighteen and work mostly in the private sphere. The religious lives of women are also expressed in the confines of the home. From an early age I experienced religious and intellectual yearnings that could not, ultimately, be satisfied by the community of my birth. So I broke all the rules, left home, crossed the bridge and went to college at New York University and, ultimately, six years after I graduated from college, entered rabbinical school. Consciously I wanted to be at the center of my religious tradition, where I had heretofore experienced myself as marginal. It was a kind of creative betrayal (a term coined, I think, by David Roskies) of my history, and one that was to catapult me into a very interesting personal and historical drama. While it often causes me great angst, providing great amounts of dissonance with my own inherited self-concept, history, and community, it remains ceaselessly fascinating and gratifying."

Rabbi Stacia Deutsch was ordained by the Hebrew Union College–Jewish Institute of Religion in 1995. After ordination, she spent two years as the assistant rabbi at Beth Abraham Congregation in Dayton, Ohio. She then returned to

HUC–JIR as the director of outreach education, a position she held both in Cincinnati and Los Angeles. In June 2002, Rabbi Deutsch resigned her position with the college to become a full-time fiction writer. She is the coauthor of a children's history series to be published by Simon & Schuster in Spring 2005. Rabbi Deutsch is married to Rabbi Richard Steinberg. They live in Irvine, California, and have three young children.

"I applied to rabbinical school directly out of college because becoming a rabbi opened the door to an endless number of career opportunities in the Jewish community. A rabbi can serve a congregation, teach in a day school or university, work in a Jewish community organization, or forge her own, as yet uncharted, career path. I look forward to creating a rabbinate all my own."

Rabbi Shoshana Dworsky was ordained by the Jewish Theological Seminary in New York in 1998. She served as the Marshall T. Meyer rabbinic fellow at Congregation B'nai Jeshurun, and as the first full-time rabbi of the Battery Park Synagogue, both in New York. From 2001 to 2003 she served as the first assistant rabbi at Congregation Neveh Shalom in Portland, Oregon.

"I met a woman rabbi for the first time in 1985, when Rabbi Stacy Ofner came to serve as the assistant rabbi at the synagogue in the town where I grew up. She recruited me to teach in the Hebrew school, and I discovered that I loved the Jewish classroom. This discovery turned out to be the beginning of my journey down the path that would lead to the rabbinate. For the next eight years I worked as a Jewish educator, learning as I went along. Eventually, I found myself thirsting for a more thorough Jewish education of my own, and that's when I began rabbinical school at the Jewish Theological Seminary. It was an exciting and definitive step in my life—both as an educator and as a Jew. I feel blessed to be able to continue learning, teaching, and growing, and am grateful to those brave women who blazed the trail before me."

Rabbi Denise L. Eger is the founding rabbi of Congregation Kol Ami, West Hollywood's (CA) Reform Synagogue. Rabbi Eger serves as vice-president of the Southern California Board of Rabbis. She is past chair of the Task Force on Gays and Lesbian in the Rabbinate for the Central Conference of American Rabbis. She has written extensively on gay and lesbian inclusion, AIDS, and human sexuality.

"I love my rabbinate, my community, and my congregation. I have been blessed to serve a unique community that focuses on inclusion and partnership, social change, and *tikkun olam*. Through my activism I have been able to live my Jewish values in the context of the synagogue community. This is a marvelous gift that I hope and pray I am able to share with others."

Rabbi Serena Raziel Eisenberg was ordained by the Reconstructionist Rabbinical College in 2002, where she studied as a Wexner graduate fellow. Previously,

Rabbi Eisenberg received a degree in Judaic studies with honors from Brown University and then completed a J.D./M.S.W. program at the University of California at Berkeley. She worked in diverse family welfare settings from West Africa to the Bronx and served eclectic pulpits in Montana and California. Currently, she lives in Berkeley with her husband and five sons.

"In the biblical story of Hannah, our archetypal nursing mother, I find my own mother, also named Hannah. She was raised with little Jewish education, and with far fewer choices, dedicating herself as a mother and a nurse. And so I tell this story as Hannah's daughter: now a woman rabbi reclaiming the Torah our mothers were denied, and now as a mother myself, finding sustenance in our Source."

Rabbi Sue Levi Elwell, who serves as the director of the Pennsylvania Council of the Union of American Hebrew Congregations, was ordained by the Hebrew Union College–Jewish Institute of Religion in 1986. The founding director of the Los Angeles Jewish Feminist Center and the first rabbinic director of Ma'yan: The Jewish Women's Project of the JCC of Manhattan, Rabbi Elwell is the editor of *The Open Door,* the CCAR Haggadah. A founding member of *B'not Esh,* a twenty-two-year-old Jewish feminist cooperative, she and colleagues Rebecca Alpert and Shirley Idelson edited the groundbreaking *Lesbian Rabbis: The First Generation.* A third-generation Reform Jew, she is the proud mother of two grown daughters.

"Frustrated that the rabbinate was not open to women when I graduated from college, I pursued a career in Jewish communal work and earned a doctorate in education. In 1976, I met and was inspired by Rabbi Sandy Sasso, and began to consider rabbinical school. (We later collaborated on one of the first resources for Jewish schools on the topic of Jewish women.) I feel blessed to be able to work with rabbis and congregations, strengthening holy connections and building sacred communities."

Rabbi Cindy Enger directs the Jewish Program at the Center for the Prevention of Sexual and Domestic Violence, an international interreligious organization committed to addressing the religious issues of interpersonal violence and working with communities to promote healing, justice, and social change. She received her rabbinic ordination in 2001 from the Hebrew Union College–Jewish Institute of Religion in Cincinnati and previously practiced law in Chicago.

"Growing up, my Zeyda, Jake Sheinbein, frequently invited me to the morning *minyan* at Congregation B'nai Amoona in St. Louis. 'You'll come to services; I'll give you the *ashrai,*' he said with his Yiddish accent and a big smile. When I said 'yes,' I experienced the loving embrace of an inclusive Jewish community. As an adult, I again experienced that embrace at Congregation Or Chadash in Chicago. Saying 'yes' to the *ashrai* led to the leading of Shabbat and High Holy Day services, which eventually resulted in my serving as president of the congregation and then rabbinical ordination. A photo of my Zeyda sits on the desk in my office, reminding me of him and the blessing of inclusive Jewish communities."

About the Contributors

Rabbi Rachel Esserman was ordained by the Reconstructionist Rabbinical College in 1998. She is currently copy editor and book reviewer for the Reporter Group (which publishes five Jewish newspapers in New York State and Connecticut) and is also the Jewish chaplain for Broome Developmental Disabilities Service Office, where she works with the developmentally disabled. Her book of poems, *I Stand by the River*, was published in 1998. Her writings have appeared in many publications, including *The Reconstructionist, Na'amat Women, Jewish Currents*, and *Sh'ma*. She also contributed to *The Women's Torah Commentary* (Jewish Lights).

"I was encouraged by several people to think about becoming a rabbi, but it wasn't until I was recovering from back surgery in 1990 that I seriously considered going to rabbinical school. I was lying in bed reading a book on Jewish history and realized that I had the power to change my life. It was scary making such a radical change, but my love of Judaism gave me the strength to pursue my dreams. Being a rabbi gives me the ability to share that love with others."

Rabbi Helaine Ettinger was ordained by the Hebrew Union College–Jewish Institute of Religion in New York in 1991. After serving for five years as the rabbi for a congregation in Kinnelon, New Jersey, she moved with her family to Israel. There she enjoyed becoming an active lay leader at Hod ve-Hadar Congregation in Kfar Saba. During her five years in Israel she was a teacher in the Masorti Movement's national program *Bar/Bat Mitzvah for the Special Child*, providing Jewish studies and enrichment for youth with developmental disabilities. Returning to the United States in 2001 she has enjoyed a number of simultaneous professional pursuits. She is the community outreach and program coordinator for the MetroWest Jewish Health and Healing Center in New Jersey. She has served as the rabbi to Congregation B'nai Harim in Pocono Pines, Pennsylvania, and was recently named rabbi emerita. She is a Synagogue 2000 Fellow and a board member of the Solomon Schechter Day School of Essex and Union in New Jersey. She is married to Henry Bloom and mother to Lyla, Yael, and Shai.

"My decision to become a rabbi was influenced by the female rabbinical students, now rabbis, I met during high school and college. I enjoy the fact that being a rabbi allows me to relate to people on multiple levels, for example, spiritually, emotionally, and educationally. It is a challenge to help weave all these human dimensions together into a cohesive Jewish whole and a privilege to share in other people's lives. I am indebted to my HUC–JIR professors who encouraged me to take my own abilities seriously. The ideas for this commentary were conceived jointly with the members of my study group, Lainie Blum Cogan, Cathy Lasser, and Lori Schuldiner Schor. I am incredibly fortunate to share weekly in their insights, creativity, and friendship."

Rabbi Susan P. Fendrick was ordained by the Jewish Theological Seminary of America in 1995, where she was a Wexner Graduate Fellow. She was a Hillel rabbi at American University and Brown University (from which she graduated in 1984 with a B.A. in women's studies). Her work in online Jewish education has included serving as founding editor of SocialAction.com, and as managing editor and lifecycle editor of MyJewishLearning.com, a transdenominational adult Jewish learning site. She is a frequent scholar-in-residence for organizations and institutions throughout North America, and is the author of several published essays and articles. She is a former member of the faculty of the Institute for Contemporary Midrash in the area of bibliodrama, and served as vice-chair of the National Havurah Committee (NHC).

"I first considered becoming a rabbi at age nineteen while teaching a group of b'nai mitzvah students in a small havurah school. I am grateful to my father, activist nuns, and the NHC community for providing me with the inspiration to pursue the rabbinate. I live with my husband and our five children in Newton, Massachusetts."

Rabbi Karen L. Fox was ordained by the Hebrew Union College–Jewish Institute of Religion in 1978. She became interested in the rabbinate in the early seventies, especially in informal educational settings. Rabbis Haim Asa and Richard Levy expressed ongoing joy and challenge in their work and that appealed to her. She served as the first woman regional director of the Union of American Hebrew Congregations, from 1978 to 1982 and then moved to California. For over ten years, she has served Wilshire Boulevard Temple in Los Angeles for over thirteen years in various capacities as camp director and rabbi. She is also a California-licensed marriage and family psychotherapist. She is the author of *Seasons for Celebration*. Rabbi Fox is married to Michael Rosen and is the mother of two musicians.

"As the child of Holocaust survivors, I was aware of my Judaism from an early age, mostly in informal educational settings. Later I was inspired by Rabbis Haim Asa and Richard Levy, whose joy in the challenges of their work appealed to me. Aside from the Judaic, historic, and Hebrew scholarship involved, there are aspects of counseling and education that are tremendously satisfying and have led me into a full and wonderful career. The most important part of my life is my family, my husband and two sons."

Rabbi Shoshana Boyd Gelfand was ordained by the Jewish Theological Seminary of America in 1993, where she studied in the first class of Wexner fellows. She currently serves as vice president of the Wexner Heritage Foundation. She graduated magna cum laude from Bryn Mawr College and was a MacCracken fellow at New York University. Rabbi Gelfand has served as assistant rabbi at Congregation Anshe Emet in Chicago, and has also worked as scholar-in-residence at the JCC of Staten Island and the Brandeis Bardin Institute. She has served on the Rabbinical Assembly's Committee on Jewish Law and Standards, and the JTS Task Force on Jewish Religious Leadership. She has published articles in *The Journal of Synagogue Music*, *The Jewish Spectator*, *Masoret*, and *Sh'ma*, where she also serves on the advisory board. She also has an essay in *The Women's Torah Commentary* (Jewish Lights).

"I originally came from a small Southern town in the Baptist Bible Belt and knew virtually nothing about Judaism. I had intended to study philosophy and music in college, but instead met an incredible professor, Dr. Samuel T. Lachs, who brought me to his *havurah* and sent me to study at JTS. I intended to go for a summer, but loved it so much that I stayed for rabbinical school and have never looked back!"

Rabbi Laura Geller was ordained by the Hebrew Union College–Jewish Institute of Religion in 1976, the third woman to be ordained in the Reform Movement. She was the first woman to become the senior rabbi of a large metropolitan congregation, Temple Emanuel of Beverly Hills, California. Prior to coming to Temple Emanuel, Rabbi Geller served for fourteen years as the Hillel director of the University of Southern California and for four years as the director of the American Jewish Congress, Pacific Southwest Region. While at Hillel, Rabbi Geller co-organized the award-winning 1984 conference "Illuminating the Unwritten Scroll: Women's Spirituality and Jewish Tradition" and facilitated the first interdisciplinary Jewish Feminist Research Group. At the American Jewish Congress she cofounded the Los Angeles Jewish Feminist Center, which became a model for others around the country. Rabbi Geller serves on the corporation of Brown University and the Board of Directors of the Hebrew Union College–Jewish Institute of Religion. Rabbi Geller has received many honors, including the ACLU of Southern California Award for Fostering Racial and Cultural Harmony and the California State Legislature Woman of the Year Award. She is the mother of two wonderful children, Joshua and Elana.

"As an undergraduate at Brown University, I was influenced by two Protestant ministers who taught me through their example that spirituality and social justice enrich each other. Their example, along with wonderful professors of religious studies, challenged me to think about my own tradition. I went to Hebrew Union College as much to learn to be Jewish as to become a rabbi. Because my own undergraduate experience was so central in forming my spiritual identity, I chose to begin my career in Hillel, where I could work with other young people at such a crucial stage in their lives. As I grew older, I came to understand the need to create synagogues that could be centers of spirituality, community, and sources of *tikkun olam*, so I chose to go into congregational work."

Rabbi Elaine Rose Glickman received her master of arts in Hebrew letters (1997) and rabbinic ordination (1998) from the Hebrew Union College–Jewish Institute of Religion. At HUC, she was the recipient of the Snyder, Ziegler, and Stern Prizes for academic excellence. She is also a magna cum laude graduate of Tufts University in Medford, Massachusetts. Rabbi Glickman is the author of *Haman and the Jews* and the project editor of *B'chol L'vavcha*. Her sermons and poetry have also appeared in the *CCAR Journal* and the *American Rabbi*. The former rabbi of the I. Weiner Jewish Secondary School in Houston, Rabbi Glickman now stays home to care for her husband, Rabbi Brenner J. Glickman, and their sons, Moses Aaron and Leo Baeck Glickman.

"Since I was small, I have loved to study and write, and Judaism has long been a central part of my life. During my years at Tufts University, I began to study Judaism from a formal, academic perspective. The things I learned intrigued me, but also troubled me; the God who slew Judah's son (Gen. 38:7) was a far cry from the open-armed, always-smiling God to whom I had been introduced at religious school. I began to grapple with theodicy, with why an all-powerful and all-loving God permits atrocity and suffering in this world. While I have certainly not solved this dilemma, I have been fortunate to have my rabbi, Samuel E. Karff, help me understand that part of being Jewish is wrestling with these issues and holding fast to God as we do so. I became a rabbi because it was my way of continuing to wrestle, of continuing to hold fast to God."

Rabbi Elizabeth W. Goldstein received her ordination from the Hebrew Union College–Jewish Institute of Religion in New York in 2001. At present, she is working on a doctorate in the field of Hebrew Bible at the University of California at San Diego. She has been teaching adult Jewish education in the San Diego area in several different forums. The writings of Jewish and Christian feminists as well as her interaction with female clergy were the two most influential factors in her decision to become a rabbi. Education and pastoral care are the areas of the rabbinate she finds most meaningful. She hopes to use her love for the study and teaching of the Hebrew Bible to foster learning both inside and outside the Jewish community. Furthermore, she hopes to promote conversation among Jews and Christians about the role of the Hebrew Bible in our society.

"I am grateful to Rabbi Yael Romer, who planted the seed for my becoming a rabbi during my teenage years. I am also most grateful to mentors from HUC–JIR, Rabbis Nancy Wiener, Carol Balin, and Andrea Weiss, who each modeled ways of balancing the rabbinate and an academic life. I became a rabbi because I knew from a young age that only one path existed for me. I hope always to be part of the many facets of rabbinic life that constantly provide me with richness and inspiration."

Rabbi Elyse M. Goldstein received her B.A. in Judaic studies from Brandeis University, and was ordained by the Hebrew Union College–Jewish Institute of Religion in New York in 1983. As a rabbinical student, she served Temple Beth Or of the Deaf, and became proficient in sign language. After being a happy and fulfilled pulpit rabbi for eight years, first at Holy Blossom Temple in Toronto and then at Temple Beth David in Canton, Massachusetts, she entered the newly growing field of Jewish adult education as the founding rabbinic director and Rosh Yeshiva of Kolel: The Adult Centre for Liberal Jewish Learning in Toronto in 1991, where she still serves today. She was the first woman to be elected president of the interdenominational Toronto Board of Rabbis. She is the author of *ReVisions:*

Seeing Torah through a Feminist Lens (Jewish Lights) and *Seek Her Out: A Textual Approach to the Study of Women and Judaism* (UAHC Press) and the editor of *The Women's Torah Commentary* (Jewish Lights).

"I am a teacher by nature, and the rabbinate offers me the perfect opportunity to teach what I love: Judaism and the joy of Jewish living. My adult students have become my congregation, but not a congregation in the synagogue sense; through them I have experienced a paradigm shift in what it means to be a rabbi. I find such joy in teaching through writing as well. I feel that my books have entered into the hearts and minds of so many people I would otherwise never get to meet, and thus I have been a kind of rabbi to my readers, too."

Rabbi Jennifer Elkin Gorman was ordained at the Jewish Theological Seminary of America in 1996. She received her B.A. from Brandeis University, where she majored in sociology, focusing on the American Jewish community. Lacking women rabbis as role models, it did not occur to her to enter the rabbinate until a friend suggested it late in her junior year. After ordination she followed her heart—and her husband—as he served as a chaplain in the U.S. Navy. Rabbi Gorman has earned the title "Submarine Lady of the Submarine Force" for her service as an adjunct rabbi at the Aloha Jewish Chapel, Pearl Harbor, Hawaii, jumping in when needed, such as the Shabbat after the USS *Greeneville* collided with the *Ehime Maru*. She also co-authored a special CD-ROM on *t'fillah* for the U.S. Naval Academy's Jewish cadets. Today Rabbi Gorman teaches a women's Torah study and speaks to groups about her experience with the military and beyond.

"While I hadn't had a regular paid position until recently, I've truly accomplished what I went into the rabbinate to do. I wrote in my seminary application essays that I wanted to change the world by reaching out to one person at a time. As a volunteer rabbi in a military setting I've been able to do just that. I've been a Jewish role model, rabbi, and educator to people who are searching for a spiritual home. The majority of our military are ages eighteen to twenty-one. Not only did I fulfill a rabbinic role, but I helped provide a Jewish home for so many sailors, soldiers, airmen and women, and marines. I've been able to see the difference I've made in their lives, and I know they'll carry that with them into adulthood."

Rabbi Tina Grimberg was ordained as a Reform rabbi by the Hebrew Union College–Jewish Institute of Religion in 2001. She is currently serving Congregation Darchei Noam in Toronto. Her background is in family therapy, and her work involves counseling interfaith couples and their children. In her work as a therapist and as a rabbi, Rabbi Grimberg employs storytelling, puppetry, and art. She was born in Kiev, Ukraine, and was the first female soviet émigré to be ordained in North America. Rabbi Grimberg is passionate about her husband, her work, and her tango.

"Becoming a rabbi was a natural progression for me. In 1979, fleeing anti-Semitism and a bleak Soviet reality, my family made their way to America. Perfect strangers, volunteers from the Reform Jewish community, hosted us. They visited our home daily, they helped us to fill out our first job applications and they brought us to our first High Holiday services. My family remained forever grateful. Their generous efforts planted the seeds for my future rabbinate. I became a family therapist and practiced that art with utmost devotion. However, I wanted to continue with my education. My love for Jewish tradition and learning, and my dedication to the mental health of people around me, brought me to the doors of Hebrew Union College. My work in the rabbinate embodies all of the above."

Rabbi Ilana Berenbaum Grinblat was ordained by the University of Judaism's Ziegler School of Rabbinic Studies in 2001. At Ziegler, she developed a passion for Jewish text study and Talmud in particular, which earned her the David Aronson Award for Excellence in Rabbinic Literature. She now serves as rabbi of Temple Beth Shalom in Long Beach, California. She is also teaching a Midrash course for the rabbinical students at the University of Judaism. She is married to Tal Grinblat, a franchise lawyer.

"My father is a rabbi so I was raised with the rabbinate in my blood in a lot of ways. Though my childhood experiences were influential, I realized that I wanted to be a rabbi in college. I spent two semesters of college abroad, teaching in a rural Ecuadorian schoolhouse and studying African art and culture in Ghana. I enjoyed community building abroad, but I realized that one is ultimately most effective in one's own communities. My decision to become a rabbi goes back to one simple moment in my life. When I was in college, I took out a piece of paper and asked myself, What do I want to be when I grow up? And I wrote one word on the piece of paper. The word was *whole*. I realized that this meant I wanted to become a rabbi, because it combined all the things that I love—teaching, writing, ritual, counseling, and community building."

Rabbi Susan Gulack was ordained by the Academy for Jewish Religion in 1986. She has served Conservative congregations in New Mexico, New York, and Connecticut. After fourteen years in the pulpit, she switched to chaplaincy. She currently serves as the chaplain of three New York State prisons, the Capital District Psychiatric Center, and the Stratton Veterans Administration Hospital. She lives in Albany, New York, with her two sons, Avraham Yonahand and Yoran Elkhanan.

"I grew up on an Army Base in Frankfurt am Main, Germany. My mother was principal of the Hebrew School, so I spent a lot of time hanging out in the base chapel. I knew then that I wanted to be a rabbi. I figured that, just like women doctors, there had to be women rabbis, I just hadn't met them yet. By the time I became Bat Mitzvah, the first women were in rabbinical school, so I knew that it was a real possibility for me. I came to my career choice as an adult, because my love of Judaism continued as well as my love of teaching and working with people. I just couldn't see myself doing anything else."

477

About the Contributors

Rabbi Rachel Sabath-Beit Halachmi was ordained by the Hebrew Union College–Jewish Institute of Religion in New York in 1995, and is currently working toward a Ph.D. in modern Jewish theology. She is director of lay leadership education and a scholar at the Shalom Hartman Institute and teaches at HUC–JIR in Jerusalem. She is the coauthor of two books, *Preparing Your Heart for the High Holy Days* and *Striving Toward Virtue: A Contemporary Guide for Jewish Ethical Behavior*. During the summer and the High Holidays, she has served as the rabbi of Congregation Shirat HaYam in Nantucket for the past eight years.

"I was inspired toward the rabbinate through intense study of text and my personal experiences of prayer. The texts, the prayers, and many of the male and female feminist leaders I encountered assured me that those who open entrances to holiness for others must themselves be ethical and just."

Rabbi Jill Hammer, Ph.D., was ordained by the Jewish Theological Seminary in 2001 and received her doctorate in social psychology from the University of Connecticut in 1995. She is currently a senior associate at Ma'yan: The Jewish Women's Project of the Jewish Community Center in Manhattan. She is a poet, author, and creator of modern midrash. Her first book is titled *Sisters at Sinai: New Tales of Biblical Women*. Her works also appear in many anthologies and journals. She is the former editor of *Living Text: The Journal of Contemporary Midrash.*

"I was interested in Jewish text and ritual from an early age. I finally decided to pursue the rabbinate when I discovered that I was spending more time learning Torah and praying with my Jewish community than I was in my graduate studies. The process of creating new midrash inclusive of once-silent voices, an important part of my life as a writer, has become a crucial part of my rabbinate as well. My path to becoming a rabbi has been deeply connected to my experience of the Divine feminine. My sense is that part of my life's work is to help bring that presence more deeply into the world. I have been influenced on my journey by rabbis, poets, drummers, storytellers, and creatures of all sorts."

Rabbi Joanne Yocheved Heiligman was ordained by the Reconstructionist Rabbinical College in 1989. She is the rabbi of Congregation Shalom Aleichem in Columbia, Maryland, where she lives with her husband, Gary, and their three children, David, Naomi, and Phoebe. Rabbi Heiligman's special interests are in helping Jews find their own unique Jewish paths, and working to build bridges among Jews of all movements to foster Jewish unity.

"I have loved Judaism from my earliest childhood. When I first thought of becoming a rabbi, I didn't think it was possible for a woman. I thank the women who preceded me and opened the minds and doors of our community so that I can do what I love. I see our tradition as a vast treasure hidden from many modern Jews. I can think of nothing more exciting that exploring this heritage and sharing it with other Jews."

Rabbi Sharyn H. Henry was ordained by the Hebrew Union College–Jewish Institute of Religion in 1988. She has served congregations in Kansas City and Pittsburgh and is currently rabbi/educator at Rodef Shalom Congregation in Pittsburgh. She is married to Dennis Grinberg and is the mother of two sons.

"I became a rabbi because it was the *one* way in which I imagined I would be able to answer the needs of my heart, my soul, and my mind. In the twenty-some years since I made that decision, I have never once imagined being anything else. It is my honor to be among those who transmit Torah from one generation to the next, and to do so in ways that help bring meaning and sustenance to the lives of Jews."

Rabbi Devorah Jacobson is the director of pastoral care at the Jewish Geriatric Services in Longmeadow, Massachusetts. She is the first rabbi hired by this organization to develop and direct the pastoral care program for its Jewish nursing home, assisted living, and other continuum-of-care facilities. She was ordained by the Hebrew Union College–Jewish Institute of Religion in New York in 1982. For over sixteen years, she worked as a college chaplain/Hillel director. She currently serves on the boards of the Food Bank of Western Massachusetts and the Pioneer Valley Habitat for Humanity. She has taught classes for many years in Talmud, Jewish spirituality, and gender and Judaism. She lives in Amherst, Massachusetts, with her nine-year-old son, Jacob Mooney, and her partner, Margaret Mastrangelo.

"I entered rabbinical school in 1975 because I was passionate about Jewish learning and wanted to keep studying. I decided to become a rabbi after my second year of rabbinical school. It was at that point that I took a two-year leave from HUC to work as the student rabbi at UC–Santa Barbara. It was because of that fortuitous and incredibly fulfilling experience that I felt more certain about the rabbinic path."

Rabbi Beth Janus was ordained by the Hebrew Union College–Jewish Institute of Religion in 2001. During her years at seminary she was certified as a hospital chaplain and served as the intern for the Commission on Social Action of Reform Judaism. Currently she is working as the first assistant rabbi at Temple Beth El in Santa Cruz, California, where she is able to combine her passion for Judaism with environmental justice. She is married to Seth Lieberman.

"I decided to become a rabbi toward the end of college. The Jewish women at my liberal college tended to see Judaism as sexist and archaic. I wanted to teach other Jews that Judaism could be relevant, spiritual, and empowering to women and men."

Rabbi Linda Joseph was ordained by the Cincinnati campus of the Hebrew Union College–Jewish Institute of Religion in 1994 and received a master's in Jewish education from the Los Angeles campus of HUC–JIR in 1995. She has served three pulpits—Bentleigh Progressive Synagogue in Melbourne, Australia; the Jewish Congregation of Kinnelon in Kinnelon, New Jersey; and Temple Beth El of Boca Raton in Florida, where she is currently an associate rabbi. Her passions include Jewish texts, teaching, storytelling, meditation, art, her dog Rashi, and her cat Khazar. Linda Joseph is the second Australian woman ordained and the first ordained woman rabbi to lead a solo pulpit in Australia.

"Becoming a rabbi was a process that developed out of my family's professional and voluntary commitment to, and participation in, Progressive Judaism in Australia, and the diverse rabbis and rabbinical students who became personal family friends over the years. Their enthusiasm and creativity led me to contemplate a rabbinical life in my early twenties, because I too had found a passion in Judaism and the Jewish people. In my late twenties, Rabbi Sam Joseph from the Cincinnati campus was on sabbatical in Australia and heard of my accomplishments in both the Melbourne and Sydney Jewish community, and encouraged me to contemplate anew a career in the rabbinate."

Rabbi Jane Kanarek was ordained by the Jewish Theological Seminary in 1998. She has taught Bible and Rabbinics for JTS's Project Judaica at Russian State Humanities University, as well as worked for the Joint Distribution Committee in Moscow, Russia. In addition, she has been the Yeshiva Senior Fellow at the Conservative Yeshiva in Jerusalem. While at JTS, she chaired the committee that helped choose the language through which the *imahot*, the matriarchs, would be added to the *Amidah*. She was also the first rabbinical intern at *Isha El Akhota*—the JTS Women's Center. Her areas of interest include Talmud and legal theory. Currently, Rabbi Kanarek is a doctoral student at the University of Chicago. She is the recipient of a Wexner graduate fellowship. Balak was her Bat Mitzvah *parashah*.

"I decided to become a rabbi in college, at Brown University. Particularly influential in my decision was the Hillel rabbi, Alan Flam, and my discovery that the rabbinate enabled me to combine the ancient with the modern and my love of books with my love of teaching."

Rabbi Karyn D. Kedar was ordained by the Hebrew Union College–Jewish Institute of Religion in 1985. Immediately after ordination she immigrated to Israel and later became the first woman rabbi to serve in Jerusalem. After living and working in Israel for ten years, she returned to her native America, most recently serving as the regional director of the Great Lakes Region of the Union of American Hebrew Congregations. She is currently the senior rabbi at Congregation B'nai Jehoshua Beth Elohim. Rabbi Kedar is author of God Whispers: Stories of the Soul, Lessons of the Heart and Our Dance with God: Finding Prayer, Perspective and Meaning in the Stories of Our Lives (both Jewish Lights). She lives with her husband, Ezra, and their three children, Talia, Shiri, and Ilan, in the Chicago area.

"To be a rabbi is a great honor. I like that it demands creativity. It deepens my faith by integrating my work with my beliefs. It demands of me compassion, and it has me on a constant search for meaning and purpose and different ways to teach all those things."

Rabbi Lynne A. Kern was ordained by the Ziegler School of Rabbinics at the University of Judaism in Los Angeles in 2001. Before entering the seminary, Rabbi Kern worked as a journalist for twelve years for the *New York Times*, the *Washington Post*, the *Louisville Courier-Journal*, and the *Kansas City Star and Times*. While at the *Kansas City Star*, she won a Pulitzer Prize for her coverage of the tragic collapse of the Hyatt Hotel. After her career in journalism, she worked as the creative director for a direct marketing advertising agency, specializing in business-to-business, high-technology campaigns. Currently, she is the founder and director of Timbrels Through Torah, a women's institute of Jewish learning in Westlake Village, California. She lives in Calabasas with her husband and three teenaged children.

"I have wanted to become a rabbi since I was a teen. Not too long ago, I found a diary from when I was about twelve years old. The title of the diary was, 'Notes from the Rabbi Lynne.' The glitch was that the Conservative movement was not ordaining women at the time I graduated from university. So, I had to choose another path."

Rabbi Zoe Klein is an author, a poet, and a rabbi. She was ordained by the Hebrew Union College–Jewish Institute of Religion in 1998, having pursued the rabbinate out of a passion for ancient texts, mythology, and sermonic, liturgical, and poetical forms. Currently, Rabbi Klein serves Temple Isaiah in Los Angeles as associate rabbi.

"Whether watching rain streak moonlit lines across my window, or tears well and spill in my mirror, since childhood I've stood in wonder of creation. I chose the rabbinate in order to devote myself to the service of the One Who gave me breath. I chose the rabbinate because I wanted to offer the days of my life and my deeds toward humankind as my sincerest prayer of gratitude to God."

Rabbi Myriam Klotz graduated from the Reconstructionist Rabbinical College in 1999. Rabbi Klotz is on the faculty at the Rabbinic Program for the Spirituality Institute, is cofounder and codirector of the Torah Yoga Institute at Elat Chayyim Jewish Retreat Center, and teaches courses on Judaism and Healing. She is the first out lesbian editor for the forthcoming Reconstructionist Rabbi's Manual. Rabbi Klotz is rabbinic supervisor for internship programs at the Reconstructionist Rabbinical College (RRC), is a Spiritual Director at the RRC, and was the founding rabbinic director of the Kimmel-Spiller Jewish Healing Center of the Jewish Family Service of Delaware.

"I decided to become a rabbi in the early '90s after a circuitous process that began when I was a teenager along with my quest for connection with God and my roots. I was lucky to have had mentors who guided me. There were several important influences, including my high school English teacher David Purdum, who first took my spiritual journey seriously and helped to provide meaningful language and framework to articulate it; Dr. David Blumenthal, who likewise took time out of a busy life to nurture sensitively and lovingly my curiosity and hunger for greater depth of knowledge and spiritual connection with God, through Jewish tradition; Rabbi Hershel Matt, *z"l*, who encouraged me greatly to pursue the rabbinic path and who, by his sensitivity, humility, and *menschlichkeit*, was a model; Dr. Judith Plaskow, who believed in my potential and helped to guide and articulate the feminist lens, which was central to integrity and staying power for my rabbinic aspirations; and Emilie Conrad, founder of Continuum, who helped teach me about the sacredness of the oceanic."

Rabbi Alison B. Kobey received her undergraduate degree from Tufts University and her master's and rabbinic ordination, *smichah*, from the Hebrew Union College–Jewish Institute of Religion in Cincinnati in 2000. She currently serves as associate rabbi and director of lifelong Jewish learning at Temple B'rith Kodesh in Rochester, New York, and is a member of various local and regional boards, including the Center for Youth and the New York State Concerned Clergy for Choice.

"My home rabbi, Henry Zoob, told me that I should become a rabbi at my Bat Mitzvah ceremony. At the time, I laughed out loud, thinking it could not be more different from my own ideas. At my confirmation ceremony, Rabbi Zoob again commented that I should be a rabbi and, again, I smiled with amusement. But he knew more about me than I did about myself. At Tufts University and upon meeting Rabbi Sharon Cohen-Anisfeld, I decided to seriously explore the rabbinate. It became the perfect occupation for me, combining my many loves and passions into one profession."

Rabbi Elisa Koppel is the dean of Jewish life at the American Hebrew Academy, a Jewish, pluralistic boarding school in Greensboro, North Carolina. Previously, she served as the assistant rabbi at the Community Synagogue in Port Washington, New York. She was ordained by the Hebrew Union College–Jewish Institute of Religion in New York in 2001. She was raised in a family where Judaism was very important, and became Jewishly active from a young age, attending Camp Harlam both as a camper and counselor and being active in synagogue life at Temple Emanu El in Westfield, New Jersey. As an active member of NFTY (the North American Federation of Temple Youth), she began to meet a number of rabbis, all of whom influenced her Judaism. Rabbi Charles Kroloff, her home rabbi, was one of the greatest of these influences, and continues to serve as a mentor.

"Somewhere in the back of my mind, I knew from high school that I wanted to be a rabbi. I knew so many wonderful people who were rabbis, and saw in the rabbinate the realization of many aspects of life that appealed to me. I didn't fully realize the idea, though, until shortly after my graduation from Brandeis University, while I was working for the Youth Division of the UAHC."

Rabbi Danielle Leshaw is the rabbi and executive director of Hillel at Ohio University in southeastern Ohio. She graduated from and was ordained by the Reconstructionist Rabbinical College in Philadelphia in 2002.

"I'm a Hillel rabbi because of my own college experience. Rabbi Barton Lee of Arizona State University, and his family—Marcie, Nira, and Noam—encouraged me to strengthen my Jewish identity and consider a life of Jewish service and study."

Rabbi Valerie Lieber was ordained by the Hebrew Union College–Jewish Institute of Religion in 1995. She served as rabbi and educator of Temple Beth Ahavath Sholom in Brooklyn for seven years and currently is the first woman rabbi of Temple Israel of Jamaica in Queens, New York. In addition to teaching, Rabbi Lieber has spent much of her time on social justice issues in the New York metropolitan area.

"I decided to become a rabbi as a student at Swarthmore College, a devoutly secular institution. Largely cut off from Jewish practice during those years, I realized just how central being Jewish was to my identity. I had encountered women rabbis growing up, and was particularly inspired by Rabbi Amy Perlin, who served as a student rabbi in a small congregation where my family spent the summers. My goal was to make the Reform Judaism I loved relevant to my generation."

Rabbi Vicki Lieberman received her B.A. from Columbia University, and her M.A. in Judaic studies and rabbinical ordination from the Jewish Theological Seminary of America in 1993. She served as the first woman rabbi at a pulpit in Woonsocket, Rhode Island. She has been an editor of a Behrman House textbook and currently writes and edits curricula for several St. Louis Jewish schools. Rabbi Lieberman and her husband, Cantor Robert Lieberman, have two children, Tovah and Joshua.

"I knew becoming a rabbi would enable me to learn and to teach Judaism and be involved in the spiritual, educational, and emotional growth of a community. Being a community educator enables me to be home more with my children."

Rabbi Jessica Locketz was ordained by the Hebrew Union College–Jewish Institute of Religion in 1999. As a student rabbi, she served congregations in Beckley, West Virginia; Paducah, Kentucky; and Lombard, Illinois. Following the completion of her studies, she spent three years at Rodef Shalom Congregation in Pittsburgh, where one of her favorite activities was singing with the preschool students. When not singing, Rabbi Locketz spent her time making connections and building relationships within the congregation and the greater Jewish community—two of the things she enjoys most as a rabbi. She is currently serving as associate rabbi of Beth El Hebrew Congregation in Alexandria, Virginia.

"As a high school student and a member of NFTY [the North American Federation of Temple Youth], I was voted by my region as 'the most likely to become a rabbi' for two years in a row. Of course, I did not take the end of the year superlatives seriously, but perhaps the recognition by my peers of my love for Judaism planted the seed for my future in the rabbinate. As a rabbi, I feel extremely fortunate that my life's work allows me to do what I love—being Jewish! It also affords me the opportunity to share that love of tradition and ritual with others. I get to help create sacred moments. I am thankful for every chance I receive to help bring God's presence into our lives."

Rabbi Nina H. Mandel is a 2003 graduate of the Reconstructionist Rabbinical College. She is currently the rabbi of Congregation Beth El in Sunbury, Pennsylvania. She also holds a master's degree in anthropology from New York University and prior to studying for the rabbinate worked as a consultant to community development agencies in New York City and Vermont. Her article, "Spirituality, Baking and the Queen of Heaven," appeared in the Fall 2002 issue of *Nashim*.

"One reason I decided to become a rabbi is that I am a woman and I have nephews. I know that my nieces will get all the support they need to grow up without limitations because of their gender. On the other hand, I want my nephews to know that there is a place for women in spiritual leadership roles in the Jewish world. I want all of them to be able to say, "My aunt is a rabbi" not "My aunt is a woman rabbi."

Rabbi Vivian (Vivie) Mayer was raised in a modern Orthodox home in New York. She lived in Israel and in North Carolina, where she was a teacher of Torah. She attended the Reconstructionist Rabbinical College, completing her education there and receiving ordination in 1996. Since then she has been teaching and serving a Conservative congregation in Danbury, Connecticut.

"I chose to be a rabbi because I feel I have access to a rich and beautiful language that not everybody understands. In my work I see myself as a translator, interpreting ancient wisdom into contemporary language, as well as interpreting contemporary wisdom and discoveries back into a Jewish framework. I was most influenced to take this path by my rabbi in Durham, North Carolina, Steve Sager, who gave me a glimpse into what I could become. I was most supported and encouraged by my life-partner Danny Deutsch, who has been a most honest friend, walking with me along the challenging path of truth."

Rabbi Rachel Leila Miller is a Conservative rabbi currently serving as the educational director of Congregation B'nai Shalom in Walnut Creek, California. In 2001, she was ordained by the Ziegler School of Rabbinic Studies, at the University of Judaism. Rabbi Miller is an avid knitter, reader, and writer, who dabbles in yoga.

"I was initially lured into the rabbinate by a love of text study. At the time, I was studying film theory and criticism and realized that I wanted to use those skills to examine an infinitely more important text—the Torah. Once I arrived at rabbinical school, I slowly realized a deeper motivation: I want to share with others the sanctuary with which Judaism and Jewish community have provided me in my life's struggles."

Rabbi Michelle Missaghieh, the daughter of a Persian-Jewish man and a New York woman, is most likely the first Persian female rabbi. She attended the University of Michigan in Ann Arbor, where she graduated with honors in women's studies and Judaic studies, and the Hebrew Union College–Jewish Institute of Religion, where she was ordained as a rabbi in 1996. She has worked at the Jewish Community Center in Manhattan and, since 1996, has been the associate rabbi at Temple Israel of Hollywood in Los Angeles. Rabbi Missaghieh is married to Bruce Ellman, and they are the proud parents of two daughters, Jael and Sivan.

"When I was a teenager I quickly found my calling in life. I remember the excitement and comfort I felt when I entered my synagogue, engaged in Jewish textual learning on youth group retreats, and talked to my rabbi about his work as a counselor, teacher, and leader. Yet it wasn't until I was in college and interned at the Union of American Hebrew Congregations in New York that I met a rabbi who was an attractive woman, married with two children, and a professional, that I understood that my dream could be a reality. What I didn't know then, but experience now, is the deep sense of honor I feel when fellow Jews open their hearts and souls to me in times of joy and crises. This is a gift that impacts my growth as a human being in endless ways."

Rabbi Nancy Rita Myers was ordained by the Hebrew Union College–Jewish Institute of Religion in New York in 1997. Her rabbinical thesis was a translation, together with Dr. Martin Cohen, of the Renaissance philosopher Elijah del Medigo's work *Behinat Hadat: Understanding the Religion.* Since her ordination, she served for six years as the associate rabbi of Temple Chai in Long Grove, Illinois. One of her passions is teaching and creating adult programming. At present, Rabbi Myers is taking a year to teach and work on a novel featuring the judge Deborah. She is married to Paul Prunty and they have two children, Gabriel and Shane Myers Prunty.

"My rabbi growing up, Joseph Herzog, was the one who introduced me to the rabbinate. He encouraged my questions, skepticism, and enthusiasm and thus fostered in me a great love for our tradition. It was his teachings, as well as the love of my family, that ultimately led me to become a rabbi. I feel blessed by my profession and the encouragement of so many wonderful people around me."

Rabbi Sheryl Nosan-Blank, R.J.E., was ordained by the New York campus of the Hebrew Union College–Jewish Institute of Religion in 1993. Sheryl serves

Temple Beth Torah in Granada Hills, California, where she is the congregation's first female rabbi. She was also the first female rabbi to serve Congregation Har Zion in suburban Toronto and Congregation Beth Am in Teaneck, New Jersey. At each of her congregations, Rabbi Nosan-Blank has focused on Jewish education. Her ongoing studies include Hasidic literature, Bible, and woman's issues, as well as classical texts.

"I decided to become a rabbi during my college years when I realized that I wanted to continue learning and teaching that which I was most passionate about: Judaism. But that's not all. Growing up in a small town without a rabbi or a real religious school, I always felt that I missed out on Jewish learning. Later, I overcompensated by going to rabbinical school! My greatest Jewish influences were my parents. My father taught me to read Hebrew and my mother taught me to light candles and say blessings. I continue to spend each Shabbat and holiday that I can with my parents, who were so influential in my becoming a rabbi and have filled my life with blessings."

Rabbi Debra Orenstein was ordained by the Jewish Theological Seminary in 1990. She is the author or editor of six books, including the award-winning Lifecycles book series: *Lifecycles 1: Jewish Women on Life Passages and Personal Milestones*; *Lifecycles 2: Jewish Women on Biblical Themes in Contemporary Life*; and the forthcoming *Lifecycles 3: Jewish Women on Holy Days and Communal Celebrations*. Rabbi Orenstein is spiritual leader of Makom Ohr Shalom, a synagogue in Tarzana, California, celebrating traditions of Jewish meditation and spirituality. She is also an accomplished actress, an instructor at the University of Judaism, and a renowned teacher and scholar-in-residence across North America. Her rabbinate represents both the inherited tradition and its flexibility in every age. A seventh-generation rabbi, she is also an alumna of the Jewish Theological Seminary's first class to include women.

"I decided to go into the family business and become a rabbi at age eight, before women were being ordained, when I had the pleasure of teaching my fourth-grade Bible class. The teacher, Mr. Rachman, encouraged anyone who got 100 percent on the Bible homework to lead the class, and I ended up teaching for a good portion of the year. My father set a wonderful example as a rabbi, and also recruited my sister and me to lead Junior Congregation. Through no merit of my own, I absorbed early and effortlessly the deep love for Jews and Judaism that my family showed and spread. I dedicate my essay to my beloved friend and mentor, Dr. Elieser Slomovic, whose scholarship, teaching, and shining goodness are a gift to the world."

Rabbi Melinda Panken was ordained by the Hebrew Union College–Jewish Institute of Religion in 1996 and is currently the senior rabbi of Temple Shaari Emeth in Manalapan, New Jersey. She spent the early years of her life at the Stephen Wise Free Synagogue in New York City, where Rabbi Sally Preisand served as the first ordained woman rabbi.

"I feel blessed to have been part of the first generation to grow up assuming that women could and should be rabbis. Rabbi Preisand, and those who followed in her footsteps, inspired me to pursue my path as a rabbi and leader for the Jewish people."

Rabbi Barbara Rosman Penzner graduated from the Reconstructionist Rabbinical College in 1987. She serves as rabbi of Temple Hillel B'nai Torah in West Roxbury, Massachusetts, and is a founding board member of Mayyim Hayyim: Living Waters Mikveh and Education Center, in the Boston area. Following two years in Israel as a Jerusalem fellow, Rabbi Penzner served as president of the Reconstructionist Rabbinical Association. Rabbi Penzner's essay is dedicated to the memory of Janis Ruth Coulter, z"l, one of her students. Janis was killed in a terrorist attack at the Hebrew University of Jerusalem on July 31, 2002, the day the first draft of this manuscript was completed. Janis was a student of the Book of Ruth, with whom she identified as a Jew by Choice. May her memory be a blessing.

"Never having met a woman rabbi until 1980, I was drawn to the rabbinate as a means of combining my love of Jewish learning and observance with my desire to bring new meanings to Jewish thought and tradition. I have found great satisfaction in combining the calling of rabbi with the joys of being mother to Aviva and Yonah and partner to Brian Rosman."

Rabbi Hara E. Person is the editorial director of the UAHC Press. Ordained by the Hebrew Union College–Jewish Institute of Religion in 1998, she is a Phi Beta Kappa graduate of Amherst College and holds an M.A. in fine arts from New York University/International Center of Photography. Rabbi Person teaches at many synagogues and conferences, and coleads an ongoing Shabbat morning Torah study group. She has had essays published in several books, including in *The Women's Torah Commentary* (Jewish Lights), and is the coeditor, along with Rabbi Richard Address, of *That You May Live Long: Caring for Aging Parents, Caring for Ourselves*. Rabbi Person lives in Brooklyn with her husband and two children.

"I am a first-generation Reform Jew, and was the first girl in my congregation to wear a tallit when I became Bat Mitzvah. I decided to become a rabbi when I was around eleven, because my rabbi was one of the only people I knew at that time who was outwardly proud to be Jewish and knowledgeable about Judaism. I remember being told that the first woman had just become a rabbi, and being stunned because I had never realized that I *couldn't* become one. I changed my mind several times, and spent a while living in Israel and going to art school before my head realized what my heart already knew—that I wanted to be a rabbi and use my skills and my passion for the good of the Jewish community and the future of Judaism."

Rabbi Marsha J. Pik-Nathan, Ph.D., lives in the Mount Airy section of Philadelphia. Rabbi Pik-Nathan earned her doctorate in clinical psychology from Washington University in St. Louis in 1987, and graduated from the

Reconstructionist Rabbinical College where she was ordained in 1996. Rabbi Pik-Nathan has held a variety of rabbinic positions, including directing the Hillel Program at Bryn Mawr, Haverford, and Swarthmore Colleges; congregational work; and geriatric chaplaincy for Jewish Family and Children's Services. Currently, she divides her time among caring for her three children—Shira, Eitana, and Noah—a private practice in psychology, teaching in academic settings and at the Melton Adult Mini School in Philadelphia, and working with rabbinical students at the Reconstructionist Rabbinical College as a spiritual director.

"I was inspired to study for the rabbinate by the role model of a woman who served as my Hillel rabbi in graduate school. While I had always been in awe of my (male) congregational rabbi during childhood, I had not seen the rabbinate as a path for me until I saw a woman in that role. Studying for the rabbinate allowed me to deepen and expand my work with people, adding the rich layers of Judaism and thereby becoming involved in the many joys and rhythms of people's lives. I am grateful for the opportunities that allowed me to realize this dream."

Rabbi Amber Powers serves as rabbi of Temple Menorah Keneseth Chai in northeast Philadelphia and is the Mid-Atlantic Regional Director for the Jewish Reconstructionist Federation. She was ordained by the Reconstructionist Rabbinical College in 2002 and holds a B.A. degree in Jewish studies from Emory University. She is an alumna of the Wexner Fellowship Program for Jewish Professionals.

"I was deeply involved in a Jewish youth group (BBYO) in high school. Though our local activities were primarily social, the summer programs I attended gave me a chance to experience a vibrant Jewish religious life filled with spirited communal prayer, keeping kosher, Torah study, and observing Shabbat. I returned home knowing that I wanted to continue to live a more fully Jewish life. That desire led me to become a Jewish studies major in college. When friends and mentors began suggesting that I go to rabbinical school, I was both excited and intimidated. I soon decided to take my mother's advice: 'Don't pick a career that you'll be just good at. Do something that you have a passion for and will love doing.' I feel blessed to have found that in the rabbinate."

Rabbi Geela Rayzel Raphael was ordained by the Reconstructionist Rabbinical College in 1997. A Wexner graduate fellow, she has also studied at Indiana University, Brandeis, Pardes, and Hebrew University. Currently she is the rabbinic director of Faithways, an Interfaith Family Support with JFCS Philadelphia, and consults with the Jewish Women's Spirituality Institute of the Bux-Mont JCC. Rabbi Raphael is a songwriter/liturgist and sings with MIRAJ, an a cappella trio. "Bible Babes A-beltin'" is Rayzel's solo recording. She is a member of two Jewish women's feminist collaboratives—B'not Aish and Achayot Or. She is a devout Rosh Chodesh celebrant. Rabbi Raphael teaches classes on biblical women, new rituals, angels, Rosh Chodesh, wild Jewish women, spirituality, and power. She used a medium to conjure up the Witch of Endor to help her write this piece.

"My journey to the rabbinate was a progressive one. I had been active in Jewish communal activities since my teenage years—in BBYO [B'nei B'rith Youth Organization] and Hillel at the Indiana University. This led to my first master's degree from Brandeis in Jewish communal service. From there I headed to Toronto to become a Hillel director at York University for eleven years (the first female). After a sabbatical year at Pardes in Jerusalem, I realized my love for Torah and Israel and could not ignore the 'still, small voice' that was urging me to go to rabbinical school. Stranded in a village in Thailand after an overland trek, I bartered with God—'Save me and I will go to rabbinical school.' I once had a dream where I was being called to serve as 'Priestess to Shekhinah,' and this has become my soul's mission."

Rabbi Laura M. Rappaport juggles her duties as chaplain resident at St. Luke's Regional Medical Center and Idaho Elks' Rehabilitation Hospital in Boise, Idaho; rabbi for Congregation Kol Shalom in Bainbridge Island, Washington; and mother of Tanya (12) and Rosa (9) Fink. She derives great pleasure from these pursuits, as she does from living and thriving in beautiful Boise, her beloved home for the past decade.

"There is nothing sadder to me than speaking with people who regret their choice of career and long to be able to start all over again. I am immensely blessed to serve in a role that has never failed to satisfy the deepest longings of my heart: to learn, to teach, and to preach about Judaism as a rabbi. From my earliest years, Jewish wisdom has touched my soul with its vibrancy, its wit, its pragmatism, and its love of life and humanity. My most spiritual moments have occurred when singing Hebrew songs, when touching the Torah scroll, when sharing Eastern European foods with relatives in my grandparents' Bronx apartment, when reading a poignant and relevant insight from an eight-hundred-year-old rabbinic text, or when laughing at the terrible, annual family jokes during Pesach seder. This has never been a job. Being a rabbi is part and parcel of my very being."

Rabbi Rochelle Robins was ordained by the Hebrew Union College–Jewish Institute of Religion in 1998. She is cofounder and currently serves as executive director of Bat Kol: A Feminist House of Study, which began as the first feminist yeshiva in Jerusalem. In addition to offering Jewish feminist text study in diverse communities, Rabbi Robins is beginning a new Bat Kol project called InterActions, an interfaith study program for adults in the United States who are interested in cross-cultural coalition-building ventures. Rabbi Robins is also a supervisor in training in clinical pastoral education. At present, she serves as a chaplain supervisor for Catholic Health East at Holy Redeemer Hospital in Huntingdon Valley, Pennsylvania.

"My first influence into the rabbinate was my father, *z"l*, who was also an HUC–JIR graduate. My parents and grandparents have handed down a true prophetic vision of Judaism that upholds social action, human values, and tradition as a means toward perfecting the world. Whether I am teaching biblical or rabbinic text, writing grants, providing pastoral care, or supervising chaplains, my rabbinate at its core is focused on the continual opportunity each one of us is provided to create a life of wholeness and health. 'In God's goodness, God continually renews the act of creation.' As beings created in the image of God, we have the ability to cocreate with God and renew our lives at each moment. This is the essence of both my own learning and teaching."

Rachel Jacoby Rosenfield earned her master's degree in comparative literature from UC–Berkeley, with a focus on ancient and modern Hebrew literature. Her studies included several years in Israel, as a volunteer on OTZMA, at the Pardes Institute, and at Hebrew University in Jerusalem. She is a Jewish educator and has taught extensively in the San Francisco Bay Area, as a graduate student at UC–Berkeley where she won awards for "teaching excellence," and in the New York metropolitan area. She also worked as the Judaic studies coordinator at the Brandeis Hillel Day School in Northern California, where she designed curricula and programs to inspire children and their families to engage in text study. She lives in Riverdale, New York, with her husband Paul and her children Maayan and Yonah.

Rabbi Deborah J. Schloss was ordained by the Jewish Theological Seminary of America in 1996 and currently works at the Emery/Weiner School in Houston. She was the first full-time female Conservative pulpit rabbi in Canada, at Congregation Shaarey Zedek in Winnipeg, Manitoba (for the "frozen chosen"), and was also an assistant rabbi at Congregation Beth Yeshurun in Houston. She holds a double master's degree in Jewish communal service and public administration from Hebrew Union College–Jewish Institute of Religion and the University of Southern California. She lives with the two loves of her life, her wonderfully supportive husband Sheldon and their precious daughter Priya.

"I first considered the rabbinate as a career during my senior year of undergraduate studies at Brandeis University, sensing it would enable me to live a meaningful life and integrate my passions for Jewish learning, God, being available to others, mysticism, asking ultimate life questions, and social action within one rubric. I continually appreciate the uniquely challenging and spiritually satisfying path that I've been directed to sometimes follow and other times lead."

Rabbi Ilene Schneider, Ed.D., a 1976 graduate of the Reconstructionist Rabbinical College in Philadelphia, was one of the first six women ordained as rabbis in the United States. She earned her bachelor's degree from Simmons College and her master's and doctoral degrees in education from Temple University. She resides in Marlton, New Jersey, with her husband, Rabbi Gary M. Gans, and their sons, Natan and Ari.

"I was participating in a communal dinner on an Erev Shabbat in the fall of 1969, my senior year of college, when one of my friends mentioned that the

Reconstructionist movement had opened a rabbinical school the previous year. That chance comment opened before me a wealth of possibilities I'd never before considered. The decision I made that evening was one that helped me define who I was and how I could best serve the Jewish community."

Rabbi Beth L. Schwartz was born and raised in Philadelphia. She received her B.A. degree in history from the State University of New York at Binghamton and an M.Ed. in guidance and counseling from George Mason University in Fairfax, Virginia. After working as a consultant to the U.S. Department of Education and as a systems analyst for the Federal Home Loan Mortgage Corporation, she attended the Hebrew Union College–Jewish Institute of Religion in Cincinnati, where she received a M.A.H.L. degree and was ordained in 1999. Prior to attending rabbinical school, she was a longtime member, teacher, and served as president of Temple Ner Shalom in Woodbridge, Virginia. Rabbi Schwartz currently serves as rabbi of Temple Beth El in Knoxville, Tennessee. She is a member of the executive committee of the Knoxville Ministerial Association, a member of the board of the Knoxville Region of the National Conference for Community and Justice, and a founding member of the Clergy Task Force on Family Violence in Knoxville. Rabbi Schwartz is married to Larry Washington. They have two grown children, Leah Washington-Lofgren and Daniel Washington.

"I chose the rabbinate after many years of active membership and leadership positions in congregational life. I grew into the role of spiritual leadership through the necessity of congregational circumstances, encouraged by Rabbis Judith Z. Abrams and Jonathan R. Katz, who helped me to realize who I was becoming, and who I could be. The rabbinate allows me to combine my strengths as teacher, preacher, *shelicha tzibbur*, and writer in ever-changing, ever-growing, and ever-interesting ways."

Rabbi Rona Shapiro is a rabbi and educator who currently serves as a senior associate at Ma'yan: The Jewish Women's Project, a program of the JCC in Manhattan. She is the creative director and editor of ritualwell.org, a Web site for new, innovative Jewish ritual, which was recently nominated for the prestigious Webby award. Previously, she served for ten years as the executive director of Berkeley (CA) Hillel. She has also written and published numerous articles. Rabbi Shapiro was ordained by the Jewish Theological Seminary in 1990, among the first classes of Conservative women rabbis. She resides with her husband and their two daughters, Noa and Hallel, in Brooklyn.

"I believe that Jewish feminism, through the creation of new ritual, the reexamination of theology and God language, and the empowerment of women as rabbis and leaders in the Jewish community, has transformed the Jewish landscape over the last thirty years. I believe that the Judaism of the future, in which our daughters and granddaughters are fully empowered as leaders and changemakers, will look vastly different from the Judaism we know. We are privileged to live in such exciting times."

About the Contributors

Rabbi Chana Thompson Shor was ordained by the Jewish Theological Seminary in 1995. She grew up in Boulder, Colorado, and earned her B.A. in religion from Swarthmore College in Pennsylvania. Currently, she is a Ph.D. candidate in the Department of Bible and Ancient Semitic Languages, also at JTS, and the mother of twin boys. Her rabbinic work in the past two years has been primarily online; she is a teacher of Bible for JTS's Kaminer Distance Learning Center, and has researched/written/edited content for its online Bible courses. She completed a full cycle of online teaching of Tanakh as the rabbi/scholar-in-residence for the United Synagogue of Conservative Judaism's Perek Yomi listserv, and, most recently, she joined the editing staff of MyJewishLearning.com.

"When I was in college, I met a woman who was planning to apply to HUC, which greatly inspired me. At the time, I was newly interested in Judaism (having been raised a good Secular Humanist), but already gravitating toward the Conservative movement—which was not yet, though as it turned out, was about to begin, ordaining women. The impracticality of considering ordination was no particular deterrent to my interest at the time, however, and I spent a good part of my college career exploring and researching the role of women in Judaism. Post-college, I worked for a Hillel rabbi, and his good, practical example and influence served as a catalyst as well. At first I entered the Jewish Theological Seminary as a graduate student, but ultimately entered the rabbinical school, and, postordination, have continued there to work on a Ph.D. in Bible. In addition to working as a teacher of Bible and an editor, I am also preoccupied at the moment with the gestation of twin girls (our second set of twins; the first set, Shaul and Ephraim, just turned three). I see, as the primary objective of my rabbinate, the incorporation and translation of critical methods of biblical study into a modern (religious/spiritual) Jewish context."

Rabbi Amy Joy Small has been the rabbi of Congregation Beth Hatikvah in Chatham, New Jersey, since 1997. She was ordained by the Reconstructionist Rabbinical College (RRC) in 1987. She holds an M.A. from RRC and an M.A. in education from Villanova University. She has served the Reconstructionist Rabbinical Association (RRA) as secretary, treasurer, board member-at-large, and first vice president, and she currently serves as president of the Association. She is past chairperson of the Jewish Reconstructionist Federation (JRF) Education Commission, has served on the national board of the Coalition for the Advancement of Jewish Education (CAJE) and chaired conferences for CAJE (Delaware Valley Regional Educators' Conference), JRF (Educators' Conference), and the RRA (national convention). Rabbi Small was also the president of Planned Parenthood of Southwestern Michigan. She has served on the editorial board of *Machshavot*, the Journal of the Chicago Board of Rabbis. Rabbi Small was previously the dean of academic administration and director of the education program at the RRC, the rabbi of Temple B'nai Shalom in Benton Harbor, Michigan, and B'nai Yisrael Reconstructionist Congregation, in South Bend, Indiana. Prior to that, Rabbi Small was the education director for religious schools in Margate, New Jersey; Broomall, Pennsylvania; and Vineland, New Jersey.

"I decided to become a rabbi in the summer of 1972 when I was fourteen years old, as soon as I learned of the first ordination of a woman at HUC that spring. (Thank you, Sally Preisand and Sandy Sasso, for paving the way!) It was a circuitous journey for a while, as my family and rabbis were not supportive. Unfortunately, the phenomenon of female rabbis was still so new and "radical" to them that even the rabbis I knew regarded my interest in the rabbinate as little more than a source of amusement. I was strongly encouraged to train to be a Jewish educator instead. Fortunately, I followed my heart, and after a brief and successful entry into a career in Jewish education, I pursued rabbinical training. I am most proud to be raising my three children in this generation. Now that we have crossed this and many other gender divides, my sons and my daughter can all freely follow their hearts with support and encouragement. Now, when I say something one of my teenagers may consider wise, but not something they wanted to hear, they are wont to reply, 'Oh, Imma, you are such a rabbi!' What greater joy could there be?"

Rabbi Karen Soria was ordained in 1981 by the Hebrew Union College–Jewish Institute of Religion in Cincinnati. Within a month of ordination, she was overseas, serving at Temple Beth Israel, in Melbourne, as Australia's first female rabbi. Returning to the States after eight years, she served Congregation Beth Shalom in Winter Haven, Florida, and was the founding rabbi of Bat Yam-Temple of the Islands, on Sanibel Island. In 1992 Rabbi Soria became the second female rabbi on active duty in the Navy, and over the next four years she became the first to be stationed overseas (in Okinawa, Japan), to serve and be deployed with a Marine unit, and to serve at CREDO, the Navy's retreat ministry. Upon her return stateside, Rabbi Soria served at the historic Commodore Levy Chapel and later the Naval Medical Center in Norfolk, Virginia. She was the director of CREDO Norfolk, the first female chaplain to be appointed to that position since the program's inception in 1971, and at present she is taking a sabbatical—walking the dog, pulling up carpet, gardening, kayaking, renewing her soul—and finding her place in the Jewish community of Victoria.

"Rabbis Samuel Sandmel and Theodore Levy inspired me to become a rabbi. They believed in me and encouraged me. I wanted to learn and to teach, to invite others into the treasures of Judaism that I had found. I wanted to emulate my namesake, Yocheved, whose teaching and love inspired her son Moses. Over the years I have discovered, as the Hasidic folk tale tells, that the most precious and unexpected wonders lie within each of us. We, too, are the burning bush, and the ground of our being is holy."

Rabbi Wendy Spears was ordained by the Hebrew Union College–Jewish Institute of Religion in 1991. After serving congregations for three years, she established a freelance rabbinic practice serving unaffiliated Jews in the Los Angeles area. She has learned sign language to aid in outreach to deaf Jews. She also teaches regularly on Judaism, spirituality, and feminist issues, in addition to being a full-time wife and mother. Her original midrash on Rachel and Leah was published in the summer 1997 issue of the CCAR *Journal,* commemorating twenty-five years of women in the rabbinate.

"My decision to become a rabbi was influenced by two Hillel rabbis who were my teachers during my college years, Rabbis Laura Geller and Patricia Karlin-Neumann. They opened my eyes to the feminist issues within Judaism and helped me understand that change can occur within a community by those who are patient and steadfast. Their joy and love for Judaism coincided with my own; their inspired teaching and heartfelt examples of living Judaism made a career in the rabbinate seem possible and fulfilling. It has been a meaningful and joyful journey."

Rabbi Carol E. Stein was ordained in 1999 by the Jewish Theological Seminary in New York after beginning her studies at the University of Judaism in 1992. After practicing law in Sacramento, California, for fourteen years, this eager student sought more advanced Jewish learning. She completed four units of CPE and, following her first experience of conducting a baptism together with a Christian clergyperson, in a hospital's neonatal intensive care unit, wrote an article published in the *Journal of Pastoral Care* (Winter 2001).

"I felt an overwhelming urge to study Torah in all its amazing facets. My seminary education was the beginning of that. I cannot say that I *chose* the rabbinate, because it was the learning that hooked me and the teaching that keeps me. I am currently involved extensively in adult education and am delighted with the need to keep learning in order to teach."

Rabbi Margot Stein is an award-winning singer-songwriter with five CDs of original Jewish music to her credit. Co-recipient of a Philadelphia Federation Continuity Grant to develop Friday Night Alive! with her musical troupe, "Shabbat Unplugged," Rabbi Stein composes and performs with the female a cappella trio, MIRAJ, and teaches Jewish ethics at the Florence Melton Adult Mini-School. A founding member of Kolot: The Center for Jewish Women's and Gender Studies at the Reconstructionist Rabbinical College, she has served on the center's board since its inception.

"I became a rabbi as part of my quest to bring the transformative, healing, and connective powers of music and liturgy to the Jewish people. Many of us, having experienced a distant, often alienating Judaism in our youth, seek a more joyous, immanent experience of God. The voice can be like wings upon which our soul soars. In particular, I have become deeply committed to helping women free our voices and find hidden parts of ourselves, bringing this new authenticity and authority into Jewish life."

Rabbi Andrea Carol Steinberger is a daughter and granddaughter of Holocaust survivors and a first-generation American. She was ordained in 1997 by the Hebrew Union College–Jewish Institute of Religion in Cincinnati. Upon graduation, she served as rabbi at Temple Israel in Columbus, Ohio—and was recognized by the Ohio State Senate as the first female rabbi in Columbus. Today she works as a rabbi at the Hillel at the University of Wisconsin in Madison. She is married to Greg Steinberger. They have two daughters, Abigail and Emma.

"I grew up in Cincinnati and was fortunate enough to learn from many rabbinical students, who were studying at the Hebrew Union College–Jewish Institute of Religion in Cincinnati, and were my Sunday School teachers and student interns at the Valley Temple. Rabbi Judith Z. Abrams and Rabbi Randi Musnitzky, in particular, were my role models as teachers and as women. I spent every summer possible at Goldman Union Camp Institute in Zionsville, Indiana, and learned how a rabbi can be a role model—even in the way he builds a campfire—from Rabbi Ronald Klotz. I am indebted to Rabbi Peter Knobel and Rabbi Eleanor Smith, at Beth Emet Synagogue in Evanston, Illinois, who cared for my family upon our move to Chicago, and to Rabbi Gary Zola, of HUC–JIR in Cincinnati, who urged me to teach religious school at Beth Emet, under the direction of Fran Pearlman, where I decided to become a rabbi."

Rabbi Shira Stern was ordained by the Hebrew Union College–Jewish Institute of Religion in New York in 1983, and spent fourteen years in the pulpit. She was named emerita of the Monroe Township (NJ) Jewish Center, when she retired. She was a cocoordinator of the Women's Rabbinic Network and served on the board of the Commission of Social Action. She has been an active social justice advocate in women's rights and human rights. In addition to her political activism in the pro-choice movement, she has been widely featured in the print and television media on a variety of topics and has taught courses at Rutgers University. She is a Certified Jewish Chaplain and is membership chair of the National Association of Jewish Chaplains. She has been a hospital and hospice chaplain, director of the Joint Chaplaincy Program of Greater Middlesex County (NJ) and is currently the director of the Jewish Institute for Pastoral Care in New York City, part of the HealthCare Chaplaincy.

"I became a rabbi to make an impact on my community on every level, from womb to tomb, wearing many hats and fulfilling a number of roles: teacher, counselor, cantorial soloist, storyteller, dreamer, and catalyst for change. My goal is twofold: to teach others to teach themselves and to refine my own skills so that my learning continues."

Rabbi Mira Wasserman was ordained by the Hebrew Union College–Jewish Institute of Religion in 1998 after undergraduate study at Barnard College, the Jewish Theological Seminary, and Hebrew University. Since her ordination, she has served as rabbi of Congregation Beth Shalom in Bloomington, Indiana. Her children's story, *Too Much of a Good Thing,* was published in 2003. She and her husband are raising two boys.

"For me, the rabbinate seemed the perfect fusion of text study and work with people. My four parents, Judy and Rabbi David Wortman, and Howard and Ricki Wasserman, provided models and encouragement."

Rabbi Pamela Wax was ordained by the Hebrew Union College–Jewish Institute of Religion in New York in 1994. Her rabbinical thesis was titled "The Daughters of Tzelophehad Revisited: The Daughter in Jewish Inheritance Law." She has served as a hospital chaplain, as a congregational rabbi, as an inveterate teacher of Introduction to Judaism classes in various venues, and as assistant director of the UAHC Department of Adult Jewish Growth, where she created adult education materials for the Reform movement. Currently, Rabbi Wax serves as the spiritual care coordinator for Westchester (NY) Jewish Community Services. Rabbi Wax is a writer of midrash and personal essay and the author of the chapter on *Parashat Pinchas,* "Daughters and Inheritance Law," in *The Women's Torah Commentary* (Jewish Lights).

"I decided to become a rabbi at a time when the convergence of my identity as a Jewish liturgist and prayer leader, as a writer, as a teacher, as a counselor, and as a feminist and social activist screamed out at me to be woven together into some meaningful whole. I consider my decision to become a rabbi to be my personal, metaphorical havdalah candle, a braiding together of varied talents, interests, and strands of self into a unified whole."

Rabbi Nancy Wechsler-Azen was ordained by the Hebrew Union College–Jewish Institute of Religion, New York campus, in 1990. Her rabbinical thesis is titled "Rabbinic Attitudes Toward Healing." She was the founding rabbi of Temple Kol Ami in Thornhill, Ontario. She has written and taught extensively on healing, Jewish spirituality, and feminism. She has published works in *Keeping Posted,* and *Reform Judaism,* and is a contributing author for *Life-Lights,* a publication of Jewish Lights, as well as *The Women's Torah Commentary* (Jewish Lights). She has served on the UAHC staff, been assistant director of the Commission on Religious Living, and taught for the National Center for Jewish Healing. She has initiated healing programming in synagogues throughout America and Canada. Rabbi Wechsler-Azen has been developing a curriculum in spiritual parenting and leads workshops. Her spiritual home is Congregation Beth Shalom in Carmichael, California, where she and her husband, Rabbi David Wechsler-Azen, share the pulpit. She has the privilege of parenting five wonderful children, Max, Sammy J., Aryeh, Eliza, and Lily.

"I started to take my spiritual calling seriously in my later years of college. Until then I had simply basked in Jewish communal life, having spent years and years at Jewish summer camps as camper, counselor, and songleader. My role models were rabbinical students who were simultaneously vibrant artists, lawyers, activists, dancers, and musicians. They demonstrated how spiritual vitality was the core for leading a pro-active life. I continue to find energy and joy through a blend of storytelling, counseling, teaching, and singing. As I find myself in my middle-aged years, more and more I seek peace as the essence of healing. These are the tools of my life in building and living in communities of participatory Judaism."

Rabbi Paula Jayne Winnig has served as the spiritual leader of Temple Sinai of Long Island in Lawrence, New York, since 1983. She has previously served congregations in Floral Park and Roslyn, New York; Los Angeles; and Auckland, New Zealand. She received her ordination from the Hebrew Union College–Jewish Institute of Religion in 1986 and her M.A.H.L. in 1983. She is an honors graduate from the University of Wisconsin–Madison, with a degree in political science. She also studied as a visiting graduate student to the Hebrew University's department of Talmud. She has been active in many community organizations and is the first female president of the New York Association of Reform Rabbis. She is the mother of two sons, Karmi and Shai Knight-Winnig.

"Growing up in Wausau, Wisconsin, my Jewish identity was formed both by the positive influence of my parents' insistence on creating a meaningful, active Jewish life, and the negative influence of living as a minority in a small town where most activities centered on the churches. I was fortunate that I always felt good about my Jewish connections and maximized them through my participation in the B'nai B'rith Youth Organization, which helped me see just how big the Jewish world really was and how many ways one could connect with it. As a lifelong social activist, I originally assumed I would become involved in international relations and work as a lawyer helping the downtrodden. While in college, however, I saw that there were plenty of people willing to save the world, but few who wished to help save, educate, and celebrate the *Jewish* world. I decided that I still wanted to save the world, but that I needed to do so from the center of the Jewish community. I also knew that I needed to expand my Jewish knowledge in order to properly serve our people. Becoming a rabbi gave me the opportunity to commingle all aspects of my life. I am able to live a fully Jewish life, serve our people, and help improve the world. I find each day deeply fulfilling and blessed by the opportunities I have been given to serve as a rabbi."

Rabbi Julie Wolkoff, D.Min., was ordained by the Hebrew Union College– Jewish Institute of Religion in New York in 1982. She received her doctor of ministry degree from HUC–JIR in 1996. She is the director of Judaic activities at Gann Academy–The New Jewish High School of Greater Boston in Waltham, Massachusetts. She previously served as the director of chaplaincy services for the United Jewish Federation of Northeastern New York. She also worked as an AIDS Care Team Coach for Eddy Visiting Nurse Services in Troy, New York. In that capacity she worked with seventeen church- and synagogue-based AIDS

Care Teams who provided nonmedical support services for HIV/AIDS patients and their households. Rabbi Wolkoff is a past president of the Capital District Board of Rabbis and a past chair of the City of Troy Commission on Human Rights. She served as a congregational rabbi for thirteen years and was extensively involved in pastoral and educational work.

"I decided to become a rabbi when I was sixteen. The desire came as a result of my youth group involvement, the example of the rabbis involved in regional youth group activities and my complete and utter fascination with Jewish texts."

Rabbi Hanna Gracia Yerushalmi was ordained in 1996 by the Hebrew Union College–Jewish Institute of Religion in Cincinnati. Upon graduation, she served as the first woman associate rabbi at Reform Congregation Beth Or in suburban Philadelphia for five years. She is married to Rabbi Ari Goldstein, and together they are raising their daughters Sela Shulamit and Nava Meira. Currently, Rabbi Yerushalmi works full-time as a mother and part-time editing and writing. She has the distinct honor of this "first": Her wedding on July 7, 2000, was the first in which a rabbi father-of-the-bride (Rabbi Isaac Yerushalmi) and a rabbi father-of-the-groom (Rabbi David Goldstein) officiated at the marriage ceremony of their children, the groom-rabbi and the bride-rabbi. This "first" even received a minor mention that auspicious morning on National Public Radio, when the "four rabbis" were referred to as a good name for a band!

"I was inspired to love and revere my Sephardic Jewish heritage by my parents, who were born and raised in Turkey. My two sisters and brother and I were taught to chant Shir HaShirim during Pesach, savor the taste of pomegranate at the New Year, and take deep pride in the scholarly achievements of our people. I consider myself a product of the Reform movement. I taught religious school in Cincinnati, attended a UAHC camp in Wisconsin, and was active in Hillel and the Judaic Studies Program at the University of Cincinnati. Becoming a rabbi is a natural extension of my love for the Jewish people and heritage. Along with the fulfillment I get from being a mother and wife, the rabbinate offers me the ultimate fulfillment of my life."

Rabbi Mary Lande Zamore was ordained by the Hebrew Union College–Jewish Institute of Religion in New York in 1997. Now an associate rabbi, she has served Temple Emanu-El of Westfield, New Jersey, since her last year of rabbinical school. She is a past editor of the CCAR Newsletter (2000–2001), has served on several CCAR committees, and is currently a member of the joint ACC-CCAR editorial board for a new officiant's manual. She has received fellowships from ARIL and the STAR Tech Foundation. Rabbi Zamore is the first fully functioning female *mashgihah*, overseeing a New Jersey bakery from 1997 to 2001. She is married to Dr. Terje Z. Lande and is the mother of two-year-old Aryeh.

"I am a fourth-generation Reform Jew whose family has always been religious and involved in the synagogue. I always knew that I would be an active layperson.

However, it did not occur to me to become a rabbi until I befriended a young man in college who wanted to become a Catholic priest. I never asked whether a woman could become a rabbi, because my parents always exposed me to women who broke gender barriers. I remember my father, a lawyer, taking me to meet a female judge when I was six years old. Rabbi Sally Priesand's name was lauded in our household. Yet Rabbi Helene Ferris, then serving at Stephen Wise Free Synagogue, was the first woman rabbi I ever saw in person on the bimah. It was inspirational."

Children's Books

Because Nothing Looks Like God
By Lawrence and Karen Kushner
What is God like? The first collaborative work by husband-and-wife team Lawrence and Karen Kushner introduces children to the possibilities of spiritual life. Real-life examples of happiness and sadness invite us to explore, together with our children, the questions we all have about God, no matter what our age.
11 x 8½, 32 pp, Full-color illus., Hardcover, ISBN 1-58023-092-X **$16.95** *For ages 4 & up*

Also Available: **Because Nothing Looks Like God Teacher's Guide**
8½ x 11, 22 pp, PB, ISBN 1-58023-140-3 **$6.95** *For ages 5–8*

Board Book Companions to *Because Nothing Looks Like God*
5 x 5, 24 pp, Full-color illus., SkyLight Paths Board Books, **$7.95** each *For ages 0–4*

What Does God Look Like? ISBN 1-893361-23-3
How Does God Make Things Happen? ISBN 1-893361-24-1
Where Is God? ISBN 1-893361-17-9

The 11th Commandment: Wisdom from Our Children
by The Children of America
"If there were an Eleventh Commandment, what would it be?" Children of many religious denominations across America answer this question—in their own drawings and words.
8 x 10, 48 pp, Full-color illus., Hardcover, ISBN 1-879045-46-X **$16.95** *For all ages*

Jerusalem of Gold: Jewish Stories of the Enchanted City
Retold by Howard Schwartz. Full-color illus. by Neil Waldman.
A beautiful and engaging collection of historical and legendary stories for children. Each celebrates the magical city that has served as a beacon for the Jewish imagination for three thousand years. Draws on Talmud, midrash, Jewish folklore, and mystical and Hasidic sources.
8 x 10, 64 pp, Full-color illus., Hardcover, ISBN 1-58023-149-7 **$18.95** *For ages 7 & up*

The Book of Miracles: A Young Person's Guide to Jewish Spiritual Awareness
By Lawrence Kushner. All-new illustrations by the author.
6 x 9, 96 pp, 2-color illus., Hardcover, ISBN 1-879045-78-8 **$16.95** *For ages 9–13*

In Our Image: God's First Creatures
By Nancy Sohn Swartz
9 x 12, 32 pp, Full-color illus., Hardcover, ISBN 1-879045-99-0 **$16.95** *For ages 4 & up*

From SKYLIGHT PATHS PUBLISHING

Becoming Me: A Story of Creation
By Martin Boroson. Full-color illus. by Christopher Gilvan-Cartwright.
Told in the personal "voice" of the Creator, a story about creation and relationship that is about each one of us. In simple words and with radiant illustrations, the Creator tells an intimate story about love, about friendship and playing, about our world—and about ourselves.
8 x 10, 32 pp, Full-color illus., Hardcover, ISBN 1-893361-11-X **$16.95** *For ages 4 & up*

Ten Amazing People: And How They Changed the World
By Maura D. Shaw. Foreword by Dr. Robert Coles. Full-color illus. by Stephen Marchesi.
Black Elk • Dorothy Day • Malcolm X • Mahatma Gandhi • Martin Luther King, Jr. • Mother Teresa • Janusz Korczak • Desmond Tutu • Thich Nhat Hanh • Albert Schweitzer • This vivid, inspirational, and authoritative book will open new possibilities for children by telling the stories of how ten of the past century's greatest leaders changed the world in important ways.
8½ x 11, 48 pp, Full-color illus., Hardcover, ISBN 1-893361-47-0 **$17.95** *For ages 7 & up*

Where Does God Live? By August Gold and Matthew J. Perlman
Using simple, everyday examples that children can relate to, this colorful book helps young readers develop a personal understanding of God.
10 x 8½, 32 pp, Full-color photo illus., Quality PB, ISBN 1-893361-39-X **$8.95** *For ages 3–6*

Children's Books
by Sandy Eisenberg Sasso

Adam & Eve's First Sunset: God's New Day

Engaging new story explores fear and hope, faith and gratitude in ways that will delight kids and adults—inspiring us to bless each of God's days and nights.

9 x 12, 32 pp, Full-color illus., Hardcover, ISBN 1-58023-177-2 **$17.95** *For ages 4 & up*

But God Remembered

Stories of Women from Creation to the Promised Land

Four different stories of women—Lillith, Serach, Bityah, and the Daughters of Z—teach us important values through their faith and actions.

9 x 12, 32 pp, Full-color illus., Hardcover, ISBN 1-879045-43-5 **$16.95** *For ages 8 & up*

Cain & Abel: Finding the Fruits of Peace

Full-color illus. by Joani Keller Rothenberg

Shows children that we have the power to deal with anger in positive ways. Provides questions for kids and adults to explore together.

9 x 12, 32 pp, Full-color illus., Hardcover, ISBN 1-58023-123-3 **$16.95** *For ages 5 & up*

God in Between

Full-color illus. by Sally Sweetland

If you wanted to find God, where would you look? This magical, mythical tale teaches that God can be found where we are: within all of us and the relationships between us.

9 x 12, 32 pp, Full-color illus., Hardcover, ISBN 1-879045-86-9 **$16.95** *For ages 4 & up*

God's Paintbrush

Wonderfully interactive, invites children of all faiths and backgrounds to encounter God through moments in their own lives. Provides questions adult and child can explore together.

11 x 8½, 32 pp, Full-color illus., Hardcover, ISBN 1-879045-22-2 **$16.95** *For ages 4 & up*

Also Available: **God's Paintbrush Teacher's Guide**

8½ x 11, 32 pp, PB, ISBN 1-879045-57-5 **$8.95**

God's Paintbrush Celebration Kit

A Spiritual Activity Kit for Teachers and Students of All Faiths, All Backgrounds

Additional activity sheets available:

8-Student Activity Sheet Pack (40 sheets/5 sessions), ISBN 1-58023-058-X **$19.95**

Single-Student Activity Sheet Pack (5 sessions), ISBN 1-58023-059-8 **$3.95**

In God's Name

Full-color illus. by Phoebe Stone

Like an ancient myth in its poetic text and vibrant illustrations, this award-winning modern fable about the search for God's name celebrates the diversity and, at the same time, the unity of all people.

9 x 12, 32 pp, Full-color illus., Hardcover, ISBN 1-879045-26-5 **$16.95** *For ages 4 & up*

Also Available as a Board Book: **What Is God's Name?**

5 x 5, 24 pp, Board, Full-color illus., ISBN 1-893361-10-1 **$7.99** *For ages 0–4 (A SkyLight Paths book)*

Also Available: **In God's Name video and study guide**

Computer animation, original music, and children's voices. 18 min. **$29.99**

Also Available in Spanish: **El nombre de Dios**

9 x 12, 32 pp, Full-color illus., Hardcover, ISBN 1-893361-63-2 **$16.95** *(A SkyLight Paths book)*

Noah's Wife: The Story of Naamah

When God tells Noah to bring the animals of the world onto the ark, God also calls on Naamah, Noah's wife, to save each plant on Earth. Based on an ancient text.

9 x 12, 32 pp, Full-color illus., Hardcover, ISBN 1-58023-134-9 **$16.95** *For ages 4 & up*

Also Available as a Board Book: **Naamah, Noah's Wife**

5 x 5, 24 pp, Full-color illus., Board, ISBN 1-893361-56-X **$7.95** *For ages 0–4 (A SkyLight Paths book)*

For Heaven's Sake: Finding God in Unexpected Places

9 x 12, 32 pp, Full-color illus., Hardcover, ISBN 1-58023-054-7 **$16.95** *For ages 4 & up*

God Said Amen: Finding the Answers to Our Prayers

9 x 12, 32 pp, Full-color illus., Hardcover, ISBN 1-58023-080-6 **$16.95** *For ages 4 & up*

Current Events/History

The Story of the Jews: A 4,000-Year Adventure—A Graphic History Book
Written & illustrated by Stan Mack
Through witty, illustrated narrative, we visit all the major happenings from biblical times to the twenty-first century. Celebrates the major characters and events that have shaped the Jewish people and culture.
6 x 9, 288 pp, illus., Quality PB, ISBN 1-58023-155-1 **$16.95**

The Jewish Prophet: Visionary Words from Moses and Miriam to Henrietta Szold and A. J. Heschel   *By Rabbi Michael J. Shire*   6½ x 8½, 128 pp, 123 full-color illus., Hardcover, ISBN 1-58023-168-3 **$25.00**

Shared Dreams: Martin Luther King, Jr. & the Jewish Community
By Rabbi Marc Schneier. Preface by Martin Luther King III.
6 x 9, 240 pp, Hardcover, ISBN 1-58023-062-8 **$24.95**

"Who Is a Jew?": Conversations, Not Conclusions   *By Meryl Hyman*
6 x 9, 272 pp, Quality PB, ISBN 1-58023-052-0 **$16.95**

Ecology

Ecology & the Jewish Spirit: Where Nature & the Sacred Meet
Edited by Ellen Bernstein   6 x 9, 288 pp, Quality PB, ISBN 1-58023-082-2 **$16.95**

Torah of the Earth: Exploring 4,000 Years of Ecology in Jewish Thought
Vol. 1: Biblical Israel: One Land, One People; Rabbinic Judaism: One People, Many Lands
Vol. 2: Zionism: One Land, Two Peoples; Eco-Judaism: One Earth, Many Peoples
Edited by Rabbi Arthur Waskow
Vol. 1: 6 x 9, 272 pp, Quality PB, ISBN 1-58023-086-5 **$19.95**
Vol. 2: 6 x 9, 336 pp, Quality PB, ISBN 1-58023-087-3 **$19.95**

Grief/Healing

Against the Dying of the Light: A Parent's Story of Love, Loss and Hope
By Leonard Fein
In this unusual exploration of heartbreak and healing, Leonard Fein chronicles the sudden death of his 30-year-old daughter and shares the hard-earned wisdom that emerges in the face of loss and grief.
5½ x 8½, 176 pp, Hardcover, ISBN 1-58023-110-1 **$19.95**

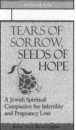

Grief in Our Seasons: A Mourner's Kaddish Companion   *By Rabbi Kerry M. Olitzky*
4½ x 6½, 448 pp, Quality PB, ISBN 1-879045-55-9 **$15.95**

Healing of Soul, Healing of Body: Spiritual Leaders Unfold the Strength & Solace in Psalms   *Edited by Rabbi Simkha Y. Weintraub, C.S.W.*
6 x 9, 128 pp, 2-color illus. text, Quality PB, ISBN 1-879045-31-1 **$14.95**

Jewish Paths toward Healing and Wholeness: A Personal Guide to Dealing with Suffering   *By Rabbi Kerry M. Olitzky. Foreword by Debbie Friedman.*
6 x 9, 192 pp, Quality PB, ISBN 1-58023-068-7 **$15.95**

Mourning & Mitzvah, 2nd Edition: A Guided Journal for Walking the Mourner's Path through Grief to Healing   *By Anne Brener, L.C.S.W.*
7½ x 9, 304 pp, Quality PB, ISBN 1-58023-113-6 **$19.95**

The Perfect Stranger's Guide to Funerals and Grieving Practices
A Guide to Etiquette in Other People's Religious Ceremonies   *Edited by Stuart M. Matlins*
6 x 9, 240 pp, Quality PB, ISBN 1-893361-20-9 **$16.95**   *(A SkyLight Paths book)*

Tears of Sorrow, Seeds of Hope: A Jewish Spiritual Companion for Infertility and Pregnancy Loss   *By Rabbi Nina Beth Cardin*
6 x 9, 192 pp, Hardcover, ISBN 1-58023-017-2 **$19.95**

A Time to Mourn, A Time to Comfort: A Guide to Jewish Bereavement and Comfort   *By Dr. Ron Wolfson*   7 x 9, 336 pp, Quality PB, ISBN 1-879045-96-6 **$18.95**

When a Grandparent Dies: A Kid's Own Remembering Workbook for Dealing with Shiva and the Year Beyond   *By Nechama Liss-Levinson, Ph.D.*
8 x 10, 48 pp, 2-color text, Hardcover, ISBN 1-879045-44-3 **$15.95**   *For ages 7–13*

Abraham Joshua Heschel

The Earth Is the Lord's: The Inner World of the Jew in Eastern Europe
5½ x 8, 128 pp, Quality PB, ISBN 1-879045-42-7 **$14.95**

Israel: An Echo of Eternity *New Introduction by Susannah Heschel*
5½ x 8, 272 pp, Quality PB, ISBN 1-879045-70-2 **$19.95**

A Passion for Truth: Despair and Hope in Hasidism
5½ x 8, 352 pp, Quality PB, ISBN 1-879045-41-9 **$18.99**

Holidays/Holy Days

7th Heaven: Celebrating Shabbat with Rebbe Nachman of Breslov
By Moshe Mykoff with the Breslov Research Institute
Based on the teachings of Rebbe Nachman of Breslov. Explores the art of consciously observing Shabbat and understanding in-depth many of the day's traditional spiritual practices.
5⅛ x 8¼, 224 pp, Deluxe PB w/flaps, ISBN 1-58023-175-6 **$18.95**

The Women's Passover Companion
Women's Reflections on the Festival of Freedom
Edited by Rabbi Sharon Cohen Anisfeld, Tara Mohr, and Catherine Spector
A groundbreaking collection that captures the voices of Jewish women who engage in a provocative conversation about women's relationships to Passover as well as the roots and meanings of women's seders.
6 x 9, 352 pp, Hardcover, ISBN 1-58023-128-4 **$24.95**

The Women's Seder Sourcebook
Rituals & Readings for Use at the Passover Seder
Edited by Rabbi Sharon Cohen Anisfeld, Tara Mohr, and Catherine Spector
This practical guide gathers the voices of more than one hundred women in readings, personal and creative reflections, commentaries, blessings, and ritual suggestions that can be incorporated into your Passover celebration as supplements to or substitutes for traditional passages of the haggadah.
6 x 9, 384 pp, Hardcover, ISBN 1-58023-136-5 **$24.95**

Creating Lively Passover Seders: A Sourcebook of Engaging Tales, Texts & Activities
By David Arnow, Ph.D.
7 x 9, 416 pp, Quality PB, ISBN 1-58023-184-5 **$24.99**

Hanukkah, 2nd Edition: The Family Guide to Spiritual Celebration
By Dr. Ron Wolfson. Edited by Joel Lurie Grishaver.
7 x 9, 240 pp, illus., Quality PB, ISBN 1-58023-122-5 **$18.95**

The Jewish Family Fun Book: Holiday Projects, Everyday Activities, and Travel Ideas
with Jewish Themes *By Danielle Dardashti and Roni Sarig. Illus. by Avi Katz.*
6 x 9, 288 pp, 70+ b/w illus. & diagrams, Quality PB, ISBN 1-58023-171-3 **$18.95**

The Jewish Gardening Cookbook: Growing Plants & Cooking for
Holidays & Festivals *By Michael Brown*
6 x 9, 224 pp, 30+ illus., Quality PB, ISBN 1-58023-116-0 **$16.95**;
Hardcover, ISBN 1-58023-004-0 **$21.95**

Passover, 2nd Edition: The Family Guide to Spiritual Celebration
By Dr. Ron Wolfson with Joel Lurie Grishaver
7 x 9, 352 pp, Quality PB, ISBN 1-58023-174-8 **$19.95**

Shabbat, 2nd Edition: The Family Guide to Preparing for and Celebrating the Sabbath
By Dr. Ron Wolfson 7 x 9, 320 pp, illus., Quality PB, ISBN 1-58023-164-0 **$19.95**

Sharing Blessings: Children's Stories for Exploring the Spirit of the Jewish Holidays
By Rahel Musleah and Michael Klayman
8½ x 11, 64 pp, Full-color illus., Hardcover, ISBN 1-879045-71-0 **$18.95** *For ages 6 & up*

Inspiration

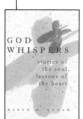

God in All Moments
Mystical & Practical Spiritual Wisdom from Hasidic Masters
Edited and translated by Or N. Rose with Ebn D. Leader
Hasidic teachings on how to be mindful in religious practice and how to cultivate everyday ethical behavior—*hanhagot*.
5½ x 8½, 192 pp, Quality PB, ISBN 1-58023-186-1 **$16.95**

The Dance of the Dolphin: Finding Prayer, Perspective and Meaning in the Stories of Our Lives *By Karyn D. Kedar* 6 x 9, 176 pp, Hardcover, ISBN 1-58023-154-3 **$19.95**

The Empty Chair: Finding Hope and Joy—Timeless Wisdom from a Hasidic Master, Rebbe Nachman of Breslov *Adapted by Moshe Mykoff and the Breslov Research Institute* 4 x 6, 128 pp, 2-color text, Deluxe PB w/flaps, ISBN 1-879045-67-2 **$9.95**

The Gentle Weapon: Prayers for Everyday and Not-So-Everyday Moments— Timeless Wisdom from the Teachings of the Hasidic Master, Rebbe Nachman of Breslov *Adapted by Moshe Mykoff and S. C. Mizrahi, together with the Breslov Research Institute* 4 x 6, 144 pp, 2-color text, Deluxe PB w/flaps, ISBN 1-58023-022-9 **$9.95**

God Whispers: Stories of the Soul, Lessons of the Heart *By Karyn D. Kedar* 6 x 9, 176 pp, Quality PB, ISBN 1-58023-088-1 **$15.95**

An Orphan in History: One Man's Triumphant Search for His Jewish Roots *By Paul Cowan. Afterword by Rachel Cowan.* 6 x 9, 288 pp, Quality PB, ISBN 1-58023-135-7 **$16.95**

Restful Reflections: Nighttime Inspiration to Calm the Soul, Based on Jewish Wisdom *By Rabbi Kerry M. Olitzky & Rabbi Lori Forman* 4½ x 6½, 448 pp, Quality PB, ISBN 1-58023-091-1 **$15.95**

Sacred Intentions: Daily Inspiration to Strengthen the Spirit, Based on Jewish Wisdom *By Rabbi Kerry M. Olitzky and Rabbi Lori Forman* 4½ x 6½, 448 pp, Quality PB, ISBN 1-58023-061-X **$15.95**

Kabbalah/Mysticism/Enneagram

Seek My Face: A Jewish Mystical Theology
By Dr. Arthur Green
This classic work of contemporary Jewish theology, revised and updated, is a profound, deeply personal statement of the lasting truths of Jewish mysticism and the basic faith claims of Judaism. A tool for anyone seeking the elusive presence of God in the world. 6 x 9, 304 pp, Quality PB, ISBN 1-58023-130-6 **$19.95**

Zohar: Annotated & Explained
Translation and annotation by Dr. Daniel C. Matt. Foreword by Andrew Harvey, SkyLight Illuminations series editor.
Offers insightful yet unobtrusive commentary to the masterpiece of Jewish mysticism that explains references and mystical symbols, shares wisdom of spiritual masters, and clarifies the *Zohar's* bold claim: We have always been taught that we need God, but in order to manifest in the world, God needs us.
5½ x 8½, 160 pp, Quality PB, ISBN 1-893361-51-9 **$15.95** *(A SkyLight Paths book)*

Cast in God's Image: Discover Your Personality Type Using the Enneagram and Kabbalah *By Rabbi Howard A. Addison* 7 x 9, 176 pp, Quality PB, Layflat binding, 20+ journaling exercises, ISBN 1-58023-124-1 **$16.95**

Ehyeh: A Kabbalah for Tomorrow *By Dr. Arthur Green* 6 x 9, 224 pp, Hardcover, ISBN 1-58023-125-X **$21.99**

The Enneagram and Kabbalah: Reading Your Soul *By Rabbi Howard A. Addison* 6 x 9, 176 pp, Quality PB, ISBN 1-58023-001-6 **$15.95**

Finding Joy: A Practical Spiritual Guide to Happiness *By Dannel I. Schwartz with Mark Hass* 6 x 9, 192 pp, Quality PB, ISBN 1-58023-009-1 **$14.95**; Hardcover, ISBN 1-879045-53-2 **$19.95**

The Gift of Kabbalah: Discovering the Secrets of Heaven, Renewing Your Life on Earth *By Tamar Frankiel, Ph.D.*
6 x 9, 256 pp, Quality PB, ISBN 1-58023-141-1 **$16.95**; Hardcover, ISBN 1-58023-108-X **$21.95**

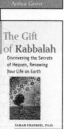

The Way Into Jewish Mystical Tradition *By Lawrence Kushner* 6 x 9, 224 pp, Hardcover, ISBN 1-58023-029-6 **$21.95**

Life Cycle

Parenting

The New Jewish Baby Album: Creating and Celebrating the Beginning of a Spiritual Life—A Jewish Lights Companion
By the Editors at Jewish Lights. Foreword by Anita Diamant. Preface by Sandy Eisenberg Sasso.
A spiritual keepsake that will be treasured for generations. More than just a memory book, *shows you how—and why it's important*—to create a Jewish home and a Jewish life. Includes sections to describe naming ceremony, space to write encouragements, and pages for writing original blessings, prayers, and meaningful quotes throughout.
8 x 10, 64 pp, Deluxe Padded Hardcover, Full-color illus., ISBN 1-58023-138-1 **$19.95**

The Jewish Pregnancy Book: A Resource for the Soul, Body & Mind during Pregnancy, Birth & the First Three Months
By Sandy Falk, M.D., and Rabbi Daniel Judson, with Steven A. Rapp
Includes medical information on fetal development, pre-natal testing and more, from a liberal Jewish perspective; prenatal *Aleph-Bet* yoga; and ancient and modern prayers and rituals for each stage of pregnancy.
7 x 10, 208 pp, Quality PB, b/w illus., ISBN 1-58023-178-0 **$16.95**

Celebrating Your New Jewish Daughter: Creating Jewish Ways to Welcome Baby Girls into the Covenant—New and Traditional Ceremonies
By Debra Nussbaum Cohen 6 x 9, 272 pp, Quality PB, ISBN 1-58023-090-3 **$18.95**

The New Jewish Baby Book: Names, Ceremonies & Customs—A Guide for Today's Families *By Anita Diamant* 6 x 9, 336 pp, Quality PB, ISBN 1-879045-28-1 **$18.95**

Parenting As a Spiritual Journey: Deepening Ordinary and Extraordinary Events into Sacred Occasions *By Rabbi Nancy Fuchs-Kreimer*
6 x 9, 224 pp, Quality PB, ISBN 1-58023-016-4 **$16.95**

Embracing the Covenant: Converts to Judaism Talk About Why & How
Edited and with introductions by Rabbi Allan Berkowitz and Patti Moskovitz
6 x 9, 192 pp, Quality PB, ISBN 1-879045-50-8 **$16.95**

The Guide to Jewish Interfaith Family Life: An InterfaithFamily.com Handbook
Edited by Ronnie Friedland and Edmund Case 6 x 9, 384 pp, Quality PB, ISBN 1-58023-153-5 **$18.95**

Making a Successful Jewish Interfaith Marriage: The Jewish Outreach Institute Guide to Opportunities, Challenges and Resources
By Rabbi Kerry Olitzky with Joan Peterson Littman 6 x 9, 176 pp, Quality PB, ISBN 1-58023-170-5 **$16.95**

The Perfect Stranger's Guide to Wedding Ceremonies
A Guide to Etiquette in Other People's Religious Ceremonies *Edited by Stuart M. Matlins*
6 x 9, 208 pp, Quality PB, ISBN 1-893361-19-5 **$16.95** *(A SkyLight Paths book)*

How to Be a Perfect Stranger, 3rd Edition
The Essential Religious Etiquette Handbook
Edited by Stuart M. Matlins and Arthur J. Magida
The indispensable guidebook to help the well-meaning guest when visiting other people's religious ceremonies.
A straightforward guide to the rituals and celebrations of the major religions and denominations in the United States and Canada from the perspective of an interested guest of any other faith, based on information obtained from authorities of each religion. Belongs in every living room, library, and office.
6 x 9, 432 pp, Quality PB, ISBN 1-893361-67-5 **$19.95** *(A SkyLight Paths book)*

Divorce Is a Mitzvah: A Practical Guide to Finding Wholeness and Holiness When Your Marriage Dies *By Rabbi Perry Netter. Afterword by Rabbi Laura Geller.*
6 x 9, 224 pp, Quality PB, ISBN 1-58023-172-1 **$16.95**

A Heart of Wisdom: Making the Jewish Journey from Midlife through the Elder Years
Edited by Susan Berrin. Foreword by Harold Kushner. 6 x 9, 384 pp, Quality PB, ISBN 1-58023-051-2 **$18.95**

So That Your Values Live On: Ethical Wills and How to Prepare Them
Edited by Jack Riemer and Nathaniel Stampfer 6 x 9, 272 pp, Quality PB, ISBN 1-879045-34-6 **$18.95**

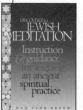

Meditation

The Handbook of Jewish Meditation Practices
A Guide for Enriching the Sabbath and Other Days of Your Life
By Rabbi David A. Cooper
Easy-to-learn meditation techniques for use on the Sabbath and every day, to help us return to the roots of traditional Jewish spirituality where Shabbat is a state of mind and soul. 6 x 9, 208 pp, Quality PB, ISBN 1-58023-102-0 **$16.95**

Discovering Jewish Meditation: Instruction & Guidance for Learning an Ancient
Spiritual Practice *By Nan Fink Gefen, Ph.D.* 6 x 9, 208 pp, Quality PB, ISBN 1-58023-067-9 **$16.95**

A Heart of Stillness: A Complete Guide to Learning the Art of Meditation
By Rabbi David A. Cooper
5½ x 8½, 272 pp, Quality PB, ISBN 1-893361-03-9 **$16.95** *(A SkyLight Paths book)*

Meditation from the Heart of Judaism: Today's Teachers Share Their
Practices, Techniques, and Faith *Edited by Avram Davis*
6 x 9, 256 pp, Quality PB, ISBN 1-58023-049-0 **$16.95**

Silence, Simplicity & Solitude: A Complete Guide to Spiritual Retreat at Home
By Rabbi David A. Cooper
5½ x 8½, 336 pp, Quality PB, ISBN 1-893361-04-7 **$16.95** *(A SkyLight Paths book)*

Three Gates to Meditation Practice: A Personal Journey into Sufism,
Buddhism, and Judaism *By Rabbi David A. Cooper*
5½ x 8½, 240 pp, Quality PB, ISBN 1-893361-22-5 **$16.95** *(A SkyLight Paths book)*

The Way of Flame: A Guide to the Forgotten Mystical Tradition of Jewish Meditation
By Avram Davis 4½ x 8, 176 pp, Quality PB, ISBN 1-58023-060-1 **$15.95**

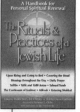

Ritual/Sacred Practice

The Jewish Dream Book
The Key to Opening the Inner Meaning of Your Dreams
By Vanessa L. Ochs with Elizabeth Ochs; Full-color Illus. by Kristina Swarner
Vibrant illustrations, instructions for how modern people can perform ancient Jewish dream practices, and dream interpretations drawn from the Jewish wisdom tradition help make this guide the ideal bedside companion for anyone who wants to further their understanding of their dreams—and themselves.
8 x 8, 120 pp, Full-color illus., Deluxe PB w/flaps, ISBN 1-58023-132-2 **$16.95**

The Rituals & Practices of a Jewish Life: A Handbook for Personal Spiritual
Renewal *Edited by Rabbi Kerry M. Olitzky and Rabbi Daniel Judson*
6 x 9, 272 pp, illus., Quality PB, ISBN 1-58023-169-1 **$18.95**

The Book of Jewish Sacred Practices: CLAL's Guide to Everyday & Holiday
Rituals & Blessings *Edited by Rabbi Irwin Kula and Vanessa L. Ochs, Ph.D.*
6 x 9, 368 pp, Quality PB, ISBN 1-58023-152-7 **$18.95**

Science Fiction/
Mystery & Detective Fiction

Mystery Midrash: An Anthology of Jewish Mystery & Detective Fiction
Edited by Lawrence W. Raphael. Preface by Joel Siegel.
6 x 9, 304 pp, Quality PB, ISBN 1-58023-055-5 **$16.95**

Criminal Kabbalah: An Intriguing Anthology of Jewish Mystery & Detective Fiction
Edited by Lawrence W. Raphael. Foreword by Laurie R. King.
6 x 9, 256 pp, Quality PB, ISBN 1-58023-109-8 **$16.95**

More Wandering Stars: An Anthology of Outstanding Stories of Jewish Fantasy and
Science Fiction *Edited by Jack Dann. Introduction by Isaac Asimov.*
6 x 9, 192 pp, Quality PB, ISBN 1-58023-063-6 **$16.95**

Wandering Stars: An Anthology of Jewish Fantasy & Science Fiction
Edited by Jack Dann. Introduction by Isaac Asimov.
6 x 9, 272 pp, Quality PB, ISBN 1-58023-005-9 **$16.95**

Spirituality

The Alphabet of Paradise: An A–Z of Spirituality for Everyday Life
By Rabbi Howard Cooper
In twenty-six engaging chapters, Cooper spiritually illuminates the subjects of our daily lives—A to Z—examining these sources by using an ancient Jewish mystical method of interpretation that reveals both the literal and more allusive meanings of each. 5 x 7¾, 224 pp, Quality PB, ISBN 1-893361-80-2 **$16.95** *(A SkyLight Paths book)*

Does the Soul Survive?: A Jewish Journey to Belief in Afterlife, Past Lives & Living with Purpose *By Rabbi Elie Kaplan Spitz. Foreword by Brian L Weiss, M.D.*
Spitz relates his own experiences and those shared with him by people he has worked with as a rabbi, and shows us that belief in afterlife and past lives, so often approached with reluctance, is in fact true to Jewish tradition.
6 x 9, 288 pp, Quality PB, ISBN 1-58023-165-9 **$16.95**; Hardcover, ISBN 1-58023-094-6 **$21.95**

First Steps to a New Jewish Spirit: Reb Zalman's Guide to Recapturing the Intimacy & Ecstasy in Your Relationship with God
By Rabbi Zalman M. Schachter-Shalomi with Donald Gropman
An extraordinary spiritual handbook that restores psychic and physical vigor by introducing us to new models and alternative ways of practicing Judaism. Offers meditation and contemplation exercises for enriching the most important aspects of everyday life. 6 x 9, 144 pp, Quality PB, ISBN 1-58023-182-9 **$16.95**

God in Our Relationships: Spirituality between People from the Teachings of Martin Buber *By Rabbi Dennis S. Ross*
On the eightieth anniversary of Buber's classic work, we can discover new answers to critical issues in our lives. Inspiring examples from Ross's own life— as congregational rabbi, father, hospital chaplain, social worker, and husband— illustrate Buber's difficult-to-understand ideas about how we encounter God and each other. 5½ x 8½, 160 pp, Quality PB, ISBN 1-58023-147-0 **$16.95**

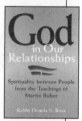

The Jewish Lights Spirituality Handbook: A Guide to Understanding, Exploring & Living a Spiritual Life *Edited by Stuart M. Matlins*
What exactly is "Jewish" about spirituality? How do I make it a part of my life? Fifty of today's foremost spiritual leaders share their ideas and experience with us.
6 x 9, 456 pp, Quality PB, ISBN 1-58023-093-8 **$19.99**; Hardcover, ISBN 1-58023-100-4 **$24.95**

Bringing the Psalms to Life: How to Understand and Use the Book of Psalms
By Dr. Daniel F. Polish
6 x 9, 208 pp, Quality PB, ISBN 1-58023-157-8 **$16.95**; Hardcover, ISBN 1-58023-077-6 **$21.95**

God & the Big Bang: Discovering Harmony between Science & Spirituality
By Dr. Daniel C. Matt 6 x 9, 216 pp, Quality PB, ISBN 1-879045-89-3 **$16.95**

Godwrestling—Round 2: Ancient Wisdom, Future Paths
By Rabbi Arthur Waskow 6 x 9, 352 pp, Quality PB, ISBN 1-879045-72-9 **$18.95**

One God Clapping: The Spiritual Path of a Zen Rabbi *By Rabbi Alan Lew with Sherril Jaffe*
5½ x 8½, 336 pp, Quality PB, ISBN 1-58023-115-2 **$16.95**

The Path of Blessing: Experiencing the Energy and Abundance of the Divine
By Rabbi Marcia Prager 5½ x 8½, 240 pp., Quality PB, ISBN 1-58023-148-9 **$16.95**

Six Jewish Spiritual Paths: A Rationalist Looks at Spirituality *By Rabbi Rifat Sonsino*
6 x 9, 208 pp, Quality PB, ISBN 1-58023-167-5 **$16.95**; Hardcover, ISBN 1-58023-095-4 **$21.95**

Soul Judaism: Dancing with God into a New Era
By Rabbi Wayne Dosick 5½ x 8½, 304 pp, Quality PB, ISBN 1-58023-053-9 **$16.95**

Stepping Stones to Jewish Spiritual Living: Walking the Path Morning, Noon, and Night *By Rabbi James L. Mirel and Karen Bonnell Werth*
6 x 9, 240 pp, Quality PB, ISBN 1-58023-074-1 **$16.95**; Hardcover, ISBN 1-58023-003-2 **$21.95**

There Is No Messiah... and You're It: The Stunning Transformation of Judaism's Most Provocative Idea *By Rabbi Robert N. Levine, D.D.*
6 x 9, 192 pp, Hardcover, ISBN 1-58023-173-X **$21.95**

These Are the Words: A Vocabulary of Jewish Spiritual Life *By Dr. Arthur Green*
6 x 9, 304 pp, Quality PB, ISBN 1-58023-107-1 **$18.95**

Spirituality/Lawrence Kushner

The Book of Letters: A Mystical Hebrew Alphabet
Popular Hardcover Edition, 6 x 9, 80 pp, 2-color text, ISBN 1-879045-00-1 **$24.95**
Deluxe Gift Edition with slipcase, 9 x 12, 80 pp, 4-color text, Hardcover, ISBN 1-879045-01-X **$79.95**
Collector's Limited Edition, 9 x 12, 80 pp, gold foil embossed pages, w/limited edition silkscreened print, ISBN 1-879045-04-4 **$349.00**

The Book of Miracles: A Young Person's Guide to Jewish Spiritual Awareness
All-new illustrations by the author
6 x 9, 96 pp, 2-color illus., Hardcover, ISBN 1-879045-78-8 **$16.95** *For ages 9–13*

The Book of Words: Talking Spiritual Life, Living Spiritual Talk
6 x 9, 160 pp, Quality PB, ISBN 1-58023-020-2 **$16.95**

Eyes Remade for Wonder: A Lawrence Kushner Reader
Introduction by Thomas Moore
6 x 9, 240 pp, Quality PB, ISBN 1-58023-042-3 **$18.95;** Hardcover, ISBN 1-58023-014-8 **$23.95**

God Was in This Place & I, i Did Not Know
Finding Self, Spirituality and Ultimate Meaning
6 x 9, 192 pp, Quality PB, ISBN 1-879045-33-8 **$16.95**

Honey from the Rock: An Introduction to Jewish Mysticism
6 x 9, 176 pp, Quality PB, ISBN 1-58023-073-3 **$16.95**

Invisible Lines of Connection: Sacred Stories of the Ordinary
5½ x 8½, 160 pp, Quality PB, ISBN 1-879045-98-2 **$15.95**

Jewish Spirituality—A Brief Introduction for Christians
5½ x 8½, 112 pp, Quality PB Original, ISBN 1-58023-150-0 **$12.95**

The River of Light: Jewish Mystical Awareness
6 x 9, 192 pp, Quality PB, ISBN 1-58023-096-2 **$16.95**

The Way Into Jewish Mystical Tradition
6 x 9, 224 pp, Hardcover, ISBN 1-58023-029-6 **$21.95**

Spirituality/Prayer

Pray Tell: A Hadassah Guide to Jewish Prayer
By Rabbi Jules Harlow, with contributions from Tamara Cohen, Rochelle Furstenberg, Rabbi Daniel Gordis, Leora Tanenbaum, and many others
A guide to traditional Jewish prayer enriched with insight and wisdom from a broad variety of viewpoints—from Orthodox, Conservative, Reform, and Reconstructionist Judaism to New Age and feminist. Offers fresh and modern slants on what it means to pray as a Jew, and how women and men might actually pray. 8½ x 11, 400 pp, Quality PB, ISBN 1-58023-163-2 **$29.95**

My People's Prayer Book Series
Traditional Prayers, Modern Commentaries
Edited by Rabbi Lawrence A. Hoffman
Provides diverse and exciting commentary to the traditional liturgy, helping modern men and women find new wisdom in Jewish prayer, and bring liturgy into their lives.

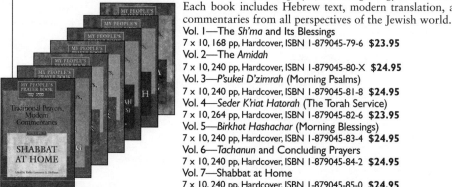

Each book includes Hebrew text, modern translation, and commentaries from all perspectives of the Jewish world.
Vol. 1—The *Sh'ma* and Its Blessings
7 x 10, 168 pp, Hardcover, ISBN 1-879045-79-6 **$23.95**
Vol. 2—The *Amidah*
7 x 10, 240 pp, Hardcover, ISBN 1-879045-80-X **$24.95**
Vol. 3—*P'sukei D'zimrah* (Morning Psalms)
7 x 10, 240 pp, Hardcover, ISBN 1-879045-81-8 **$24.95**
Vol. 4—*Seder K'riat Hatorah* (The Torah Service)
7 x 10, 264 pp, Hardcover, ISBN 1-879045-82-6 **$23.95**
Vol. 5—*Birkhot Hashachar* (Morning Blessings)
7 x 10, 240 pp, Hardcover, ISBN 1-879045-83-4 **$24.95**
Vol. 6—*Tachanun* and Concluding Prayers
7 x 10, 240 pp, Hardcover, ISBN 1-879045-84-2 **$24.95**
Vol. 7—Shabbat at Home
7 x 10, 240 pp, Hardcover, ISBN 1-879045-85-0 **$24.95**

Spirituality/The Way Into... Series

The Way Into... Series offers an accessible and highly usable "guided tour" of the Jewish faith, people, history and beliefs—in total, an introduction to Judaism that will enable you to understand and interact with the sacred texts of the Jewish tradition. Each volume is written by a leading contemporary scholar and teacher, and explores one key aspect of Judaism. *The Way Into...* enables all readers to achieve a real sense of Jewish cultural literacy through guided study.

The Way Into Encountering God in Judaism *By Neil Gillman*
6 x 9, 240 pp, Hardcover, ISBN 1-58023-025-3 **$21.95**

Also Available: **The Jewish Approach to God: A Brief Introduction for Christians**
By Neil Gillman 5½ x 8½, 192 pp, Quality PB, ISBN 1-58023-190-X **$16.95**

The Way Into Jewish Mystical Tradition *By Lawrence Kushner*
6 x 9, 224 pp, Hardcover, ISBN 1-58023-029-6 **$21.95**

The Way Into Jewish Prayer *By Lawrence A. Hoffman*
6 x 9, 224 pp, Hardcover, ISBN 1-58023-027-X **$21.95**

The Way Into Torah *By Norman J. Cohen*
6 x 9, 176 pp, Hardcover, ISBN 1-58023-028-8 **$21.95**

Spirituality in the Workplace

Being God's Partner
How to Find the Hidden Link Between Spirituality and Your Work
By Rabbi Jeffrey K. Salkin. Introduction by Norman Lear.
6 x 9, 192 pp, Quality PB, ISBN 1-879045-65-6 **$17.95**

The Business Bible: 10 New Commandments for Bringing Spirituality & Ethical
Values into the Workplace *By Rabbi Wayne Dosick*
5½ x 8½, 208 pp, Quality PB, ISBN 1-58023-101-2 **$14.95**

Spirituality and Wellness

Aleph-Bet Yoga
Embodying the Hebrew Letters for Physical and Spiritual Well-Being
By Steven A. Rapp. Foreword by Tamar Frankiel, Ph.D., and Judy Greenfeld. Preface by Hart Lazer
7 x 10, 128 pp, b/w photos, Quality PB, Layflat binding, ISBN 1-58023-162-4 **$16.95**

Entering the Temple of Dreams
Jewish Prayers, Movements, and Meditations for the End of the Day
By Tamar Frankiel, Ph.D., and Judy Greenfeld
7 x 10, 192 pp, illus., Quality PB, ISBN 1-58023-079-2 **$16.95**

Minding the Temple of the Soul
Balancing Body, Mind, and Spirit through Traditional Jewish Prayer, Movement, and
Meditation *By Tamar Frankiel, Ph.D., and Judy Greenfeld*
7 x 10, 184 pp, illus., Quality PB, ISBN 1-879045-64-8 **$16.95**
Audiotape of the Blessings and Meditations: 60 min. **$9.95**
Videotape of the Movements and Meditations: 46 min. **$20.00**

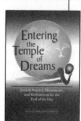

Spirituality/Women's Interest

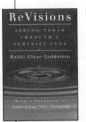

Lifecycles, Vol. 1: Jewish Women on Life Passages & Personal Milestones
Edited and with introductions by Rabbi Debra Orenstein
6 x 9, 480 pp, Quality PB, ISBN 1-58023-018-0 **$19.95**

Lifecycles, Vol. 2: Jewish Women on Biblical Themes in Contemporary Life
Edited and with introductions by Rabbi Debra Orenstein and Rabbi Jane Rachel Litman
6 x 9, 464 pp, Quality PB, ISBN 1-58023-019-9 **$19.95**

Moonbeams: A Hadassah Rosh Hodesh Guide *Edited by Carol Diament, Ph.D.*
8½ x 11, 240 pp, Quality PB, ISBN 1-58023-099-7 **$20.00**

ReVisions: Seeing Torah through a Feminist Lens *By Rabbi Elyse Goldstein*
5½ x 8½, 224 pp, Quality PB, ISBN 1-58023-117-9 **$16.95**

White Fire: A Portrait of Women Spiritual Leaders in America
By Rabbi Malka Drucker. Photographs by Gay Block.
7 x 10, 320 pp, 30+ b/w photos, Hardcover, ISBN 1-893361-64-0 **$24.95** *(A SkyLight Paths book)*

Women of the Wall: Claiming Sacred Ground at Judaism's Holy Site
Edited by Phyllis Chesler and Rivka Haut
6 x 9, 496 pp, b/w photos, Hardcover, ISBN 1-58023-161-6 **$34.95**

The Women's Haftarah Commentary: New Insights from Women Rabbis on
the 54 Weekly Haftarah Portions, the 5 Megillot & Special Shabbatot
Edited by Rabbi Elyse Goldstein 6 x 9, 560 pp, Hardcover, ISBN 1-58023-133-0 **$39.99**

The Women's Torah Commentary: New Insights from Women Rabbis on the 54
Weekly Torah Portions *Edited by Rabbi Elyse Goldstein*
6 x 9, 496 pp, Hardcover, ISBN 1-58023-076-8 **$34.95**

The Year Mom Got Religion: One Woman's Midlife Journey into Judaism
By Lee Meyerhoff Hendler
6 x 9, 208 pp, Quality PB, ISBN 1-58023-070-9 **$15.95**; Hardcover, ISBN 1-58023-000-8 **$19.95**

See Holidays for *The Women's Passover Companion: Women's Reflections on
the Festival of Freedom* and *The Women's Seder Sourcebook: Rituals &
Readings for Use at the Passover Seder.*

Travel

Israel—A Spiritual Travel Guide: A Companion for the Modern Jewish Pilgrim
By Rabbi Lawrence A. Hoffman 4¾ x 10, 256 pp, Quality PB, illus., ISBN 1-879045-56-7 **$18.95**
Also Available: **The Israel Mission Leader's Guide** ISBN 1-58023-085-7 **$4.95**

12 Steps

100 Blessings Every Day
**Daily Twelve Step Recovery Affirmations, Exercises for Personal Growth &
Renewal Reflecting Seasons of the Jewish Year**
By Rabbi Kerry M. Olitzky. Foreword by Rabbi Neil Gillman.
Using a one-day-at-a-time monthly format, this guide reflects on the rhythm of
the Jewish calendar to help bring insight to recovery from addictions and com-
pulsive behaviors of all kinds. Its exercises help us move from *thinking* to *doing.*
4½ x 6½, 432 pp, Quality PB, ISBN 1-879045-30-3 **$15.99**

Recovery from Codependence: A Jewish Twelve Steps Guide to Healing Your Soul
By Rabbi Kerry M. Olitzky 6 x 9, 160 pp, Quality PB, ISBN 1-879045-32-X **$13.95**

Renewed Each Day: Daily Twelve Step Recovery Meditations Based on the Bible
By Rabbi Kerry M. Olitzky and Aaron Z.
Vol. 1—Genesis & Exodus:
6 x 9, 224 pp, Quality PB, ISBN 1-879045-12-5 **$14.95**
Vol. 2—Leviticus, Numbers & Deuteronomy:
6 x 9, 280 pp, Quality PB, ISBN 1-879045-13-3 **$14.95**

Twelve Jewish Steps to Recovery
A Personal Guide to Turning from Alcoholism & Other Addictions—Drugs, Food,
Gambling, Sex...
By Rabbi Kerry M. Olitzky and Stuart A. Copans, M.D. Preface by Abraham J. Twerski, M.D.
6 x 9, 144 pp, Quality PB, ISBN 1-879045-09-5 **$14.95**

Theology/Philosophy

Aspects of Rabbinic Theology
By Solomon Schechter. New Introduction by Dr. Neil Gillman.
6 x 9, 448 pp, Quality PB, ISBN 1-879045-24-9 **$19.95**

Broken Tablets: Restoring the Ten Commandments and Ourselves
Edited by Rachel S. Mikva. Introduction by Lawrence Kushner. Afterword by Arnold Jacob Wolf.
6 x 9, 192 pp, Quality PB, ISBN 1-58023-158-6 **$16.95**; Hardcover, ISBN 1-58023-066-0 **$21.95**

Creating an Ethical Jewish Life
A Practical Introduction to Classic Teachings on How to Be a Jew
By Dr. Byron L. Sherwin and Seymour J. Cohen
6 x 9, 336 pp, Quality PB, ISBN 1-58023-114-4 **$19.95**

The Death of Death: Resurrection and Immortality in Jewish Thought
By Dr. Neil Gillman 6 x 9, 336 pp, Quality PB, ISBN 1-58023-081-4 **$18.95**

Evolving Halakhah: A Progressive Approach to Traditional Jewish Law
By Rabbi Dr. Moshe Zemer
6 x 9, 480 pp, Quality PB, ISBN 1-58023-127-6 **$29.95**; Hardcover, ISBN 1-58023-002-4 **$40.00**

Hasidic Tales: Annotated & Explained
By Rabbi Rami Shapiro. Foreword by Andrew Harvey, SkyLight Illuminations series editor.
5½ x 8½, 240 pp, Quality PB, ISBN 1-893361-86-1 **$16.95** *(A SkyLight Paths Book)*

A Heart of Many Rooms: Celebrating the Many Voices within Judaism
By Dr. David Hartman
6 x 9, 352 pp, Quality PB, ISBN 1-58023-156-X **$19.95**; Hardcover, ISBN 1-58023-048-2 **$24.95**

Judaism and Modern Man: An Interpretation of Jewish Religion
By Will Herberg. New Introduction by Dr. Neil Gillman.
5½ x 8½, 336 pp, Quality PB, ISBN 1-879045-87-7 **$18.95**

Keeping Faith with the Psalms: Deepen Your Relationship with God Using the
Book of Psalms *By Daniel F. Polish*
6 x 9, 272 pp, Hardcover, ISBN 1-58023-179-9 **$24.95**

The Last Trial
On the Legends and Lore of the Command to Abraham to Offer Isaac as a Sacrifice
By Shalom Spiegel. New Introduction by Judah Goldin.
6 x 9, 208 pp, Quality PB, ISBN 1-879045-29-X **$18.95**

A Living Covenant: The Innovative Spirit in Traditional Judaism
By Dr. David Hartman 6 x 9, 368 pp, Quality PB, ISBN 1-58023-011-3 **$18.95**

Love and Terror in the God Encounter
The Theological Legacy of Rabbi Joseph B. Soloveitchik
By Dr. David Hartman
6 x 9, 240 pp, Quality PB, ISBN 1-58023-176-4 **$19.95**; Hardcover, ISBN 1-58023-112-8 **$25.00**

Seeking the Path to Life
Theological Meditations on God and the Nature of People, Love, Life and Death
By Rabbi Ira F. Stone 6 x 9, 160 pp, Quality PB, ISBN 1-879045-47-8 **$14.95**

The Spirit of Renewal: Finding Faith after the Holocaust
By Rabbi Edward Feld 6 x 9, 224 pp, Quality PB, ISBN 1-879045-40-0 **$16.95**

Tormented Master: *The Life and Spiritual Quest of Rabbi Nahman of Bratslav*
By Dr. Arthur Green 6 x 9, 416 pp, Quality PB, ISBN 1-879045-11-7 **$19.99**

Your Word Is Fire: The Hasidic Masters on Contemplative Prayer
Edited and translated by Dr. Arthur Green and Barry W. Holtz
6 x 9, 160 pp, Quality PB, ISBN 1-879045-25-7 **$15.95**

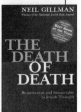

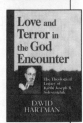
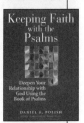

I Am Jewish
Personal Reflections Inspired by the Last Words of Daniel Pearl
Almost 150 Jews—both famous and not—from all walks of life, from all around
the world, write about Identity, Heritage, Covenant/Chosenness and Faith,
Humanity and Ethnicity, and *Tikkun Olam* and Justice.
Edited by Judea and Ruth Pearl
6 x 9, 304 pp, Hardcover, ISBN 1-58023-183-7 **$24.99**

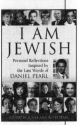

About Jewish Lights

People of all faiths and backgrounds yearn for books that attract, engage, educate, and spiritually inspire.

Our principal goal is to stimulate thought and help all people learn about who the Jewish People are, where they come from, and what the future can be made to hold. While people of our diverse Jewish heritage are the primary audience, our books speak to people in the Christian world as well and will broaden their understanding of Judaism and the roots of their own faith.

We bring to you authors who are at the forefront of spiritual thought and experience. While each has something different to say, they all say it in a voice that you can hear.

Our books are designed to welcome you and then to engage, stimulate, and inspire. We judge our success not only by whether or not our books are beautiful and commercially successful, but by whether or not they make a difference in your life.

For your information and convenience, at the back of this book we have provided a list of other Jewish Lights books you might find interesting and useful. They cover all the categories of your life:

Bar/Bat Mitzvah	Life Cycle
Bible Study / Midrash	Meditation
Children's Books	Parenting
Congregation Resources	Prayer
Current Events / History	Ritual / Sacred Practice
Ecology	Spirituality
Fiction: Mystery, Science Fiction	Theology / Philosophy
Grief / Healing	Travel
Holidays / Holy Days	Twelve Steps
Inspiration	Women's Interest
Kabbalah / Mysticism / Enneagram	

Stuart M. Matlins, Publisher

Or phone, fax, mail or e-mail to: **JEWISH LIGHTS Publishing**
Sunset Farm Offices, Route 4 • P.O. Box 237 • Woodstock, Vermont 05091
Tel: (802) 457-4000 • Fax: (802) 457-4004 • www.jewishlights.com
Credit card orders: **(800) 962-4544** (8:30AM–5:30PM ET Monday–Friday)
Generous discounts on quantity orders. SATISFACTION GUARANTEED. Prices subject to change.